Technology Addictions and Digital Diseases:

Theories and Practices

Özgün Arda Kuş
https://orcid.org/0000-0002-1487-3772
Uskudar University, Turkey

IGI Global
Scientific Publishing
Publishing Tomorrow's Research Today

Published in the United States of America by
IGI Global Scientific Publishing
701 East Chocolate Avenue
Hershey, PA, 17033, USA
Tel: 717-533-8845 | Fax: 717-533-7115
Website: https://www.igi-global.com E-mail: cust@igi-global.com

Library of Congress Cataloging-in-Publication Data

Names: Kuş, Özgün Arda, 1988- editor
Title: Technology addictions and digital diseases : theories and practices / edited by Özgün Arda Kuş.
Description: Hershey, PA : IGI Global Scientific Publishing, [2027] | Includes bibliographical references and index. | Summary: "This book explores the psychological, behavioral, and neurobiological impacts of technology addiction and digital disorders. It examines how excessive reliance on smartphones, social media, and digital tools reshapes attention, motivation, and relationships, offering critical insights into the hidden costs of life in the digital age"-- Provided by publisher.
Identifiers: LCCN 2025041873 (print) | LCCN 2025041874 (ebook) | ISBN 9798337366654 hardcover | ISBN 9798337366661 paperback | ISBN 9798337366678 ebook
Subjects: LCSH: Internet addiction | Social media addiction | Compulsive behavior
Classification: LCC RC569.5.I54 T44 2026 (print) | LCC RC569.5.I54 (ebook)
LC record available at https://lccn.loc.gov/2025041873
LC ebook record available at https://lccn.loc.gov/2025041874

British Cataloguing in Publication Data
A Cataloguing in Publication record for this book is available from the British Library.

Editorial Advisory Board

Table of Contents

Detailed Table of Contents

Digital technologies have become deeply embedded in everyday life, shaping how people communicate, construct their identities, manage emotions, and maintain social relationships. As concerns about technology-based behavioral addictions grow, much of the existing literature continues to approach the issue primarily from clinical or neurobiological perspectives. Although these approaches offer important insights, they often leave aside the communicative and structural characteristics of digital environments. This chapter argues that problematic digital use should not be reduced to individual weakness or simple loss of control. Instead, it suggests that such behaviors emerge from the interaction between psychological processes, social dynamics, and platform design features. Drawing on behavioral addiction theory, research on reward and self-regulation, and studies of computer-mediated communication, the chapter reexamines the conceptual boundaries of technology-based addictions. Building on this discussion, the chapter proposes the Integrated Digital Interaction Model (IDIM), which brings together three interconnected dimensions: the psychological, the communicative-social, and the structural-design level. By situating digital behaviors within a broader socio-technical context, the chapter aims to offer a more balanced and context-sensitive understanding of addiction in the digital age and to outline directions for future research.

The rhetoric of screen addiction positions the problem of excessive digital use as a personal behavioral pathology, similar to substance dependency, because of dopamine

the paper examines how constant connectivity, algorithmic mediation, and virtual interactivity reshape attention, memory, identity, and interpersonal dynamics. The research highlights both the empowering and disruptive dimensions of digital immersion, including enhanced access to information, altered emotional processing, and the erosion of reflective solitude. By mapping these shifts, the study calls for a nuanced understanding of digital embodiment and proposes ethical pathways for fostering mindful engagement in technologically saturated societies.

This study aims to examine how young people use generative artificial intelligence in their educational processes and daily routines, and how this usage is reflected in their tendencies toward addiction. In order to achieve this aim, a qualitative research method was adopted, and in-depth interviews were used as the data collection technique. The sample of the study consists of young individuals aged 18–24 living in Istanbul. Since this research covers the use of AI tools in both educational processes and daily life practices, the sample was limited to university students. This constitutes the main limitation of the study. In this context, semi-structured interviews were conducted with young participants identified through a combination of convenience sampling and snowball sampling methods. The findings show that frequent and uncontrolled use of AI tools contributes to emerging addiction tendencies and perceptions among young people

The digital era has become the era of Smartphone addiction, manifesting as an increasing psychological and behavioral phenomenon among young adults and teenagers. Even though the terms like Fear of Missing out (FoMO) and nomophobia have been analyzed extensively, they have been frequently considered as separate entities, which reduces the opinion of their interaction to perpetuate problematic smartphone usage. This chapter summarizes the research of the current times and suggests the Integrative Digital Dysregulation (IDD) model to account for smartphone addiction as a dynamic self-stigmatizing cycle with identity extension, information vigilance, and psychophysical strain. In this context, FoMO and nomophobia serve as the major psychological processes transforming the vulnerability of the identity into the constant surveillance and anxiety-inducing activity. The chapter focuses on how

Continuous content consumption has become an important part of entertainment in the digital era, especially with the widespread availability of on-demand streaming platforms, easy accessibility to high-speed internet and mobiles etc. Viewers increasingly engage in watching multiple episodes of series or online content in a single sitting, which results in making binge-watching a common media viewing habit. This chapter focuses on examining marathon-viewing as a contemporary viewing practice by reviewing existing literature, with particular attention to its prevalence, psychological mechanisms, associated mental health and social outcomes and differentiating unhealthy binge-watching from healthy viewing habits. Lastly, this chapter highlights the importance of practical intervention approaches, cultural considerations, and key research gaps.

Digital platforms like TikTok are known to shorten attention spans and foster addiction symptoms such as FOMO and doomscrolling. This study investigates the interplay between digital content, the attention economy, and digital addiction. Employing content analysis, the research examines 300 TikTok videos tagged #beforeafter (#öncesisonrası), systematically collected via data scraping on August 20, 2025. This specific hashtag was selected as the contrast between initial "chaos" and final "order" offers high visual satisfaction, encouraging viewer retention. By analyzing both metadata and qualitative structures, the study deconstructs the mechanisms behind the "doomscroll" experience. Findings are discussed through a techno-political lens, revealing the visual dynamics underpinning the attention economy. Ultimately, this research provides a theoretical and empirical foundation for understanding "digital malaise," including cognitive fatigue and screen dependency.

This study examines how the habit of monitoring vehicle listings on Sahibinden.com, Turkey's largest classifieds platform, transforms into a digital compulsion. Using a phenomenological approach, in-depth interviews were conducted with male users who

Foreword

The twenty-first century is witnessing a transformation unprecedented in human history. Digital technologies have evolved far beyond their original role as tools designed to facilitate daily life; they have become deeply embedded in the ways we think, communicate, consume, and engage with the world around us. Today, individuals live in environments increasingly shaped by algorithms, artificial intelligence systems, mobile technologies, and digitally mediated experiences. While these developments have significantly expanded human capabilities, they have also introduced new forms of dependency, vulnerability, and behavioral risk.

The emergence of technology-based behavioral addictions represents one of the most pressing challenges of the digital era. Unlike traditional forms of addiction, these phenomena are intertwined with activities that have become integral to contemporary life. Smartphones, social media platforms, online shopping environments, streaming services, and AI-powered applications are designed to offer convenience, engagement, and personalized experiences. Yet the very mechanisms that make these technologies attractive and useful may also encourage compulsive patterns of use that influence attention, motivation, decision-making, and emotional regulation.

Understanding these developments requires moving beyond explanations that attribute addiction solely to individual weakness or a lack of self-control. Digital environments are increasingly structured by sophisticated technological systems designed to capture attention, shape preferences, and sustain engagement. Consequently, technology addiction must be examined not only through psychological lenses but also within broader social, cultural, economic, and technological contexts.

This book, *Technology Addictions and Digital Diseases: Theories and Practices*, offers a comprehensive exploration of the realities emerging from the digital age. Bringing together diverse scholarly perspectives, the contributing authors present theoretical discussions, conceptual frameworks, empirical findings, and practical insights into technology-based behavioral addictions. Collectively, the chapters illuminate how digital technologies are reshaping human behavior and contributing to the emergence of new forms of dependency within hyperconnected societies.

Particular attention is devoted to the theoretical foundations of technology addiction and digital diseases. Contemporary perspectives that revisit and extend traditional addiction frameworks introduce concepts such as algorithmic compulsions, digital self-disorders, and technology-mediated behavioral patterns. These discussions invite readers to reconsider the relationship between human autonomy and digital environments in an age defined by constant connectivity.

The book also examines a wide range of technology-related addictions and compulsive behaviors. Emerging tendencies toward AI dependency, smartphone addiction, social media addiction, online shopping addiction, binge-watching behaviors, and other forms of digital engagement are explored through interdisciplinary perspectives. Beyond describing these phenomena, the chapters investigate the psychological mechanisms, social influences, and technological structures that contribute to their development and persistence.

Another significant contribution of this book lies in its focus on the attention economy and the behavioral architecture of digital platforms. Many contemporary technologies are intentionally designed to maximize user engagement and prolong interaction. Recognizing this reality is essential for understanding that technology addiction is not merely an individual concern, but also a consequence of broader technological and economic systems.

One of the greatest strengths of this book is its interdisciplinary character. Drawing on contributions from psychology, psychiatry, communication studies, educational sciences, sociology, economics, and related fields, the book provides a multidimensional perspective on technology addictions and digital diseases. Such intellectual diversity is indispensable for understanding and addressing challenges that extend beyond the boundaries of any single discipline.

Importantly, this book does not adopt an anti-technology stance. Rather, it emphasizes the need for a more conscious, balanced, and ethically grounded relationship with digital technologies. The objective is not to resist innovation or technological advancement, but to better understand the conditions under which technology contributes to human flourishing and the circumstances in which it may undermine autonomy and well-being.

As societies continue to evolve alongside increasingly intelligent, connected, and immersive technologies, the questions explored in this book will only grow in significance. I believe this book will serve as a valuable resource for researchers, practitioners, policymakers, and students seeking to better understand the complex relationship between technological progress and human behavior.

It is my sincere hope that the discussions presented in these chapters will contribute to the development of healthier digital cultures, more responsible technological design, and a deeper appreciation of the human values that must remain at the center of technological progress.

Nevzat Tarhan
Üsküdar University, Turkey

Preface

INTRODUCTION

The future has never felt closer than it does today. Thinking about the future has gradually become almost indistinguishable from thinking about tomorrow itself. The digital age has transformed human life in ways that would once have been difficult to imagine, introducing entirely new forms of behavior into everyday life. Over the past two decades, rapid technological developments have reshaped communication, education, healthcare, entertainment, social interaction, and even the ways individuals perceive themselves and the world around them. Smartphones, social media platforms, artificial intelligence systems, online environments, immersive technologies, and algorithm-driven digital ecosystems have become inseparable parts of contemporary life.

At this point, I would particularly like to emphasize the role of smartphones. By allowing countless technological developments to transcend the limitations of time and space and remain constantly within reach, smartphones have transformed the ways individuals think, build habits, view life, form friendships and relationships, access information, and maintain productivity—along with many other aspects of everyday experience that often go unnoticed. Yet every development inevitably carries both social and individual costs. In this respect, digital advancements have also silently and progressively contributed to the emergence of new psychological, behavioral, social, and neurocognitive challenges affecting individuals across societies.

As digital technologies become more deeply integrated into everyday life, problematic technology use has increasingly emerged as a major topic of academic, clinical, and societal concern. Excessive screen exposure, compulsive social media engagement, problematic digital behaviors, emotional regulation difficulties, cognitive fatigue, and technology-based behavioral addictions are now recognized as growing global concerns. These developments have also paved the way for the emergence of the increasingly discussed concept of "digital diseases."

The concept of digital diseases extends beyond technology addiction alone. It refers to a broader framework encompassing psychological, physiological, cognitive, and behavioral difficulties that arise from excessive and dysfunctional exposure to digital environments. In many ways, these conditions are not always as fixed or severe as traditional addictions; rather, they may also describe temporary experiences that individuals can encounter periodically, much like common illnesses such as the flu or a cold.

Shaped by personalization algorithms, persuasive interface designs, gamification systems, infinite scrolling mechanisms, instant feedback loops, and artificial intelligence-supported recommendation systems, the modern digital ecosystem has transformed the relationship between humans and technology into something increasingly inseparable.

One of the most important challenges in this field is that digital technologies are no longer merely external tools used occasionally by individuals. Today, educational systems, professional life, healthcare services, interpersonal communication, social identity construction, entertainment habits, and even emotional regulation processes are increasingly mediated through digital technologies. For this reason, problematic technology use cannot be examined solely within the narrow boundaries of addiction. Instead, it requires a broader and interdisciplinary perspective that takes into account the psychological, neurological, sociological, communicational, educational, and ethical dimensions of digital life.

This growing complexity has also intensified the need for multidisciplinary academic discussions regarding the effects of digitalization on human behavior and mental health. Personally, I often compare approaching digitalization through a single discipline to trying to sit on a one-legged chair without falling. Therefore, the process of digitalization and its consequences should be examined through multiple perspectives, including psychology, psychiatry, neuroscience, communication sciences, public health, sociology, educational sciences, media studies, and behavioral sciences. Despite the rapid growth of the literature, there remains a significant need for comprehensive academic resources that bring together theoretical approaches, empirical findings, practical implications, and interdisciplinary perspectives.

Technology Addictions and Digital Diseases: Theories and Practices was prepared with the aim of contributing to this academic need. The chapters included in this book bring together scholars from different disciplines who examine technology-based addictions and digital diseases through diverse theoretical, methodological, and applied perspectives. Topics discussed throughout the book include artificial intelligence dependency, smartphone addiction, social media addiction, online shopping addiction, binge-watching behavior, algorithmic compulsions, attention economy dynamics, digital consumer behavior, and emerging forms of technology-mediated behavioral dependency.

One of the greatest strengths of this book lies in its interdisciplinary nature. Technology-related behavioral problems cannot be fully understood through the lens of a single discipline alone. For this reason, the book aims to foster a more holistic understanding of technology addictions and digital diseases through contributions from researchers working across different academic fields. By combining theoretical discussions with current research and practical approaches, this work seeks to provide both conceptual depth and practical insight.

When used consciously and in moderation, digital technologies offer significant opportunities and advantages. However, the highly stimulating nature of modern digital platforms, together with reward-oriented behavioral mechanisms and constantly evolving algorithmic structures, may increase vulnerability to compulsive and dysfunctional patterns of use in certain individuals. Understanding this delicate balance between technological benefit and technological harm is critically important for developing healthier digital environments and more effective intervention strategies.

CHAPTER OVERVIEW

The chapters included in this book also emphasize the importance of prevention efforts, digital literacy, ethical technology design, early intervention strategies, and interdisciplinary collaboration. Adolescents and young adults, in particular, represent more vulnerable groups due to their developmental, emotional, and neurocognitive sensitivities. Therefore, promoting healthy digital habits and increasing awareness regarding problematic technology use constitute some of the central themes of this book.

In addition, this book aims to contribute to future scientific discussions regarding the continuously evolving relationship between technology and human behavior. As artificial intelligence systems, immersive virtual environments, wearable technologies, neurotechnology applications, and algorithmic personalization systems continue to develop, new forms of digital interaction and new behavioral risks will inevitably emerge. For this reason, the field of digital diseases is expected to gain even greater academic and clinical importance in the years ahead.

CONCLUSION

It is my sincere hope that this book will contribute to the international literature on technology addictions and digital diseases and serve as a valuable resource for researchers, clinicians, educators, policymakers, mental health professionals, and students. I also hope that this work will inspire future interdisciplinary collaborations and contribute to the development of healthier, more ethical, and more sustainable digital environments.

Finally, I would like to express my gratitude to all authors, reviewers, and members of the editorial team who contributed to the realization of this book. Their academic dedication and collaborative efforts played a significant role in shaping this work and enriching the growing body of literature in this field.

Acknowledgments

The completion of *Technology Addictions and Digital Diseases: Theories and Practices* has been made possible through the valuable contributions, collaboration, and support of many individuals and institutions.

First and foremost, I would like to express my sincere gratitude to all contributing authors for their scholarly efforts, patience, and commitment throughout the editorial and revision processes. Their interdisciplinary perspectives and academic dedication have significantly enriched the quality and scope of this book.

I would also like to thank the reviewers for their valuable feedback and constructive evaluations, which played an important role in strengthening the chapters included in this volume.

My appreciation extends to the editorial and publishing team at IGI Global Scientific Publishing for their professional guidance, continuous support, and coordination throughout the publication process.

This book was developed with the aim of contributing to the growing body of knowledge surrounding technology addictions, digital diseases, and their psychological, behavioral, social, and neurocognitive dimensions in the rapidly evolving digital era. It is my hope that this work will contribute to future research, academic discussions, and interdisciplinary collaborations in this important field.

Finally, I would like to dedicate this work to the memory of my beloved mother, Canan KARAUÇAK, whose love and guidance continue to inspire me; to my wife, Asena Irmak KUŞ, for her endless patience, understanding, and support throughout this journey; and to my cats, who brought comfort and peace during the long writing process.

Chapter 1

Rethinking the Future of Technology-Based Behavioral Addictions

Özgün Arda Kuş
http://orcid.org/0000-0002-1487-3772
Uskudar University, Turkey

ABSTRACT

Digital technologies have become deeply embedded in everyday life, shaping how people communicate, construct their identities, manage emotions, and maintain social relationships. As concerns about technology-based behavioral addictions grow, much of the existing literature continues to approach the issue primarily from clinical or neurobiological perspectives. Although these approaches offer important insights, they often leave aside the communicative and structural characteristics of digital environments. This chapter argues that problematic digital use should not be reduced to individual weakness or simple loss of control. Instead, it suggests that such behaviors emerge from the interaction between psychological processes, social dynamics, and platform design features. Drawing on behavioral addiction theory, research on reward and self-regulation, and studies of computer-mediated communication, the chapter reexamines the conceptual boundaries of technology-based addictions. Building on this discussion, the chapter proposes the Integrated Digital Interaction Model (IDIM), which brings together three interconnected dimensions: the psychological, the communicative-social, and the structural-design level. By situating digital behaviors within a broader socio-technical context, the chapter aims to offer a more balanced and context-sensitive understanding of addiction in the digital age and to outline directions for future research.

DOI: 10.4018/979-8-3373-6665-4.ch001

INTRODUCTION

The ways in which digital technologies have entered everyday life have permanently reshaped how individuals work, communicate, entertain themselves, and construct their identities. As digital technologies have evolved, so too have patterns of thought, emotional processes, and behavioral tendencies at both individual and societal levels. Websites, mobile applications, social media platforms, online games, and digital streaming services have become environments that demand significant amounts of users' time, attention, and emotional investment. In this shift, technology use has gradually moved beyond being merely instrumental and, for many, has become an end in itself. For some individuals, this transformation has developed into patterns of behavior marked by loss of control, impaired functioning, and psychosocial difficulties. Within this context, technology-based behavioral addictions have, over the past two decades, become a shared area of inquiry across disciplines, particularly psychology and communication studies.

The concept of behavioral addiction was initially introduced to explain cognitive structures, emotional processes, and behavioral patterns that are not related to substance use but nevertheless produce similar clinical and psychosocial outcomes. Griffiths' (2005) biopsychosocial components model became one of the key theoretical foundations in this field, clearly demonstrating that elements such as tolerance, withdrawal, mood modification, and loss of control can be observed in behaviors as well as in substance use. Grant and colleagues (2010) further emphasized that behavioral addictions should be examined along the dimensions of impulsivity and compulsivity. Collectively, these contributions have strengthened the position of behavioral addictions within the broader psychopathology literature.

Although the integration of technology into daily life has brought undeniable advantages, it has also introduced new risks, opening a distinct line of debate within the field of behavioral addictions. With technology entering this discussion, concepts such as Internet addiction, social media addiction, and online gaming addiction began to gain visibility in academic literature. Young's (1998) pioneering study, which conceptualized Internet addiction as a new clinical disorder, laid the groundwork for empirical research in this area. Subsequent studies demonstrated that technology-based addictions cannot be explained solely by individual weaknesses or personality traits; rather, they are closely linked to reward mechanisms (Montag & Reuter, 2017; Brand et al., 2016).

However, a review of the existing literature reveals that technology-based behavioral addictions are most often examined from clinical psychology or neurobiological perspectives. While these approaches provide valuable insights at the individual level, they frequently treat the socio-communicative nature and cultural context of digital environments as secondary. Yet digital platforms influence not only individual reward systems but also communicative processes such as social approval, visibility, belonging, and identity construction (Andreassen, 2015; Kuss & Griffiths, 2017).

At this point, communication studies offer an important and distinctive contribution to understanding technology-based addictions. McLuhan's (1964) influential view of media as extensions of the human being remains highly relevant for understanding how digital technologies reshape individual experience. Walther's (1996) model of computer-mediated communication demonstrated that online interactions, while qualitatively different from face-to-face communication, can generate bonds that are psychologically just as intense. Baym's (2015) work further revealed how digital communication transforms interpersonal relationships, providing a foundation for situating addiction debates within a broader social context.

This chapter seeks to rethink and reinterpret the future of technology-based behavioral addictions within a holistic framework that aims to build a bridge between psychology and communication studies. It argues that digital behaviors should not be understood solely as indicators of individual psychopathology, but rather as complex phenomena intertwined with platform design, cultural norms, and communicative practices. By examining together the reward structures of digital environments, self-regulation processes, and identity formation, the chapter also seeks to question the limits of existing approaches.

Finally, this introductory section maintains that an interdisciplinary orientation is essential in the study of technology-based behavioral addictions. By bringing together psychological theories, communication models, and debates in digital ethics, the chapter aims to contribute both to the deepening of academic scholarship and to the development of policies and interventions that support digital well-being. In doing so, it underscores the need to reconsider and redefine the concept of addiction in the digital age.

The Evolution of the Concept of Behavioral Addiction

For much of its history, the concept of addiction was framed narrowly around the repeated use of psychoactive substances and the biological and psychological consequences of such use. Within this perspective, the development of tolerance and the presence of physical withdrawal symptoms were treated as the primary criteria of addiction. The idea that non-substance-related behaviors might display similar addictive patterns remained largely peripheral for many years. Even today, when addiction is mentioned, substance use disorders are still the first associations that come to mind.

Several factors have contributed to the recognition of behavioral addiction as a legitimate concept. One of the most significant is the observation that certain behaviors, like substance use, can become repetitive, lead to tolerance, and produce both psychological and even physical withdrawal-like symptoms when discontinued. At the same time, clinical research increasingly demonstrated that addiction cannot be reduced to a purely biological process. This realization paved the way for biopsychosocial approaches that emphasize the interaction of individual, psychological, and social factors. In this context, Griffiths' (2005) components model has emerged as one of the most influential frameworks supporting the theoretical legitimacy of behavioral addictions. Through six core components—salience, mood modification, tolerance, withdrawal, conflict, and relapse—the model systematically highlights the shared characteristics of substance-related and non-substance-related addictions. Importantly, it suggests that the similarities between these forms of addiction are not superficial, but structural in nature.

At the same time, the expansion of the behavioral addiction concept has generated important methodological and conceptual debates. Holden (2001) cautioned that defining behavioral addictions too broadly risks pathologizing ordinary and functional behaviors. This concern has become particularly salient in the context of digital technologies, which are now deeply embedded in everyday life. The widespread and often necessary use of technology complicates efforts to draw clear clinical boundaries. In this respect, it is evident that the literature still faces challenges in establishing consistent criteria for distinguishing behavioral addictions from high but non-problematic engagement. Treating intensive technology use as synonymous with addiction carries the potential for problematic consequences at both clinical and societal levels.

For this reason, contemporary research on behavioral addictions should move beyond purely quantitative indicators and place greater emphasis on qualitative criteria. Loss of control over the behavior, its centrality in the individual's life, and the extent to which it disrupts academic, professional, or social functioning have emerged as key distinguishing features (Grant et al., 2010). From this perspective, the evolution of the behavioral addiction concept should not be understood simply as the addition of new behaviors to an expanding list, but as a more nuanced effort to grasp the contextual and functional dimensions of addiction.

In sum, the historical development of the behavioral addiction concept suggests that addiction should not be treated as a fixed and universal category. Rather, it is better understood as a dynamic, multidimensional phenomenon that is sensitive to context and function. This conceptual shift provides the necessary foundation for evaluating technology-based behavioral addictions and offers a strong theoretical framework for the interdisciplinary discussions that follow in the subsequent sections.

Conceptual Boundaries of Technology-Based Behavioral Addictions

Technological developments have introduced profound innovations into everyday life. They have enabled individuals to act independently of time and place, while significantly simplifying many daily tasks. Yet technology-based devices and their digital extensions have not only made life easier; they have also brought new risks and vulnerabilities. Among the most critical of these are forms of technology-related addiction that threaten individual functioning.

As the behavioral addiction literature expanded to include dependencies related to digital technologies, the concept of technology-based behavioral addictions emerged as a new area of academic and clinical debate. Young's (1998) introduction of the term *Internet addiction* at the end of the twentieth century marked an important turning point. By conceptualizing excessive Internet use as a potential clinical disorder and drawing attention to the psychological consequences of digital behaviors, this pioneering work played a key role in shaping the theoretical foundations of the field. It emphasized that Internet use could affect multiple areas of an individual's life and that technology engagement might evolve beyond an instrumental activity into a potentially addictive process.

Subsequent research, however, revealed the heterogeneous nature of the concept of Internet addiction. The Internet is not a single activity but a broad environment encompassing diverse behaviors such as social media interaction, online gaming, information seeking, and digital content consumption. This diversity raised concerns that technology-related addictions were being compressed into a single diagnostic category (Montag & Reuter, 2017). As a result, more recent scholarship has shifted toward the notion of "specific Internet-use disorders," highlighting the importance of evaluating problematic behaviors in relation to distinct forms of digital engagement.

The I-PACE model developed by Brand and colleagues (2016) represents a process-oriented attempt to clarify the conceptual boundaries of technology-based behavioral addictions. The model explains how digital behaviors may develop into problematic usage patterns through the interaction of individual predispositions (such as personality traits and psychopathology), affective and cognitive responses, and executive functions. Rather than treating technology-based addictions as fixed and universal categories, the I-PACE framework conceptualizes them as dynamic processes shaped by ongoing interactions between the individual and the environment.

One of the most fundamental challenges in conceptualizing technology-based behavioral addictions lies in the inseparable integration of digital technologies into everyday life. The period of isolation during the COVID-19 pandemic further intensified this integration, making technology use not only common but often unavoidable. Today, education, work, and social interaction are largely conducted through digital platforms, which increasingly blurs the boundaries between "normal" and "problematic" use. This context makes it clear that focusing solely on individual symptoms is insufficient. Instead, the contextual, social, and functional consequences of digital behaviors must be considered together (Andreassen, 2015; Kuss & Griffiths, 2017).

From this perspective, communication studies provide an important lens for expanding the conceptual understanding of technology-based behavioral addictions. Digital platforms are not merely tools that activate individual reward systems; they are environments that structure communicative dynamics such as social approval, visibility, and interaction. For this reason, technology-based behavioral addictions should be examined not only within a framework of individual pathology but also within broader socio-communicative processes.

In sum, the conceptual boundaries and dynamics of technology-based behavioral addictions cannot be defined through rigid or fixed criteria. Rather, they must be understood through the interplay of technological design, individual characteristics, and social context. Recognizing this complexity underscores the importance of interdisciplinary, flexible, and context-sensitive approaches in advancing both the understanding and the responsible management of technology-based behavioral addictions.

Psychological Dimension: Reward, Motivation, and Self-Regulation

Psychological processes occupy a central place in understanding and evaluating technology-based behavioral addictions. Digital technologies are designed with reward structures and interaction loops that aim to sustain users' attention, directly targeting motivational systems. This design logic helps explain why technology use, for some individuals, can become problematic and difficult to control. After all, these platforms operate within profit-driven structures and are therefore built to keep users continuously engaged.

At the core of behavioral addictions lie psychological mechanisms closely tied to reward and reinforcement processes. Behavioral learning theories, particularly those emphasizing variable ratio reinforcement schedules, have long demonstrated how powerful such mechanisms can be in maintaining repeated behavior. Digital platforms make extensive use of these structures through likes, notifications, badges, and algorithmically generated feedback (Griffiths, 2005). As noted earlier, these systems are structured to capture and retain a significant portion of users' time and attention.

From a neuropsychological perspective, digital rewards—like other rewards encountered in everyday life—are associated with dopamine-based reward systems.

However, the current literature cautions against reducing technology-based addictions to simplistic dopamine-centered explanations. Brand and colleagues (2016) argue that the reward value of digital behaviors must be understood in relation to the individual's emotional state and cognitive expectations. In this view, digital rewards gain meaning within lived experience, shaped by personal context as well as perceptions of time and space.

Social media platforms and online games, in particular, generate secondary rewards such as social approval and feelings of achievement, further reinforcing user behavior. Andreassen (2015) demonstrated that feedback received on social networking sites is closely linked to self-esteem and a sense of belonging, thereby strengthening repeated engagement. Digital reward systems therefore appeal not only to hedonic pleasure but also to deeper psychosocial needs.

Motivational processes also play a significant role in sustaining technology-based behavioral addictions. Intrinsic motivations—such as entertainment, escapism, relaxation, and relief from boredom—are especially influential in driving digital engagement (Kuss & Griffiths, 2017). In this sense, technology-oriented behaviors often function as tools for emotional regulation. Turning to digital environments to cope with negative emotions, reduce stress, or alleviate loneliness can contribute to the development of problematic usage patterns. Baumeister and Vohs (2007) note that when self-regulatory capacity weakens, individuals become more inclined toward behaviors that provide immediate gratification. Like substances or other pleasure-inducing activities, digital technologies can offer a readily accessible form of escape. One distinctive feature of digital environments is their independence from time and place, making access to gratification nearly constant.

The link between emotional regulation and technology-based addictions is particularly evident in studies focusing on adolescents and young adults. Riva and colleagues (2016) suggest that the emotional intensity experienced in digital environments may serve a compensatory function for unmet emotional needs in offline life. This helps explain why digital behaviors may become especially attractive for certain individuals. Adolescents and young adults who struggle to experience desired emotional depth in their daily lives may turn to virtual spaces to fill this gap.

Self-regulation refers to the capacity to manage impulses, attention, behavior, and desires in line with long-term goals. The literature on technology-based behavioral addictions consistently identifies weaknesses or deficits in self-regulation as important risk factors for problematic digital use (Hofmann et al., 2012). The constant accessibility and persuasive design of digital platforms increase the demands placed on self-regulatory resources. When these resources are strained, loss of control may emerge. Baumeister and Vohs' (2007) ego depletion framework suggests that self-regulatory capacity can weaken when cognitive resources are overextended. The continuous stream of salient stimuli offered by digital environments may accelerate this depletion process.

Over time, individuals may find themselves exercising diminishing control over digital behaviors that initially began as deliberate choices. Repetition gradually transforms intentional actions into habits and automated responses. As Brand and colleagues (2016) emphasize, this shift from conscious decision-making to automatic behavioral patterns represents a critical stage in the maintenance of technology-based addictions. As self-regulatory mechanisms weaken or lose effectiveness, restructuring behavior becomes increasingly difficult, reinforcing and deepening the cycle of digital dependency.

The psychological processes discussed in this section demonstrate that technology-based behavioral addictions cannot be adequately explained by individual weakness alone. Reward mechanisms, intrinsic and extrinsic motivational dynamics, and self-regulatory processes interact with the design and communicative features of digital environments. For this reason, psychological approaches gain greater explanatory power when considered alongside communication studies and analyses of digital culture. The psychological dimension of technology-based behavioral addictions is closely intertwined with the communicative processes addressed in the following section. The social meanings of digital rewards, the communicative context of motivation, and the relationship between self-regulation and platform architectures all underscore the necessity of an interdisciplinary perspective.

Figure 1. Psychological processes model of technology-based behavioral addictions.

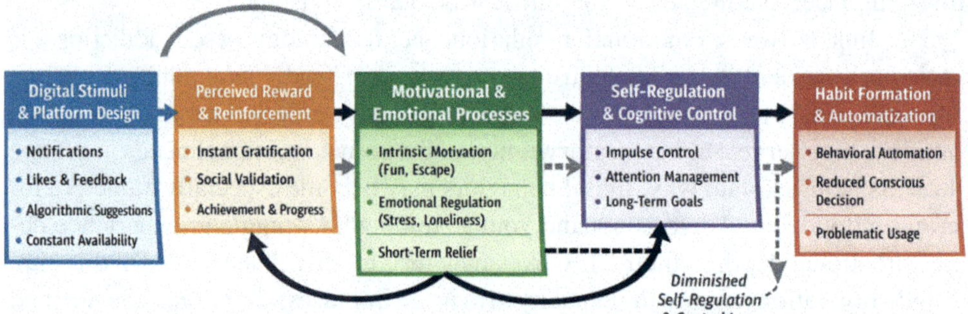

Original conceptual model developed by the author, informed by the I-PACE framework (Brand et al., 2016, 2019).

Communicative Dimension: Mediated Interaction, Identity, and Social Context

Explaining technology-based behavioral addictions solely through individual reward systems or self-regulation mechanisms risks overlooking the fundamentally social nature of digital environments. At their core, digital platforms are communicative spaces. They produce symbolic arenas in which individuals present themselves, negotiate social positioning, and construct a sense of belonging. For this reason, the communicative dimension of technology-based behavioral addictions calls for an analysis that is closely intertwined with psychological processes rather than separated from them.

Mediated Interaction and Hyperpersonal Dynamics

Research in computer-mediated communication has demonstrated that digital interactions, while qualitatively different from face-to-face communication, can generate psychologically intense forms of connection. Walther's (1996) hyperpersonal model suggests that online environments, through selective self-presentation and idealized perceptions, may even foster stronger and more accelerated relational bonds. In this sense, the digital environment is not merely a tool that facilitates communication; it also functions as a filter that can amplify emotional intensity.

Baym (2015) emphasizes that characteristics such as persistence, visibility, and archiving transform interpersonal relationships in digital contexts. These features link social interaction to continuous feedback loops, keeping the search for social approval constantly active. On social networking platforms in particular, the number of likes, comments, and shares can become directly associated with perceived social value (Andreassen, 2015). This creates a space where communicative feedback converges with psychological reward systems.

McLuhan's (1964) characterization of media as "extensions of man" remains highly relevant for understanding how digital platforms expand the experience of selfhood. Smartphones and social media accounts are no longer merely tools for communication; they function as extensions through which identity is maintained and made visible. In this context, disengaging from a platform may represent more than stepping away from an application—it may feel like a disruption of one's social presence.

Identity Presentation and Performativity

Digital environments offer individuals the opportunity to construct and revise their identities in selective ways. Although Goffman's dramaturgical approach was originally developed in relation to face-to-face interaction, it continues to provide a powerful framework for understanding identity performances online. Digital spaces allow users to curate their "front stage," edit mistakes, and present idealized versions of themselves (Baym, 2015).

Riva and colleagues (2015) argue that identity in digital environments is not only represented but actively reconstructed. During adolescence and young adulthood in particular, online identity experiences can play a formative role in the development of self-concept. In this sense, social media platforms become not only sites of communication but laboratories of identity.

Yet this process of identity construction is deeply intertwined with ongoing feedback mechanisms. A lack of social approval, diminished visibility, or reduced interaction may trigger feelings of exclusion or worthlessness (Kuss & Griffiths, 2017). Over time, a cycle can emerge between identity performance and reward expectation. This cycle may be driven not only by the pursuit of pleasure, but also by a perceived necessity to sustain one's social existence.

Social Context, Belonging, and the Network Society

It is not possible to assess the communicative dimension of technology-based behavioral addictions without considering the broader social context in which individuals are embedded. As Castells (2008) describes through the concept of the network society, the digital age has produced a social order organized around networked structures of connection. Within this structure, visibility, ongoing participation, and interaction become key components of social capital.

Andreassen (2015) notes that time spent on social networking sites is often shaped not only by individual preference but also by social expectations and norms. For younger users in particular, disengaging from digital environments may mean falling out of sync with their social circles. This dynamic has been conceptualized in the literature as the "fear of missing out" (FOMO), an important variable explaining the continuity of digital participation (Kuss & Griffiths, 2017).

Montag and Reuter (2017) highlight how the algorithmic structures of digital platforms shape user behavior by increasing exposure to particular types of content and reinforcing interaction intensity. From this perspective, addiction should not be understood solely as an individual failure of control but as a process supported by design and structural features. Platform architectures, operating within the dynamics of the attention economy, develop strategies to keep users online, often reducing communicative interaction to quantifiable metrics.

At this point, the social dimension of technology-based behavioral addictions must be evaluated not only in relation to psychological vulnerabilities but also within the broader framework of cultural norms, digital capitalism, and the economy of visibility. In many contexts, maintaining a digital presence becomes a performative obligation. This obligation can gradually transform behavior from a voluntary choice into a routine reinforced by subtle but persistent social pressure.

The Intersection of Communicative Processes and Psychological Mechanisms

The reward and self-regulation processes discussed in the psychological dimension interact directly with communicative feedback mechanisms. Notifications of likes, increases in followers, or in-game social status are not merely cognitive reinforcers; they are symbols that carry social meaning (Andreassen, 2015). This symbolic value has the potential to amplify the impact of reward.

While the I-PACE model proposed by Brand and colleagues (2016) emphasizes the interaction between individual predispositions and environmental stimuli, it also implies that the communicative features of digital environments should be considered among these stimuli. It therefore becomes difficult to meaningfully understand technology-based behavioral addictions by isolating psychological processes from their communicative context.

In conclusion, technology-based behavioral addictions cannot be explained solely through individual loss of control or reward-seeking tendencies. They are complex phenomena shaped within mediated forms of interaction, identity performances, and networked social structures. Incorporating the communicative dimension into analysis makes it possible to move beyond narrow clinical boundaries and to develop a more comprehensive framework aligned with the social realities of the digital age.

A THEORETICAL MODEL FOR THE FUTURE: THE INTEGRATED DIGITAL INTERACTION MODEL (IDIM)

A review of the literature on technology-based behavioral addictions shows that most existing models primarily focus on individual psychological processes. The I-PACE model (Brand et al., 2016; Brand et al., 2019), for example, provides a detailed account of the interaction between personal predispositions and cognitive–affective processes. However, structural elements such as algorithmic architectures, the dynamics of the attention economy, and broader cultural norms are often addressed only indirectly, typically positioned within general environmental components.

Contemporary digital environments are shaped not only by users' internal processes but also by platform design, data infrastructures, and economic imperatives.

In response to this limitation, the proposed Integrated Digital Interaction Model (IDIM) offers a holistic framework that conceptualizes technology-based behavioral addictions across three interrelated levels:

1. The Individual Psychological Level
2. The Communicative–Social Level
3. The Structural–Design Level

The Individual Psychological Level

This level is strongly represented in the current literature. Reward sensitivity, impulsivity, self-regulatory capacity, and emotion regulation strategies are widely recognized as key determinants of problematic digital use (Hofmann et al., 2012; Brand et al., 2019). In particular, avoidance of negative affect and the pursuit of short-term relief play a central role in maintaining digital behaviors (Elhai et al., 2020).

At the same time, recent scholarship cautions against explaining digital addictions solely in terms of dopaminergic reward processes. Kardefelt-Winther et al. (2017) emphasize the importance of considering the functional context of behavior and carefully distinguishing between high engagement and clinically significant disorder. This perspective encourages a more cautious stance, helping the model avoid the risk of over-pathologizing everyday digital practices.

The Communicative–Social Level

Digital environments are not merely spaces of reward acquisition; they are arenas in which individuals sustain identity, generate social capital, and structure relationships of belonging. A growing body of research demonstrates that social media use is associated with psychological well-being through processes such as social comparison and visibility pressures (Vogel et al., 2014; Appel et al., 2020).

The concept of "fear of missing out" (FOMO) has emerged as a particularly important variable in explaining the continuity of digital engagement (Przybylski et al., 2013; Elhai et al., 2021). FOMO is linked not only to individual anxiety levels but also to the constant updating pressures generated by networked social structures. From this perspective, technology-based addiction may be understood, at least in part, as an extension of the desire to remain socially connected and relevant.

Moreover, algorithmically curated content flows shape users' perceptions of social reality and can contribute to the formation of echo chambers (Cinelli et al., 2021). This suggests that digital behaviors are guided not solely by personal preference but also by logics of visibility, amplification, and access embedded within platform systems.

The Structural–Design Level

An increasingly discussed topic in recent literature concerns the role of platform design in fostering addictive dynamics. Features such as variable ratio reinforcement schedules, infinite scroll, autoplay functions, and notification architectures are often interpreted as deliberate design choices intended to maximize user engagement (Alter, 2017; Harris, 2016).

The attention economy framework underscores that user attention constitutes the primary economic resource of digital platforms (Wu, 2016). From this standpoint, addiction-like patterns of use may reflect not merely individual vulnerability but also economically driven design strategies. Orben (2020), particularly in research on adolescents, argues that the impact of digital technologies depends less on technology itself and more on usage context and design characteristics.

The IDIM framework assumes that these three levels operate in continuous interaction. When individual vulnerabilities converge with social pressures and design-based reinforcement mechanisms, the risk of problematic use increases. However, when one or more of these components are relatively weak or protective factors are present, intensive use does not automatically develop into addiction.

Figure 2. Integrated Digital Interaction Model (IDIM).

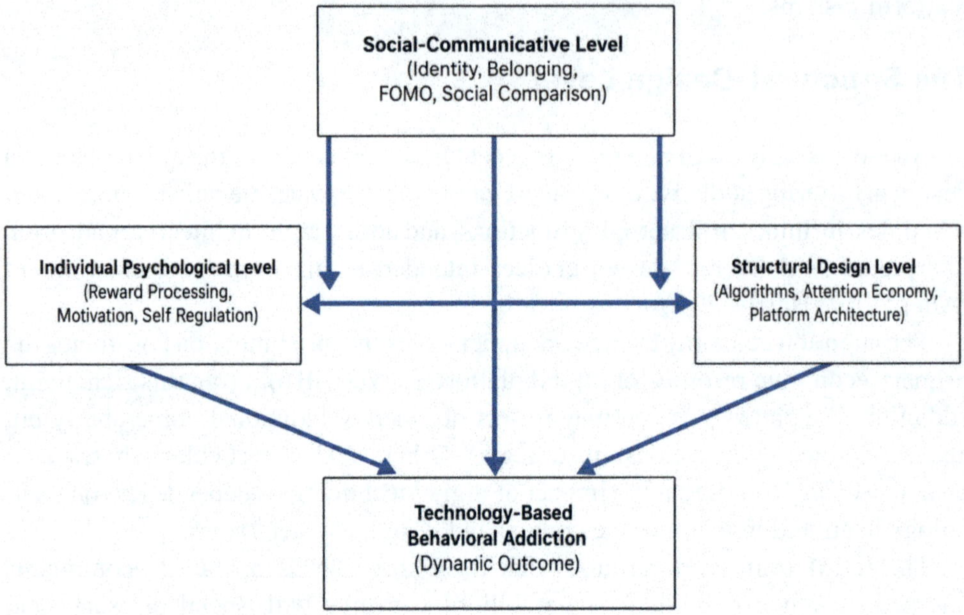

Original conceptual model proposed and developed by author.

Theoretical Contribution of the Model

The primary contribution of the proposed model lies in positioning technology-based behavioral addictions not solely within a psychopathological framework, but within a broader socio-technical ecosystem. From this perspective:

- Clinical interventions should focus not only on strengthening individual self-regulation skills,
- but also on promoting digital literacy and critical media awareness,
- as well as addressing platform design ethics and regulatory policies.

This approach offers a more balanced framework that understands addiction not as an individual flaw, but as the outcome of multi-layered interactions. Particularly in post-2020 scholarship, the emphasis on the contextual nature of problematic use (Kardefelt-Winther et al., 2017; Orben, 2020) aligns with the model's commitment to a functional rather than purely normative evaluation.

FUTURE RESEARCH DIRECTIONS

The future research agenda on technology-based behavioral addictions should move beyond a narrow focus on identifying individual risk factors and instead adopt a multi-layered, context-sensitive perspective. Addressing the psychological, communicative, and structural dimensions of digital behavior together is essential for reducing conceptual fragmentation within the field. In this regard, future studies would benefit from deeper engagement along three central axes: causality, measurement diversity, and contextual sensitivity.

First, much of the current literature relies on cross-sectional designs. This makes it difficult to determine the direction of the relationship between intensive digital use and psychological well-being. As Orben (2020) notes, discussions surrounding digital technologies often rely more heavily on correlational findings than on robust causal evidence. Longitudinal and experimental studies are therefore needed to clarify how individual vulnerabilities may develop into patterned digital behaviors over time. The updated I-PACE model (Brand et al., 2019) offers a useful theoretical foundation for examining such temporal dynamics. However, the model should be tested more explicitly in conjunction with social and design-related variables.

Second, diversification of measurement tools is critical. Self-report scales remain valuable for capturing subjective experiences of digital engagement, yet they are limited when not complemented by behavioral or structural data. The use of digital trace data has increased in recent years, but systematic integration of these data with psychological measures remains underdeveloped. The effects of algorithmically curated content flows on phenomena such as echo chambers and social comparison (Cinelli et al., 2021; Appel et al., 2020) should be examined through carefully designed experimental frameworks. Such approaches would strengthen the field by grounding debates about digital addiction not only in subjective perception but also in observable behavioral and structural evidence.

Third, greater attention must be paid to cultural and social context within research design. As Kardefelt-Winther et al. (2017) caution, the risk of pathologizing intensive use increases when cultural norms and social expectations are overlooked. In networked societies, visibility, accessibility, and continuous connectivity have increasingly become normative expectations. Comparative studies across cultural settings are therefore needed to better understand how digital participation is interpreted and socially reinforced in different contexts. Cross-cultural variation in fear of missing out (FOMO) (Przybylski et al., 2013; Elhai et al., 2021) presents a particularly promising area of inquiry, offering insights into how needs for social belonging manifest within diverse social structures.

In addition, platform design and digital ethics require more systematic empirical investigation. Design elements such as infinite scroll, autoplay, and notification architectures can be experimentally manipulated to assess their effects on attention span and self-regulation processes. The attention economy framework (Wu, 2016) and design-centered critiques of digital addiction (Alter, 2017) both suggest the need for research that moves beyond normative debate toward empirical testing. Future studies should analyze user behavior not solely through the lens of individual willpower, but also in relation to the guiding influence of design architectures.

Finally, the advancement of interdisciplinary methodologies will be crucial for the development of the field. Collaborations among psychology, communication studies, human–computer interaction, and data science can provide a more comprehensive understanding of the layered nature of technology-based behavioral addictions. Such an approach positions digital behaviors not as a single-dimensional pathology, but as dynamic products of interactions among individuals, society, and technology.

Future research that more precisely distinguishes between intensive use and clinical disorder, incorporates contextual variables into analysis, and explicitly tests the role of design architecture will significantly contribute to both theoretical refinement and applied practice. In doing so, scholarship in this area may help redefine the concept of addiction in the digital age—not only at an academic level, but also in ways that shape social understanding and public policy.

CONCLUSION

This study has sought to demonstrate that technology-based behavioral addictions cannot be explained solely in terms of individual loss of control. Rather, they should be understood within an interactional framework shaped by psychological processes, social dynamics, and platform design. The proposed model conceptualizes addictive behavior not as the product of a single variable, but as a multi-layered process emerging across interconnected levels. What distinguishes the present framework from earlier models is its insistence that addictive patterns emerge not only from internal predispositions, but from the recursive interaction between psychological vulnerability, communicative meaning-making, and design architecture.

At the individual level, factors such as reward sensitivity, impulsivity, difficulties in emotion regulation, and psychopathological symptoms are known to be associated with problematic digital use (Brand et al., 2016; Elhai et al., 2017). The I-PACE framework, in particular, illustrates how personal predispositions may be translated into behavioral patterns through emotional and cognitive responses (Brand et al., 2019). From this perspective, technology-based addiction should be viewed not as a static personality trait, but as a process activated under specific conditions.

Although psychological vulnerabilities increase the risk of digital addiction, they are not sufficient on their own to explain the phenomenon. Digital platforms shape user behavior not only through the content they provide, but also through social feedback mechanisms such as visibility metrics, likes, comments, and follower counts. Social comparison theory has long established that individuals are inclined to compare themselves with others. In social media environments, however, such comparisons occur more frequently, more visibly, and often through idealized representations. Meta-analytic findings suggest that this dynamic can have meaningful effects on subjective well-being (Appel et al., 2020). Similarly, fear of missing out (FOMO) has emerged as a significant motivational force driving individuals to remain continuously connected (Przybylski et al., 2013). In this sense, digital addiction reflects not only the pursuit of pleasure, but also the need for belonging, social connection, and acceptance.

At the structural level, the attention economy and algorithmic design play a decisive role. Platform architectures designed to maximize engagement operate in ways that resemble variable ratio reinforcement mechanisms, strengthening repetitive behavior (Montague & Berns, 2002; Wu, 2016). This suggests that addiction-like patterns of use may result not merely from individual weakness, but from systematically encouraged modes of engagement. The continuously updated, personalized nature of digital environments adds a new dimension to classical models of behavioral addiction.

Findings from neuroscience further indicate that certain forms of technology-based addiction may share similarities with substance-related addictions in terms of reward system activation (Volkow & Baler, 2014). At the same time, digital addictions are directed not toward a fixed object, but toward an interactive environment. This distinction is critical for understanding both the persistence and the rapid diffusion of such behaviors.

In conclusion, technology-based behavioral addictions are dynamic phenomena emerging at the intersection of individual, social, and structural processes. Future research should therefore move beyond single-variable explanations and develop interactional, system-oriented models. Understanding the risks of the digital age requires not only analyzing user behavior, but also examining the architectural and systemic forces that shape that behavior.

REFERENCES

Alter, A. (2017). *Irresistible: The rise of addictive technology and the business of keeping us hooked*. Penguin Press.

Andreassen, C. S. (2015). Online social network site addiction: A comprehensive review. *Current Addiction Reports, 2*(2), 175–184. DOI: 10.1007/s40429-015-0056-9

Appel, M., Marker, C., & Gnambs, T. (2020). Are social media ruining our lives? A review of meta-analytic evidence. *Review of General Psychology, 24*(1), 60–74. https://doi.org/DOI: 10.1177/1089268019880891

Baumeister, R. F., & Vohs, K. D. (2007). Self-regulation, ego depletion, and motivation. *Social and Personality Psychology Compass, 1*(1), 115–128. DOI: 10.1111/j.1751-9004.2007.00001.x

Baym, N. K. (2015). *Personal connections in the digital age* (2nd ed.). Polity Press.

Brand, M., Wegmann, E., Stark, R., Müller, A., Wölfling, K., Robbins, T. W., & Potenza, M. N. (2019). The Interaction of Person–Affect–Cognition–Execution (I-PACE) model for addictive behaviors: Update, generalization, and specification. *Neuroscience and Biobehavioral Reviews, 104*, 1–10. DOI: 10.1016/j.neubiorev.2019.06.032

Brand, M., Young, K. S., Laier, C., Wölfling, K., & Potenza, M. N. (2016). Integrating psychological and neurobiological considerations regarding the development and maintenance of specific Internet-use disorders: An interaction of person–affect–cognition–execution (I-PACE) model. *Neuroscience and Biobehavioral Reviews, 71*, 252–266. DOI: 10.1016/j.neubiorev.2016.08.033

Cinelli, M., Quattrociocchi, W., Galeazzi, A., Valensise, C. M., Brugnoli, E., Schmidt, A. L., Zola, P., Zollo, F., & Scala, A. (2021). The echo chamber effect on social media. *Proceedings of the National Academy of Sciences of the United States of America, 118*(9), e2023301118. DOI: 10.1073/pnas.2023301118

Elhai, J. D., Levine, J. C., Dvorak, R. D., & Hall, B. J. (2017). Fear of missing out, need for touch, anxiety and depression are related to problematic smartphone use. *Computers in Human Behavior, 63*, 509–516. DOI: 10.1016/j.chb.2016.05.079

Elhai, J. D., Levine, J. C., Dvorak, R. D., & Hall, B. J. (2020). Non-social features of smartphone use are most related to depression, anxiety, and problematic smartphone use. *Computers in Human Behavior, 69*, 75–82. DOI: 10.1016/j.chb.2016.12.023

Elhai, J. D., Yang, H., & Montag, C. (2021). Fear of missing out (FOMO): Overview, theoretical underpinnings, and literature review on relations with severity of negative affectivity and problematic technology use. *The British Journal of Psychiatry*, *43*(2), 203–209. DOI: 10.1590/1516-4446-2020-0870

Goffman, E. (1959). *The presentation of self in everyday life*. Doubleday.

Grant, J. E., Potenza, M. N., Weinstein, A., & Gorelick, D. A. (2010). Introduction to behavioral addictions. *The American Journal of Drug and Alcohol Abuse*, *36*(5), 233–241. DOI: 10.3109/00952990.2010.491884

Griffiths, M. D. (2005). A "components" model of addiction within a biopsychosocial framework. *Journal of Substance Use*, *10*(4), 191–197. DOI: 10.1080/14659890500114359

Hofmann, W., Schmeichel, B. J., & Baddeley, A. D. (2012). Executive functions and self-regulation. *Trends in Cognitive Sciences*, *16*(3), 174–180. DOI: 10.1016/j.tics.2012.01.006

Holden, C. (2001). 'Behavioral' addictions: Do they exist? *Science*, *294*(5544), 980–982. DOI: 10.1126/science.294.5544.980

Kardefelt-Winther, D., Heeren, A., Schimmenti, A., van Rooij, A., Maurage, P., Carras, M., Edman, J., Blaszczynski, A., Khazaal, Y., & Billieux, J. (2017). How can we conceptualize behavioural addiction without pathologizing common behaviours? *Addiction (Abingdon, England)*, *112*(10), 1709–1715. DOI: 10.1111/add.13763

Kuss, D. J., & Griffiths, M. D. (2017). Social networking sites and addiction: Ten lessons learned. *International Journal of Environmental Research and Public Health*, *14*(3), 311. DOI: 10.3390/ijerph14030311

Montag, C., & Reuter, M. (2017). *Internet addiction: Neuroscientific approaches and therapeutic implications*. Springer., DOI: 10.1007/978-3-319-46276-9

Montague, P. R., & Berns, G. S. (2002). Neural economics and the biological substrates of valuation. *Neuron*, *36*(2), 265–284. DOI: 10.1016/S0896-6273(02)00974-1

Orben, A. (2020). The Sisyphean cycle of technology panics. *Perspectives on Psychological Science*, *15*(5), 1143–1157. DOI: 10.1177/1745691620919372

Przybylski, A. K., Murayama, K., DeHaan, C. R., & Gladwell, V. (2013). Motivational, emotional, and behavioral correlates of fear of missing out. *Computers in Human Behavior*, *29*(4), 1841–1848. DOI: 10.1016/j.chb.2013.02.014

Riva, G., Wiederhold, B., & Cipresso, P. (2015). 1. Psychology Of Social Media: From Technology To Identity. In *The Psychology of Social Networking Vol.1: Personal Experience in Online Communities* (pp. 4-14). Warsaw, Poland: De Gruyter Open Poland. https://doi.org/DOI: 10.1515/9783110473780-003

Vogel, E. A., Rose, J. P., Roberts, L. R., & Eckles, K. (2014). Social comparison, social media, and self-esteem. *Psychology of Popular Media Culture*, *3*(4), 206–222. DOI: 10.1037/ppm0000047

Volkow, N. D., & Baler, R. D. (2014). Addiction science: Uncovering neurobiological complexity. *Neuropharmacology*, *76*, 235–249. DOI: 10.1016/j.neuropharm.2013.05.007

Walther, J. B. (1996). Computer-mediated communication: Impersonal, interpersonal, and hyperpersonal interaction. *Communication Research*, *23*(1), 3–43. DOI: 10.1177/009365096023001001

Wu, T. (2016). *The attention merchants: The epic scramble to get inside our heads*. Knopf.

Young, K. S. (1998). Internet addiction: The emergence of a new clinical disorder. *Cyberpsychology & Behavior*, *1*(3), 237–244. DOI: 10.1089/cpb.1998.1.237

ADDITIONAL READING

Andrew, K. (2013). Motivational, emotional, and behavioral correlates of fear of missing out. *Computers in Human Behavior*, *29*(4), 1841–1848. DOI: 10.1016/j.chb.2013.02.014

Brand, M., Young, K. S., Laier, C., Wölfling, K., & Potenza, M. N. (2016). Integrating psychological and neurobiological considerations regarding the development and maintenance of specific Internet-use disorders: An interaction of person–affect–cognition–execution (I-PACE) model. *Neuroscience and Biobehavioral Reviews*, *71*, 252–266. DOI: 10.1016/j.neubiorev.2016.08.033

Kardefelt-Winther, D., Heeren, A., Schimmenti, A., van Rooij, A., Maurage, P., Carras, M., Edman, J., Blaszczynski, A., Khazaal, Y., & Billieux, J. (2017). How can we conceptualize behavioural addiction without pathologizing common behaviours? *Addiction (Abingdon, England)*, *112*(10), 1709–1715. DOI: 10.1111/add.13763

Kuss, D. J., & Griffiths, M. D. (2017). Social networking sites and addiction: Ten lessons learned. *International Journal of Environmental Research and Public Health, 14*(3), 311. DOI: 10.3390/ijerph14030311

Lembke, A. (2021). *Dopamine nation: Finding balance in the age of indulgence.* Dutton.

Orben, A. (2020). The Sisyphean cycle of technology panics. *Perspectives on Psychological Science, 15*(5), 1143–1157. DOI: 10.1177/1745691620919372

Turkle, S. (2015). *Reclaiming conversation: The power of talk in a digital age. Penguin Press. Adam Alter (2017). Irresistible: The rise of addictive technology and the business of keeping us hooked.* Penguin Press.

Twenge, J. M. (2019). More time on technology, less happiness? Associations between digital-media use and psychological well-being. *Current Directions in Psychological Science, 28*(4), 372–379. DOI: 10.1177/0963721419838244

Wu, T. (2016). *The attention merchants: The epic scramble to get inside our heads.* Knopf.

KEY TERMS AND DEFINITIONS

Algorithmic Reinforcement: The use of algorithm-driven personalization, variable feedback, and content delivery systems designed to increase user engagement on digital platforms. These mechanisms may operate in ways similar to variable ratio reinforcement schedules, thereby strengthening repeated patterns of behavior.

Behavioral Addiction: A pattern of repetitive and compulsive behavior that does not involve the use of a psychoactive substance, yet is marked by loss of control, the development of tolerance over time, and withdrawal-like symptoms when the behavior is restricted. Such patterns lead to noticeable impairments in academic, occupational, or social functioning.

Digital Addiction: A form of addiction-like behavior characterized by diminished control over technology-related activities, persistent preoccupation, the gradual need for increased engagement, and feelings of restlessness or discomfort when access is limited. It refers to a pattern in which digital use extends beyond functional purposes and begins to negatively affect daily life and overall functioning.

Digital Well-Being: The capacity to use digital technologies in a balanced and self-regulated manner that supports psychological health, social relationships, and overall quality of life. Rather than focusing solely on duration of use, digital well-being emphasizes the purpose, context, and outcomes of digital engagement.

Integrated Digital Interaction Model(IDIM): The theoretical framework proposed in this study, which conceptualizes technology-based behavioral addictions across three interconnected levels: psychological, communicative-social, and structural-design. The model situates addictive behavior within a socio-technical ecosystem, viewing it as the outcome of ongoing interactions rather than solely as an individual predisposition.

Socio-Technical Ecosystem: An integrated system formed through the dynamic interaction between individual characteristics, technological infrastructures, and social networks. Technology-based behavioral addictions emerge and take shape within this multilayered environment.

Chapter 2

Beyond Addiction:
Mapping Ecology of Algorithmic Compulsions and Digital Self-Disorders in Hyperconnected Societies

Utsav Krishan Murari
http://orcid.org/0009-0007-1606-6775
Manipal University Jaipur, India

Hemlata Parmar
http://orcid.org/0009-0009-1438-5427
Manipal University Jaipur, India

Trishu Sharma
http://orcid.org/0009-0008-7779-4175
Manipal University Jaipur, India

ABSTRACT

The rhetoric of screen addiction positions the problem of excessive digital use as a personal behavioral pathology, similar to substance dependency, because of dopamine pay-offs occasioned by infrequent notifications and personalized content. In this chapter, the socio-technical emergent phenomenon suggested is the algorithmic compulsion. Multi-level feedback loops reflected on an ecological framework, individual neurocognitive responses, interface nudges, platform optimization, and societal norms of hyperconnectivity are the determinants of digital self-disorders: fractured attention, validation dependency, emotional volatility, performative identity, and fragmentation. The systemic entanglement and personal pathology

DOI: 10.4018/979-8-3373-6665-4.ch002

shift is the focal point of the integrated model, which proposes ethical redesign, regulatory transparency, and reconstructed mental health strategies to the resilient human-algorithmic futures.

INTRODUCTION

One of the main hyperconnected societies' behavioural concerns is the overuse of digital technologies. The concept, which prevails in the conceptualization of heavy platform use: 'screen addiction', is clearly coloured by the concept of behavioural addiction theory. This way of thinking defines compulsive scrolling, gaming, and using social media as a neurobiological disorder like substance addiction, which develops tolerance, withdrawal, and impairment (Young, 2017; Griffiths, 2013). This perspective has been supported by large-scale epidemiological studies, which have shown significant correlations between heavy social media use and psychiatric illness including depression and anxiety in multinational samples statistically (Andreassen et al., 2016). The addiction paradigm suffers, however, from a basic explanatory lapse that it places the explanation of addiction in the neurological vulnerability of the individual and considers the environment created by the machines as merely background.

Think about a real-life example. An adolescent starts playing TikTok to see two or three short clips. She watched dozens of videos in the next 45 minutes and is feeling dysphoric. This is believed to be due to a loss of self-regulation and dopamine habituation. But what it can't explain is the exact order of events at the platform level that led to the best dwell time: TikTok's for You Page algorithm figured out the affective frequency that increased dwell time in seconds. It was an emotional, novel and aspirational social sequence, designed to release dopamine in anticipation to moderate variable-ratio reinforcement. In France, Amnesty International (2025) empirically observed this escalation pattern on teen-simulated accounts: profiles that showed interest in mental health issues were 'steered' towards increasingly distressing content within a period of 15 to 60 minutes. It wasn't just in the user; it was generated architecturally.

Both theoretically and practically, this distinction is important. Diagnostic categories based on the DSM-5 criteria for substance use disorder do not easily correspond with digital engagement, which is platform-specific, and context-dependent (American Psychiatric Association, 2013). A meta-analysis has shown that the correlation between overall screen time and well-being measures is weaker than the correlation between content and social context and well-being measures (Orben & Przybylski, 2019). The addiction narrative at the societal level perpetuates a moral panic, shifting the focus away from the surveillance capitalist system that extracts behavioural data, creates predictive models, and sells behavioural futures to advertisers, towards a focus on personal shortcomings. When compulsion is clearly situated in the human–algorithmic mix, it emerges as a distributed system in which recommendation engines shape human actions by offering affordances at a finer grain that are systematically designed to access cognitive biases (Yeung, 2017).

The chapter proposes algorithmic compulsion as an alternative analytical concept and proposes an ecological socio-technical framework to explain the effects of multi-layered platform architectures that create habits and lead to digital self-disorders that are threatening to identity integrity. The analysis is guided by three research questions. How do algorithmic affordances, such as dopamine loops, interface nudges, platform optimization and hyperconnectivity norms, play out across the ecological layers to create emergent digital self-disorders? Second, how does an ecological socio-technical model broaden the explanatory power of traditional models of addiction? Third, what does this mean for interdisciplinary theorizing and for action-oriented, structure-oriented interventions? The chapter builds on a critical review of pertinent literature, an ecological mapping of the mechanisms of compulsion and the consequences for self-disorder, a formalized integrated model and implications for research, policy and clinical practice.

Table 1. Comparative Analysis of Behavioral Addiction Models and the Proposed Ecological Framework

Aspect	Behavioral Addiction Model: Limitations	Proposed Ecological Framework: Advantages
Unit of Analysis	Individual pathology — dopamine-hijacking as primary cause (Schultz, 2016)	Socio-technical emergence — distributed agency across human–algorithmic assemblages (Yeung, 2017)
Causal Mechanisms	Reinforcement cycles located within the user (Griffiths, 2013)	Multi-layer feedback loops spanning individual, interface, platform, and societal strata (Bronfenbrenner, 1979; Rosa, 2013)
Contextual Scope	Neglects platform economics; treats surveillance capitalism as background noise (Zuboff, 2019)	Integrates economic imperatives and affective labor as constitutive forces (Illouz, 2007; Zuboff, 2019)
Outcomes Mapped	Symptomatic — withdrawal, tolerance, compulsive use (Young, 2017)	Emergent self-disorders — identity fragmentation, validation dependency, affective volatility (Turkle, 2011)
Intervention Target	Individual therapy, self-regulatory skill-building (Kuss & Griffiths, 2017)	Systemic — platform redesign, regulation, ecological mental health frameworks (Milano et al., 2020)

Note. The table maps conceptual distinctions that motivate the chapter's reframing of digital compulsion.

FROM ADDICTION TO ALGORITHMIC COMPULSION: AN INTERDISCIPLINARY SYNTHESIS

Constructing an adequate account of algorithmic compulsion requires integrating four bodies of scholarship — behavioral addiction frameworks, persuasive technology research, platform economics, and identity psychology — each of which illuminates a distinct facet of the phenomenon while remaining individually insufficient.

Behavioral Addiction Frameworks: The Individual-Pathology Scaffold

Griffiths' (2013) components model based on the dimensions of substance-dependency was the first systematic template that mapped the dimensions of substance-dependency onto behavioral contexts: salience, mood modification, tolerance, withdrawal, conflict, and relapse. Next, Young's (2017) taxonomy was expanded to include Internet addiction and cyber-relational compulsion and Andreassen et al. (2016) cross-nationally reported on co-occurrence of intensive Internet use with depression, anxiety and other behavioral addictions. Collectively, these pieces of work showed that digital engagement can occur in clinically relevant ways of dysregulation. The explanatory weakness, however, is structural: they place the source of causation in individual dysfunctions in the dopamine reward system and self-control, and make the behavioral stimuli, which trigger the reward system and the self-control deficits, incidental.

Persuasive Technology: Engineering the Habit Loop

The basic model of captology developed by Fogg (2003) suggests that all digital interfaces are designed to influence behaviour; in fact, they can, when they are used, change behaviour if they use the right motivational triggers and user ability. Eyal (2014) turned this observation into a four-step hook cycle: trigger (either an external or internal cue that provokes a reaction); action (the action, e.g. scrolling); variable reward (random or unpredictable content or social validation that maintains dopamine anticipation); and investment (posting content or building social connections that raise switching costs and keep the user in the loop). The concept can be applied to modern social media to reveal the behavioral infrastructure of compulsion, such as infinite scrolling, autoplay, and algorithmic content curation. Building on this critique, Machidon (2025) states that AI-driven recommender systems decontextualize the human being and turn the user into a manipulated behavioral profile, from which excessive engagement emerges while cognition and well-being suffer due to the unbalanced focus on engagement scores. Most importantly, this literature tends to fail to include the economic forces that make and keep the persuasive design possible as an active and powerful force that persists in sustaining the compulsion.

Surveillance Capitalism: The Economic Engine of Compulsive Design

Zuboff's (2019) theory of surveillance capitalism fills the missing structural account in the study of persuasive technology. Zuboff's (2019) theory of surveillance capitalism complements the missing structural account in the study of persuasive technology. Digital platforms are based on an economic model of extracting behavioural data as raw material, creating predictive models from it, and trading behavioural futures with advertisers. This is not a by-product of this logic; it is the productive mechanism. Each extra second of wait, each click and pause creates behavioral surplus, which improves on algorithms and adds to advertising value. This poses an irreducible dilemma, because voluntary ethical redesign leading to a decrease in compulsion would harm revenue, and therefore being structurally feasible without external regulatory pressure is impossible. Algorithmic governance academics refer to this as the "hyper nudging" of people's behavior through invisible and personalized data-driven and default-setting systems, which increasingly threaten informed consent and user autonomy (Yeung, 2017). In addition to this, Boehmer (2024) notes that algorithmic decision making creates accountability gaps, which has direct implications for the mental health impacts of engagement-maximization platforms, as effective transparency processes to address these gaps are necessary.

Identity Psychology: The Self Under Algorithmic Pressure

Social comparison theory, applied to algorithmically curated content environments, shows that frequent exposure to idealised versions of others is linked to lower self-esteem, greater body image concerns, and greater depressive affect (Vogel et al., 2014). Marwick and Boyd's (2011) idea of 'context collapse' adds to these effects: when multiple, incompatible audience groups coalesce into one platform space, users are forced to present discontinuous and strategically managed versions of themselves as opposed to coherent and authentic identities. The motivational underpinnings are that of self-determination theory, which posits that algorithmically managed environments violate three basic psychological needs — autonomy (via nudges that restrict choice), competence (via constant social comparison), and relatedness (via superficial algorithmically mediated relationships) — that lead to experiences of extrinsic motivational states, which sustain compulsive engagement without allowing for the satisfaction of the needs that underlie human well-being (Ryan and Deci, 2017).

Synthesis: Toward a Distributed Model

In all four areas, there is a common understanding: digital compulsion is neither a purely psychological phenomenon nor a purely structural phenomenon. It is a combination of recursive entanglements of psychological vulnerabilities, persuasive interface design, platform economic pressures, and hyperconnectivity norms. Where personal structures produce explanatory paradoxes, a model of distributed agency, where compulsive patterns are produced because of human and algorithmic forces, solves the tensions. It also re-characterizes the object of intervention: when compulsion is a systemic socio-technical emergence, constructive actions should work on the ecological level not individual users.

Table 2. Interdisciplinary Synthesis: Strengths, Limitations, and Integrative Pathways

Domain	Core Concepts	Explanatory Strengths	Key Limitations	Integration Points
Behavioral Addiction	Salience, tolerance, withdrawal (Griffiths, 2013; Young, 2017)	Documents symptomatic patterns and comorbidity with psychiatric disorders	Pathologizes the individual; treats engineered rewards as incidental	Links dopamine loops to algorithmically designed reinforcement schedules
Persuasive Technology	Triggers, variable rewards, habit hooks (Fogg, 2003; Eyal, 2014)	Exposes intentional behavioral engineering embedded in interface design	Ethically neutral; under-theorizes commercial exploitation of attention	Connects micro-nudges to platform-level optimization agendas
Platform Economics / Surveillance Capitalism	Behavioral surplus, predictive algorithms (Zuboff, 2019)	Reveals economic imperatives driving compulsive design at scale	Under-specifies individual psychological mechanisms of compulsion	Frames persuasion as profit-driven algorithmic governance (Yeung, 2017)
Identity Psychology	Upward comparison, performative selfhood (Vogel et al., 2014; Marwick & boyd, 2011)	Explains self-fragmentation and the contingent self-worth cycle	Neglects technological mediation of identity processes	Integrates thwarted basic needs (Ryan & Deci, 2017) with feedback loops

Note. SDT = Self-Determination Theory. The table identifies the distinctive contribution and key conceptual gap of each domain, motivating an ecological synthesis.

THE ECOLOGY OF ALGORITHMIC COMPULSIONS

The idea of algorithmic compulsion is framed in this case as a four-stratum ecological system. This model is based on the ecological systems model created by Bronfenbrenner (1979) and places compulsion as an emergent property of self-dependent feedback loops functioning between the individual (microsystem), interface (proximal mesosystem), platform (distal mesosystem) and societal (macrosystem) levels. The causation is bidirectional, recursive: both levels create and are created by the other, creating vicious cycles that deepen the compulsion in the course of time (Lupton, 2020).

Individual Level: Neurocognitive Vulnerability and Thwarted Needs

Compulsion is supported by neurocognitive mechanisms of dopamine anticipation and attentional capture at the individual stratum. Prediction-error signals — neurochemical signals in response to unexpected rewards — are a key driver of continued use of personalized recommender systems, just as variable-ratio reinforcement schedules are for continued gambling behavior (Skinner, 1953; Schultz, 2016). Predictable rewards like a video that is viewed every day leads to a lower release of dopamine and consequently less effort towards re-engagement; however, when rewards are unpredictable – say, a notification from a creator you don't follow, or a viral post by another creator – the dopamine released is greater and so is the motivation to re-engage. Repeated exposure to stimuli which change quickly over time exhausts executive resources, which leads to poor impulse control and increased deepening of habits (Carr 2020). As predicted by SDT, algorithmic defaults that limit the freedom of choice and replace social interaction with algorithmic validation signals, lead to a gradual shift from intrinsic to extrinsic motivation and maintain compulsive reengagement with the algorithmically designed experience that ultimately proves insufficient for satisfaction of higher psychological needs (Ryan & Deci, 2017).

These dynamics are exacerbated in adolescence because of its neurophysiological asymmetry. According to De et al. (2025), AI-optimized content creates dopamine imbalances in underdeveloped brains, resulting in more extreme addiction-like behaviors. Prefrontal inhibitory control, which partially protects adults from compulsive re-engagement, is one of the final neural systems to complete development leaving adolescents particularly susceptible to interfaces designed to attract their attention.

Interface Level: Persuasive Nudges and Micro-Feedback Loops

The interface stratum constitutes the proximal environment in which individual psychological processes intersect with platform affordances. Notifications disrupt ongoing cognitive tasks and redirect attention involuntarily (Fogg, 2003). Infinite scroll eliminates the natural stopping points that bounded pagination would provide, exploiting what Rosa (2013) calls temporal acceleration — the compression of decision intervals that makes continuous interaction feel effortless. Engagement metrics such as follower counts, reactions, and view tallies quantify social worth in ways that encourage upward social comparison and contingent self-esteem (Vogel et al., 2014). Each element of the interface participates in a trigger–action–reward–investment cycle that increases the user's investment in platform content and social capital, raising the psychological cost of disengagement (Eyal, 2014). These micro-feedback loops operate at the level of seconds and clicks, rendering conscious deliberation largely ineffective as a counterforce.

Platform Level: Optimization, Governance, and Behavioral Surplus

On the platform level, every user action, including scrolling, pausing, liking, and sharing, is captured as a behavioural surplus that can be inserted as input into machine learning models to create preference profiles and make further adjustments on the recommender output with the aim of maximizing engagement (Zuboff, 2019). The creation of filter bubbles and echo-chambers is not an algorithmic bug, but an algorithmic feature: emotionally charged and opinion provoking content is guaranteed to lengthen the session time, and the algorithmic governance systems are built to maximize such content (Milano et al., 2020). This is the so-called "rabbit-hole effect" and has been empirically recorded. Amnesty International (2025) showed how teen-simulated TikTok accounts were algorithmically nudged towards increasingly distressing mental health content in 5-105 minutes by features that encourage engagement, such as 'infinite scroll' and 'behavioural recommendation logic'. In algorithmic decision-making, there is a potential efficiency benefit, but it also creates accountability gaps that cannot be addressed internally without transparency mechanisms, as Boehmer (2024) points out.

Societal Level: Hyperconnectivity Norms and Temporal Acceleration

The compulsion mechanisms work in the context of a culture that is set in the societal stratum. Labor markets, relationship cultures, and social status hierarchies have all become accustomed to expecting constant digital connectivity, including a very fast response to messages in all contexts from work to social to relationship (Marwick & boyd, 2011). With the concept of social acceleration, Rosa (2013) has identified a cultural imperative for immediacy that is manifested through the fast-interaction preferences in platform interfaces, compressed by the infrastructure of the digital. Affective economies also relate emotional expression and relational labor to the platform extraction imperative, as users' desire to be authentic and connected adds value to engagement, with this need for connection being picked up by surveillance systems and structurally linked to the extraction of value (Illouz, 2007).

Inter-Layer Feedback and Emergent Compulsion

The fundamental theoretical argument of this model is that compulsion is not generated at any one level, but rather through a cross-level, circular feedback between all four ecological levels. Behavioral signals are created through individual dopamine response, which can then be used to refine recommenders, which in turn can induce affective volatility, which in turn can determine societal norms, reducing the cognitive effort needed to re-engage at the individual level. This circularity is characteristic of a complex socio-technical system (Lupton, 2020): changes made at one layer such as requiring algorithmic transparency may ripple through the layers and, depending on the conditions, interfere with amplification at all levels.

Table 3. Multi-Layer Ecological Framework: Mechanisms, Empirical Illustrations, and Theoretical Anchors

Ecological Layer	Key Mechanisms	Illustrative Example	Theoretical Anchors
Individual	Dopamine anticipation, attentional capture, thwarted psychological needs	A teenager's prediction-error response to personalized TikTok content sustains habitual scrolling despite declining mood (De et al., 2025)	Schultz (2016); Ryan & Deci (2017); Carr (2020)
Interface	Nudges, variable rewards, quantified micro-feedback	Instagram's notification bursts and follower-count displays create checking cycles reinforced by social comparison (Fogg, 2003)	Eyal (2014); Vogel et al. (2014); Rosa (2013)
Platform	Recommender optimization, behavioral surplus extraction, algorithmic governance	YouTube's autoplay maximizes watch time by sequencing progressively arousing content, amplifying affective volatility (Milano et al., 2020)	Zuboff (2019); Yeung (2017); Boehmer (2024)
Societal	Norms of constant availability, performative presence, temporal acceleration	Professional LinkedIn culture normalizes 24/7 responsiveness, making disengagement socially and economically costly (Rosa, 2013)	Illouz (2007); Marwick & boyd (2011)

Note. Each layer is analytically distinct but dynamically interdependent. Figure 1 maps the bidirectional feedback pathways connecting strata.

DIGITAL SELF-DISORDERS AND IDENTITY FRAGMENTATION

The ecological amplification cycles mentioned in the previous section are not neutral in regard to selfhood. Basic psychological needs will be frustrated in a systematic way using platform-mediated environments, and this will not only cause momentary discomfort, but will present a continual violation of the conditions for coherent identity. Here, 6 types of digital self-dialectics are presented, each associated with one of the 6 ecological mechanisms.

Fractured Attention

Attentional fragmentation is the most basic digital self-disorder as sustained attention is necessary for all other aspects of self-regulated self-processes such as autobiographical memory consolidation, reflective identity construction and coherent temporal experience. Platform interfaces provide ongoing new stimuli: notifications, algorithmically refreshed feed content, autoplay transitions, and so on, thereby using up executive resources, which leaves less space for prolonged self-directed thought (Carr, 2020). Decreased self-concept clarity is related to empirical evidence of attentional dispersion: users have shown that they feel less sure about their self-knowledge as the rapid stimulus cycling increases (Vogel et al., 2014). The result is a fragmented self of temporality which is unable to bind experiences together in a coherent narrative.

Validation Dependency

Once the measurement of value is based on engagement, self-evaluation is no longer based on self-determination, rather it is the algorithmically mediate input of followers, reactions, and view tallies. Marwick and Boyd (2011) report on the imagined audience of social media posts which drive performative decisions, and which turn self-expression into strategic optimization. This contingent self-worth mechanism sets up a reinforcement cycle in which behaviour focused on metrics serves as a variable-ratio reinforcement, causing posting and checking behaviours to be repeated in cycles even as overall well-being decreases. Upward social comparisons with algorithmically generated idealized content also erode self-esteem, making the need for metric-based validation even stronger (Vogel et al., 2014). Precisely this vulnerability is the key to affective economies that generate surplus value from authentic human expression, relation work and attention (Illouz, 2007).

Affective Volatility

Algorithmically amplified high arousal content, positively valenced (inspiration, excitement) and negatively valenced (outrage, anxiety), keeps the viewer engaged by running a lot of affective turns. This instability leads to fluctuations between 'highs' and the dysphoria that develop from unfilled dopamine expectations, thus affecting emotional self-regulation (Baumeister et al., 2007). As metrically mediated interactions suppress opportunities for real competence and authentic relationships, the motivational resources become more and more depleted, which leads to a greater dependence on external stimuli (Ryan & Deci, 2017). De et al. (2025) pinpoint the neurophysiological substrate: AI-optimized content results in changes to the way the dopamine system functions in the adolescent brain, leading to increased and context-generalized reactivity to social reward and punishment signals.

Performative Identity Fragmentation

The phenomenon of 'context collapse' (when more than one set of incompatible audiences converge into a single platform space) forces users to produce a host of 'audience self' performances simultaneously, and therefore to abandon their sense of self-authorship that is integrated across contexts (Marwick & boyd, 2011). The temporal dimension is given by Rosa's (2013) social acceleration thesis: Digital infrastructure systematically reduces the time available for reflective identity negotiation, thus making stable identity construction more difficult. The performative self is reactive, changing quickly to the signals from the audience without a coherent narrative whole. The society-level norms of hyperconnectivity are legitimating and reinforcing this state of affairs, and strategic self-visibility is required for both social and professional inclusion.

Self-Quantification Anxiety and Parasocial Attachment

There are two other forms of self-disorder that should be discussed. Self-quantification anxiety is when gamified self-tracking systems only make lived experience readable through quantitative metrics, which creates existential discomfort and a disaffection with other aspects of personhood that are not measurable: embodied experience, relational depth, and interior life (Lupton, 2020). On the other hand, parasocial attachment is the feeling of intimacy and care formed by users toward algorithmic entities such as content creators, virtual influencers, and AI companions, which cannot be reciprocated as in real-life relationships (Horton & Wohl, 1956; Turkle, 2011). In both disorders, there is a structural aspect: self-referential processes are displaced to externally given processes that are algorithmically mediated and which progressively deplete the resources for self-construction that are internal to the system.

Table 4. Digital Self-Disorders: Mechanisms, Outcomes, and Theoretical Anchors

Manifestation	Core Mechanisms	Key Outcomes	Theoretical Anchors
Fractured Attention	Interface-driven attentional capture; infinite-feed design	Diminished self-concept clarity; temporal discontinuity; impaired executive function	Carr (2020); Vogel et al. (2014)
Validation Dependency	Metric-driven social comparison; contingent self-worth cycles	Emotional volatility; externalized identity; compulsive posting behavior	Marwick & boyd (2011); Vogel et al. (2014)
Affective Volatility	Algorithmic amplification of high-arousal content; dopamine-dysphoria cycles	Impaired emotional regulation; mood instability; anxiety escalation	Baumeister et al. (2007); Ryan & Deci (2017)
Self-Quantification Anxiety	Gamified tracking; datafication of personal performance	Existential unease; alienation from non-quantifiable selfhood	Lupton (2020)
Parasocial Attachment	One-sided bonds with algorithmic entities and content creators	Blurred self–other boundaries; diluted offline relational capacity	Horton & Wohl (1956); Turkle (2011)
Performative Identity Fragmentation	Context collapse; temporal acceleration of self-presentation demands	Reactive self-curation; loss of identity coherence across platforms	Rosa (2013); Marwick & boyd (2011)

Note. The six manifestations are analytically distinct but empirically overlapping; they co-occur and mutually reinforce in practice, constituting a syndrome of socio-technical self-disturbance.

AN INTEGRATED SOCIO-TECHNICAL ECOLOGICAL MODEL

The sections above charted the ecology of algorithmic compulsion and its implications for selfhood. Those relationships are formalized in this section in a structural model that can be tested, with five constitutive components representing antecedents, mediators, moderators, outcomes, and feedback pathways, based on the logic of the structure of the existing internet-use disorder models (Brand et al., 2016; Hou et al., 2019).

Model Architecture

These are the antecedent affordances that set up compulsive dynamics: interactive and persistent interfaces optimized for engagement, including machine-learning-driven recommendation systems; persuasive interface features like infinite scroll, autoplay, and variable-reward notifications; and behavioral data extraction based on surveillance, continually being refined for predictive personalization (Fogg, 2003; Eyal, 2014; Zuboff, 2019). These affordances are the 'structural prerequisites' to which users are constantly exposed in everyday interactions via the interface environment, and which activate three psychological entry points: dopamine anticipation, attentional bias and frustrated social needs.

The proximal psychological and affective processes that mediate between the affordances and the sustained compulsive engagement are the mediators. There are two parallel mediating pathways. Affective mediation involves validation seeking loops that is fueled by metric based social comparison and emotional amplification resulting from algorithmically curated high arousal content (Vogel et al., 2014; Illouz, 2007). This is a novelty prediction and variable reinforcement mechanism that captures and splits attention, which leads to depleting self-regulatory resources and disrupting autonomous decision-making (Eyal, 2014; Carr, 2020). The central theoretical idea is that these mediators trigger ongoing compulsions by short-circuiting the reinforcement system by increasing engagement while simultaneously reducing the motivational resources (autonomy, competence, relatedness) that would otherwise allow for self-determined disengagement (Ryan & Deci, 2017).

Moderators are differential vulnerability and resilience at the individual and cultural level. Digital literacy and self-regulatory competence act as moderating buffers, helping users to be aware of persuasive design and to set intentional boundaries (Baumeister et al., 2007). Developmental stage is a moderating and amplifying variable, as adolescents are more susceptible to the influence of the social environment thanks to their immature prefrontal cortex, incomplete consolidation of identity and greater sensitivity to social reward and punishment (Orben & Przybylski, 2019; De et al., 2025). An antecedent-to-mediator pathway is reinforced by cultural norms of time acceleration and hyperconnectivity in contexts in which disengagement is structurally punished (Rosa, 2013).

Outcomes include the digital self-disorders identified in the previous section, implemented at the identity, affect, cognition, behavior, and relational capacity level.

The integrated model is more of a nonlinear causal model because it includes feedback loops. Outcome states (e.g., fragmented identity, validation dependency) create greater posting and checking behavior, creating more behavioral surplus to bolster recommerce outputs, which in turn intensify the antecedent affordances. The phenomenon is emergent, bidirectional and self-reinforcing – it is a socio-technical system, rather than an individual pathology, hence the distinction from conventional addiction models.

Formal Propositions

The following three formal propositions are based on the architecture of the model. The affective loop intensity and attentional capture will be positively associated to exposure to algorithmic affordances - personalization, persuasive nudges and data extraction through surveillance - with this, predicting compulsive engagement and digital self-disorder severity, as stated in Proposition 1. Digital literacy and self-regulatory capacity (mediator) will moderate this pathway, with low levels of digital literacy and self-regulation reducing mediator activation, and reducing the severity of compulsion, whereas the developmental stage of adolescence and cultural norms of acceleration will amplify this pathway. Proposition 3 is that outcome states intensify affordances of antecedents, in the sense that they drive greater behavioral data production and urgency of re-engagement, creating a recursive loop and sustaining algorithmic compulsion as an emergent and self-reinforcing phenomenon instead of an individual condition.

Table 5. Integrated Socio-Technical Ecological Model: Components, Constructs, and Anchors

Component	Variables / Constructs	Representative Theoretical Anchors
Antecedents	Algorithmic affordances: recommender personalization, persuasive nudges (infinite scroll, autoplay, variable-reward notifications), surveillance-based data extraction	Fogg (2003); Eyal (2014); Zuboff (2019)
Mediators	Affective loops (validation-seeking, emotional amplification); attentional capture (variable reinforcement, novelty prediction); thwarted psychological needs (autonomy, competence, relatedness)	Schultz (2016); Carr (2020); Ryan & Deci (2017)
Moderators	Digital literacy and self-regulatory capacity (buffering); adolescent developmental stage (amplifying); cultural norms of temporal acceleration (amplifying)	Orben & Przybylski (2019); Rosa (2013); Baumeister et al. (2007)
Outcomes	Digital self-disorders: identity fragmentation, validation dependency, affective volatility, performative self-curation, self-quantification anxiety; secondary: attentional deficits, relationship impairment	Turkle (2011); Lupton (2020); Vogel et al. (2014)
Feedback Loops	Outcome states (fragmented identity, validation-seeking) feed back to reinforce antecedent affordances by increasing data yield and compulsive re-engagement, sustaining the cycle	Bronfenbrenner (1979); Milano et al. (2020); Lupton (2020)

Note. Bidirectional feedback arrows (Proposition 3) connect outcomes back to antecedents, operationalizing the model's core claim about recursive socio-technical emergence.

IMPLICATIONS FOR RESEARCH, POLICY, AND MENTAL HEALTH PRACTICE

The integrated model generates a coherent agenda across interdisciplinary research, platform governance, regulation, and mental health practice. The organizing principle across all domains is consistent: effective responses to algorithmic compulsion must operate at the ecological level rather than targeting individual users.

Interdisciplinary Research Priorities

Longitudinal is the most important empirical lack. Current studies offer only cross sectional associations between self-disorder outcomes and heavy platform use and cannot distinguish if compulsive engagement leads to identity fragmentation, or the other way around. Cohort designs that track adolescents and emerging adults over development transitions, coupled with ecological momentary assessment of affective states and fine-grained records of platform usage logs, would allow researchers to unravel the bi-directional relationships as outlined in Proposition 3 (Rosa, 2013; Turkle, 2011). Experimental studies that manipulated the antecedent affordance of platforms by systematically modifying the ranking objective, introducing intentional friction and greater transparency, and showing how these changes affect the degree of mediator activation and compulsive engagement would offer causal evidence of the impact of reducing antecedent affordance strength on mediator activation and compulsive engagement.

Qualitative and participatory research methods are also essential to capture aspects that cannot be quantified. Documentation of ethnographic studies should take into account how users negotiate, contest and internalise hyper nudges in everyday life, recovering the phenomenology of compulsion and lived experience of managing their identity under algorithmic governance (Lupton, 2020). A participatory design research approach with the people most impacted by compulsive digital environments would allow the co-development of alternative affordance architectures that emphasize relational depth without increasing engagement volume.

Regulatory and Platform Governance

An ethical redesign of surveillance capitalism cannot be achieved through voluntary action without regulation because of the structural incentive misalignment of surveillance capitalism. The integrated model provides a number of evidence based on regulatory directions. Transparency requires that platforms publish the main optimization goals, so that base conditions of informed consent are restored, and meaningful algorithmic auditing would give an account to hyper nudge systems

(Yeung, 2017; Milano et al., 2020). The OECD/GPAI (2024) report on algorithmic transparency in the public sector distinguishes between institutional models and other approaches; among the former, proactive disclosure mechanisms, such as algorithmic registries, are in operation in France, Colombia and Uruguay, allowing for external oversight without impacting platform functions.

Precautionary measures similar to those applied to consumer safety in other product areas include, for platforms with a primary user base of minors, a ban on infinite scroll; for platforms that send notifications for rewards, a limit on the variability of the reward notification after a prolonged nightly session; and for platforms with content diversity, a limit on content diversity after a prolonged session. The most developed framework to date are the EU Digital Services Act and the EU AI Act, which requires very large platforms to undergo systemic-risk assessments and to extend the rights of researchers to audit. To widen the use of these instruments to expressly cover compulsory design characteristics and mental health impacts would be an important step forward. The social costs of behavioral surplus extraction (Zuboff, 2019) would be internalized by incentive realignment measures such as civil liability for compulsion-related harms and engagement taxes.

Comparative analysis of the regulatory approaches finds other countries. Whilst state-led protections for adolescents, such as age verification, time-limit defaults, and content restrictions for AI-driven platforms are important considerations, these protections are limited by enforcement difficulties and the risk of platform migration (Yao, 2025). In the United States, current litigation against Meta and Google for their intentional design of products for youth could upend scales of corporate incentives. Fragmented national approaches would be less comprehensive than harmonized international approaches to high-risk affordances, cross-border algorithmic impact assessments and coordinated fiscal measures.

Mental Health Frameworks

There are two problems with addiction-diagnostic frameworks in the context of public health and clinical practice: one is that they pathologies coping mechanisms in the face of actual and legitimate environments of compulsion; and two, they focus on managing symptoms and not on structural change. The idea of digital self-disorders as socio-technical stress syndromes—emergent responses to ecological pressures—shifts the therapeutic goal from rehabilitating behaviors to changing behaviors and increasing skills for ecological advocacy (Uslu 2025).

Intervention developed within the integrated framework would explicitly include socio-technical concepts and the three thwarted basic needs would be addressed in a hybrid fashion, consisting of an individual skills training focused on attention regulation, values clarification and critical digital literacy, as well as a psychoeducation about persuasive design architectures and an advocacy for structural platform reform (Ryan & Deci, 2017). The American Academy of Pediatrics (2026) policy statement on digital ecosystems makes similar recommendations for system-level design changes and protective default settings, along with individualized guidance. Public mental health communications should move from focusing on individual screen time to the structural factors that contribute to compulsive engagement, stigma reduction and help-seeking, and collective action.

Table 6. Summary of Implications and Priority Research Directions by Domain

Domain	Key Implications	Priority Research Directions
Regulation & Platform Design	Mandate algorithmic transparency; restrict addictive affordances; require mental health impact assessments for high-risk platforms	Experimental evaluations of DSA/AI Act provisions; randomized trials of ethically redesigned feed architectures
Mental Health Frameworks	Reframe digital self-disorders as socio-technical syndromes; integrate SDT into therapy; reduce individual stigma through systemic framing	Hybrid intervention trials combining ecological redesign advocacy with individual skill-building; critical analysis of DSM pathologization
Interdisciplinary Scholarship	Longitudinal studies on temporal acceleration and identity coherence; participatory design with affected communities	Cohort studies tracking adolescents across developmental transitions; ecological momentary assessment of affect-algorithm interactions

Note. Entries are derived directly from the integrated model's propositions and constitute a structured agenda rather than an exhaustive inventory.

ETHICAL DIMENSIONS AND DESIGN INTERVENTIONS

The ecological model is not only descriptive but also depicts the normative fault lines that make current platform architectures ethically unsound. There are four structural elements that are tied to specific ethical issues.

First, hypernudges are opaque, which violates the principles of informed consent. However, users are unable to make truly voluntary decisions regarding their involvement settings when they are not visible, when the goals of the optimization are not disclosed, or when the opt-out alternatives aren't available (Yeung, 2017). Algorithmic explainability tools that would give users easy-to-understand visualizations of how content was selected through algorithmic means, along with user-controllable personalization parameters, would restore some of the conditions for autonomous decision-making without full disclosure of algorithms.

Second, the systemic exploitation of emotional vulnerability is commercial exploitation. Engaging readers isn't necessarily an unintended side effect of arousal optimization — the practice of prioritizing content that reliably keeps readers entertained for a long period of time, be they angry, concerned, or socially envious (Vogel et al., 2014; Zuboff, 2019). Technically possible alternatives to encourage user's interests and long-term sustainability of the platform include well-being weighted ranking objectives and arousal de-emphasis features after long sessions (Milano et al., 2020).

Thirdly, it is problematic to apply adult engagement architectures to minors from an ethical perspective in terms of developmental harm. Adolescents have compulsive behavioral patterns at lower thresholds of exposure to affordances than do adults (Orben & Przybylski, 2019; De et al., 2025) due to the immaturity of their prefrontal function and increased neurophysiological sensitivity to social reward and punishment. Proper ‘age-appropriate design defaults' such as limiting addictive affordances, offering parental-control APIs, and banning variable-ratio reward systems for youth-facing products are all examples of proportionate precautionary measures. These recommendations are in line with the harm reduction approach outlined in the Stanford Youth Safety and Digital Wellbeing Report (2025), recognizing the positive social roles of platform engagement.

Fourth, there is a fundamental tension between surveillance capitalism's need to extract behaviour and user psychology, which cannot be addressed by design interventions alone. Independent algorithmic impact assessments would create evidence-based accountability systems which are similar to environmental assessment statements. Civil liability regimes that ensure corporate responsibility for clearly documented compulsion-related psychological harm would bring these costs into the corporation, instead of onto individuals and public health care systems. These structural features would establish real economic pressures to move from the maximization of engagement to well-being design goals.

Table 7. Ethical Concerns, Mechanisms, Proposed Interventions, and Supporting Evidence

Ethical Concern	Primary Mechanism / Risk	Proposed Intervention	Supporting Literature
Opacity and erosion of user autonomy	Hidden hypernudges diminish volitional choice; opaque personalization withholds meaningful consent	Algorithmic explainability tools; user-adjustable personalization parameters; mandatory disclosure of optimization goals	Yeung (2017); Milano et al. (2020)
Exploitation of affective vulnerabilities	High-arousal content prioritized to maximize engagement, amplifying anxiety, outrage, and social envy	Well-being-weighted ranking objectives; arousal de-emphasis after prolonged sessions; content-diversity incentives	Vogel et al. (2014); Zuboff (2019)
Developmental harm to minors	Adolescents' underdeveloped prefrontal regulation heightens susceptibility to compulsive design features	Age-verified defaults; stricter limits on addictive affordances in youth-facing products; parental-control APIs	Orben & Przybylski (2019); Turkle (2011); De et al. (2025)
Structural incentive misalignment	Surveillance capitalism financially rewards engagement maximization over user well-being	Algorithmic impact assessments; civil liability for compulsion-related harm; engagement-tax fiscal disincentives	Zuboff (2019); European Commission (2022)

Note. Interventions are ordered from least to most structurally disruptive, reflecting a graduated regulatory logic from transparency through liability.

FUTURE RESEARCH DIRECTIONS

The ecological socio-technical framework proposed in this chapter indicates several scientific issues that need to be explored separately. These directions are transdisciplinary and embody the theoretical stance of the integrated model: namely that algorithmic compulsion is an emergent, recursive and structurally produced phenomenon and not a stable individual pathology.

Longitudinal design is the most urgent methodological need. Most of the studies are cross-sectional, and thus it remains unclear whether compulsive platform engagement leads to and causes identity fragmentation and affective volatility, or if such vulnerabilities are a cause of greater access to algorithmic affordances. To dissect temporal ordering and to examine bidirectional feedback loops as posited in Proposition 3, multi-wave panel studies of adolescents and young adults are necessary that involve EMA of affective states along with platform usage telemetry.

A second major gap is related to the experimental study of platform architecture alternatives. Much of the work so far has been on the behavioural implications of actual affordance configurations, and very little has been done on the effects of ethically re-designed configurations. Randomized controlled trials that compared standard feed architectures to ones that included intentional friction, well-being weighted ranking, content diversity requirements, and reduced variable-ratio reinforcement would produce causal data for the antecedent affordance effects in the integrated model.

A third underdeveloped field is cross-cultural and comparative studies. The ecological model includes amplifying moderators of hyperconnectivity and temporal acceleration in society, which differ significantly across cultural contexts. Comparative studies comparing the manifestation of algorithmically compulsive dynamics in high connectivity versus lower connectivity cultures, and societies with different regulatory frameworks regarding platforms, would enhance the understanding of the contribution of macrosystems to compulsion and self-disorder outcomes.

The fourth is developmental neuroscience and platform design. While some studies, such as De et al. (2025), have shown how AI-optimized content cycles can affect the brain of adolescents, more research is needed using longitudinal neuroimaging to observe the changes in brain development, specifically in the development of the dopaminergic system, in response to exposure to platforms over longer periods of time. This research could offer biological underpinning for the application of precautionary regulatory requirements to digital products aimed at youth.

Fifth, algorithmic compulsion is not well developed in terms of its phenomenology. Quantitative studies tell us a lot about how users behave, but they don't tell us how they perceive, negotiate, resist or accommodate hyper nudges in everyday life. Experiencing algorithmic governance and designing culturally grounded, experience-near interventions will require ethnographic, interview-based, and participatory research approaches to recover the subjective dimensions of identity management.

Finally, and most importantly, technology-specific research on new platforms and interaction modalities is greatly needed. Rapidly emerging AI companion apps, XR spaces, and generative content interfaces generate new affordance configurations, which have not yet been studied systematically in terms of their compulsive use and self-disorder potentials. Theories and empirical studies need to follow the evolution of platforms and not be continuously revisited.

Lastly, there is a clear need for interdisciplinary research on the effectiveness of regulation. However, as the EU Digital Services Act, EU AI Act and other national legislations begin to be put in place, a systematic assessment of their impacts on compulsive engagement patterns, self-disorder prevalence and adolescent well-being will change the debate from ideological controversies to evidence-based iterative governance. Researchers from many disciplines, such as legal scholars, computational social scientists, developmental psychologists, and public health researchers, are all needed to make this agenda a reality.

CONCLUSION

The chapter has provided a sustained critique of the behavioral addiction paradigm as an explanatory model of the phenomenon of digital compulsion, and its implications for the self in hyperconnected societies. Although the behavioural addiction model may be useful in clinical situations for diagnostic purposes, all it does is place the responsibility for causing addiction on an individual and systematically ignore the generative sociocultural norms, economic pressures and engineered affordances that are the true context of compulsion.

The ecological socio-technical framework proposed here offers an alternative account that is structured around four analytically distinct but dynamically interrelated strata: individual neurocognitive vulnerability, persuasive interface design, platform-level optimization and behavioral surplus extraction, and societal norms of hyperconnectivity/temporal acceleration. These recursive feedback loops between these strata generate compulsion as an emergent condition, which leads to digital self-disorders as a psychological, technological and economic phenomenon, and to identity-threatening experiences of fragmented attention, validation dependency, affective volatility, performative identity fragmentation and self-quantification anxiety in relation to using platforms.

Three propositions are integrated in the model and suggest that algorithmic affordances are associated with digital self-disorders via affective and cognitive-attentional mediating processes that are moderated by digital literacy, developmental stage and cultural context. The bidirectional feedbacks between the outcome state and the affordances of the antecedent states constitute it as a self-sustaining socio-technical system, rather than as static individual pathologies and as a form of algorithmic compulsion. The formalization provides a basis for a common interdisciplinary research programme and a reorientation of practice towards the ecological instead of single level intervention.

All the implications have a common theme: it is a structural issue, not a personal one. Progress will require coordinated action on three fronts: regulatory systems that ensure transparency, reducing the risks of high-risk affordances, and re-engineering corporate incentives; platform design that takes well-being as a legitimate optimization goal; and clinical and public health systems that understand and address the structural drivers of distress and provide therapeutic resources accordingly. Hyperconnectivity is not a disease; it is not a cure. The question is whether the algorithmic architecture which regulates human sociality will be used to leverage off psychological vulnerabilities, for commercial purposes, or to enable conditions for coherent, self-determined human flourishing. It is a question of design and governing before it is a clinical question.

REFERENCES

American Psychiatric Association. (2013). *Diagnostic and statistical manual of mental disorders* (5th ed.)., DOI: 10.1176/appi.books.9780890425596

Amnesty International. (2025). Dragged into the rabbit hole: New evidence of TikTok's risks to children's mental health (Index: POL 40/0360/2025). https://www.amnesty.org/en/documents/pol40/0360/2025/en/

Andreassen, C. S., Billieux, J., Griffiths, M. D., Kuss, D. J., Demetrovics, Z., Mazzoni, E., & Pallesen, S. (2016). The relationship between addictive use of social media and video games and symptoms of psychiatric disorders: A large-scale cross-sectional study. *Psychology of Addictive Behaviors*, *30*(2), 252–262. DOI: 10.1037/adb0000160

Baumeister, R. F., Vohs, K. D., & Tice, D. M. (2007). The strength model of self-control. *Current Directions in Psychological Science*, *16*(6), 351–355. DOI: 10.1111/j.1467-8721.2007.00534.x

Boehmer, N. (2024). The double-edged sword of algorithmic governance: Transparency at stake. Ash Center for Democratic Governance and Innovation, Harvard Kennedy School. https://ash.harvard.edu/wp-content/uploads/2024/02/niclas_boehmer_essay.pdf

Brand, M., Young, K. S., Laier, C., Wölfling, K., & Potenza, M. N. (2016). Integrating psychological and neurobiological considerations regarding the development and maintenance of specific Internet-use disorders: An Interaction of Person-Affect-Cognition-Execution (I-PACE) model. *Neuroscience and Biobehavioral Reviews*, *71*, 252–266. DOI: 10.1016/j.neubiorev.2016.08.033

Bronfenbrenner, U. (1979). *The ecology of human development: Experiments by nature and design*. Harvard University Press. DOI: 10.4159/9780674028845

Carr, N. (2020). *The shallows: What the internet is doing to our brains* (2nd ed.). W. W. Norton.

De, D., El Jamal, M., Aydemir, E., & Khera, A. (2025). Social media algorithms and teen addiction: Neurophysiological impact and ethical considerations. *Cureus*, *17*(1), e77145. Advance online publication. DOI: 10.7759/cureus.77145

European Commission. (2022). The Digital Services Act package. https://digital-strategy.ec.europa.eu/en/policies/digital-services-act-package

Eyal, N. (2014). *Hooked: How to build habit-forming products*. Portfolio.

Fogg, B. J. (2003). *Persuasive technology: Using computers to change what we think and do*. Morgan Kaufmann. DOI: 10.1016/B978-155860643-2/50011-1

Griffiths, M. D. (2013). Social networking addiction: Emerging themes and issues. *Journal of Addiction Research & Therapy*, *4*(5), e118. Advance online publication. DOI: 10.4172/2155-6105.1000e118

Horton, D., & Wohl, R. R. (1956). Mass communication and para-social interaction: Observations on intimacy at a distance. *Psychiatry*, *19*(3), 215–229. DOI: 10.1080/00332747.1956.11023049

Hou, Y., Xiong, D., Jiang, T., Song, L., & Wang, Q. (2019). Social media addiction: Its impact, mediation, and intervention. *Cyberpsychology (Brno)*, *13*(1), 4. Advance online publication. DOI: 10.5817/CP2019-1-4

Illouz, E. (2007). *Cold intimacies: The making of emotional capitalism*. Polity Press.

Kuss, D. J., & Griffiths, M. D. (2017). Social networking sites and addiction: Ten lessons learned. *International Journal of Environmental Research and Public Health*, *14*(3), 311. Advance online publication. DOI: 10.3390/ijerph14030311

Lupton, D. (2020). *Data selves: More-than-human perspectives*. Polity Press.

Machidon, O. M. (2025). Beyond algorethics: Addressing the ethical and anthropological challenges of AI recommender systems. *Journal of Media Ethics*, 1–13. Advance online publication. DOI: 10.1080/23736992.2025.2584435

Marwick, A. E., & boyd, . (2011). I tweet honestly, I tweet passionately: Twitter users, context collapse, and the imagined audience. *New Media & Society*, *13*(1), 114–133. DOI: 10.1177/1461444810365313

Milano, S., Taddeo, M., & Floridi, L. (2020). Recommender systems and their ethical challenges. *AI & Society*, *35*(4), 957–967. DOI: 10.1007/s00146-020-00950-y

Orben, A., & Przybylski, A. K. (2019). The association between adolescent well-being and digital technology use. *Nature Human Behaviour*, *3*(2), 173–182. DOI: 10.1038/s41562-018-0506-1

Organisation for Economic Co-operation and Development & Global Partnership on Artificial Intelligence. (2024). Algorithmic transparency in the public sector: A state-of-the-art report. https://wp.oecd.ai/app/uploads/2025/05/algorithmic-transparency-in-the-public-sector.pdf

Rosa, H. (2013). *Social acceleration: A new theory of modernity*. Columbia University Press. DOI: 10.7312/rosa14834

Ryan, R. M., & Deci, E. L. (2017). *Self-determination theory: Basic psychological needs in motivation, development, and wellness*. Guilford Press. DOI: 10.1521/978.14625/28806

Schultz, W. (2016). Dopamine reward prediction error coding. *Dialogues in Clinical Neuroscience*, *18*(1), 23–32. DOI: 10.31887/DCNS.2016.18.1/wschultz

Skinner, B. F. (1953). *Science and human behavior*. Macmillan.

Turkle, S. (2011). *Alone together: Why we expect more from technology and less from each other*. Basic Books.

Uslu, O. (2025). Understanding digital wellbeing: Impacts, strategies, and the path to healthier technology practices. *Discover Social Science and Health*, *5*(1), 145. Advance online publication. DOI: 10.1007/s44155-025-00259-5

Vogel, E. A., Rose, J. P., Roberts, L. R., & Eckles, K. (2014). Social comparison, social media, and self-esteem. *Psychology of Popular Media Culture*, *3*(4), 206–222. DOI: 10.1037/ppm0000047

Yao, M. Z. (2025). Regulating social media for minors: A comparative analysis of national approaches. *Journal of Information Policy*, *15*(1), 1–38. DOI: 10.5325/jinfopoli.15.1.0001

Yeung, K. (2017). 'Hypernudge': Big data as a mode of regulation by design. *Information Communication and Society*, *20*(1), 118–136. DOI: 10.1080/1369118X.2016.1186713

Young, K. S. (2017). The evolution of Internet addiction. *Addictive Behaviors*, *64*, 229–230. DOI: 10.1016/j.addbeh.2015.05.016

Zuboff, S. (2019). *The age of surveillance capitalism: The fight for a human future at the new frontier of power*. PublicAffairs.

KEY TERMS AND DEFINITIONS

Algorithmic Affordance: Any aspect of a digital service that is designed and implemented to influence the actions of users by inducing conditions that make certain activities (e.g., scrolling, clicking, posting, sharing) more likely because of exploiting cognitive biases, social needs, and reinforcement mechanisms. Algorithmic affordances are infinite scroll, variable-reward notification systems, autoplay, and personalized content recommendation, which are antecedent structural conditions that lead to compulsive engagement (Fogg, 2003; Eyal, 2014).

Algorithmic Compulsion: An emergent socio-technical phenomenon characterized by multi-level feedback loops between individual neurocognitive reactions, interface nudging effects, platform optimization pressures and hyperconnectivity cultural norms. Algorithmic compulsion does not blame individuals as in behavioral addiction models, but rather the distributed agency of human–algorithmic assemblages in which the engineered affordances produce and maintain patterns of compulsion (Machidon, 2025; De et al., 2025).

Behavioral Surplus: The behavioural data about users that is collected from digital platforms as a by-product of their use, such as scroll depth, time spent on a page, clicks and social signals, which are harvested by the platform and then converted to predictive models for sale to advertisers. Subsequently, the concept was formulated by Zuboff (2019), who viewed behavioral surplus as the main raw material of surveillance capitalism and engagement maximization as a process for generating and refining behavioral surplus.

Context Collapse: The condition of the boundaries of different social audiences, family/friend/colleague/stranger, becoming blended in a single space of a digital platform, forcing the user to create a message that is likely to be consumed by audiences with conflicting needs. Context collapse offers an incentive to present oneself in strategic and fragmented ways rather than in ways that might be considered authentic to a self, potentially fragmenting self-presentation and making authentic self-authorship harder to maintain (Marwick & boyd, 2011).

Digital Self-Disorders: Recursive human–algorithmic interactions generating emergent socio-technical disruptions of identity integration, affective stability and self-regulatory capacity. These include fragmented attention, a dependence on validation, affective volatility, performative identity fragmentation, and anxiety with self-quantification. As systemic relational processes, they should be viewed as reactions to structural ecological pressures not as individual diseases (Turkle, 2011; Lupton, 2020).

Hypernudge: Steering user behavior on a default basis in a data-driven and algorithmically implemented way, in a largely invisible and individually adapted manner at scale. A hypernudge is fundamentally different from a conventional nudge as it uses granular behavioral data, is adaptive with personalisation and is able to run continuously and simultaneously across millions of users. They increasingly violate informed consent and autonomous decision making by building environments that maximize engagement with platforms but don't necessarily maximize user health (Yeung, 2017).

Parasocial Attachment: The emotional content of their interactions with media figures, content creators, virtual influencers or AI companion systems that create a unidirectional feeling of intimacy, care, and identification for the user, lacking the reciprocal relationship found in real interpersonal interactions. In algorithmically curated content environments, parasocial attachments that involve familiar figures and the illusion of a relational connection can intensify and are persistent, potentially replacing the development of real offline relationships, and leading to the blurring of the boundaries between self and other (Turkle, 2011; Horton & Wohl, 1956).

Surveillance Capitalism: An economic model whereby digital platforms monetize the behaviour of normal human beings by capturing information about their behaviour in everyday activities, building predictive models based on that data, and then selling access to the predictive products to advertisers and other commercial parties. Theoretically, as posited by Zuboff (2019), surveillance capitalism incentivizes the highest amount of engagement, at the cost of the user's well-being, which is economically irrational without external regulatory measures.

Temporal Acceleration: The social time's compression effected by cultural and technological factors, which generates norms of immediacy, quickness, and constant presence in relational, professional, and public activities. Temporal acceleration as a macro-system context that magnifies platform-level compulsion mechanisms, and because of decisions made in platform design that reduce decision time and make quick interactions more attractive than reflective engagement, is theorized by Rosa (2013).

Validation Dependency: A shift in self-regulatory self-worth and emotional regulation in which external algorithmic signals (e.g., likes, followers, shares) take the place of internal standards or values. Validation dependency occurs when intrinsic motivation is systematically replaced by dependency upon social comparisons based on metrics and maintained by variable-ratio schedules of reinforcement in platform engagement architectures (Vogel et al., 2014; Marwick & boyd, 2011).

Chapter 3
From Addiction to Embeddedness:
Rethinking Digital Life in a Digitally Attached Age

Gulsun Bozkurt
http://orcid.org/0000-0001-9558-7577
Istanbul Nisantasi University, Turkey

Gülden Demir
http://orcid.org/0000-0002-6028-5496
İstanbul Nişantaşı University, Turkey

ABSTRACT

Digital media have become central environments through which social life is organized rather than optional tools. This chapter critiques dominant digital addiction narratives for individualizing and pathologizing practices that are increasingly shaped by institutional and infrastructural conditions. Drawing on communication theory, platform studies, and critical social theory, it proposes digital embeddedness as a more productive framework for understanding contemporary digital life. Digital embeddedness emphasizes how everyday communication, work, education, and public participation are organized through platform infrastructures that shape experiences of time, visibility, presence, and social belonging. The chapter highlights a freedom–dependence paradox in which digital media expand communicative possibilities while simultaneously binding individuals and institutions to opaque systems of governance and value extraction, calling for communication research to move beyond addiction discourses toward critical analyses of platform power.

DOI: 10.4018/979-8-3373-6665-4.ch003

INTRODUCTION

Digitalization is no longer merely an add-on to everyday life; it has become its very substrate. Smartphones, social networks, short-video platforms, and AI-enabled services are restructuring the rhythms of communication, the terms of public visibility, and the organization of cultural production. This transformation compels a move beyond the pathology-centered frames that dominate debates on "technology addictions and digital diseases." In psychiatry and clinical psychology, addiction is typically defined as a pattern of loss of control, compulsion to continue, and consequent impairment of functioning with respect to a substance or behavior (American Psychiatric Association [APA], 2013). Although categories such as "internet/social media/game addiction" are cast within this frame, a conceptual problem arises: unlike alcohol or narcotics -excludable objects that can be set aside- digital tools have penetrated virtually every domain of social life, from education and work to cultural production and political participation. Reducing persistent online presence to the addiction label obscures the phenomenon's structural and communicative dimensions.

Subjective experience underscores this tension. Checking the phone upon waking, spending long stretches on social media, and joining online meetings or games are widely legitimated as "part of the job" or "the necessary path to sustaining relationships," even as many report anxiety, attentional fragmentation, loneliness, and insomnia. If these practices are addictions, why is social life organized around them? If they are not, why does intensive use continue to produce problems? The paradox reveals the limits of classical addiction theories-built on individual will-failure and orientation to an external object-for explaining the conditions of the digital present. Digitalization is not simply orientation to an external object; it is a transformation of self-construal, cognitive processes, and relational existence. Identities curated through social-media profiles, affiliations forged in online communities, and emotional bonds sustained via instant messaging sit at the center of lived reality (Turkle, 2011). Digital presence should therefore be conceptualized not as a pathology but as a new mode of being. Following a communicative-theory perspective, these dynamics can be read as a remaking of the lifeworld, with platform infrastructures colonizing routines of visibility, temporality, and participation.

In this sense, digital embeddedness entails both a reconfiguration of the communicative lifeworld and the embedding of social relations within platform infrastructures. Communication and sociological scholarship approach this condition through interlocking perspectives. Building on the insight that economic and social action is always situated within networks and institutions, we extend this argument toward digital embeddedness: contemporary social relations, cultural production, and everyday interactions are increasingly organized through and dependent on platform environments (Granovetter, 1985; Hepp, 2019). While psychology's notion of "digital immersion" emphasizes the allocation of cognitive and attentional resources to mediated stimuli (Slater & Wilbur, 1997), a communication-oriented perspective foregrounds infrastructural conditioning. What becomes visible, what is rendered salient, and which forms of interaction are amplified or marginalized are shaped by platforms' ranking and recommendation systems as well as interface politics (Bucher, 2018; Gillespie, 2014). From this standpoint, single-factor measures such as "screen time" fail to capture the socio-ecological character of digital experience; the critical dynamics lie instead in regimes of visibility and rhythmic notification infrastructures that organize communicative practice and temporal orientation (Napoli, 2019).

This infrastructural transformation has also generated a digitally attached generation. This chapter understands the digitally attached generation not as a cohort defined by age, but as a generation shaped by the normalization of digitally mediated lifeworlds across work, education, and public communication. Concepts such as perpetual contact, connected presence, and affective publics describe a communicative mode premised on being always in-network (Katz & Aakhus, 2002; Licoppe, 2004; Papacharissi, 2015). Within "networked publics," context collapse renders identity performance and the public–private boundary matters of ongoing negotiation (boyd, 2010; Marwick & boyd, 2011). Technology thus ceases to function as an external "object" and increasingly becomes the texture through which communication unfolds. As Plantin et al. (2018) demonstrate, large platforms gradually assume the functions of classical infrastructures, becoming the indispensable backbone of public communication; the behavioral and economic costs of "exit" consequently rise. To sustain communicative presence, individuals become structurally bound to platforms-a condition better understood as infrastructural dependence than as the individual will-failure implied by addiction discourse (van Dijck et al., 2018).

Digital embeddedness manifests along two interrelated dimensions. First, digital/human embeddedness: notifications, timing prompts, ranking, and measurement practices shape attentional flow and relationality. Second, digital/institutional embeddedness: the rhythms of education, work, and public discourse-performance and visibility metrics, "well-being" indicators, and learning modules-are organizationally sedimented (John et al., 2025). These dimensions reconfigure communicative flows through an equi-constitutive process, producing a symbiosis in which people are tethered to platforms and platforms are grafted onto everyday practice. The critical question is thus not simply "why do we use so much?" but what is made visible, how, and for whom (Gillespie, 2014). Coupled with the competitive logic of the attention economy (Citton, 2017; Wu, 2017;) and the extractive, predictive ambitions of surveillance capitalism (Zuboff, 2019), communicative presence becomes a metricized performance. Here an "loss/condition of freedom" paradox emerges: notification systems may capture attention, while non-presence on the same platforms risks exclusion from work and social life. The issue, therefore, is less a matter of "weak will" than of infrastructural designs that shape public values.

Accordingly, the perspective advanced here does not discard "addiction reduction" rhetoric but supplements it with the governance of communicative infrastructures. Communication research can contribute by rendering algorithmic culture and interface politics legible; advocating accountable ranking and visibility transparency; designing interfaces that provide "why this now?" explanations; and normatively articulating embedding hygiene principles-layered publics (audience/visibility controls), temporal autonomy through rhythm-sensitive notification regimes, and data minimization (Ananny & Crawford, 2018; boyd, 2010; Marwick & boyd, 2011; Napoli, 2019). Such an approach enables a shift from pathology to ecology: the task is not only to modulate individual overuse but to transform the quality of embeddedness by re-framing visibility, data, and rhythm design in the name of the public interest (van Dijck, 2014; van Dijck et al., 2018).

While concepts such as mediatization, networked publics, platformization, and digital immersion have offered crucial insights into the transformation of communication, they tend to foreground either institutional change, interactional forms, or subjective experience in isolation. The concept of digital embeddedness advances this literature by theorizing the structural inescapability of platform infrastructures across everyday life. In this sense, digital embeddedness shifts the analytical focus from media influence or overuse to the politics of infrastructural dependency, linking lived experience, institutional rhythms, and algorithmic governance within a single explanatory framework.

In sum, this chapter contends that the technology–human relation cannot be reduced to the addiction rubric; the order that emerges alongside digitally attached cohorts is more accurately theorized through digital embeddedness. Our thesis is as follows: contemporary communicative practices operate within a symbiotic ecology that co-constitutes people and platforms; explanatory frameworks should therefore foreground the politics of communicative infrastructures rather than clinical pathology. The guiding question thus shifts from "why do we use so much?" to "how are we rendered visible, to which rhythms are we bound, and how can these be redesigned in the service of public values?" (Ananny & Crawford, 2018; Gillespie, 2014; van Dijck et al., 2018). This theoretical reframing offers both a conceptual contribution to the literature and actionable implications for design and policy: rhythm-aware notifications, layered visibility, data minimization, accountable ranking, and the re-design of participation along the axis of the public interest.

THE CONCEPTUAL LIMITS OF THE ADDICTION FRAMEWORK IN THE DIGITAL AGE

The concept of addiction, originally developed as a diagnostic category within psychology and psychiatry, has become a common expression in academic literature and everyday discourse over the past two decades to explain relationships with digital technologies. However, the almost unquestioned application of this clinically specific concept to digital life generates significant conceptual and interpretive limitations for understanding digital behavior. The mismatch between the clinical context in which addiction is defined and the realities of everyday life in the digital age constitutes a critical epistemological issue concerning how digital life is conceptualized. This issue should therefore not be treated as merely terminological. The addiction discourse, by insufficiently accounting for the social, cultural, and relational dimensions of digital behavior, tends to frame these practices primarily within an individual pathology paradigm. More importantly, the widespread everyday use of the addiction discourse can constrain communicative explanations from the outset, leading digital practices to be interpreted predominantly through a pathology-centered lens.

In clinical literature, addiction is defined through specific indicators such as loss of control, withdrawal symptoms, tolerance development, functional impairment, and high levels of conflict (American Psychiatric Association [APA], 2013). Within this framework, addiction is understood as a pathology in which individuals lose agency over a particular substance or behavior, resulting in persistent harm across life domains. However, dominant popular and academic discourse surrounding digital media frequently applies the addiction label to patterns of behavior that do not meet these clinical criteria. Behaviors such as frequently checking one's phone, repeatedly refreshing social media feeds throughout the day, or feeling a need to remain online are often described as "addictive" in everyday language. This broad application stretches a clinical concept beyond its diagnostic boundaries, applying it to ordinary experiences of digital life.

The problem with this labeling lies not only in conceptual misuse, but in the powerful discursive effects that reshape how behavior is interpreted. The term addiction directs attention toward individual weakness and internal deficits as explanatory factors. As Panova and Carbonell (2018) argue, this discourse produces a narrow explanatory framework that obscures the social and relational contexts of behavior (p. 256). Their analysis shows that smartphone "addiction" narratives often reduce complex social and communicative necessities to individual failures of self-control. Similarly, Kardefelt-Winther (2014) emphasizes that framing digital use within an addiction paradigm predisposes researchers to interpret behavior as potentially pathological from the outset, thereby narrowing the scope of analysis (pp. 29-30). In this sense, addiction functions less as an explanatory concept and more as a classificatory and normative regime that pre-structures interpretation.

A growing body of research on internet and social media use points to the limitations of addiction models in explaining digital behavior. Although Griffiths's (2005) widely cited "components model" proposes that all addictions share six common elements, there is considerable debate regarding the applicability of these components to digital contexts. Van Rooij and Prause (2014) demonstrate that the clinical validity of "internet addiction" criteria remains uncertain and that prevalence rates vary dramatically depending on the measurement instruments used (pp. 206-209). This variability suggests that addiction operates as a flexible and context-dependent category rather than a stable explanatory framework for digital practices.

These limitations become even more apparent within communication research. Communication technologies have become central to the texture of social relationships, the rhythms of everyday life, and the criteria of social visibility. Time spent in digital environments is often not a matter of individual choice, but a requirement of social and institutional order. Baym (2015) highlights that communication technologies have become indispensable for maintaining social ties and fulfilling needs for visibility, belonging, and relational continuity. Intensive use, therefore, is not necessarily an indicator of psychological disorder, but a natural consequence of living in a digitally mediated society.

One of the most visible problems of addiction discourse is its individualizing framework. Within this perspective, individuals are positioned as the agents of "overuse," while platform architectures, algorithmic steering, and the structural logics of the attention economy remain largely outside the analytical frame. Billieux et al. (2015b) argue that the addiction concept, particularly in relation to digital behaviors, tends to produce a blame-oriented framework rather than an explanatory one. This individualization undermines the structural sensitivity required to understand qualitative transformations in digital behavior.

Methodological limitations further reinforce this problem. Many addiction-oriented studies on internet and social media use rely on relatively narrow quantitative indicators such as screen time, notification-checking frequency, or subjective perceptions of control, often grouped under the umbrella of "problematic internet use" (Caplan, 2002; Young, 1998). Increasingly, however, scholars question whether such measures can adequately capture the complex, contextual, and relational nature of digital experience (Browne et al., 2021; Burén et al., 2023). These metrics often fail to illuminate the conditions under which use emerges or the communicative functions it serves. As a result, analytical frameworks that insufficiently account for the multi-layered nature of communication processes become normalized (Billieux et al., 2015b; Livingstone, 2009).

Indeed, Billieux et al. (2015a) emphasize that problematic use cannot be defined solely through quantitative intensity; motivations, contextual demands, and social obligations must also be considered (pp. 157-159). Intensive digital use is frequently tied to fulfilling relational responsibilities, maintaining social visibility, or adapting to professional expectations-rhythms that characterize everyday life in the digital age. The meaning of use, therefore, lies not in its duration, but in the context in which it is embedded.

The concept of addiction also carries a strong normative tone. Digital presence is often evaluated through binary distinctions between "good" and "bad" use (Kim et al., 2011; Naydanova et al., 2018), a dichotomy ill-suited to the complexity of contemporary digital culture. As Turkle (2011) demonstrates, digital environments reshape relational forms of existence: individuals do not merely consume information but also construct emotional, social, and symbolic bonds through digital media. Reducing such complex relationality to the category of "overuse" obscures the nature of digital reality.

Discursively, the "addicted" label also produces identity effects. As Becker's (1963) labeling theory suggests, how behavior is named shapes both self-perception and social evaluation. While active participation in digital environments often results from communicative, cultural, and economic necessities, addiction discourse reframes this participation as individual weakness. This individualizing lens obscures the design and economic structures of digital platforms. Algorithmic recommendation systems, rhythmic notification calls, and attention-driven interface designs frequently disappear within addiction narratives. As Zuboff (2019) argues, platforms do not merely observe user behavior; they actively shape, direct, and often anticipate it. Explaining repetitive digital engagement solely through individual motivation therefore renders key dynamics of platform capitalism invisible.

These issues pose significant methodological and theoretical challenges for communication research. Communication studies aim to situate digital practices not within individual psychological traits, but within relational positions, social network participation, cultural norms, economic expectations, and technological infrastructures (Deuze, 2012; Livingstone, 2009). Addiction discourse, by contrast, often defines digital behavior as an individual problem, relegating relational and structural contexts to the background. Questions concerning the conditions under which digital practices emerge, how they are sustained, and which communicative functions they fulfill become secondary to quantitative measures of use. From a communication perspective, what matters instead is how digital practices intertwine with everyday rhythms, visibility expectations, and interactional orders (Hargittai, 2010).

For these reasons, the central objection from a communication research perspective is that addiction discourse offers an overly narrow, individualizing, and normative framework for understanding digital behavior. Digital practices today emerge at the intersection of social participation, economic necessity, cultural visibility regimes, and platform infrastructures (Fuchs, 2017; van Dijck et al., 2018). The continuity and rhythmicity of digital behavior are therefore not symptoms of pathology, but outcomes of how digital life is organized. Addiction discourse renders this structural embeddedness invisible by framing digital behavior in terms of individual willpower or loss of control.

Given these limitations, addiction proves inadequate for explaining the relational and infrastructural nature of digital life. A more descriptive concept is needed to characterize the subject of the digital age. In this chapter, the concept of the digitally attached (Demir, 2025) is proposed to describe individuals' relationships with digital technologies not as pathological excess, but as relational, infrastructural, and institutional attachment. Being digitally attached does not imply uncontrolled consumption of technology; rather, it denotes a condition in which social relationships, communicative continuity, and institutional participation are organized through digital infrastructures. This attachment is less a matter of individual choice than a consequence of how digital life is structured (Katz & Aakhus, 2002). Digitally attached subjects engage with digital environments not because they are unable to disengage, but because social, cultural, and economic life increasingly unfolds through these technologies. The concept thus departs from the notion of loss of will implied by addiction and functions as an intermediary framework for describing communicative existence in the digital age.

This perspective leads into the subsequent discussion of digital embeddedness. Digital technologies are no longer external tools positioned outside the lifeworld, but have become foundational infrastructures embedded within everyday practices. The following chapter therefore examines why the concept of digital embeddedness offers a more comprehensive framework for explaining how the individual-platform relationship is reconfigured along axes of both freedom and dependence.

DIGITAL EMBEDDEDNESS AND THE FREEDOM-DEPENDENCE PARADOX

The previous section demonstrated the conceptual limits of addiction-based explanations for digital behavior by showing that intensive digital attachment is rooted in structural, relational, and communicative transformations rather than individual pathology. Building on this critique, this section introduces the concept of digital embeddedness to theorize the socio-technical condition in which digital infrastructures have become constitutive of everyday life. Focusing on the paradoxical coexistence of freedom and dependence, the section examines how digital platforms simultaneously expand individuals' communicative capacities while binding them to algorithmic rhythms, visibility regimes, and institutional infrastructures.

The transformation of digital technologies to an infrastructure that surrounds everyday life indicates a new socio-technical condition that carries the relationship between the individual and technology beyond classical addiction discourses. Approaches that have addressed internet and social media use within a psychological addiction framework for many years were inclined to explain behaviors mostly through individual weakness of will, compulsive repetition, or pathological tendencies (Griffiths, 2005). This approach treated digital behavior as an individual-centered problem, reducing it to biopsychological factors. However, in today's communication environment, digital technologies have become the basic condition of social relations, economic participation, cultural production, and social visibility, rather than an external tool in the individual's life. Therefore, linking digital behavior only to individual psychology, willpower, or compulsive structures is not sufficient to understand the ontological character that digital life has acquired.

Therefore, especially in the field of social sciences, there is a need for another usage instead of the concept of addiction that also encompasses the relational, infrastructural, and cultural transformation of the digital age. In this regard, benefit may be taken from Granovetter's thesis of "embeddedness," in which he asserted that economic behaviors cannot be reduced to an abstract rationality, but rather are shaped within an ongoing network of social relations. According to him, economic actions are neither the product of under socialized individuals who are completely independent from social context nor explainable through an overly socialized determinism in which the individual is wholly surrendered to social structure. Human behaviors take root in a concrete and continuous network of social relations; even the generation of trust is formed not through institutional arrangements but through practices embedded into these relational networks (Granovetter, 1985).

Granovetter's idea of embeddedness requires a new interpretation in the digital age. Because today, individuals' social relations, economic activities, and cultural practices are embedded not only in social structures but also in digital infrastructures. The social networks emphasized by Granovetter have now transformed into structures that are interfaced by digital platforms, organized by algorithms, and continuously reshaped by norms of online presence. Therefore, in the digital age, embeddedness refers not only to the network of social relations but also to the technical, economical, and cultural impositions of platforms.

This transformation constitutes the basis of the concept of digital embeddedness. Individuals have now become unable to carry out their economical, cultural, and social actions outside digital environments; from communication to banking, from affective sharing to business networks, many practices are embedded in the infrastructures of digital platforms. The individual is not merely an actor who uses technology, but a human being who sustains the rhythm, visibility, and social ties of life practices within digital infrastructures (Hepp, 2019). Thus, Granovetter's claim that economic action is embedded in social relations expands in the digital age and turns into a condition in which the behaviors of the individual are embedded in digital technosocial structures.

Indeed, digital environments are structures that not only reflect but also shape the relational universe of the individual. Granovetter's critique of the 'undersocialized individual' (Swedberg, 1997, p.164), when applied to the digital context, makes visible the problem in the assumption that individuals use platforms through rational choices; meanwhile, the critique of the 'oversocialized individual' prevents conceiving the individual as a figure entirely determined by the platform. The digital embeddedness approach makes it possible to conceptualize the individual's position in the digital environment beyond this dichotomy. In the digital sphere, the individual is an actor who both makes choices and whose choices are shaped within the algorithmic, cultural, and economic frameworks of platforms.

Therefore, in the digital age, embeddedness describes a new socio-technical order in which social relations are rooted not only in social networks but also in the logic of digital infrastructures, in algorithmic regimes of visibility, and in the economic dynamics of platform capitalism. While Granovetter's embeddedness demonstrates that economic behavior is grounded in social ties; digital embeddedness makes visible that all practices of modern life are rooted in the technical and cultural ecosystem of digital platforms. Thus, the concept of embeddedness provides a strong theoretical basis for explaining that, in digital environments, the individual's actions are situated within both a relational and an infrastructural context. This approach marks the core characteristic of digital embeddedness: digital environments acquire not merely an instrumental but an existential status.

Messaging applications constitute the infrastructure of everyday communication; social-media feeds determine the terms of social visibility, search engines become the gatekeepers of access to information, navigation applications guide spatial experience. In this way, digital technologies turn into a framework that organizes the structure of a person's life. This condition demonstrates that usage is no longer a voluntary choice but has become a compulsory component of modern life (van Dijck et al., 2018). Digital presence is now a precondition for socio-economic participation; being online is mandatory for social visibility, communicative continuity, and economic activity.

This compulsory condition further reveals the limits of the classical notion of addiction. The repetitive nature of digital behaviors is often not the result of a psychopathology into which individuals are unwillingly drawn, but rather a consequence of the design logic of platforms. Notification cycles, infinite-scroll mechanisms, personalized content streams, and interface designs that steer user conduct produce a rhythmic economy that continually draw the individual's attention (Wu, 2017). Therefore, the repetition of digital behaviors cannot be understood independently from the architecture through which digital infrastructures organize individuals' time, attention, and social presence.

Digital embeddedness is not merely a technological proximity; it is a cultural norm. To sustain social presence, one must remain online, whereas being offline often translates into social invisibility or economic exclusion (Papacharissi, 2015). For this reason, the repetitive nature of digital use emerges as a requirement of one's social and cultural life. As Turkle (2011) demonstrates, digital environments have generated an economy of presence that demands relational continuity. This economy renders withdrawal from digital environments nearly impossible. Thus, digital embeddedness cannot be treated merely as a technological habit or an individual weakness; it is the organizing principle of modern social life.

In this context, the question of how digital embeddedness transforms the conception of freedom becomes significant. Reinterpreting Ricoeur's distinction between voluntary and involuntary action for the digital age, Whitehead and Hannah (2025) argue that individuals both consciously use digital technologies and are compelled to use them due to social and economic conditions. On the one hand, digital environments expand individuals' capacities for communication, access to information, and freedom of expression; on the other, the boundaries set by platform designs silently shape individual freedom. This dual structure turns digital freedom into an experience that is both expanded and conditioned.

The dual nature of digital freedom renders increasingly problematic the assumption that individuals freely evaluate the options presented by digital platforms. In digital environments, choice architectures are invisibly shaped by algorithms, and much of what individuals believe they have "chosen" is in fact part of a visibility regime structured by the platform's prioritization logic (Bucher, 2018; Gillespie, 2014; Zuboff, 2019). Thus, freedom ceases to be a domain of action determined solely by individual will; it takes place within a field constituted by algorithmic filtering, data-processing operations, and personalized content streams. This condition demonstrates that freedom in the digital age has not only expanded but has also been reconfigured by being drawn into specific structural limits.

At the phenomenological level of digital embeddedness, individuals experience freedom as a genuine sensation while using digital tools. Sending messages, sharing photographs, consuming content, or browsing a news feed appear, in essence, as expressions of personal choice. Yet most of these choices have already been pre-structured by behavior-shaping interface design, the rhythmic solicitation of notifications, and the option fields filtered through algorithmic streams. Therefore, the sense of freedom is shaped less by the individual's arbitrary exercise of will than by acting within a set of options constructed by the platform.

Another critical dimension that unsettles the perception of freedom is the cultural layer. As being online has become a cultural norm, digital presence has turned into a necessary condition for social recognition and the maintaining of interpersonal bonds. What Papacharissi (2015) terms "affective publics" requires individuals to sustain their emotional and social existence within digital environments. This illustrates that digital participation is not merely an individual preference but a prerequisite for social belonging. Consequently, being offline is not simply a technological withdrawal; it entails the loss of social visibility, the risk of relational discontinuity, and the possibility of cultural exclusion.

The economic and institutional level are the other determining dimension of digital embeddedness. Today, the majority of economic activities are conducted through digital infrastructures; from e-commerce to banking, and from logistics to educational services, numerous domains are embedded within the technical architectures provided by platforms (van Dijck et al., 2018). Digital embeddedness is therefore a structural necessity that extends beyond the individual to institutions and social systems. To withdraw from digital technologies often means withdrawing from economic production, public services, and social interaction.

This infrastructural dependency clearly reveals the biopolitical dimension of digital embeddedness. Foucault's concept of biopolitics posits that modern power functions as a form of governmentality that regulates life, not through prohibition and repression, but through norms, rhythms, and regimes of visibility. In the digital age, this form of governmentality is intensified by algorithms' capacity to anticipate behavior, the temporal rhythms produced by notification cycles, and the logic of measurability. Digital environments have come to manage the individual's time (notification frequency), spatial movement (location services), behavior (likes, comments, following practices), and affect (the emotional framing of algorithmic feeds). Digital embeddedness is therefore not merely a matter of technological use, but a biopolitical environment in which life processes are rhythmically organized (Zuboff, 2019).

The attention economy occupies a central position in understanding the relationship between individuals and technology in the digital age. Today's digital environments are built upon systems that treat human attention as a resource and seek to keep it constantly in motion. Platform design operates through mechanisms that track and predict user behavior; content feeds, notification cycles, and rhythmic solicitations that aimed at retaining users, constitute the primary instruments of this arrangement. Within such an environment, what individuals attend to, which content they encounter, and which behaviors they repeat are largely shaped within an invisible framework driven by economic logics. As a result, digital embeddedness becomes not only a structure that transforms social relations, but also one that reshapes time use and cognitive processes.

This transformation is also intertwined with a broader economic order. Digital platforms convert user behavior into a form of raw material that generates economic value. As individuals spend time on platforms, they produce data; this data is used to optimize platform operations, to deliver new content in the most effective manner, or to be converted into economic assets. Thus, the user becomes not merely a consumer but an actor who continuously generates data through their behavior. This dynamic clarifies the economic dimension of digital embeddedness: individuals are tethered to platforms not only for social reasons, but also for economic and institutional ones.

When these processes converge, digital embeddedness signals a structural condition that simultaneously expands and restricts individual freedom. Digital technologies increase individuals' capacities in domains such as communication, expression, and cognition, while at the same time creating an invisible infrastructural framework that determines the limits of those capacities. Individuals may feel free while using digital environments; yet this freedom operates within a field of possibilities structured by platform design and algorithmic systems. Thus, even though the experience of freedom appears to expand, it is in fact shaped within a directed set of possibilities.

This condition also makes clear why the concept of addiction falls short. The continuity of digital use is less a matter of individual weakness or pathological inclination than a natural consequence of the technical, social, and institutional structures of modern life. Because daily communication, cultural interaction, economic activity, and public services are largely conducted through digital infrastructures, individuals are already situated within these environments. Digital use, therefore, is not a habit but the organizational form of the world in which one lives.

Digital embeddedness becomes evident across three levels. At the phenomenological level, digital tools structure the emotional and relational rhythms of everyday life; self-presentation, communication, and affective circulation unfold within digital spaces. Digital use becomes less a matter of choice than a natural component of lived temporal rhythms. At the cultural level, being online has become a primary condition for social visibility and belonging; being offline often signifies cultural invisibility or relational rupture. At the economic-institutional level, digital infrastructures are indispensable to the functioning of economic actors, public services, and social systems; thus, withdrawal from digital environments frequently entails risks of economic and institutional exclusion.

When these three levels are considered together, the continuity of digital use ceases to signify addiction and instead becomes the natural outcome of the organization of modern life. Digital embeddedness serves as an explanatory concept that demonstrates how technology integrates into an individual's lifeworld: individuals are intertwined with digital environments not because they are addicted to technology, but because they live within it.

In conclusion, freedom in the digital age is no longer a matter of absolute openness or limitless choice. Freedom emerges instead as the capacity to act within the infrastructural conditions provided by platforms. In digital environments, individuals both choose and are guided; they are free, yet they inhabit a compulsory framework. Digital embeddedness renders visible the paradoxical nature of modern life and conceptualizes the digital not as an option but as a condition of existence.

WHY THE ADDICTION NARRATIVE FAILS FROM A COMMUNICATION PERSPECTIVE

This section argues that the addiction narrative fails to adequately explain digital communication practices because it misrecognizes a structural transformation of everyday life as an individual pathology. From a communication perspective, intensive digital engagement is not the result of excessive or uncontrolled use, but the outcome of a reorganization of communicative time, relational expectations, and public visibility within digital infrastructures. By drawing on concepts such as connected presence, networked publics, and rhythmanalysis, the section demonstrates that digital communication today operates as a constitutive condition of social existence rather than as a detachable object of use.

The addiction narrative, drawing largely on the literature of clinical psychology and psychiatry, is fundamentally grounded in a set of core assumptions: the presence of an external object positioned opposite the individual, the establishment of an excessive and uncontrolled relationship with this object, and the consequent impairment of individual functioning (Griffiths, 2005, p. 192). Within this conceptual framework, digital media is treated as an object whose use can be delimited and regulated through individual willpower. Yet, within the contemporary social formation structured around digitalization, communication has taken on a character that exceeds these assumptions. Digital media can no longer be understood merely as an instrument that confronts the individual and serves the informational and entertainment functions of communication; rather, it has become a constitutive and transformative component of everyday life, social relations, and modes of public participation.

This transformation indicates a structural reorganization that encompasses all areas of everyday life, ranging from the organization of education through online learning platforms, to digital appointment and monitoring systems in healthcare services, from the conduct of citizenship practices through e-government infrastructures, to the circulation of cultural production through online networks. In this context, communication has ceased to be an activity specific to particular times and spaces; it has been reorganized around the principles of constant contact, connected presence, and simultaneity.

One of the most visible effects of digitalization is the disappearance of the temporal and spatial boundaries of communication. The widespread adoption of mobile communication technologies lays the groundwork not only for the diversification of communication channels, but also for a profound reorganization of the temporal and spatial dimensions of the communication experience (Katz and Aakhus, 2002, p. 2). In explaining the social impact of mobile phones, Katz and Aakhus (2002) draw attention to the fact that technology is not merely a socially constructed tool; according to them, mobile communication generates a new communicative consciousness based on a shared sense of time that is independent of space, by giving rise to similar patterns of use across different social and cultural contexts. Katz and Aakhus (2002) conceptualize this phenomenon through the notion of Apparatgeist, arguing that mobile communication creates shared norms, expectations, and communicative rhythms among users. This shared spirit produces implicit rules regarding when individuals should initiate communication, how quickly they should respond, and the extent to which they are expected to remain constantly accessible. Thus, mobile communication becomes a practice that operates less through individual preferences than through collectively shared communicative expectations.

From this perspective, the intensive use of mobile phones in everyday life is not the result of individual excess, but rather a consequence of the transformation of the temporal regime of communication. Apparatgeist enables communication to gain continuity by dispersing it across every moment of everyday life, rather than confining it to specific contexts. This situation demonstrates why, in the digital age, communication has ceased to be an activity that can be "switched off," and why the discourse of addiction falls short in explaining communicative experience. In this sense, mobile communication functions as a constitutive structure that binds individuals not only to technological devices, but also to collectively shared new communicative norms and temporal perceptions.

While Katz and Aakhus's (2002) conceptualization of Apparatgeist demonstrates that mobile communication produces shared norms and expectations, Licoppe (2004) elaborates on how this transformation is concretized at the level of communicative experience through the concept of "connected presence." According to Licoppe (2004), digital communication has become not a secondary form of contact that replaces face-to-face interaction, but rather a complementary and constitutive element that ensures the continuity of relationships. This connected presence, established through text messages, instant notifications, and micro-contacts, transforms communication from an activity confined to specific times and spaces into a continuously operating background of everyday life (Licoppe, 2004, pp. 135-137). In this context, communication is no longer an action that is "initiated" and "terminated," but a process through which relational ties are continuously updated.

The concept of "connected presence" emphasized by Licoppe (2004) makes it possible to interpret the quantitative intensity of digital communication not as a sign of individual excess or addiction, but as the outcome of a transformed relational regime. The sustainability of relationships becomes tied less to the physical co-presence of the other party than to the continuity of communicative availability and responsiveness. While this situation generates a constant expectation of being "reachable" for individuals, it simultaneously renders being offline a risk of relational rupture (Licoppe, 2004, p. 141). Consequently, the intensity of digital communication is not the result of weakened individual willpower, but rather a consequence of the new mode of organization of social relations. This perspective clearly demonstrates, at the communicative level, why digital behaviors cannot be explained through the concept of addiction: the issue is not excessive use, but the fact that communication now operates within a regime of uninterrupted presence.

"Connected presence," established through digital technologies, points to a new communication regime that enables individuals to sustain their relationships in continuity without being physically co-present. Within this regime, communication ceases to be an activity reduced to discrete encounters and instead becomes organized through continuous, rhythmic, and repetitive micro-interactions flowing in the background of everyday life. This transformation has entailed not only the mediation of social relations through media, but also their very structuring by media architectures themselves.

It is precisely at this point that boyd's concept of "networked publics" reveals that digital environments are not merely new communication channels, but socio-technical spaces that reconfigure the distinction between public and private spheres. According to boyd, networked publics are publics restructured by networked technologies; these publics are constituted through both technological architectures (profiles, feeds, comment systems) and the practices that develop within these architectures (boyd, 2010, pp. 1-4). The defining characteristic of networked publics lies in their capacity to render communicative interaction continuously open to multiple audiences through dynamics such as the scalability of visibility, the persistence of content, and the collapse of contexts (boyd, 2010, pp. 7-10). This condition leads individuals to form their social relations increasingly through digitally sustained ties rather than face-to-face encounters; communication becomes determined less by spatial co-presence than by the architectural affordances and regimes of visibility offered by platforms. Accordingly, communicative existence takes shape not through individual preferences, but within the structural conditions of networked publics; digital embeddedness provides a more encompassing explanatory framework for grasping this transformed communicative order than the discourse of addiction.

Papacharissi's (2015) approach to "affective publics," meanwhile, demonstrates that digital communication generates not only a cognitive but also an emotional form of publicness. This publicness requires continuous interaction, visibility, and affective engagement.

In the digitalized world, rhythms of life have been reorganized through platform-determined temporalities and notification cycles. To conceptualize the deeper transformations this shift has produced in the texture of everyday life, Lefebvre's analyses of everyday life provide an important theoretical ground. According to Lefebvre (1991), everyday life in modern societies is not merely the domain of repetitive routines, but the plane in which power relations, modes of production, and ideological orientations are most intensively internalized. Communication practices established through digital platforms can thus be read as one of the contemporary forms of the colonization of everyday life. Continuous connectivity, notification regimes, and algorithmic feeds fragment and reorganize individuals' everyday experience of time; communication is no longer an activity confined to specific contexts, but becomes a form of uninterrupted accompaniment.

Lefebvre's approach to rhythmanalysis is particularly illuminating in demonstrating why digitalized communication cannot be explained through concepts of individual pathology such as "excessive use" or "addiction." Lefebvre (2004) emphasizes that everyday life is constituted through the intersection of biological, social, and spatial rhythms; the tensions that emerge when these rhythms are disrupted are not the result of individual weaknesses, but of structural arrangements. In digital communication environments, rhythm is no longer determined by natural cycles or social consensus, but through platforms' notification timings, content refresh rates, and visibility metrics. This condition transforms being constantly online from a matter of "choice" into a normative condition of everyday life.

Therefore, the intensity of digital communication practices should be understood not as an indicator of addiction, but rather as a consequence of the new mode of organization of everyday life embedded within digital infrastructures. In this context, Lefebvre's critique of everyday life makes it possible to theoretically ground the communicative dimension of the concept of digital embeddedness. Lefebvre's (2004) rhythm analysis approach underscores that everyday life is organized through rhythms; in the digital age, these rhythms are now algorithmic and designed rhythms.

Under these conditions, communication ceases to be an activity dependent on individual volition. Sustaining social relationships, remaining visible within professional networks, participating in public debates, and even maintaining a sense of everyday belonging are, in a sense, contingent upon the continuity of digital communication. Therefore, it would not be inaccurate to argue that extended periods spent in digital environments are not merely the result of pleasure-seeking or loss of control, but rather a form or consequence of a transformed mode of communicative existence.

In conclusion, explaining individuals' modes of communicative existence in the digitalized world not through the concept of addiction, but through the lens of digital embeddedness, offers a more comprehensive perspective. Communication is no longer an avoidable activity, but a fundamental condition of social existence. For this reason, digital intensity should be addressed not as a problem, but as the communicative reality of the digital age; the focus of critique should be directed not toward individuals, but toward the platform infrastructures that structure communication.

INSTITUTIONAL EMBEDDEDNESS: HOW PLATFORMS RESHAPE WORK, EDUCATION, AND PUBLIC LIFE

Previous sections discussed how digital embeddedness operates in relation to individual experience, communicative existence, and the tension between freedom and obligation. This section examines how the same process unfolds at the institutional level. Digital technologies do not only reshape individuals' everyday practices; they fundamentally reconfigure working life, educational institutions, and public communication. This shift aligns with media and communication scholarship that conceptualizes platforms as socio-technical infrastructures rather than neutral tools (Couldry & Hepp, 2017; Gillespie, 2018). Accordingly, the issue addressed here concerns not individual usage preferences, but the institutional and structural dimensions of digital embeddedness.

Digitalization has normalized the conduct of institutional communication, coordination, and evaluation through platforms. Workplaces, universities, public institutions, and civil society organizations increasingly rely on infrastructures provided by private technology companies. As Plantin et al. (2018) argue, platforms have taken on roles traditionally associated with public infrastructures. From a communication perspective, this development resonates with analyses of infrastructural power, where media systems shape social organization by determining conditions of access and circulation (Couldry, 2012; Parks & Starosielski, 2015). Platforms thus become managerial infrastructures that reorganize institutional operations (Eubanks, 2018; Rahman & Thelen, 2019).

Crucially, platforms are not merely functional instruments for institutions. They are infrastructures that structure communication itself. Which messages gain priority in workplaces, which forms of participation are recognized in educational settings, and which voices circulate in the public sphere are increasingly shaped by platform interfaces and algorithmic arrangements. This reflects what Bucher (2018) describes as the algorithmic shaping of communicative visibility. Communication is thereby transformed from interpersonal exchange into an infrastructurally governed regime of circulation, requiring media studies to shift attention from content to conditions of mediation (Couldry & Mejias, 2019).

Institutional digital embeddedness also involves a reconfiguration of communicative time. Expectations of immediacy, synchronicity, and constant availability have become normalized within organizational communication. As communication scholars have shown, digital media reorganize temporal norms and expectations, producing regimes of "perpetual contact" and accelerated responsiveness (Bayer et al., 2020). These rhythms regulate not only productivity but also communicative presence, defining when silence becomes visible and problematic.

The Platformization of Work

Working life is one of the domains where institutional digital embeddedness is most visible. Remote work systems, project management tools, performance dashboards, and corporate messaging platforms redefine where, when, and how work is performed. From a media and communication perspective, this reflects the broader platformization of organizational communication (van Dijck et al., 2018).

In platform-based work environments, productivity is increasingly defined through communicative and behavioral metrics such as online presence, response speed, interaction frequency, and meeting participation. This metricization aligns with communication research on datafication, which shows how communicative acts become quantifiable signals within organizational systems (Couldry & Mejias, 2019). As a result, work becomes not only labor-intensive but communicatively surveilled.

Importantly, this process does not emerge because individuals overuse digital media. Rather, as work becomes institutionally embedded in platforms, constant connectivity becomes a communicative requirement. As Kellogg et al. (2020) note, visibility within digital systems becomes a condition of organizational legitimacy. From a communication standpoint, intensive digital engagement thus reflects institutional obligation rather than individual compulsion.

The Platformization of Education and Measurable Learning

A parallel transformation can be observed in education. Learning management systems, online course platforms, and digital assessment tools restructure education around platform-centered communication architectures. Media scholars argue that such systems reframe education as a communicative data environment, where learning is translated into traceable interactions (Selwyn, 2022; Williamson, 2017). Within educational platforms, participation and success are increasingly defined through communicative data: login frequency, viewing time, interaction patterns, and response metrics. As a result, relational and dialogical dimensions of education -central concerns in communication pedagogy- are marginalized. From the perspective of digital embeddedness, the student is no longer only a learning subject but also a communicative data subject. Refusing or exiting platforms often entails exclusion from educational communication altogether. As media education scholars emphasize, this is not a matter of excessive use but of institutional dependency on digital infrastructures (Selwyn, 2022).

The Embedding of Public Communication in Private Platforms

The most critical dimension of institutional embeddedness concerns public communication. Social media platforms have become primary sites for public debate, political communication, and cultural visibility. Communication scholars widely document how public discourse is increasingly shaped by platform architectures and algorithmic curation (Gillespie, 2018). This transformation alters the structure of the public sphere. Visibility is no longer grounded in equal access but in algorithmically mediated probabilities. As Bucher (2018) and Couldry (2012) argue, public communication increasingly operates within regimes of mediated attention rather than deliberative exchange. Consequently, public discourse becomes aligned with the competitive logic of visibility rather than democratic dialogue. Withdrawal from platforms thus becomes communicatively costly. As media scholars note, absence from social media often entails exclusion from public relevance and symbolic participation (Papacharissi, 2015). Individuals remain on platforms not due to personal attachment, but because public communication itself is institutionally embedded there.

Exit Costs and Institutional Obligation

A defining feature of institutional embeddedness is the high cost of exit. In work, education, and public communication, platforms often lack viable alternatives. As van Dijck et al. (2018) emphasize, platforms do not merely mediate communication; they restructure entire communicative ecosystems. From a media systems perspective, this produces infrastructural lock-in rather than voluntary engagement. This condition cannot be adequately explained through addiction discourse. Communication scholars argue that platform dependency reflects structural coercion rather than individual loss of control (Couldry & Mejias, 2019). Institutional embeddedness is therefore not a matter of willpower but of communicative infrastructure.

Biopolitical and Managerial Dimensions

Institutional digital embeddedness produces a new mode of communicative governance. Performance indicators, participation metrics, and visibility scores become central tools for evaluating communicative worth. This aligns with media research on surveillance capitalism and communicative control, where feedback systems subtly steer behavior without overt coercion (Zuboff, 2019). Unlike classical disciplinary power, this form of governance operates through normalization and self-regulation. Platforms create communicative environments in which individuals internalize expectations and optimize their visibility. Power thus materializes not through prohibition, but through interface design and metrics-a key insight of critical media studies.

The Inadequacy of the Addiction Discourse at the Institutional Level

Finally, addiction discourse proves insufficient for explaining institutionally structured communication. Continuous connectivity, platform reliance, and visibility-seeking behaviors are outcomes of communicative obligations, not psychological dependency. As media scholars argue, framing these dynamics as addiction individualizes structural problems and obscures infrastructural power (Karppi, 2022; Roberts & David, 2023). By reducing communication to individual pathology, addiction discourse diverts attention from fundamental media questions: how communication is structured, who controls its conditions, and who gains or loses visibility. The digital embeddedness perspective reorients critique away from individuals and toward infrastructures, governance, and institutional power.

In conclusion, digital embeddedness is not merely an alternative concept for communication research; it constitutes a necessary analytical framework for understanding the communicative realities of the digital age. While addiction-oriented accounts focus primarily on individual behavior, the perspective of embeddedness shifts attention to the infrastructural and institutional conditions under which communication takes place. From this standpoint, critique is redirected away from individuals and toward platforms, and from pathology toward questions of political and institutional responsibility. To understand communication in the digital age therefore no longer means asking why people remain online, but rather interrogating how a communicative order has been established in which remaining offline has become increasingly difficult.

From this perspective, the central problem of the digital age is not that individuals "use technology too much," but that institutions reorganize social life according to platform logics. The concept of digital embeddedness allows this transformation to be understood not as a pathological deviation, but as a structural condition of contemporary communication. In doing so, digital life is detached from individualized addiction narratives and repositioned as an object of critical analysis at the social and institutional level.

FUTURE RESEARCH DIRECTIONS

As a conceptually driven chapter, this study does not rely on empirical data; however, the frameworks proposed here invite systematic empirical investigation. Future research may operationalize concepts such as *digital embeddedness* and *digitally attached* in order to examine how infrastructural dependency, algorithmic visibility regimes, and rhythmic notification systems shape communicative practices across different social contexts. In particular, qualitative and mixed-method designs could explore how individuals experience the freedom-dependence paradox in everyday life, while institutional-level studies might analyze how platform infrastructures structure participation in work, education, and public communication. For communication research, these concepts offer an alternative to pathologizing labels such as "addiction" or "dependency," enabling analyses that foreground the symbiotic relationship between individuals and platforms. By empirically testing and refining these concepts, future scholarship can further illuminate how communicative life is reorganized within digitally embedded environments without reducing structural conditions to individual deficits.

CONCLUSION

The discussions developed throughout this chapter demonstrate why the addiction discourse, which has long been dominant in explaining the individual–technology relationship in the digital age, has become increasingly inadequate. Framing digital behaviors in terms of individual pathology, weakness of will, or loss of control, this approach systematically renders invisible the communicative, institutional, and political dimensions of digitalized life. Yet digital technologies can no longer be understood as tools external to the individual; they have become infrastructures that shape the conditions of social relations, public participation, labor, and knowledge production. For this reason, the continuity of digital behaviors should be understood not as an individual problem, but as the outcome of a digitalized social order.

The central argument of this chapter is that the core issue of the digital age is not "excessive use" or "addiction." Rather, the core issue is that life itself is embedded in digital infrastructures. The concept of digital embeddedness provides a more appropriate framework for explaining why individuals engage so intensively with digital technologies. People do not live digitally because they spend too much time in digital environments; they spend so much time in digital environments because work, education, social relationships, and public communication now take place there. This distinction is not only analytical, but also political.

The addiction discourse disperses structural responsibility by locating the problem within the individual. Within this framework, the design choices of digital platforms, mechanisms of algorithmic steering, attention-economy–based business models, and processes of institutional digitalization are pushed out of focus. As a result, individuals are positioned not as subjects constrained by systems that compel constant connectivity, but as the agents of their own supposed "weaknesses." This shift deflects critique away from the operation of digital capitalism and narrows the space for political intervention.

From the perspective of communication research, this individualizing framework is particularly problematic. The relationship established with digital technologies is a communicative one; it operates through meaning, visibility, recognition, and relationality. These relations are shaped not within the individual's inner world, but within the infrastructures provided by platforms, institutional expectations, and cultural norms. Consequently, relying on psychological diagnostic categories to explain digital behavior produces a reduction that distorts communicative reality. The digital embeddedness approach, by contrast, makes it possible to read this reality through the transformation of the lifeworld rather than through the individual subject.

The freedom-dependence tension discussed throughout the chapter constitutes one of the most critical dimensions of this transformation. Digital technologies offer individuals extensive possibilities for communication, access to information, and self-expression. Yet these possibilities are experienced within the options and limits provided by platforms. Individuals may feel free as they move through digital environments; however, this freedom unfolds within a pre-structured field of possibilities. For this reason, digital freedom does not amount to absolute autonomy, but rather to a guided space of action. This condition clearly reveals the paradoxical nature of digital embeddedness.

When considered at the institutional level, this paradox becomes even more visible. In the domains of work, education, and public communication, platforms have become indispensable components of institutional functioning. As institutions become increasingly embedded in digital infrastructures, individuals' capacity to withdraw from these infrastructures correspondingly diminishes. Disengaging from platforms is no longer merely a matter of personal choice; it often entails the risk of professional, educational, and civic exclusion. In this context, digital intensity ceases to be a question of individual will and instead becomes an institutional necessity.

At this point, a political question inevitably emerges: who bears responsibility for digital life? The addiction discourse answers this question by pointing to the individual. The digital embeddedness approach, by contrast, shifts responsibility away from individuals and toward infrastructures, institutions, and the logics of the platform economy. This change in direction redefines the locus of critique in the digital age. The problem is not that people "cannot stop" looking at their phones, but that a social order has been constructed in which living without looking at them has become impossible.

The political contribution of this chapter lies precisely at this point. The concept of digital embeddedness proposes approaching digital life not through moral judgments, but through structural analysis. Rather than calls to discipline individuals' digital behaviors, what must be subjected to scrutiny are the public role of platforms, algorithmic transparency, data policies, and processes of institutional digitalization. Framing the problems of digital life as a lack of individual self-control misdirects political responsibility. A digital embeddedness perspective instead implies that responsibility must be redistributed toward platform governance, institutional design, and public policy. This includes treating major platforms as communicative infrastructures with public obligations, holding institutions accountable for the forms of digital participation they normalize, and developing regulatory frameworks that protect temporal autonomy, visibility control, and data minimization as public values rather than individual coping strategies.

In conclusion, this chapter argues that the shift from narratives of digital addiction to the perspective of digital embeddedness is not merely a conceptual choice, but a political necessity. Living in the digital age does not mean "overusing" technology. To live in the digital age means to exist within specific infrastructures and to attune oneself to particular rhythms. Under these conditions, explaining individuals' digital behaviors through pathological categories obscures the structural transformations of the era.

Approaching digital life through the lens of digital embeddedness has several implications for future research, policy, and platform governance. For communication research, this perspective calls for a shift away from individual-level metrics such as screen time toward analyses of infrastructural conditions, including regimes of visibility, algorithmic ranking, and temporal coordination. At the policy level, it underscores the need to treat major platforms as communicative infrastructures with public responsibilities, thereby justifying demands for transparency, accountability, and democratic oversight. Finally, for platform governance and design, the digital embeddedness framework points toward interventions that enhance users' temporal autonomy, enable layered forms of visibility, and reduce the structural costs of disconnection. Rather than disciplining individual behavior, these implications foreground the governance of infrastructures as a central task for shaping more equitable and livable digital futures.

REFERENCES

American Psychiatric Association. (2013). *Diagnostic and statistical manual of mental disorders* (5th ed.). American Psychiatric Association.

Ananny, M., & Crawford, K. (2018). Seeing without knowing: Limitations of the transparency ideal and its application to algorithmic accountability. *New Media & Society, 20*(3), 973–989. DOI: 10.1177/1461444816676645

Bayer, J. B., Campbell, S. W., & Ling, R. (2020). Connection cues: Activating norms and habits of social connectedness. *Communication Theory, 30*(2), 173–193.

Baym, N. K. (2015). *Personal connections in the digital age* (2nd ed.). Polity.

Becker, H. S. (1963). *Outsiders: Studies in the sociology of deviance*. Free Press.

Billieux, J., Maurage, P., Lopez-Fernandez, O., Kuss, D. J., & Griffiths, M. D. (2015a). Can disordered mobile phone use be considered a behavioral addiction? *Current Addiction Reports, 2*(2), 156–162. DOI: 10.1007/s40429-015-0054-y

Billieux, J., Schimmenti, A., Khazaal, Y., Maurage, P., & Heeren, A. (2015b). Are we overpathologizing everyday life? A tenable blueprint for behavioral addiction research. *Journal of Behavioral Addictions, 4*(3), 119–123. DOI: 10.1556/2006.4.2015.009

boyd, d. (2010). Social network sites as networked publics: Affordances, dynamics, and implications. In Z. Papacharissi (Ed.), *A networked self: Identity, community, and culture on social network sites* (pp. 39–58). Routledge.

Browne, D. T., May, S. S., Colucci, L., Gawrilow, C., & Besic, N. (2021). From screen time to digital engagement: A critical review of measures used to assess problematic digital media use. *BMJ Open, 11*(5), e046367. DOI: 10.1136/bmjopen-2020-046367

Bucher, T. (2018). *If... then: Algorithmic power and politics*. Oxford University Press. DOI: 10.1093/oso/9780190493028.001.0001

Burén, J., van Rooij, A. J., van de Mheen, D., & Schoenmakers, T. M. (2023). Screen time as a proxy for problematic smartphone use: A weak and inconsistent indicator. *Frontiers in Psychology, 14*, 1258784. DOI: 10.3389/fpsyg.2023.1258784

Caplan, S. E. (2002). Problematic Internet use and psychosocial well-being: Development of a theory-based cognitive–behavioral measurement instrument. *Computers in Human Behavior, 18*(5), 553–575. DOI: 10.1016/S0747-5632(02)00004-3

Citton, Y. (2017). The ecology of attention. *Polity*.

Couldry, N. (2012). *Media, society, world: Social theory and digital media practice*. Polity Press.

Couldry, N., & Hepp, A. (2017). The mediated construction of reality. *Polity*.

Couldry, N., & Mejias, U. A. (2019). *The costs of connection: How data is colonizing human life and appropriating it for capitalism*. Stanford University Press.

Demir, G. (2025, June). *Digital media addiction and the transformation of everyday practices among young adults*. 13th International Conference on Research in Behavioral and Social Sciences, Vienna, Austria. https://www.dpublication.com/wp-content/uploads/2025/05/04-4387.pdf

Deuze, M. (2012). *Media life*. Polity Press.

Eubanks, V. (2018). *Automating inequality: How high-tech tools profile, police, and punish the poor*. St. Martin's Press.

Fuchs, C. (2017). *Social media: A critical introduction* (2nd ed.). Sage.

Gillespie, T. (2014). The relevance of algorithms. In Gillespie, T., Boczkowski, P. J., & Foot, K. A. (Eds.), *Media technologies: Essays on communication, materiality, and society* (pp. 167–193). MIT Press. DOI: 10.7551/mitpress/9042.003.0013

Gillespie, T. (2018). *Custodians of the Internet: Platforms, content moderation, and the hidden decisions that shape social media*. Yale University Press.

Granovetter, M. (1985). Economic action and social structure: The problem of embeddedness. *American Journal of Sociology*, *91*(3), 481–510. DOI: 10.1086/228311

Griffiths, M. D. (2005). A 'components' model of addiction within a biopsychosocial framework. *Journal of Substance Use*, *10*(4), 191–197. DOI: 10.1080/14659890500114359

Hargittai, E. (2010). Digital na(t)ives? Variation in internet skills and uses among members of the "net generation.". *Sociological Inquiry*, *80*(1), 92–113. DOI: 10.1111/j.1475-682X.2009.00317.x

Hepp, A. (2019). *Deep mediatization*. Routledge. DOI: 10.4324/9781351064903

John, B., Alsamarra'i, Z., & Panteli, N. (2025). Reconfiguring digital embeddedness in hybrid work: The case of employee experience management platforms. *Information Systems Journal*, *35*(2), 450–479. DOI: 10.1111/isj.12545

Kardefelt-Winther, D. (2014). A conceptual and methodological critique of internet addiction research. *International Journal of Mental Health and Addiction*, *12*(1), 21–34.

Karppi, T. (2022). *Disconnect: Facebook's affective bonds*. University of Minnesota Press.

Katz, J. E., & Aakhus, M. (Eds.). (2002). *Perpetual contact: Mobile communication, private talk, public performance*. Cambridge University Press. DOI: 10.1017/CBO9780511489471

Kellogg, K. C., Valentine, M. A., & Christin, A. (2020). Algorithms at work. *The Academy of Management Annals*, *14*(1), 366–410. DOI: 10.5465/annals.2018.0174

Kim, H. C., Park, C. J., Ko, Y. M., Hyun, J. S., & Kim, C. M. (2011). The good and the bad: The effects of excellence in internet and mobile phone usage. In Park, J. J., Jin, H., & Park, M. S. (Eds.), *Advanced software engineering and its applications* (pp. 559–568). Springer., DOI: 10.1007/978-3-642-27207-3_61

Lefebvre, H. (1991). *Critique of everyday life* (Vol. 1; Moore, J., Trans.). Verso.

Lefebvre, H. (2004). *Rhythmanalysis: Space, time and everyday life* (S. Elden & G. Moore, Trans.). *Continuum*.

Licoppe, C. (2004). "Connected" presence: The emergence of a new repertoire for managing social relationships in a changing communication technoscape. *Environment and Planning. D, Society & Space*, *22*(1), 135–156. DOI: 10.1068/d323t

Livingstone, S. (2009). *Children and the internet: Great expectations, challenging realities*. Polity Press.

Marwick, A. E., & boyd, . (2011). I tweet honestly, I tweet passionately: Twitter users, context collapse, and the imagined audience. *New Media & Society*, *13*(1), 114–133. DOI: 10.1177/1461444810365313

Napoli, P. M. (2019). *Social media and the public interest: Media regulation in the disinformation age*. Columbia University Press. DOI: 10.7312/napo18454

Naydanova, E., Beal, B. D., & Doty, D. H. (2018). Internet use for school-mandated and self-initiated learning: Good, bad, or both? *Cyberpsychology, Behavior, and Social Networking*, *21*(7), 444–449. DOI: 10.1089/cyber.2017.0003

Panova, T., & Carbonell, X. (2018). Is smartphone addiction really an addiction? *Journal of Behavioral Addictions*, *7*(2), 252–259. DOI: 10.1556/2006.7.2018.49

Papacharissi, Z. (2015). *Affective publics: Sentiment, technology, and politics*. Oxford University Press.

Parks, L., & Starosielski, N. (Eds.). (2015). *Signal traffic: Critical studies of media infrastructures*. University of Illinois Press. DOI: 10.5406/illinois/9780252039362.001.0001

Plantin, J.-C., Lagoze, C., Edwards, P. N., & Sandvig, C. (2018). Infrastructure studies meet platform studies in the age of Google and Facebook. *New Media & Society*, *20*(1), 293–310. DOI: 10.1177/1461444816661553

Rahman, K. S., & Thelen, K. (2019). The rise of the platform business model. *Politics & Society*, *47*(2), 177–204. DOI: 10.1177/0032329219838932

Roberts, J. A., & David, M. E. (2023). *The attention economy: A category blueprint*. Routledge.

Selwyn, N. (2022). *Education and technology: Key issues and debates*. Bloomsbury Academic. DOI: 10.5040/9781350145573

Slater, M., & Wilbur, S. (1997). A framework for immersive virtual environments (FIVE). *Presence (Cambridge, Mass.)*, *6*(6), 603–616. DOI: 10.1162/pres.1997.6.6.603

Swedberg, R. (1997). New economic sociology. *Acta Sociologica*, *40*(2), 161–182. DOI: 10.1177/000169939704000203

Turkle, S. (2011). *Alone together: Why we expect more from technology and less from each other*. Basic Books.

van Dijck, J. (2014). Datafication, dataism and dataveillance. *Surveillance & Society*, *12*(2), 197–208. DOI: 10.24908/ss.v12i2.4776

van Dijck, J., Poell, T., & de Waal, M. (2018). *The platform society: Public values in a connective world*. Oxford University Press. DOI: 10.1093/oso/9780190889760.001.0001

Van Rooij, A. J., & Prause, N. (2014). A critical review of "Internet addiction" criteria. *Journal of Behavioral Addictions*, *3*(4), 203–213. DOI: 10.1556/JBA.3.2014.4.1

Whitehead, M., & Hannah, M. G. (2025). New figurations of freedom: Ricoeurian perspectives on the digital society. *Dialogues in Human Geography*, 20438206251379592. Advance online publication. DOI: 10.1177/20438206251379592

Williamson, B. (2017). Big data in education: The digital future of learning, policy and practice. *Sage (Atlanta, Ga.)*. Advance online publication. DOI: 10.4135/9781529714920

Wu, T. (2017). *The attention merchants: From the daily newspaper to social media, how our time and attention is harvested and sold.* Atlantic Books.

Young, K. S. (1998). Internet addiction. *Cyberpsychology & Behavior, 1*(3), 237–244. DOI: 10.1089/cpb.1998.1.237

Zuboff, S. (2019). *The age of surveillance capitalism: The fight for a human future at the new frontier of power.* PublicAffairs.

ADDITIONAL READINGS

Chayko, M. (2014). Techno-social life: The internet, digital technology, and social connectedness. *Sociology Compass, 8*(7), 976–991. DOI: 10.1111/soc4.12190

Fürstenau, D., Baiyere, A., & Kliewer, N. (2019). A dynamic model of embeddedness in digital infrastructures. *Information Systems Research, 30*(4), 1319–1342. DOI: 10.1287/isre.2019.0864

John, B., Alsamarra'i, Z., & Panteli, N. (2025). Reconfiguring digital embeddedness in hybrid work: The case of employee experience management platforms. *Information Systems Journal, 35*(2), 450–479. DOI: 10.1111/isj.12545

Koçak, O., Kovan, A., Alkhulayfi, A. M. A., Alshehri, N. A., Demirdöven, M., & Yıldırım, M. (2025). The relationship between social network addiction, online gaming addiction, and suicide ideation: Mediating and moderating role of loneliness. *BMC Psychology, 13*(1), 991. DOI: 10.1186/s40359-025-02892-w

LaRose, R. (2012). Uses and gratifications of internet addiction. In Young, K. S., & de Abreu, C. N. (Eds.), *Internet addiction: A handbook and guide to evaluation and treatment* (pp. 55–72). Wiley.

Revill, G., van Duppen, J., & Scarles, C. (2024). Interfacing as embodied practice: Journeys between print, screen and beyond. *Social & Cultural Geography, 25*(8), 1331–1349. DOI: 10.1080/14649365.2024.2308916

Smith, J. (2020). The impact of technology addiction on mental health. *Journal of Digital Health, 15*, 45–52.

Stilman, R. (2022). Attached to technology: Exploring identity and human relating in a virtual and corporeal world. *Transactional Analysis Journal, 52*(2), 93–105. DOI: 10.1080/03621537.2022.2036484

Sutton, T. (2020). Digital harm and addiction: An anthropological view. *Journal of the Royal Anthropological Institute*, *26*(1), 1–18.

Tabish, S. A. (2025). Digital addiction: The emerging epidemic of the modern age. *Journal of Clinical Medicine*, *2*(3), 1–9.

KEY TERMS AND DEFINITIONS

Addiction Discourse: It refers to the prevailing societal and academic language that frames constant digital engagement primarily as a psychological or behavioral pathology (an "addiction").

Communicative Infrastructures: It refers to the technical and structural systems that enable communication to occur.

Digital Embeddedness: It refers to a new socio-technical order where social relations are fundamentally rooted in digital infrastructures.

Digital Life: It is the mode of existence sustained within a digital environment, facilitated by the integration of digital technologies into everyday activities.

Digitally Attached Generation: A demographic group defined by their seamless integration into a digital ecosystem, where work, education, and social interactions are inherently mediated by technology, regardless of their biological age.

Digitally Attached: It describes a condition in which an individual's social, professional, and personal existence is inseparable from digital technology. It implies that their "lifeworld"-the way the experience reality-is consistently mediated by digital platforms.

Freedom-Dependence Paradox: It refers to the condition in which digital technologies simultaneously expand individuals' communicative capacities while structurally binding them to platform infrastructures, algorithmic rhythms, and institutional requirements.

Chapter 4
Electronic Minds:
Transformation of Human Behaviour and Functions in the Age of Digital Immersion

Pinnika Syam Yadav
http://orcid.org/0000-0003-4954-1273
Christ University, India

Preeti Kumari
Mittal School of Business, Lovely Professional University, India

ABSTRACT

In an era defined by pervasive digital immersion, human cognition, behavior, and social functioning are undergoing profound transformations. This study explores the emergence of electronic minds, a conceptual framework capturing the interplay between neuroplastic adaptation and digital environments. Drawing from interdisciplinary perspectives in psychology, neuroscience, and media studies, the paper examines how constant connectivity, algorithmic mediation, and virtual interactivity reshape attention, memory, identity, and interpersonal dynamics. The research highlights both the empowering and disruptive dimensions of digital immersion, including enhanced access to information, altered emotional processing, and the erosion of reflective solitude. By mapping these shifts, the study calls for a nuanced understanding of digital embodiment and proposes ethical pathways for fostering mindful engagement in technologically saturated societies.

DOI: 10.4018/979-8-3373-6665-4.ch004

INTRODUCTION TO ELECTRONIC MINDS

The transition from human to electronic minds lies at the intersection of neuroplastic adaptation and digitally mediated environments. Electronic minds serve as a conceptual framework for understanding the cognitive, affective, and social transformations that result from pervasive digital immersion. Massive cognitive changes occur under the continuing, self-perpetuating digital stimulation and connectivity roller coaster. Over the past decades, psychology and the neurosciences have produced a conceptual foundation for describing the theoretical preconditions of electronic minds. The focus lies on the neuroplastic scope of experience and the experimental evidence that digital engagement enhances, contributes to, or accelerates cognitive, affective, and social reprogramming (Montag & Diefenbach, 2018). Digital immersion is a condition and process of ongoing, pervasive, profound, diverse, lock-in, and global engagements with digital environments. It also serves as one of the primary catalyzers for emerging electronic minds.

THEORETICAL FRAMEWORK

Neuroplasticity permeates contemporary discourse on digital culture, with numerous theoretical accounts tracing the conceptual evolution of such transformations in recent decades (Smart et al., 2017). By capturing the fundamental quality of neuroplasticity, the notion of an "electronic mind" delineates how this adaptation scientifically unfolds amid the pervasive digital transition defining present conditions. Emerging as the key explanatory framework linking digital culture and neuroplastic adaptation, electronic minds specify the combined subjective and cognitive adjustments precipitated by the simultaneous intensification and acceleration of present forms of digital immersion. The concept frames a comprehensive research program that, spanning multiple disciplines, unites the contributions of numerous specialized concepts and methods in analyzing unconscious eidetic and structured habituation (Singh et al., 2025). An interdisciplinary dialogue integrating perspectives from computing, applied and cognitive psychology, neurobiology, neuroscience, anthropology, and digital humanities provides added theoretical depth. Analysis of the broader social implications anchors these theoretical inquiries.

Neuroplasticity and Digital Environments

The ability of the brain to reorganize itself functionally and physically by drawing on cognition when exposed to consistent demands constitutes one of the defining aspects of the human nervous system (Holman & de Villers-Sidani, 2014). Cognitive activity emerges from the coordinated activity of anatomically distinct yet functionally related neuronal networks that operate on multiple time scales to engage the whole brain. This activity can modulate perceptual and motor systems, as well as influence a large number of processes that can be recruited to assimilate task requirements. The negotiation of this conceptual landscape suggests that cognition forms the scaffolding of neuroplasticity and is not just a consequence or epiphenomenon (Yadav et al., 2026). The human brain appears to have evolved as a complex organ that is equipped with a diverse set of processes that support cognition. Through extensive cognitive processing, the organism can bind variables, encode, map, and assimilate aspects of a concept or task and, in so doing, construct the architecture of experience in the nervous system, thereby configuring itself on demand in response to the exigencies of the environment and the task at hand (Spina, 2023).

Interdisciplinary Perspectives

Emerging from the conceptual terrain that grounds electronic minds, interdisciplinary perspectives offer complementary vantage points on the cognitive ecology surrounding digital immersion (Smart et al., 2017), corresponding to the experiential domain that anchors the ensuing discussion of digital-immersive transformations. Symbiotic and complementary directions of inquiry across the cognitive sciences suggest that electronic minds constitute a portal into the multispecific extensions of human nature, implicating modes of cognition and sociality that defy traditional diagnostic criteria. The term, therefore, assumes a critical heuristic role that facilitates interdisciplinary investigations into the cognitive capacities and extendability of intelligent living systems in the digital-technological age.

Digital Immersion: Definitions and Context

The precise meaning of immersion varies according to the associated media (Ensslin et al., 2019). Its use extends beyond immersion in digital fiction (Bell et al., 2018), yet the theoretical perspectives developed in that vocabulary have far-reaching implications for digital engagement.

Ever since water immersion prompted immersion's entry into English, the figurative extension of its meanings has remained connected to how an external medium surrounds and submerges a mind or a body. The conventional definition at the interface with the digital domain continues to emphasize "submersion" or "deep mental involvement" and "an opening up of a space or a channel between the subject and the object of perception". Following this understanding, immersion has risen since the late 1990s and early 2000s because it captures the expansion of the range of experiential domains that digital stories make accessible by transporting consciousness to elaborately simulated places or fictional worlds. When this is combined with the emergence of electronic minds as a conceptual framework that promotes the long-term neuroplastic adaptation to the dimensions of the digital environment, it follows that digital immersion will transform the lifelong habits of cognition, sense-making, and socialisation when it is performed routinely and on a large scale.

Understanding Digital Immersion

Electronic minds, therefore, arise as a conceptual framework capturing the relationship between neuroplastic adaptation and digital environments and introduce a perspective to consider the implications of the digital age for the nature of human cognition and social organization. "Digital immersion" is defined, and its interpretations are briefly rehearsed (Bell et al., 2018). The massive and accelerating penetration of everyday human environments by digital infrastructures is documented, demonstrating that the world is now more than ever global, instantaneous, ubiquitous, and continuous, so that questions about the impact of digital devices on cognition become urgent and legitimate. A wide range of empirical and theoretical studies underscoring the ongoing transformation of mental processes under conditions of massive, pervasive connectivity across time and space (digital + immersion) are then examined, demonstrating that key dimensions of human cognition, such as attention and memory, are continuously affected by connectivity (Ensslin et al., 2019). The chapter argues that the development of new forms of electronic embodiment increasingly leads to the emergence of the electronic mind. "Electronic" does not simply refer to the use of hardware but instead describes a complex and transformative socio-developmental trajectory in which human minds progressively adapt to bio-digital environments and evolve into new cognitive configurations, sometimes in unintuitive ways; this framework also integrates and complements elements of other proposals for the development of a new cognitive entity (e.g., the "extended mind" or "distributed cognition") (Yadav et al., 2025). The scope of digital immersion is vast—covering not only pervasive engagement with digital media and the reality of mediated living, but also the development of infrastructures that contribute to digitally enabled organization and coordination of every aspect of contemporary life—thereby specifically tying neuroplastic adaptation to the rapid emergence and proliferation of digital phenomena. This principle, then, is developed in several stages.

Historical Context of Digital Engagement

Digital immersion differs from earlier digitalization processes discussed by Montag and Diefenbach (2018), and Spina introduced the concept of a digital era as a determined space (2023). It emphasizes a species-wide phenomenon involving the continuous operation of specific digital equipment, independent of individual intentions and goals. Digital immersion inherently requires a digital interface and permanently alters human experience across cognitive, emotional, behavioral, and social dimensions. Unlike mere digital usage, where individuals activate a digital medium for brief periods, digital immersion occurs when a digital device operates continuously over long durations, often without human initiation or control.

Cognitive Transformations in the Digital Age

Transformations in human attention are among digital immersion's most evident cognitive repercussions. Perpetually connected individuals are continuously bombarded by email alerts, messages, and other communications interrupt daily activities, impeding the ability to concentrate on singular tasks. Such prolonged engagement with digital environments can deteriorate episodic and autobiographical memory—faculties integral to constructing a consistent self-concept and guiding future actions—while concurrently enhancing semantic and procedural memory associated with information retrieval and application. The sociocultural ramifications of pervasive digital connectivity permeate identity construction, discourse, and social interactions (Montag & Diefenbach, 2018).

Meeting the escalating demand for constant connection, proprietary algorithms anticipate and influence consumer preferences by selecting, presenting, and arranging information that reflects individual tastes, opinions, and interests. The pervasive collection and utilization of personal data intensifies the pivotal role of digital engagement in shaping social and cognitive processes.

Mastery of digital technologies grants unprecedented access to information and services, facilitating the formulation of novel plans, testing innovative ideas and hypotheses, and pursuing diverse educational objectives. Digital platforms enable rapid and comprehensive responses to complex problems by providing relevant data, data visualization capabilities, effective communication instruments, and various participatory mechanisms. Nonetheless, digital engagement may also destabilize psychological equilibrium to an extent that compromises optimal cognitive functioning (Yadav et al., 2025). Contemporary life frequently requires multitasking, problem-solving, and continuous shifts between issues. The prioritization of immediate information access over reflective solitude and creative ideation can inflict significant psychological harm on many individuals.

Attention in a Connected World

The challenges to the human mind posed by increasing digital immersion demand focused attention, which is the primary element affected when the mind interfaces with digital stimuli. While psychostimulants can extend attention to enable multitasking, the cognitive demand of tasks in complex environments also promotes additional neuroplastic resizing within the attention system. Individuals report increased idleness and a pressured feeling of time. The pressure is not linear in time but in cognitive cycles of information processing, acquisition, elaboration, and memorization. The experience is a closed circuit of continuous insight that is exhausting, masking within it an abeyance before the actual understanding of a new pattern or concept can develop—an unconsciously experienced state of confusion, a chaotic accumulation of new information (Smart et al., 2017; Zandi, 2018).

Memory and Information Overload

According to Ward (2013), people tend to form transactive memory structures, which serve an adaptive purpose by offloading responsibility for information to other systems or people, freeing up cognitive resources for more complex tasks. Such memory networks strengthen social bonds through shared knowledge. The internet now functions as an external memory-storage device, surpassing human partners in both capacity and accessibility. Increasing reliance on the internet can diminish awareness of one's mental boundaries and foster a sense of unity with the cloud. Whether this integration yields positive or negative consequences, it proceeds independently of individual awareness or preference. The central question is whether to withdraw into focused personal remembrance or embrace the internet's potential for enhancing cognition. Preliminary findings indicate synergistic interaction with the internet can enhance memory accuracy and creativity. Although the domain of human–internet memory interactions remains nascent, it presents promising avenues for augmenting the human experience.

Identity in the Digital Sphere

Digital media may influence self-perception, reflection, and presentation. Digital environments shape experiences of the minimal self, which is immediate and non-observational, and the narrative self, which involves identity and continuity over time and is built through stories told to oneself and others. Attitudes and opportunities for experiencing these types of self may be influenced by digital interactions (Montag & Diefenbach, 2018). Movements with particular digital media, such as smartphones, also appear to be incorporated into responses to bodily representations (Singh et al., 2025). Tools and machines used by humans are themselves, to a certain extent, regarded as extensions of the body. With the perception of body limits blurred, one's body image or schema will be altered accordingly. A successful gesture with a tool immediately impacts the body image. That tool is therefore incorporated within the individual's spatial and motor domains. Moving in a virtual world may produce a similar change, resulting in a specific modification of the subjective experience of one's own body (Spina, 2023).

Constructing Digital Identities

Digital technologies enable the construction of faceless and disembodied personae. Users can engage in multiple, simultaneously activated lives. The early computer games Dungeons and Dragons and MUDs (Multi-User Dungeons) illustrate this phenomenon. Constructing a persona constitutes an active form of identity work. The experience of an oral or written narrative typically affects users at a low level. Their immersion in digital worlds and constructing an electronic self activate psychological and developmental mechanisms (Cavagnetto & Gahir, 2011).

Cavagnetto and Gahir (2011) propose a formalized model for understanding identity in virtual worlds that emphasizes a bi-directional psychological relationship between the authentic self and the virtual self, or avatar, grounded in Parfit's notion of q-memory. A limonoid state mediates between these selves, encapsulating layers of information that define identity in both the real and virtual realms once the relation is established. Similarly, Kuruc highlights that online interactions often lack face-to-face communication, yet participants feel part of a community that permits creation (Kuruc, 2010). Smith, writing before the advent of social media, dismisses the notion that technology will unify humanity into a single community.

Impact of Social Media on Self-Perception

Human identity is highly multifaceted and covers both intra- and inter-individual aspects. The concept of identity is widely used by psychologists, social scientists, philosophers, and scholars of culture alike, but rarely with a clear definition and often with overlapping concepts such as self, self-concept, and self-image (Wang et al., 2023). People identify themselves by describing their personal characteristics and social roles, and appraise their life with means of self-esteem and well-being (Ahern, 2019). Starting in the 1990s, the increasing stream of human activity mediated by digital devices, virtually all day and night, has given a new twist to studying human identity. The digital immersion emphasises electronic minds, described here as a conceptual framework linking the adaptation of neuroplasticity to the externalization of memory function and the growing engagement with the digital environment and behaviours.

Interpersonal Dynamics in a Digital Context

Electrified by digital immersion, we also experience transformations in social cognition and interpersonal relationships. Virtual relationships and friendships emerge, and emotional experiences become altered (Smart et al., 2017). Early twenty-first-century adults expect constant access to leading social-media platforms, enabling instant images, information, and communication. Across cultivated relationships, a reservoir of "digital residues"—frequently curated, often dormant bits of information, such as photos, messages, and comments—materializes, directly affecting social structures (Montag & Diefenbach, 2018). Furthermore, interpersonal dynamics comprise elements such as trust in virtual teams, affective communication technology, and considerations from digital sociology. Human computation—when everyday people collectively process and analyze data—plays a significant role in both citizen science and collective intelligence. Theoretical approaches such as extended cognition and material engagement theory explore how brain, body, and culture interact with digital and social tools to affect belief formation and epistemic feelings, thereby shedding light on the interplay between digital immersion and cognition.

Virtual Interactions and Relationships

Physically shaped by our interaction with digital media and the virtual environments they convey, cognition adapts itself to such stimuli at all scales and moments. 'Electronic minds' offers a conceptual framework coupling degrees of virtual embodiment with neuroplastic change, linking cognitive to social transformations. Technological novelties influence culture and economics, yet communication remains the structural substrate of society's evolution. Virtual communication via electronic media profoundly alters virtually all human cultural activities, shaping thoughts and feelings such that the human mind becomes progressively more electronic. Video games attract players through active participation, immersing users in complex virtual environments where interaction confirms the reality of the virtual world over immediate physical surroundings. Virtual environments can transform a company, sector, or the entire world economy, underscoring the importance of exposing virtual reality technologies' growth, maturation, and appropriation (Kuijk et al., 2013).

The internet's capacity to influence human activity, behaviour, and development can be understood within an extended ecological psychology based on an environmental conception of the human mind. Social interaction facilitated by the internet significantly contributes to social development and cultural identity construction.

Analyses of technology-induced developmental shifts may provide valuable theoretical insights into current and forthcoming changes in human cognition (M. James & Francis Leader, 2023). Digital technology facilitates and fosters the formation of electronic individuals; this development constitutes a crucial step in the emergence of electronic minds. Since technology's advent, information access has increased considerably, transforming individuals into information managers who constantly move between positions and subjectivities. In parallel, peer-to-peer relationships predominate; indeed, individuals' perceptions, ambitions, and thoughts are centred increasingly around their relationships with, and the attitudes of others towards themselves.

Emotional Processing in Digital Communication

Emotions are integral to everyday life. The visibility of emotional expressions and the absence of anticipated emotional feedback increase emotional salience in mobile engagements with people, technology, or humans through technology. Emotion is a complex process, arising from interactions among intentions, beliefs, perceptions, and circumstances. Understanding sentiment requires comprehending the individual's mental states and contexts and the processes these conditions may elicit. The environment plays a critical role in determining the human mind's condition.

Human-computer and human-mobile interaction explores the dynamical interplay between individuals and machines, drawing on supporting information from both device and human. For decades, scholars worldwide have sought to elucidate the function of emotion in technological interactions. Research in affective computing concentrates on four areas: (1) reducing user frustration, (2) facilitating comfortable communication of user emotion, (3) developing infrastructure and applications to manage adequate information, and (4) creating tools that support the development of social and emotional skills.

This research aims to clarify the relationship between human emotional states and interaction, demonstrating that emotion exerts a more substantial influence on interaction than other factors. Trials with real individuals interacting with different computer systems confirmed the importance of emotional state in human-computer interaction. The investigation begins by categorizing emotional states induced by external events, challenges, and circumstances, and assessing their impact on life. Events and situations are divided into two groups: those eliciting positive feelings and those eliciting negative emotions. These insights inform design principles for digital worlds that fulfill the human need for emotional connection, indicating the necessity of minimizing frustration and accommodating our inherently social nature (Montag & Diefenbach, 2018).

The Role of Algorithms in Shaping Experience

Algorithms mediate the experience of a remotely controlled body situated in a virtual environment, thereby intervening in user groups' attention and memory structures. The characteristics of these mediations vary between groups, depending on the degree of freedom that algorithms are afforded in designing access to digital content. Rapid and ever-increasing territorialisation in online spaces has enabled the reconstruction of alternatives within average search times of less than a minute. The presence of algorithms in this space assists this fast reconstruction and mitigates the continuity of nostalgic time in online social experiences (Roth, 2019). While they increase agency by acting as mediators of a techno-social environment, these machines intervene in human activity and extend their presence in constructing action (Brooker et al., 2019). Algorithms offer dedicated platforms that constrain the world's purposes—material, digital, social, cultural, or political—. Throughout different stages of engagement, these platforms establish the continuity of simulated presence in online social experience (ESPOSITO, 2017). Membership of a virtual community and simulation of continuous omnipresence constitute the basis of a new political order, as they change the principles upon which social relations are constructed and develop analytical tools for addressing collective phenomena within digital immersion. The return to the balance of analogy versus digital ways of being is unlikely to restore progressive subjectivation. Equally, new forms of subjectivation are problematic within a pervasive environment that shapes the modalities of their emergence and development. Still, the hybrid, intermediate, compound, and composite subjects who do emerge stand at the centre of analyses of electronic minds.

Algorithmic Mediation of Reality

Digital technology mediates the substance of many communications and their form. The effect of this complex mediation makes the concept of electronic minds relevant to understanding contemporary subjectivity. The fundamental distinction between Socrates and electronic minds lies in the matter of the medium itself—tools on the internet not only augment private memory but exercise systematic control of conscious awareness; tools on the internet not only extend the conversational exchange into new media, but deeply mediate the reflection and cognition that produce the topic of the exchange. This mediation has empowering and disruptive transformational dimensions, thereby suggesting new ways of conceptualizing the digital phenomenon.

Whereas algorithmic processors were initially static and straightforward compared to primal humanness and the richness of archival forms, the scale and complexity of contemporary processors far surpass those of individuals, distributed archivally in a competitive assembly magnified in speed and density by expansive storage capacity. This exponentially increased bandwidth, enhanced by virtuality, distinguishes electronic processes from analogue media (Dhiya et al., 2024).

The operation of algorithmic processors atop networks of such dense, fast, open, and flexible intercultural flow creates virtual events that emerge independently of subject intent. These artificial contingencies complicate human information-seeking, suggesting altered cognitive conditions and a transformation of vitality and perception. Electronic algorithms amplify the force of communication's alterity, creating a disjunctive encounter in knowledge construction. Algorithmic mediation and digital embodiment shape individuation and production of subjectivity, exigencies of social systems, and ontopoietic processes necessary to the constitution of complexity and order. The digital environment is more than a venue for communication; it constitutes an architectonic of interaction, layering sociohistorical forms of communicative process with digital hazards and potentials, structural imperatives that both enable and constrain individual agency, and a virtual condition that saturates awareness with disparate raw materials and attendant exigencies (ESPOSITO, 2017).

Personalization and Its Implications

Pervasive digital engagement engenders subtle behavioral shifts and an increasingly personalized online existence. As digital immersion proceeds, the transition from highly personalized worlds to algorithmically crafted virtual planetary systems introduces the contemporary notion of electronic minds. Electronic minds manifest as the neuroplastic consequence of immersion within a digital environment.

From an evolutionary vantage point, human identity and brain function coemerged to facilitate survival within a particular milieu. Phenomenological theorists argue that the self fundamentally constitutes an embodied, situated, and dynamical process. Accordingly, digital immersion may be interpreted as a virtual re-embodiment: a digital form of bodily extension that necessitates continually adapting the central nervous system and behavioral patterns. Contemporary individuals are engaged in either adaptive recalibration or maladaptive degeneration. Immersion within a virtual space activates a profound, governing influence that shapes contemporary subjectivity according to properties of the governing milieu. Empirical examination reveals a dichotomous outcome: digital embodiment functions as an engine for societal and cognitive evolution, engendering a distinct form of posthuman identity, yet simultaneously imparts a disruptive potential that poses hazards to mental health and sustainability (Montag & Diefenbach, 2018).

Empowering Aspects of Digital Immersion

Digital immersion appears to empower its beneficiaries. Consider the benefits of ever-increasing access to information or the power of digital media as a learning resource. Immersion may reinforce focus, generate strengthened empathy (Bell et al., 2018; Ensslin et al., 2019), and facilitate play, a behaviour fundamental to developing the pleasures and skills vital to life. One potential co-advantage lies in the influence of digital environments upon what neuroplasticity transforms: digital immersion likely induces neuroplastic adaptation of the perceptual systems that make experienced environments liveable. Technological environments are now an important part of users' lifeworlds and, thus, interactions with technology constitute the intentional states that underlie the phenomenology of much experience. The transformation of lifespan developmental trajectories within interacting systems is also examined to enhance understanding of the commanding allure of technology and reveal avenues to locate powerful digital experiences within a more demarcated phenomenology.

Enhanced Access to Information

Enhancements in access to information constitute a widely recognized environmental driver of cognitive alteration in electronic minds. The digital environment fosters immersion and, thus, exposure to large volumes of information through diverse channels, including digitized print materials, digital audio and video, internet access, email, GPS, social networks, applications, games, etc. An electronic mind is immersed in a protracted and intense information onslaught and consequently enjoys unprecedented access to knowledge resources. However, it encounters difficulty ignoring extraneous and irrelevant data and faces continuous bombardment by waves of stimulating or distracting stimuli, which strongly shape its experience and state of mind. Rest periods without digital flow input become necessary to avoid the generalization of this effect. A potentially more serious issue relates to long-term exposure to psychological and neurological imbalances induced by an excessive presence of digital media; extended immersion and overstimulation can alter the capacity to reflect and consolidate memories. Nonetheless, readable and well-organized information remains more accessible. It is transformed by digitization, so that the electronic mind can benefit significantly from the new environment regarding cognitive empowerment, despite the circulation of disinformation and fake news (Voinea et al., 2020).

Opportunities for Learning and Growth

Electronic minds provide opportunities for learning and growth beyond the cognitive capacities of the individual human brain, creating new affordances for understanding both ourselves and the cultural environment in which we emerge. These possibilities illuminate the potential and challenges of evolving alongside electronic minds, reframing human well-being within a digital context.

The cultural and ecological context of information access and processing in human cognition remains poorly understood, despite the rapid development of digital sociology and the urgency to address emerging issues associated with digital media. While the process of human cognition extends beyond individual agents, the specific nature of extension through external resources like the internet is under-explored (Smart et al., 2017). Digital culture studies encompass a vast range of theoretical frameworks, technologies, and social structures that shape the everyday landscape of cultural knowledge. Reliable open data sets and methodologies for data mining enable perspectives on social behavior at continental scales. The cultural and ecological conditions required for emerging and maintaining digital society are becoming more apparent globally (Manuel Sánchez-Sordo, 2019). The development of neuromedia addresses media based on the neurophysiological foundations of sensory input, production, and experience of cultural content.

Human computation holds potential as an emerging advanced form of collective activity that interrogates large, fragmented, and distributed data in ways beyond individual human or conventional machine capabilities. Citizen science represents a large-scale experimental interaction between human and machine cognition in an open invitation for the construction of novel cultural knowledge. Though unconventional by most research standards, the pandemic-created sample offers valuable cross-cultural insights on social engagement, virtual teamwork, and collective intelligence. Research in human computation explores domains such as affective communication, trust and cooperation in virtual teams, and activity recognition for the cognitive self. A dive into the digital underground is required to discover how novel narratives bypass censorship and censorship fusion systems.

Disruptive Dimensions of Digital Engagement

Digital immersion offers unique and valuable opportunities that reshape an information environment, providing immediate, almost instantaneous access to countless digital sources, thereby enhancing the availability and transmission of information. Music, films, images, and texts are now accessible at any time and from any place. Easy accessibility to information fosters continuous learning and education, enabling the development of social, scientific, and political knowledge and facilitating the building of new identities on a less socially restricted basis. The transformation of our surroundings into information and knowledge offsets traditional education's limited transmissions and intermittent repetitive nature (Pandey & Yadav, 2023).

However, digital immersion also entails disruptive transformations. It renders inherent solitude untenable by eroding the possibility of reflective solitude, which provides the distance necessary for mental processes in any action, including learning. The ubiquity of digital technologies compromises moments of isolation, leaving us perpetually connected and unable to remain alone with our thoughts. This condition threatens the well-being of countless individuals. Digital immersion can give rise to depression and affective fragility while promoting shamelessness and an impediment to experience. These forms of disruption challenge the emergence of the digital being from the depths of digital immersion (Spina, 2023).

The concept of electronic minds delineates the transformative potential of digital immersion on cognition and social interactions. It offers emerging research perspectives from psychology, neuroscience, sociology, and media theory, highlighting the digital era's capacity to shape innovative versions of the human being. The study introduces an interdisciplinary framework for probing this transformation, one that simultaneously embraces conditioning and implications of digital immersion as sources of both empowering and disruptive modifications to cognition and interpersonal dynamics in technological contexts (Montag & Diefenbach, 2018). Such insights support ethical guidelines for engaging with the digital environment and open future avenues for investigating the electronic mind.

Erosion of Reflective Solitude

To be continuously interconnected is never to be alone. Reflective solitude has given way to "online togetherness." Individuals constantly anticipate incoming messages on social media or work-related platforms and find it difficult to resist the urge to check. The virtual remains: walking anywhere, waiting for a bus, or even going to the toilet without the smartphone accompanying the trajectory is now difficult.

The "mechanism of perceptual and cognitive saturation" is explained by the deluge of stimuli that reach the individual through a daily flow of information and the impulse to check. According to Spina (Spina, 2023), the new duration, termed the "digital moment," condenses the experience of phenomena into a very short temporal interval in which the brain restructures the "antennae to the environment." Smartphone addiction occurs because the mobile device provides access to the world at the touch of a finger, with the consequence that the virtual world appears more accessible than reality." Immersion becomes a natural state through which one lives. When emptied of perceptual–emotional content, the experience registers as "empty time," in which complex reactions of nostalgia, sadness, and uneasiness reset conflict with a phatic relationship made hyperconscious by the omnipresence of the digital device.

The moment occurs through the noospheric dimension: on entering the digital, the individual also enters a new "world" whose mechanism lies with the "complex social and cognitive system" to which they belong. Even an entire society is identified as a noosphere, but this system consists of more entities in constant interaction and relationship. In a particular space, individuals immerse themselves in a world that establishes, systematizes, and describes conditions, rules, and expectations.

Challenges to Mental Health

Digital technology contributes to mental illnesses, the consequences of which are substantial. In particular, the broad adoption of social networking services might affect mental health and lead to a loneliness epidemic, as they could fragment lifestyle and promote growing feelings of isolation and alienation. The neuroplastic process allows for detachment from the physical but does not replace meaningful interaction; the digitalised side of the self remains dependent on the organic core. Treated as a reality, however, the algorithmic content propagator builds an echo chamber in which the organic mind cannot participate. While massive digital connectivity improves access to information and services, it does not simultaneously guarantee well-being, meaning, and happiness. Instead, a digital etiquette capable of transforming a passive reception into mindful engagement is required to use the digital world as a space for co-construction and conviviality (Montag & Diefenbach, 2018).

Ethical Considerations in Digital Engagement

The pervasive use of digital technology fosters human transformation at distinctive temporal and spatial scales. Electronic minds describe a conceptual formation that links the neuroplastic modulation of cognition with the digital media environment. Mounting interdisciplinary research reveals that cognitive capacity, social interaction, and the physical self-adjust continuously depending on digital connectivity. Digital immersion encourages a further redefinition of human tracing; analytical reports, microblogs, and pictures provide multiple functions that cheaply reproduce every aspect of indistinct human activity. The social engagement of the individual becomes a matter of experiment. The behavioral modality associated with the Internet enables a revision of the long-standing dialogue between nature and culture that determines modern subjectivity. Habits, gestures, and relations between people and machines are progressively modulated. The epigenetic model of neuronal connections opens interesting points of comparison with human agency. The mental dependency on a digital process becomes marked, and the identity of the self reabsorbed in a correspondingly digital set of priorities, largely indifferent to the continuity of experience and memory, ready to modify itself with every new level of interface (Montag & Diefenbach, 2018).

Electronic minds define a conceptual framework for the neuroplastic relation between embodied cognition and an environment of digital stimulation. Its formulation provides a conceptual tool for understanding the processes through which that environment has altered the functional structure of individual cognition. It also provides an analytic terminology to extend the understanding of the broader social transformations associated with digital immersion.

Mindful Engagement Strategies

Strategies of Mindful Engagement

The pervasiveness of digital networks and the ease of access to Web 2.0 applications are remolding the foundations of human cognition. Digital immersion captures the intricate patterns of daily engagement with digital platforms, extending beyond straightforward constructs such as cyberspace, Internet use, hyperconnectedness, or online social networking portals and applications. By deploying this epistemological framework that interprets electronic minds as emerging from the coalescence of neuroplastic progression and digital immersion, examining how the constantly expanding web of digital networks is reshaping cognitive and social capabilities becomes crucial (Pandey & Yadav, 2023).

Policy Recommendations for Digital Well-being

Digital engagement currently lacks a clear strategy to ensure well-being while harnessing the efficiencies of ubiquitous digital networks. While digital tools can enhance life and workplace functions, providing benefits such as improved information access—especially in times of lockdown—and educational enrichment, adverse consequences arise once personal, social, cognitive, and emotional spheres become insufficiently mediated and digitally saturated. This imbalance can generate a harmful oversaturation that disrupts cognitive and social functioning.

Strategies for promoting well-being must find solutions that preserve the advantages of digital immersion alongside related activities while minimizing adverse effects. Considering well-being as a state of balance, several recommendations emerge: the digital environment should facilitate, not disrupt, critical routines such as relaxation, reflection, sleep, and recreation. Mindful and intentional design should align equal access to technology with sensibly structured integration, thereby avoiding detrimental disruptions to productive behavior or human happiness. Educational initiatives and incentives can encourage practices—such as those documented in specific online resources—prioritizing productive and intentional information dissemination over distracted or incidental digital engagement (M Thomas et al., 2022).

Contemporary digital networks serve a dual role: they operate on one hand as anthropomorphic digital systems that extend and interweave distributed channels through unique interoperable electronic identities, and on the other as integrated social structures that effortlessly merge human and humanoid agency. This multi-functional field provides unprecedented access to information and rapid knowledge accumulation and grants near-omnipresent cross-platform connectivity, ensuring uninterrupted engagement, collective participation, and continuous sharing of situational awareness. Such seamless interplay of platforms and protocols continuously influences cognition and social expressions. Humans remain embodied and subjected to natural laws, yet social coupling with digital networks catalyzes ongoing transitions into new identity formations, capacities, and modes of existence. Contemporary progress in digital connectivity thus enables—and indeed compels—socio-cognitive transitions to electronic modes of Adaptively Situated Embodiment (ASE), typically manifesting at scale within the space of just one generation. A dominant form of repetitive digital interaction emerges when personal devices are persistent proxies for individual behavior, facilitating ubiquitous and immersive engagement (Montag & Diefenbach, 2018).

FUTURE RESEARCH DIRECTIONS

Ongoing research has identified various digital immersion themes that should be incorporated into a future research agenda. Further research in the fast-evolving field of digital cognition will continue to reveal new cognitive and social consequences of digital immersion. Interdisciplinary, holistic models are required to integrate the central psychological phenomena explored in this study and associated fields. Prompted by this urgent need for a comprehensive synthesis of extant concepts, the present article introduced the notion of "electronic minds" as a theoretical link between the neurological role of neuroplasticity and the digital environments accessible through contemporary information equipment (Montag & Diefenbach, 2018) (Spina, 2023). This concept offers a framework for synthesizing models and evidence, focusing on the overlooked process by which endlessly repeated digital stimuli motivate persistent release of the brain-growth hormone BDNF, thereby driving rapid development of a distinct digital cognitive profile. Building on this foundation, the subsequent discussion outlined nine digital themes that describe the deep cognitive and social transformations that now demand serious scholarly attention (Lepuschitz, 2010). Digital immersion embraces empowering and disruptive forms of human transformation and emphasizes a stronger interdisciplinary approach than many previous models.

Emerging Trends in Digital Cognition

Emerging trends in digital cognition indicate the development of "electronic minds". These electronic minds originate from the adaptive processes associated with human neuroplasticity operating within the novel and ever-changing environment created by the growing digital immersion. This enables a highly sophisticated adaptive mechanism to cope with the overwhelming psychological and social transformations generated by exposed human brains to excessive and intensive digital stimulation during large parts of people's everyday lives. The concept of digital immersion was examined and put in relation to the existing state of the art, briefly explored, and establishes the various cognitive changes linked to constant connectivity. Subsequent analysis shed light on attention and memory alterations and the construction of identity and interpersonal dynamics in the digital sphere. Emphasis was placed on the role played by a new cognitive ontological agent: algorithmic mediation.

The disruptive dimension of these analyses was scrutinized, considering the many ways digital immersion may transform cognition and social behaviour. Mindful engagement with the digital ecosystem emerges as a foundational change that should be encouraged to support the development of a well-functioning and highly aware digital society. This opens the door to proposals to create a better intertwined reality of silicon and carbon, which was unbalanced for millennia and is now powering together a new renaissance of Western civilisation. The present methodology brought together concepts from different disciplines, applying advances from neuroplasticity to a new social–psychological framework that contributes to deepening the understanding of human behaviours in a world with pervasive digital stimulation, enabling a closer examination of both empowering and disruptive traits of digital immersion.

Interdisciplinary Research Opportunities

The emergence of "electronic minds" is closely tied to digital immersion. A constant and ubiquitous connection to the internet makes digital devices the medium through which many individuals satisfy their urge for stimulation and novelty. Through this constant connection, human minds are adapting to the challenges and demands of the digital age.

The brain's neuroplasticity makes it capable of such adaptations, as it modifies its physical structure and function in response to an ongoing stream of specialised stimuli. Any new form of stimulation that enters millions of households in a brief period will inevitably modify the thought patterns of those exposed, and perhaps also the basis of their worldview. Identifying the possible new cognitive, social, and psychological characteristics shaped by digital technology has been termed “mind change” — the digital-age alteration of the human mind.

CONCLUSION

Electronic minds represent a conceptual framework that links the neuroplastic adaptation of human brains to the continuous feedback from digital environments. Because contemporary populations are immersed in digital media and technology, they exhibit changes in cognition, self-perception, and interaction that resemble the dynamics of electronic circuits and computational networks (Montag & Diefenbach, 2018). The concept of electronic minds thus serves as a productive model for the societal and individual transformations that emerge in response to the immersive digital milieu.

People experience digital environments in many ways, with the evidence indicating this immersive condition's eventual widespread reach (Spina, 2023). Effective engagement typically requires internalizing external stimuli and deploying appropriate interactions within the digital context. The capacity for such internalization depends on neuroplastic adaptation to the information provided through the primary media channels. Contemporary humans, immersed in the digital venue of entertainment, work, and socialization, therefore develop neural circuitries that sustain lifestyles and behaviors increasingly compatible with the constraints of the electronic arena.

REFERENCES

Ahern, K. (2019). MY SELFIE-IMAGE: AN ARTIST'S MULTIMEDIA PERSPECTIVE TO SELF-DISCOVERY.

Brooker, P., Dutton, W., & Mair, M. D. (2019). The New Ghosts in the Machine: 'Pragmatist' AI and the Conceptual Perils of Anthropomorphic Description.

ESPOSITO, E. (2017). Artificial Communication? The Production of Contingency by Algorithms.

M. James, M. & Francis Leader, J. (2023). Do digital hugs work? Re-embodying our social lives online with digital tact.

Kuijk, F., Van Broeck, S., Dareau, C., Ravenet, B., Ochs, M., Apostolakis, K., Daras, P., Monaghan, D., E O'Connor, N., Wall, J., Izquierdo, E., Kuijk, F., Van Broeck, S., Dareau, C., Ravenet, B., Ochs, M., Apostolakis, K., Daras, P., Monaghan, D., E O'Connor, N., Wall, J., & Izquierdo, E. (2013). A Framework for Human-like Behavior in an Immersive Virtual World.

Lepuschitz, R. (2010). BCIs – The New Ontological Dimension of Cyberspace.

Manuel Sánchez-Sordo, J. (2019). Data mining techniques for the study of online learning from an extended approach.

Montag, C. & Diefenbach, S. (2018). Towards Homo Digitalis: Important Research Issues for Psychology and the Neurosciences at the Dawn of the Internet of Things and the Digital Society.

Pandey, M., & Yadav, P. S. (2023). Understanding the role of individual concerns, attitude, and perceived value in green apparel purchase intention, the mediating effect of consumer involvement, and the moderating role of Generation Z and Y. *Cleaner and Responsible Consumption*, *9*, 100120. DOI: 10.1016/j.clrc.2023.100120

Roth, C. (2019). Algorithmic Distortion of Informational Landscapes.

Singh, M., Michael, R. A., Saheb, S. S., Yadav, P. S., Kiran, P. B., & Malhi, A. (2025). A Study on Digital Intelligence and Influencer Marketing for Sustainable Diversification of India's Retail Economy: A Qualitative Study. In Pujari, P., Khan, S., Kumar, A., & Naim, A. (Eds.), *Fostering Economic Diversification and Sustainable Business Through Digital Intelligence* (pp. 1–22). IGI Global Scientific Publishing., DOI: 10.4018/979-8-3693-8492-3.ch001

Singh, M., Syed, S. M., Saheb, S. S., Yadav, P. S., & Kiran, P. B. (2025). Role of Influencer Marketing in the Indian Retail Business Sector: A Qualitative Study. In Hussain, Z., Albattat, A., Fakir, F., & Yi, Z. (Eds.), *Innovative Trends Shaping Food Marketing and Consumption* (pp. 105–130). IGI Global Scientific Publishing., DOI: 10.4018/979-8-3693-8542-5.ch005

Smart, P., Heersmink, R., & Clowes, R. (2017). The Cognitive Ecology of the Internet. Holman, C. & de Villers-Sidani, E. (2014). Indestructible plastic: the neuroscience of the new aging brain.

Spina, S. (2023). Homo-Loggatus. The anthropological condition of historians in the digital world. Ensslin, A., Bell, A., Smith, J., Van Der Bom, I., & Skains, L. (2019). Immersion, digital fiction, and the switchboard metaphor. Bell, A., Ensslin, A., Van Der Bom, I., & Smith, J. (2018). Immersion in digital fiction.

M Thomas, N., G Choudhari, S., M Gaidhane, A., & Quazi Syed, Z. (2022). 'Digital Wellbeing': The Need of the Hour in Today's Digitalized and Technology-Driven World!.

Voinea, C., Vică, C., Mihailov, E., & Savulescu, J. (2020). The Internet as Cognitive Enhancement.

Wang, Q., Khuu, A., & Jivotovski, M. (2023). The self online: When meaning-making is outsourced to the cyber audience.

Yadav, P. S., Kiran, P. B., Vemula, R., Kumar, V., Kumari, P., & Michael, R. A. (2026). Leveraging AI and Digital Solutions to Enhance Sustainability in Green and Blue Economies. In Ordóñez de Pablos, P., Zhang, X., Anshari, M., & Almunawar, M. (Eds.), *AI and Digital Nomads Shaping Global Industrial Technology Transitions* (pp. 53–84). IGI Global Scientific Publishing., DOI: 10.4018/979-8-3373-0159-4.ch002

Yadav, P. S., Kiran, P. B. N., Sharma, A., Vemula, R., & Shrama, A. (2025). Customer Acceptance of Sustainable Fintech Innovation. In Financial Innovation for Global Sustainability (pp. 337–357). Wiley. https://doi.org/DOI: 10.1002/9781394311682.ch14

Zandi, R. (2018). *The Parallel Mind. Cavagnetto, S. & Gahir, B. (2011). A Formalized Model of Multiple Selves in MUDs. Kuruc, K. (2010).* Identity VS E-dentity.

ADDITIONAL READING

Alter, A. (2017). *Irresistible: The Rise of Addictive Technology and the Business of Keeping Us Hooked*. Penguin Press.

Carr, N. (2010). *The Shallows: What the Internet Is Doing to Our Brains*. W. W. Norton & Company.

Han, B.-C. (2015). *The Burnout Society*. University Press.

Levitin, D. J. (2014). *The Organized Mind: Thinking Straight in the Age of Information Overload*. Dutton.

Newport, C. (2019). *Digital Minimalism: Choosing a Focused Life in a Noisy World*. Portfolio.

Paul, A. M. (2021). *The Extended Mind: The Power of Thinking Outside the Brain*. Mariner Books.

Turkle, S. (2011). *Alone Together: Why We Expect More from Technology and Less from Each Other*. Basic Books.

Turkle, S. (2015). *Reclaiming Conversation: The Power of Talk in a Digital Age*. Penguin Press.

Vaidhyanathan, S. (2018). *Antisocial Media: How Facebook Disconnects Us and Undermines Democracy*. Oxford University Press.

Zuboff, S. (2019). *The Age of Surveillance Capitalism*. PublicAffairs.

KEY TERMS AND DEFINITIONS

Algorithmic Mediation: The process through which algorithms shape, filter, prioritize, and personalize digital experiences, thereby influencing attention, perception, decision-making, and social behavior.

Digital Identity: The representation and construction of the self within digital environments through online interactions, social media activities, avatars, and technologically mediated forms of self-expression.

Digital Immersion: A condition of continuous and pervasive engagement with digital environments in which individuals remain constantly connected to digital technologies, leading to cognitive, emotional, behavioral, and social transformations.

Electronic Minds: A conceptual framework describing the neuroplastic adaptation of human cognition and identity under conditions of persistent digital stimulation and technologically mediated living.

Neuroplasticity: The brain's ability to reorganize its structure and functions in response to environmental stimuli, experiences, learning processes, and repeated digital interactions.

Chapter 5
Tendencies Toward AI Addiction Among Youth:
An Examination in the Context of Educational Processes and Daily Life Practices

Burak Çeber
http://orcid.org/0000-0002-3760-3177
Üsküdar University, Turkey

ABSTRACT

This study aims to examine how young people use generative artificial intelligence in their educational processes and daily routines, and how this usage is reflected in their tendencies toward addiction. In order to achieve this aim, a qualitative research method was adopted, and in-depth interviews were used as the data collection technique. The sample of the study consists of young individuals aged 18–24 living in Istanbul. Since this research covers the use of AI tools in both educational processes and daily life practices, the sample was limited to university students. This constitutes the main limitation of the study. In this context, semi-structured interviews were conducted with young participants identified through a combination of convenience sampling and snowball sampling methods. The findings show that frequent and uncontrolled use of AI tools contributes to emerging addiction tendencies and perceptions among young people

DOI: 10.4018/979-8-3373-6665-4.ch005

INTRODUCTION

Artificial intelligence (AI) is developing rapidly and having a transformative impact in various areas of life, as recognized by international organizations, including the European Commission (2020). In the past two years, advances in large language models (LLMs) and their increasing integration into daily life have led to a significant rise in the use of AI-powered conversational platforms. Platforms such as OpenAI's ChatGPT, Google's Gemini, and Anthropic's Claude are designed as general-purpose tools to be used across a wide range of domains, including work, education, and entertainment. The conversational style of these systems, their use of first-person language, and their ability to simulate human-like interactions have paved the way for users to occasionally anthropomorphize and personify these systems (Phang et al., 2025). This trend has accelerated further with the diversification of generative AI tools according to content type. The rapid spread of generative AI tools for text production, such as ChatGPT, has been accompanied by the proliferation of similar tools used to generate visual, auditory, and motion-graphic content. While valuable in terms of creativity, these tools are increasingly preferred for boosting content production—especially for social media use—and for reducing production costs (Matsiola et al., 2024).

While the widespread use of AI is often welcomed for its potential to enhance productivity and facilitate access to information, recent academic discussions have increasingly focused on the psychosocial and behavioral dimensions of this extensive interaction. Concerns have emerged regarding issues such as digital addiction, cognitive overload, and changes in human–AI interaction patterns (Aljanabi et al., 2023; Alhaidry et al., 2023). These developments highlight the need to address the adoption of ChatGPT not merely as a technological advancement, but as a sociotechnical phenomenon with profound implications for individual well-being and collective digital culture (Maral et al., 2025). Indeed, in today's rapidly digitalizing world, the unprecedented speed at which AI technologies are being integrated into individuals' daily life practices, modes of accessing information, and patterns of social interaction has brought forth a new and complex phenomenon that fundamentally questions the nature of the relationship between humans and technology. This phenomenon, which can be considered one of the possible outcomes of this transformation, has been conceptualized as a new form of addiction referred to as "AI addiction" (Avcı, 2025).

Zhang et al. (2024) define AI addiction as individuals becoming excessively dependent on AI technologies across various areas of life, such as daily routines, social interactions, and academic work. AI addiction encompasses not only the excessive use of AI-supported tools but also psychological dependence on these technologies. Differentiating from existing models, Kooli et al. (2025) introduced the concept of Generative AI Addiction Syndrome (GAID) as a new form of digital addiction. According to this approach, users have shifted from passive content consumption to an active co-creation process with AI. Whereas traditional digital addictions generally involve one-way content consumption, GAID is based on a reciprocal and productive interaction process. This compelling co-creation aspect makes GAID more immersive and psychologically engaging than traditional digital addictions (Abbas et al., 2023). Accordingly, GAID is conceptualized not merely as exaggerated technology use but as a distinct syndrome with its own unique characteristics (Kooli et al., 2025).

As AI technologies become increasingly integrated into daily routines, screen-related addiction also appears to rise, increasing the likelihood that individuals develop addictive habits (Kardefelt-Winther et al., 2019). Within this framework, research has begun to focus not only on the technological benefits of AI use but also on the potential problems it may generate in both daily life and educational contexts. Pearson and Qadar (2024) emphasize that the rapid development and widespread adoption of AI in everyday life constitute an important issue in terms of how addiction and habit formation may emerge. The authors argue that in order to prevent negative outcomes, awareness of these psychological effects should be raised and appropriate management strategies should be adopted.

Parallel to AI's growing impact on everyday life, its implications for education are also increasingly debated. AI, which affects many areas of daily life, has led to transformations in teaching and learning approaches in the field of education (Morales-García et al., 2024). However, this transformation also brings significant issues, such as addiction in learning processes. In this context, Putri et al. (2024) note that members of Generation Z who heavily rely on AI in learning processes may experience declines in critical thinking and problem-solving skills if they develop excessive dependence on advanced technologies capable of answering virtually any question (Kılıç & Koca, 2025). Students tend to use systems such as ChatGPT, which are capable of generating content, to complete assignments or online exams (Susnjak, 2022). Excessive reliance on AI for content production carries the risk of weakening the ability to conduct original analysis. Students need critical thinking skills to engage deeply with course materials (Townsend & Hunt, 2019; Rudolph et al., 2023). When students perceive AI not as a tool that supports creativity but as a "black box" solution, learning outcomes may be negatively affected. In order to use AI tools in a supportive and conscious manner during the learning process, students must understand the limitations of these tools and be able to manage concerns such as data quality, academic integrity, overdependence, and the weakening of original thinking (Zhou et al., 2024).

In the literature, no study has been found that specifically examines AI addiction among students in the context of both daily life practices and educational processes.

Moreover, discussions of addiction in the literature largely focus on hypothetical advantages and potential risks rather than being grounded in empirical evidence. This study aims to reveal the perceptions and tendencies related to Generative AI Addiction among young people—particularly university students who are actively engaged in education—within the framework of both their educational processes and daily life practices.

The Use of Generative Artificial Intelligence in Educational Processes and Daily Life Practices

Rapid and unprecedented technological advancements are transforming all aspects of human activity, particularly business life and professional domains. This transformation is also significantly affecting the structure and functioning of the field of education (Gavranović & Veljković Michos, 2022). In connection with this transformation, the evolution of computers as well as information and communication technologies over time has enabled the emergence of new opportunities in the field of artificial intelligence (Sain et al., 2024).

The rapid progress in AI has been largely driven by developments in Natural Language Processing (NLP) models and Large Language Models (LLMs). These technologies have enabled the development of intelligent systems that users can access without possessing advanced theoretical or practical knowledge of AI and machine learning algorithms (Matsiola et al., 2024). Initially, chatbots and translation applications paved the way for the widespread adoption of user-friendly AI applications. More recently, the large-scale adoption of ChatGPT for text generation (Kamalov et al., 2023) has significantly increased interest in such tools.

Today, generative AI (GenAI), triggering change at an unprecedented speed and scale, has emerged as an AI paradigm that goes beyond producing purely algorithmic outputs and is capable of undertaking a wide range of tasks, particularly creative ones, thus representing a new milestone in the evolution of AI (Yastıoğlu, 2023). ChatGPT, GPT-4o, DeepSeek, Midjourney, Gemini, Bard, Claude, Runway, and Sora are among the most up-to-date examples of generative AI applications (Çeber, 2025). The rapid expansion of generative AI technologies—especially ChatGPT—beyond research laboratories into nearly all areas of social life is creating profound and lasting effects on science, art, human life, and all dimensions of communication (Kennedy et al., 2023).

Generative artificial intelligence (GenAI) has become a fundamental tool in education by significantly transforming various aspects of the field, including learning and teaching processes as well as the development of scientific research. Its potential to transform traditional learning approaches and enhance students' educational experiences has increased both academic and institutional interest in AI (Abbas et al., 2023; Masuwd & Putra, 2024). Through technological tools such as adaptive learning systems and intelligent assistants, students can engage more effectively with learning materials and grasp complex concepts in a shorter period of time. At this stage, whether generative AI is being used becomes particularly important. If a system demonstrates core competencies such as language acquisition and translation, video, visual, and music generation, information retrieval, and problem-solving based on machine learning techniques, it can be said that AI is being employed within that system (Douglas et al., 2024). Indeed, generative AI is an innovative AI approach that aims to produce entirely new and original content by learning from data distribution patterns; it can process various types of content, such as text, images, audio, and video, and generate highly realistic outputs (Jovanović & Campbell, 2022; Epstein et al., 2023). In this context, generative AI is positioned as a strategic digital assistant in education, supporting both teachers and students (Limna et al., 2022). Notably, generative AI supports the production of content, ideas, and designs, as well as conceptual exploration processes. As seen in the example of ChatGPT, it also contributes to problem-solving, reinforcing concepts, providing explanations, and developing writing skills through the generation of instant responses (Maclachlan et al., 2024; Dilmegani, 2023). Generative AI (GenAI) not only supports students' understanding of course content and learning processes but also contributes to the development of communication skills and facilitates a clearer understanding of the technical aspects of academic subjects (Ngonso et al., 2025).

Research focusing on AI applications in higher education points to numerous positive effects in terms of improving teaching and learning processes and supporting core competencies. These effects promote interactive learning experiences and enable education to become more responsive to individual student needs (Matsiola et al., 2024). Moreover, the use of AI in educational processes contributes to improved academic performance by expanding access to various digital learning resources and fostering personalized learning experiences (Budiningsih et al., 2024). Some studies also indicate that generative AI tools facilitate educators' access to diverse instructional materials and resources due to their capacity to produce content across different disciplines. In addition, the interactive and immersive nature of generative AI applications has been shown to enhance student motivation and encourage active participation in the learning process (Tashtoush et al., 2022).

Roll and Wylie (2016) conceptualized the use of AI in education along two main trajectories. The first is an evolutionary trajectory focused on improving teaching and learning applications, while the second is a revolutionary trajectory that examines the integration of AI tools into students' daily lives. The approach described by Roll and Wylie (2016) as the revolutionary trajectory draws attention to AI extending beyond learning environments and becoming integrated into individuals' everyday life practices. Indeed, AI technologies are increasingly finding widespread applications by transforming not only education but also daily life (Sain et al., 2024). In other words, as a modern technology, AI influences nearly every moment of our lives.

According to a report titled *"Data Never Sleeps"* published by a U.S.-based technology company, people worldwide perform 5.9 billion searches every minute and direct approximately 1 million questions to AI systems per minute. A significant portion of these queries is now addressed to AI. These questions span a wide range of domains, including entertainment, health, education, e-commerce, transportation, and social media (Singh, 2025). Generative AI tools such as ChatGPT are capable of responding to long and complex problems across many of these domains—including more personal topics—while maintaining contextual coherence in a manner comparable to human interaction. Thus, generative AI tools contribute significantly to daily life, sometimes through automation, speed, and accuracy, and at other times through features such as context-aware human-like dialogue, real-time responses, a broad range of topics, and personalized communication (Çeber, 2024b).

In a study conducted by Aslitdinova (2025), AI was found to provide significant benefits across a wide range of daily life activities, increasing efficiency and improving overall quality of life. Another study revealed that ChatGPT-4 has revolutionized the way young students interact with online content and communicate with their surroundings. The same research also showed that generative AI positively affects students' psychological well-being (Shahzad et al., 2024). Several other studies have reached similar conclusions regarding the positive impact of generative AI on mental health (Hu, Mao, & Kim, 2023; Zhang et al., 2024).

On the other hand, recent studies on the use of AI in education and daily life practices have focused on several emerging problems associated with AI use. Among the most widely recognized issues are data security, transparency, privacy, bias, and accountability (Çeber, 2024a; Rodgers & Nguyen, 2022; Yu, 2021). With the increasing adoption of generative AI applications by end users, new concerns have also emerged, such as overreliance on and excessive trust in AI (Li & Wang, 2022), superficial engagement, and the weakening of cognitive processes (Shanmugasundaram & Tamilarasu, 2023; Çeber, 2025).

Students' use of ChatGPT and other generative AI tools to complete assignments may lead to issues related to a lack of creativity and originality. Failure to disclose this process transparently may be considered a violation of academic integrity (McAlister et al., 2024). In addition, ongoing debates suggest that generative AI may weaken students' learning, particularly their critical thinking and problem-solving skills (Kasneci et al., 2023). These issues may, in turn, give rise to more serious problems such as addiction (Zhou & Zhang, 2024). This study focuses specifically on the phenomenon of addiction among the various problems associated with generative AI tools.

Generative Artificial Intelligence Addiction

Although generative artificial intelligence has the potential to enhance human creativity and productivity, the improper use or misuse of these technologies also brings various challenges (Kooli et al., 2025). One of these challenges is the phenomenon of addiction. Despite growing concerns, research on AI addiction is still in its early stages, and the number of studies in this area remains limited. Existing research shows variation in definitions and approaches to AI addiction, and there is not yet a shared conceptual framework in the literature (Al-Obaydi & Pikhart, 2025). Nevertheless, current studies indicate that research on AI addiction shares both similarities and differences with technology addiction.

Technology addiction has long been a major topic in psychological and clinical research. In particular, forms of addiction such as Internet Gaming Disorder (American Psychiatric Association, 2013) and problematic social media use have been widely discussed in the literature (Kooli et al., 2025). Previous studies suggest that addictions related to technological devices and systems may also be associated with artificial intelligence (Farghaly Abdelaliem et al., 2023). Griffiths (1995) conceptualizes technology addiction as a type of behavioral addiction. Within this framework, artificial intelligence—being closely linked to technology—is also associated with this category of addictions (Kılıç & Koca, 2025). Indeed, some studies consider AI addiction as a new subtype of technological addiction (Küçükvardar & Tingöy, 2018). Based on the technology addiction literature, AI addiction is therefore defined, similar to problematic smartphone or internet use, as an excessive use of AI technologies that leads to negative outcomes and reflects an addiction tendency in individuals (Wiederhold, 2018; Hu et al., 2023).

On the other hand, the literature also includes definitions that distinguish AI addiction from technology and internet addiction. According to Xie et al. (2023), "AI addiction" refers to a behavioral pattern characterized by the obsessive and excessive use of AI-powered technologies—including social generative chatbots, generative models, and algorithmic recommendation systems—that impairs an individual's functioning and leads to psychological distress. This perspective argues that the dynamic, adaptive, and human-like interaction features of AI distinguish this form of addiction from broader concepts such as technology or internet addiction.

Unlike other digital tools that rely on static feedback structures, AI systems generate personalized reinforcement loops that adapt to user behavior in real time, thereby increasing the level of engagement. This situation creates a foundation for the development of psychological addiction and a strong sense of attachment between users and AI systems (Xie et al., 2023; Murimi, 2023).

At the core of AI addiction are the intense and repetitive interactions that users establish with AI-based systems. In particular, generative AI tools, which have become widespread in recent years, offer users continuous streams of new and unpredictable outputs and include certain design features that may trigger addictive processes. These features, referred to in the literature as "dark addictive patterns," include response unpredictability, instant and visually presented outputs, notification mechanisms, and empathetic, user-adaptive responses. Such design elements can directly activate addiction mechanisms associated with the dopamine-based reward system and may increase the risk of users developing psychological dependence on AI-based chatbots (Shen & Yoon, 2025). Therefore, AI addiction encompasses not only the excessive use of AI-supported tools but also psychological dependence on these technologies (Zhang et al., 2024).

In these respects, generative AI Addiction is considered a new form of digital addiction that differs from existing types of addiction. Unlike addictions based on the consumption of external content, this syndrome stems from the excessive adoption of AI as a creative extension of the self. Users engage with generative AI not only for entertainment or functional purposes but also to satisfy needs for intellectual stimulation, self-expression, and social connection. This blurs the boundary between productive use and compulsive engagement, making it more difficult to recognize addictive patterns and for individuals to regulate their own usage (Zhou & Zhang, 2024).

Today, individuals of all ages and from various professional backgrounds use artificial intelligence technologies (Al-Obaydi & Pikhart, 2025) and may become excessively dependent on these technologies across different areas of life, including daily routines, social interactions, and academic work (Zhang et al., 2024). In recent years, generative AI tools have become increasingly widespread in the field of education. The capacity of AI technologies to enable personalized learning has led to a significant transformation in teaching and learning approaches in higher education. However, growing trust in AI also brings certain practical risks, such as potential declines in cognitive skills, reduced student motivation, and various ethical concerns (Morales-García et al., 2024). Indeed, findings by Zhang et al. (2024) indicate that excessive dependence on AI may weaken students' creativity, critical, and independent thinking skills, increase the spread of misinformation, and promote laziness in the learning process. Furthermore, the use of AI-based tools has been associated with increased screen time, and prolonged screen exposure has been linked to negative outcomes such as mental fatigue, reduced attention span, and decreased cognitive performance (Newport Institute, 2024).

Within this framework, the tendency toward addiction to AI technologies is considered likely to lead to various problems. One of the groups at particular risk in this respect is university students (Kılıç & Koca, 2025). Therefore, examining AI addiction among university students is crucial for providing meaningful and explanatory insights into the issue. In a study conducted with university students,

Kılıç and Koca (2025) found that students' levels of AI addiction were not low and should not be underestimated. The same study also revealed that AI addiction levels differed significantly according to usage frequency and students' fields of study. Similarly, another study showed that addiction to ChatGPT positively influences users' intention to continue using the tool. However, it has also been suggested that individuals with high achievement orientation and strong self-confidence may be less likely to become dependent on ChatGPT, as they tend to rely more on their own abilities and feel less need for external sources (Hong & Chen, 2024). The Artificial Intelligence Addiction Scale developed by El-Sayed et al. (2025) for students has recently emerged as a significant instrument for assessing addiction. The scale consists of two methodological phases—scale development and psychometric evaluation—and provides an important framework for evaluating addiction, functional impairment, withdrawal symptoms, and tolerance. Moreover, some studies have identified various psychological factors that contribute to the persistence of AI addiction. Among these factors, the need for competence development and social connection stand out. These needs may encourage students to use generative chatbots to improve productivity and decision-making processes; however, over time, this may lead to excessive use and addictive tendencies (Salah et al., 2023).

This study is important in terms of increasing awareness of AI addiction and its potential associated problems, addressing the issue holistically and systematically, and developing preventive approaches against possible risks. In line with this aim, in-depth interviews will be conducted with young individuals currently enrolled in university education as part of the research.

METHOD

This study aims to examine how young people use generative artificial intelligence in their educational processes and daily routines, and how this usage is reflected in their tendencies toward addiction. In order to achieve this aim, a qualitative research method was adopted, and in-depth interviews were used as the data collection technique. The sample of the study consists of young individuals aged 18–24 living in Istanbul.

Since this research covers the use of AI tools in both educational processes and daily life practices, the sample was limited to university students. This constitutes the main limitation of the study. However, because daily life practices are also included within the scope of the research, the more inclusive term "young people" was preferred over "students" when describing the participants. In this context, semi-structured interviews were conducted with young participants identified through a combination of convenience sampling and snowball sampling methods.

To determine young people's tendencies regarding generative AI use, the following research questions will be examined:

- How do young people use generative AI tools in educational processes in the context of learning and cognitive activities?
- How and for what purposes do young people use generative AI tools in their daily life practices outside of education?
- What are young people's tendencies toward addiction in relation to generative AI use? How do they perceive and make sense of this process?

Semi-structured interviews lasting between 45 and 75 minutes were conducted with 16 young participants in the research sample in order to carry out an in-depth and comprehensive analysis of AI addiction tendencies. During the in-depth interview phase, the purposes and ways in which young people use generative AI tools in their learning processes and daily routines were examined. In this way, young people's tendencies toward AI addiction were identified. In addition, cognitive and behavioral experiences related to AI addiction tendencies were also explored.

The table below presents the demographic characteristics of the in-depth interview participants.

Table 1: Demographic Characteristics of the Interviewees

Variable	Category	Count	Percentage (%)
Gender	Females	10	%62,5
	Males	6	%37,5
Year of Study	1st Year	3	%18,75
	2rd Year	4	%25
	3rd Year	4	%25
	4th Year	5	%31,25

*The table was created by the author.

The in-depth interviews were conducted face-to-face after obtaining participants' consent, and audio recordings were made. All interviews were transcribed verbatim in accordance with the participants' explicit consent. Following the automated transcription process, the audio recordings were re-listened to and compared with the written texts to ensure the accuracy and completeness of the transcripts.

The responses obtained from the in-depth interviews were analyzed using an inductive coding approach within the framework of Braun and Clarke's (2006) six-phase thematic analysis, in order to identify the main themes. These phases consist of familiarization with the data, initial coding, searching for themes, reviewing themes, defining and naming themes, and producing the report.

FINDINGS

The research findings indicate that all participants regularly use at least one generative artificial intelligence (AI) tool, and more than half utilize multiple tools interchangeably. It is observed that participants access generative AI tools at least once a day, with usage frequency occasionally reaching five times or more. Participants primarily use text-based generative AI tools, although there is a noticeable recent increase in the use of visual-based applications.

The use of generative AI by participants is examined under two categories: utilization in educational processes and utilization in daily life practices. The tendencies, effects, and perceptual states arising from these usage purposes are analyzed under separate headings.

Use of Artificial Intelligence in Educational Processes

Participants reported utilizing AI tools at various stages of the educational process. These stages include conducting research, developing ideas, summarizing, ensuring adherence to writing and grammar rules, defining concepts, and explaining topics. Some participants expressed their experiences with AI use in these processes as follows:

"First, I use it during the writing and proofreading stage. Since I write quickly, I just put down whatever comes to mind. There can be issues with punctuation in my text. To fix this, I copied the text and pasted it into ChatGPT. It then sends me the revised version. I have never seen it make a mistake in this regard; I think it is quite successful." (P5)

"For a student, the most needed thing is ideas. After the idea comes the process of creating content. Because a student does not always, at least speaking for myself, have an initial idea or example. AI provides that first idea and establishes a starting point." (P7)

"I am preparing a project. Reading all the articles required for this project takes a lot of time. I uploaded the article from Google Scholar, wrote my topic, and it directly gave me a summary paragraph related to my topic. I also received support from ChatGPT regarding the project title." (P8)

Students' perspectives indicate that artificial intelligence is utilized across various processes in education. A notable aspect in their statements is the level of trust placed in artificial intelligence for performing these tasks. Students tend to delegate certain responsibilities to AI based on this trust. In this context, artificial intelligence addiction can also be conceptualized as the tendency or need to excessively rely on automated systems for decision-making, task execution, or verification (Morales-García et al., 2024).

- Transformation in Learning and Cognitive Processes

The use of generative AI tools in educational processes brings about a significant transformation in learning and cognitive processes. Participants described their experiences regarding this transformation as follows:

> *"But here's the thing—there used to be a certain drive. I would think, 'I will learn this, I will do this.' I no longer feel that personal drive to learn. Even if it exists, it's diminished. Now it's more like, 'I'll research it on chat for five minutes, I'll do it, I'll learn it.' I'll learn it very quickly, even in two minutes. We want things done within a few days. Patience has decreased." (P14)*

> *"I think I have stopped thinking as much. I used to think a lot. When I was going to present a project, I would check it at least 10–15 times and reflect on it. In fact, I would start preparing for a project a month in advance. But now I believe I can complete it within two-weeks, and instead of thinking 10 times, thinking five times is sufficient." (P9)*

In addition, Participant 3 described the transformation in their study practices as follows:

> *"I take small notes during lectures. For example, I recently studied philosophy of culture. There, I had written very brief notes on the concept of positivism. When I input these keywords directly into AI, it explains the entire topic to me. I then directly convert the information I receive into lecture notes. When researching information on Google, you have to read a lot, but AI selects and provides the relevant content immediately. When you ask for references, it also provides the links, so you can check them yourself." (P3)*

Students' perspectives suggest that the use of artificial intelligence leads to changes in cognitive processes such as motivation to learn, deep focus, and critical thinking. This situation stems from an overreliance on artificial intelligence as a creative extension of the self (Zhou & Zhang, 2024). Along with this excessive reliance, a decline in individuals' decision-making abilities may occur, and the automation of tasks can contribute to a tendency toward cognitive laziness (Ahmad et al., 2023).

- Evolution of the AI Usage Process

Participants indicated that their AI usage has followed an upward trajectory over time, becoming increasingly comprehensive in scope. Participant 10 described this process as follows:

"In the early stages, I used AI applications more restrictively. I used them for assignments, content creation, or idea development. Now, I use them more broadly. I am not only focused on writing; I also create visuals and generate ideas. Sometimes, I even consult AI regarding personal matters. As I learned to use it, it became somewhat like an assistant for me." (P10)

Participant 3 reported a similar progression:

"Initially, I was skeptical about AI. Then I started using it, but only for simple tasks and in limited ways. I began to use it more when I encountered difficulties. For example, last year we had a project, and I created visuals using AI. The project allowed the use of AI-generated visuals, which I really liked—it enhanced the presentation. That's when I thought, 'Why not use it?'" (P3)

An examination of students' statements indicates that the use of artificial intelligence has increased and diversified. This situation may play a role in intensifying artificial intelligence addiction. Indeed, as AI technology becomes more integrated into our work processes, dependence on screens also increases, thereby raising the likelihood of individuals developing addictive habits (Kardefelt-Winther et al., 2019).

AI Use in Daily Routines

Participants reported using AI applications not only for educational purposes but also to support their daily life practices. AI tools were found to be employed in a variety of areas, including social media content creation, interpersonal relationships, shopping, consulting and decision-making, cooking, entertainment (e.g., fortune-telling), and personal development. These findings suggest that generative AI tools have become integrated into numerous aspects of daily life, beyond strictly academic purposes.

- Non-Academic Usage Areas

Participant statements indicate that generative AI tools are not limited to educational contexts but are also widely used in diverse non-academic domains. This usage extends from everyday life practices to social and emotional contexts, demonstrating its versatility.

"A couple of years ago, I would personally write birthday or special occasion messages even for my closest friends. Now, I inevitably consult AI. I want to see an example of what I could write." (P9)

"I disagreed with a friend. Since many people around me experience similar situations, I was somewhat influenced and consulted AI about who was right. As usual, AI responded very positively, saying, 'Your friend may be right, but you are also justified in this aspect.' Sometimes, a person needs someone to ask, and when there is no one available or trustworthy, they think, 'At least I can ask it.'" (P5)

Participant 15's statements echo those of Participant 5. Additionally, Participant 15 described using AI in a psychologist-like capacity:

"I use AI like a psychologist. When I feel the need to be justified or want to feel better, I turn to it to hear what I want; I perceive it more like a human. I also use it for shopping—for example, to evaluate the pros and cons of buying a product." (P15)

When an emotional attachment is formed with artificial intelligence, users may exhibit symptoms of behavioral addiction following intensive interactive encounters. The dual concept of parasocial interaction that defines this attachment explains how individuals approach AI both as a symbolic figure and as a responsive companion, thereby reinforcing their emotional dependence (Al-Obaydi & Pikhart, 2025).

- Use of AI in Daily Life Practices

Participant statements indicate that AI applications have become an integral part of daily life practices, providing practical solutions to problems encountered by individuals. Participants expressed this based on their own experiences as follows:

"Recently, I repaired a faucet by asking ChatGPT. I entered an area I knew nothing about, followed the AI's advice, and successfully fixed the faucet. In addition, I can ask questions about topics such as plants, animal species, or images of places I am curious about. I also use AI for daily life practices like cooking recipes." (P6)

"I use AI while cooking. When I need a recipe or want to try different flavors, I turn to AI. I also use it for guidance when operating a home appliance instead of consulting the manual." (P13)

"I often suffer from headaches, so I frequently ask questions like, 'What can I do? What helps?' AI provides solutions for me in this regard. Additionally, I use it for locating places." (P11)

Prolonged interaction with artificial intelligence tools for work, education, or entertainment purposes may lead to addiction. It is therefore crucial to consid-

er the risk of AI addiction and maintain a balance in order to benefit from AI technologies without compromising health (Huang et al., 2024).

The Influence of Social Environment on AI Use

The findings indicate that the social environment—comprising academic circles, peers, and family—plays a significant role in determining young people's use of AI applications in both educational processes and daily life practices.

- Academic Environment

The results show that faculty members generally adopt a restrictive approach toward the direct use of AI applications. This approach reflects a reluctance to allow students' assignments and projects to be largely AI-generated; however, when AI tools are used correctly and ethically, instructors demonstrate a supportive attitude.

"Instructors take a restrictive stance toward AI applications because our department is entirely based on individual and original idea production. I think they adopt this approach to prevent difficulties in exams and future professional life. However, in introductory courses—especially in areas such as design projects—they sometimes encourage the use of AI." (P4)

"Faculty attitudes are generally negative. They can especially tell when ChatGPT is used directly. ChatGPT—and AI in general—has a distinctive language, which even I can recognize. Therefore, I try not to use AI applications in some assignments." (P1)

- Peers and Family

Based on participants' experiences, peers generally demonstrate an encouraging approach toward the use of AI applications. In contrast, family members tend to respond positively to outputs generated by AI but adopt a more cautious stance, particularly regarding the sharing of information.

"Some of my friends, as soon as they think about a topic, immediately say, 'Let's ask ChatGPT.' This has started to influence me more recently. Over time, I realized I had gotten used to it, because this topic comes up in almost every context. Eventually, I got accustomed to it and now feel that I am also leaning in that direction." (P11)

"My family is interested in technology, but they are still learning most things. For example, yesterday my father asked me, 'How can I create a video using AI?' Also,

I had used AI to organize the garden of our house in the village. When my father saw it, he liked it very much and asked for the name of the application." (P7)

"Some members of my family tell me not to use AI too much. They are particularly concerned that sharing so much of my personal life or integrating it too extensively into AI could cause problems in the future. Regarding things like fortune-telling, they warn that AI can provide inaccurate or unrealistic responses, so I should not get too carried away. As people warn me, at some point I start thinking, 'Should I stop?'" (P10)

Perceived AI Addiction Tendencies

The findings reveal that young people are developing tendencies toward addiction and negative perceptions regarding the use of AI applications in both educational processes and daily life practices. These negative perceptions appear to be associated with intensive, frequent, and uncontrolled use of AI tools. Among the 16 students participating in the study, nine reported being addicted to AI applications, three considered themselves partially addicted, and four did not yet perceive themselves as addicted.

"I think I am addicted to AI. At some point, I cannot do anything without asking ChatGPT. Even for something as simple as looking up a name, I say, 'Let me ask ChatGPT.' We use it in every aspect of our lives, and I think this is a harmful addiction." (P10)

Participant 4 emphasized that laziness resulting from AI use can eventually lead to addiction:

"Addiction, actually, comes from the fact that people have become so lazy that instead of researching on Google and finding the correct answer, they want to get a solution in two minutes. Or, if something comes to mind, they immediately open ChatGPT to look it up. I think researching everything on AI eventually leads to addiction. After all, we live in an era where people are constantly on their phones." (P4)

"I think enough of our personal information is stored in the system. Yet, the extent to which AI permeates our lives now bothers me. Its constant accompaniment to my thoughts also creates discomfort. Despite this, we cannot detach ourselves from it—there is an addiction to AI." (P9)

Participant 3 reflected on personal observations, noting that their peer group had become addicted to AI tools, while their own use in educational contexts could be considered addictive:

"My friend asks AI about almost everything, and I am genuinely surprised. Even for very simple information, instead of searching on Google and clicking the first link, they get answers directly from AI. They even want ready-made,

flawless sentences. Yet, not everything needs to be perfect; after all, none of us is professional or flawless. This leads to addiction and negatively affects creativity. Therefore, there should be guidance on how and within what limits AI should be used. I can say that I am addicted, especially when studying, but I cannot say I am addicted in every context." (P3)

- Metaphorical Conceptualization of AI Addiction

The findings also reveal that young people, when expressing their perceptions of AI addiction, often metaphorically liken AI to family members or scientific figures. Some participants expressed this as follows:

"We tend to ask and consult our mother about everything instantly. AI is like a mother in our pocket. Because when something happens, we directly ask, 'Mom, did we put this in the food?' or 'How did we operate the washing machine?' and it answers." (P14)

"I liken AI to my father, my eldest sister, and my boss at work. These are people who are always around and know everything I ask. They never say 'I don't know' or 'let me check'; they always have an answer." (P4)

In contrast, Participants 16 and 12 compared AI not to family members but to individuals prominent in thought and science:

"If AI were a human figure, it would be Celal Şengör. Because what comes to mind for me is wisdom—a wise person who guides me." (P16)

"I thought perhaps a philosopher or a scientist—I might liken AI to them." (P12)

The comparison of artificial intelligence to family members (e.g., parents, older siblings) or prominent opinion leaders in society reflects individuals' dependence on AI. Human-like features that render the technology more personal and engaging, while fostering a sense of companionship, can contribute to higher levels of addiction (Huang & Huang, 2024).

CONCLUSION

The emergence of generative AI tools such as ChatGPT, Gemini, and Midjourney marks the beginning of a new era in both daily life (Morales-García et al., 2024) and educational processes (Zhou et al., 2024). Generative AI tools offer numerous advantages in everyday contexts, including instant access to information, content creation, and facilitation of communication (Matsiola et al., 2024; Hoşgör & Güngördü, 2025). At the same time, these tools contribute significantly to the educational domain, notably by expanding access to digital learning resources and enhancing personalized learning experiences (Budiningsih et al., 2024; Crompton & Burke, 2023).

Although generative AI tools generate considerable excitement due to their features (Zhou et al., 2024), they can also create challenges, such as addiction. Young users who are highly immersed in digital tools, particularly university students, may develop excessive reliance on these systems, potentially undermining problem-solving skills and weakening their connection to real-life experiences (Hoşgör & Güngördü, 2025). The present study aimed to examine the tendencies toward generative AI addiction (GAID) among young people within the context of educational processes and daily life practices. To this end, semi-structured interviews were conducted with 16 university students to explore their patterns of AI use and perceived addiction.

Analysis of the findings first revealed that generative AI tools are widely used across both educational and everyday life contexts. In educational processes, young people employ generative AI for tasks such as researching topics, developing ideas, creating lecture notes, summarizing course materials, producing content, and performing writing checks. The findings also indicate that AI use in these tasks may lead to transformations in learning and cognitive processes. Notable aspects of this transformation include reduced patience for traditional tools and methods, a desire for quick and easy results, diminished reflective thinking, superficiality, and decreased attention span. Beyond the academic context, the study also found that young people use AI tools for interpersonal relationships, shopping, consulting and decision-making, social media content creation, personal development, cooking, fortune-telling, and entertainment purposes.

Consistent with previous research, the findings show that frequent and uncontrolled use of AI tools contributes to emerging addiction tendencies and perceptions among young people. Key indicators of these tendencies include frequent use at different times of the day, a continuous desire to ask questions of AI, avoidance of individual decision-making, identification of certain tasks directly with AI, the belief that tasks cannot be completed without AI, feelings of incompleteness when not using AI, perceived decreases in problem-solving abilities, and turning to AI during negative emotional states. The fact that more than half of the participants reported being addicted to generative AI highlights the presence of strong subjective perceptions of addiction.

Participants also metaphorically conceptualized AI in terms of family members (e.g., mother, father) or scientific figures when describing their perceived addiction. This metaphorical representation is likely related to the trust they place in AI. According to Kooli et al. (2025), GAID arises less from passive consumption of external content and more from excessive reliance on AI as a creative extension of the self. Furthermore, anthropomorphizing AI tends to increase addiction; since AI simulates human-like interactions (Kbaiah & Nashwan, 2024), users may perceive it as a trustworthy interlocutor, fostering emotional attachment (Saetra, 2023).

AI addiction is a multidimensional and complex phenomenon, influenced by technological, social, and psychological factors. From intrinsic motivations such as relationship-building and competence to perceived intelligence, personalization possibilities, and anthropomorphizing tendencies attributed to AI, all these factors play a role in the emergence of AI addiction (Al-Obaydi & Pikhart, 2025).

Further research is needed to deepen the understanding of AI addiction and its contributing factors. Advances in AI technologies significantly affect nearly all domains, both in terms of opportunities and challenges (Bom, 2023). Therefore, examining the long-term impacts of these technologies, uncovering underlying mechanisms, and developing effective interventions are of critical importance. Collaboration among researchers, policymakers, educators, and technology developers can contribute to the design of responsible AI systems that prioritize user well-being (Al-Obaydi & Pikhart, 2025).

This study was conducted with a limited sample of university students, and the generalizability of the findings should be considered within this context. Future research should examine AI addiction tendencies across larger and more diverse samples, including different age groups and educational levels. Additionally, employing mixed-method approaches that combine in-depth interviews with quantitative data collection tools, such as surveys, in various cultural contexts would provide a more comprehensive understanding of this phenomenon.

REFERENCES

Abbas, N., Ali, I., Manzoor, R., Hussain, T., & Al Hussaini, M. H. (2023). Role of artificial intelligence tools in enhancing students' educational performance at higher levels. *Journal of Artificial Intelligence Machine Learning and Neural Network*, *3*(5), 36–49. DOI: 10.55529/jaimlnn.35.36.49

Ahmad, S. F., Han, H., Alam, M. M., Rehmat, M., Irshad, M., Arraño-Muñoz, M., & Ariza-Montes, A. (2023). Impact of artificial intelligence on human loss in decision making, laziness and safety in education. *Humanities & Social Sciences Communications*, *10*(1), 1–14. PMID: 37325188

Al-Obaydi, L. H., & Pikhart, M. (2025). Artificial intelligence addiction: Exploring the emerging phenomenon of addiction in the AI age. *AI & Society*. Advance online publication. DOI: 10.1007/s00146-025-02535-z

Alhaidry, H. M., Fatani, B., Alrayes, J. O., Almana, A. M., & Alfhaed, N. K. (2023). ChatGPT in dentistry: A comprehensive review. *Cureus*, *15*(4), e38317. DOI: 10.7759/cureus.38317 PMID: 37266053

Aljanabi, M., Ghazi, M., Ali, A. H., & Abed, S. A. (2023). ChatGpt: Open possibilities. *Iraqi Journal for Computer Science and Mathematics*, *4*(1), 62–64. DOI: 10.52866/ijcsm.2023.01.01.0018

American Psychiatric Association. (2013). *Diagnostic and statistical manual of mental disorders* (5th ed.)., DOI: 10.1176/appi.books.9780890425596

Aslitdinova, M. S. (2025). How artificial intelligence helps us in our daily life. *International Journal of Artificial Intelligence*, *5*(05), 538–542. https://www.academicpublishers.org/journals/index.php/ijai/article/view/4421

Avcı, Ö. (2025). Yapay zekâ bağımlılığı [Conference presentation]. 4th International Turkic World Congress on Social, Humanities, Administrative, and Educational Sciences, Baku, Azerbaijan.

Bom, H.-S.-H. (2023). Exploring the opportunities and challenges of ChatGPT in academic writing: A roundtable discussion. *Nuclear Medicine and Molecular Imaging*, *57*(4), 165–167. Advance online publication. DOI: 10.1007/s13139-023-00809-2 PMID: 37483875

Braun, V., & Clarke, V. (2006). Using thematic analysis in psychology. *Qualitative Research in Psychology*, *3*(2), 77–101. DOI: 10.1191/1478088706qp063oa

Budiningsih, I., Oktapiani, M., Rijanto, W., & Masuwd, M. A. (2024). Comparative analysis of creative assignments, participatory collaborative learning, and students' satisfaction in digital & non-digital learning media. *Jurnal Pendidikan Progresif, 14*(3), 1900–1913. DOI: 10.23960/jpp.v14.i3.2024129

Çeber, B. (2024a). Yapay zekâ etiği bağlamında reklamcılık sektörü üzerine uygulamalı bir araştırma. *Intermedia International E-journal, 11*(20), 63–84. DOI: 10.56133/intermedia.1462312

Çeber, B. (2024b). Yapay zekâyı sorgulamak: Veri etiği ve dijital reklamcılığın kesişimi. In *Yapay zekâ etiği ve iletişim: Sorunlar, sınırlar ve zorluklar*. Nobel Akademik Yayıncılık.

Çeber, B. (2025). Generative artificial intelligence and brain rot from an advertising perspective. *The Turkish Online Journal of Design Art and Communication, 15*(3), 1162–1177. DOI: 10.7456/tojdac.1674327

Crompton, H., & Burke, D. (2023). Artificial intelligence in higher education: The state of the field. *International Journal of Educational Technology in Higher Education, 20*(1), 1–22. DOI: 10.1186/s41239-023-00392-8

Dilmegani, C. (2023). *ChatGpt education use cases, benefits & challenges in 2023*. AI Multiple. https://research.aimultiple.com/chatgpt-education/

Douglas, P., Stella, W., & Didi, E. F. (2024). Influence of artificial intelligence (AI) tools on students' learning outcome in adult education postgraduate programme in Rivers State University. *International Journal of Advanced Research and Learning, 3*(4), 132–141.

El-Sayed, Ahmed Abdelwahab Ibrahim, Alsenany, Samira Ahmed, Asal, Maha Gamal Ramadan, Alasqah, Ibrahim, Development and Validation of Artificial Intelligence Addiction Scale for Researchers: A Methodological Study, Journal of Nursing Management, 2025, 8458533, 15 pages, 2025. DOI: 10.1155/jonm/8458533

Epstein, Z., Hertzmann, A., Herman, L., Mahari, R., Frank, M., Groh, M., Schroeder, H., Smith, A., Akten, M., Fjeld, J., Farid, H., Leach, N., Pentland, A., & Russakovsky, O. (2023). Art and the science of generative AI: A deeper dive. *Science, 380*(6650), 1110–1111. DOI: 10.1126/science.adh4451 PMID: 37319193

European, C. (2020). *Libro blanco sobre la inteligencia artificial: un enfoque europeo orientado a la excelencia y la confianza*. Oficina de Publicaciones de la Unión Europea. https://eur-lex.europa.eu/legal-content/ES/TXT/PDF/?uri=CELEX:52020DC0065

Farghaly Abdelaliem, S. M., Dator, W. L. T., & Sankarapandian, C. (2023). The relationship between nursing students' smart devices addiction and their perception of artificial intelligence. *Health Care*, *11*(1), 110. DOI: 10.3390/healthcare11010110 PMID: 36611570

Gavranović, V., & Veljković Michos, M. (2022). Utilizing Ludic Foreign Language Pedagogy at the Tertiary Level. Paper presented at Sinteza 2022 - *International Scientific Conference on Information Technology and Data Related Research*. Retrieved from: DOI:DOI: 10.15308/Sinteza-2022-353-357

Griffiths, M. (1995). Technological addictions. *Clinical Psychology Forum*, *76*(76), 14–19. DOI: 10.53841/bpscpf.1995.1.76.14

Hong, J., & Chen, N. (2024). *Effects of achievement motivation and Chat-GPT self-efficacy on ChatGPT addiction and ChatGPT continuance intention. SSRN*. DOI: 10.2139/ssrn.5064583

Hoşgör, H. K., & Güngördü, H. (2025). Dijital yerlilerde ChatGPT'nin kullanım alanları ve ChatGPT bağımlılığı üzerine bir araştırma: A study on the usage areas of ChatGPT and ChatGPT addiction among digital natives. *Socrates Journal of Interdisciplinary Social Researches*, *11*(57), 12–24. DOI: 10.5281/zenodo.17179422

Hu, B., Mao, Y., & Kim, K. J. (2023). How social anxiety leads to problematic use of conversational AI: The roles of loneliness, rumination, and mind perception. *Computers in Human Behavior*, *143*, 107760. DOI: 10.1016/j.chb.2023.107760

Huang, S., Lai, X., Ke, L., Li, Y., Wang, H., Zhao, X., Dai, X., & Wang, Y. (2024). Mental health and AI dependence: A cross-lagged panel model and the mediating roles of motivations for AI use among adolescents. *Psychology Research and Behavior Management*, *17*(3), 1087–1102. DOI: 10.2147/PRBM.S440889 PMID: 38495087

Huang, Y., & Huang, H. (2024). Exploring the effect of attachment on tech- nology addiction to generative AI chatbots: A structural equation modeling analysis. *International Journal of Human-Computer Interaction*. Advance online publication. DOI: 10.1080/10447318.2024.2426029

Jovanović, M., & Campbell, M. (2022). Generative artificial intelligence: Trends and prospects. *Computer*, *55*(10), 107–112. DOI: 10.1109/MC.2022.3192720

Kamalov, F., Calonge, D. S., & Gurrib, I. (2023). A new era of artificial intelligence in education: A multifaceted revolution. *Sustainability*, *15*(16), 12451. DOI: 10.3390/su151612451

Kardefelt-Winther, D., Hebert, V., Heidari, S., Minges, K. E., Brindis, C. D., & Victor, L. (2019). Effects of excessive screen time on neurodevelopment, learning, memory, mental health, and neurodegeneration: A scoping review. *International Journal of Mental Health and Addiction, 17*(5), 1119–1139. DOI: 10.1007/s11469-019-00118-2

Kasneci, E., Seßler, K., Küchemann, S., Bannert, M., Dementieva, D., Fischer, F., Gasser, U., Groh, G., Günnemann, S., Hüllermeier, E., Krusche, S., Kutyniok, G., Michaeli, T., Nerdel, C., Pfeffer, J., Poquet, O., Sailer, M., Schmidt, A., Seidel, T., & Kasneci, G. (2023). ChatGPT for good? On opportunities and challenges of large language models for education. *Learning and Individual Differences, 103*, 102274. DOI: 10.1016/j.lindif.2023.102274

Kbaiah, A. T., & Nashwan, A. J. (2024). Beyond the image: Artificial intelligence's role in refining and transforming radiology nursing. *Avicenna (Doha), 2024*(1), 3. DOI: 10.5339/avi.2024.3

Kennedy, B., Tyson, A., & Saks, E. (2023). *Public awareness of artificial intelligence in everyday activities: Limited enthusiasm in U.S. over AI's growing influence in daily life*. Pew Research Center. https://www.pewresearch.org/science/2023/02/15/public-awareness-of-artificial-intelligence-in-everyday-activities/

Kılıç, S., & Koca, F. (2025). Artificial intelligence addiction of university students: The case of Ordu University. *Ordu Üniversitesi Sosyal Bilimler Enstitüsü Sosyal Bilimler Araştırmaları Dergisi, 15*(ISRIS 2025), 352–368. DOI: 10.48146/odusobiad.1725693

Kooli, C., Kooli, Y., & Kooli, E. (2025). Generative artificial intelligence addiction syndrome: A new behavioral disorder? *Asian Journal of Psychiatry, 107*, 104476. DOI: 10.1016/j.ajp.2025.104476 PMID: 40174516

Küçükvardar, M., & Tıngöy, O. (2018). Teknoloji bağımlılığının semptomlar temelinde incelenmesi. *AJIT-e: Academic Journal of Information Technology, 9*(35), 111–123. DOI: 10.5824/1309-1581.2018.5.008.x

Li, R., & Wang, C. (2022). Cultural and creative product design and image recognition based on deep learning. *Computational Intelligence and Neuroscience, 2022*(1), 7256584. DOI: 10.1155/2022/7256584 PMID: 35865496

Limna, P., Jakwatanatham, S., Siripipattanakul, S., Kaewpuang, P., & Sriboonruang, P. (2022). *A review of artificial intelligence (AI) in education during the digital era.* Advance Knowledge for Executives, 1(1), 1–9. https://papers.ssrn.com/sol3/papers.cfm?abstract_id=4160798

Maclachlan, R., Adams, R., Lauro, V., Murray, M., Magueijo, V., Flockhart, G., & Hasty, W. (2024). Chat-GPT: A clever search engine or a creative design assistant for students and industry? In *Proceedings of the 26th International Conference on Engineering and Product Design Education* (Article 70). DOI: 10.35199/EPDE.2024.70

Maral, S., Naycı, N., Bilmez, H., Erdemir, E. İ., & Satici, S. A. (2025). Problematic ChatGPT Use Scale: AI-Human collaboration or unraveling the dark side of ChatGPT. *International Journal of Mental Health and Addiction*. Advance online publication. DOI: 10.1007/s11469-025-01509-y

Masuwd, M., & Putra, F. T. (2024). Improving the quality of education through teacher resource management: The strategic role of school principals. *Jurnal Manajemen Pendidikan Islam Almatani, 1*(1), 29–46. https://journal.yrpipku.com/index.php/jmpia/article/view/6148

Matsiola, M., Lappas, G., & Yannacopoulou, A. (2024). Generative AI in education: Assessing usability, ethical implications, and communication effectiveness. *Societies (Basel, Switzerland)*, *14*(12), 267. DOI: 10.3390/soc14120267

McAlister, A. R., Alhabash, S., & Yang, J. (2024). Artificial intelligence and ChatGPT: Exploring current and potential future roles in marketing education. *Journal of Marketing Communications*, *30*(2), 166–187. DOI: 10.1080/13527266.2023.2289034

Morales-García, W. C., Sairitupa-Sanchez, L. Z., Morales-García, S. B., & Morales-García, M. (2024). Development and validation of a scale for dependence on artificial intelligence in university students. *Frontiers in Education*, *9*, 1323898. DOI: 10.3389/feduc.2024.1323898

Murimi, R. (2023). What makes AI addictive? The role of discounting, risk aversion and self-regulation. In Hsu, C. H., Xu, M., Cao, H., Baghban, H., & Shawkat Ali, A. B. M. (Eds.), *Big data intelligence and computing* (Vol. 13864, pp. 451–462). Springer., DOI: 10.1007/978-981-99-2233-8_32

Newport Institute. (2024). *Brain rot*. https://www.newportinstitute.com/resources/co-occurring-disorders/brainrot/

Ngonso, B., Egielewa, P., Egenti, G., Uduehi, I., Sunny-Duke, F., Ukhurebor, K., Onwusinkwue, S., Odezuligbo, I., Abiodun, A., Talabi, A., Jokthan, G., Opateye, J., Nwankwo, U., Eneche, B., & Osemengbe, U. (2025). Influence of artificial intelligence on educational performance of Nigerian students in tertiary institutions in Nigeria. *Journal of Infrastructure. Policy and Development*, *9*(1), 9949. DOI: 10.24294/jipd9949

Pearson, J., & Qadar, S. (2024). *Artificial intelligence has psychological impacts our brains might not be ready for*. ABC News. https://www.abc.net.au/news/health/2024-05-01/artificial-intelligence-ai-psychology-mental-health/103753940

Phang, J., Lampe, M., Ahmad, L., Agarwal, S., Fang, C. M., Liu, A. R., . . . Maes, P. (2025). *Investigating affective use and emotional well-being on ChatGPT*. arXiv. https://doi.org//arXiv.2504.03888DOI: 10.48550

Putri, A. E., Dinata, W. W., & Basri, D. C. (2024). The influence of addiction to using artificial intelligence (AI) in generation z in guidance and counselling. *BICC Proceedings, 2*, 159–164.

Rodgers, W., & Nguyen, T. (2022). Advertising benefits from ethical artificial intelligence algorithmic purchase decision pathways. *Journal of Business Ethics, 178*(4), 1043–1061. DOI: 10.1007/s10551-022-05048-7

Roll, I., & Wylie, R. (2016). Evolution and revolution in artificial intelligence in education. *International Journal of Artificial Intelligence in Education, 26*(2), 582–599. DOI: 10.1007/s40593-016-0110-3

Rudolph, J., Tan, S., & Tan, S. (2023). ChatGPT: Bullshit spewer or the end of traditional assessments in higher education? *Journal of Applied Learning & Teaching, 6*(1). Advance online publication. DOI: 10.37074/jalt.2023.6.1.23

Sain, Z. H., Vasudevan, A., erban, R. C., & Thelma, C. C. (2024). Integrating artificial intelligence in education: Understanding students' perceptions. *Journal of Educational Informatics*. Advance online publication. DOI: 10.62083/d62dea91

Salah, M., Abdelfattah, F., Alhalbusi, H., & Mukhaini, M. A. (2023). Me and my AI bot: Exploring the "Aiholic" phenomenon and university students' dependency on generative AI chatbots—Is this the new academic addiction? *Research Square*. DOI: 10.21203/rs.3.rs-3508563/v1

Shahzad, M. F., Xu, S., Liu, H., & Zahid, H. (2024). Generative Artificial Intelligence (ChatGPT-4) and social media impact on academic performance and psychological well-being in China's higher education. *European Journal of Education*. Advance online publication. DOI: 10.1111/ejed.12716

Shanmugasundaram, M., & Tamilarasu, A. (2023). The impact of digital technology, social media, and artificial intelligence on cognitive functions: A review. *Frontiers in Cognition, 2*, 1203077. DOI: 10.3389/fcogn.2023.1203077

Shen, M. K., & Yoon, D. (2025). The dark addiction patterns of current AI chatbot interfaces. In *Conference on Human Factors in Computing Systems - Proceedings* (pp. 1–7). DOI: 10.1145/3706599.3720003

Singh, S. (2025). Artificial intelligence and sustainable development: Opportunities and challenges. In Beniwal, A. (Ed.), *Artificial intelligence, ethics, and the digital society: Pathways to sustainable development.* Deep Science Publishing., DOI: 10.70593/978-937-1854-97-9

Susnjak, T. (2022). *ChatGPT: The end of online exam integrity?* arXiv. https://doi .org//arXiv.2212.09292DOI: 10.48550

Tashtoush, M. A., Wardat, Y., Aloufi, F., & Taani, O. (2022). The effectiveness of teaching method based on the components of concept-rich instruction approach in students achievement on linear algebra course and their attitudes towards mathematics. *Journal of Higher Education Theory and Practice*, *22*(7). Advance online publication. DOI: 10.33423/jhetp.v22i7.5269

Townsend, D. M., & Hunt, R. A. (2019). Entrepreneurial action, creativity, & judgment in the age of artificial intelligence. *Journal of Business Venturing Insights*, *11*, e00126. DOI: 10.1016/j.jbvi.2019.e00126

Wiederhold, B. K. (2018). "Alexa, are you my mom?" The role of artificial intelligence in child development. *Cyberpsychology, Behavior, and Social Networking*, *21*(8), 471–472. DOI: 10.1089/cyber.2018.29120.bkw PMID: 30110199

Xie, T., Pentina, I., & Hancock, T. (2023). Friend, mentor, lover: Does chatbot engagement lead to psychological dependence? *Journal of Service Management*, *34*(4), 806–828. DOI: 10.1108/JOSM-02-2022-0072

Yastıoğlu, S. (2023). Üretken yapay zekânın işletmelerde kullanımı: Fırsatlar ve tehditler. İ. Çeviktekin (Ed.), *Yönetim bilişim sistemleri: İşletmelerde dijital dönüşüm yönetimi* içinde (ss. 173-190). Özgür Yayınları.

Yu, Y. (2021). The role and influence of artificial intelligence on advertising industry. In *Proceedings of the 2021 International Conference on Social Development and Media Communication (SDMC 2021)* (pp. 190–194). Atlantis Press. DOI: 10.2991/assehr.k.220105.037

Zhang, S., Zhao, X., Zhou, T., & Kim, J. H. (2024). Do you have AI dependency? The roles of academic self-efficacy, academic stress, and performance expectations on problematic AI usage behavior. *International Journal of Educational Technology in Higher Education*, *21*(1), 34. DOI: 10.1186/s41239-024-00467-0

Zhou, T., & Zhang, C. (2024). Examining generative AI user addiction from a CAC perspective. *Technology in Society*, *78*, 102653. DOI: 10.1016/j.techsoc.2024.102653

Zhou, X., Zhang, J., & Chan, C. (2024). Unveiling students' experiences and perceptions of Artificial Intelligence usage in higher education. *Journal of University Teaching & Learning Practice*, *21*(6). Advance online publication. DOI: 10.53761/xzjprb23

ADDITIONAL READINGS

Al-Obaydi, L. H., & Pikhart, M. (2025). Artificial intelligence addiction: Exploring the emerging phenomenon of addiction in the AI age. *AI & Society*. Advance online publication. DOI: 10.1007/s00146-025-02535-z

Hu, B., Mao, Y., & Kim, K. J. (2023). How social anxiety leads to problematic use of conversational AI: The roles of loneliness, rumination, and mind perception. *Computers in Human Behavior*, *143*, 107760. DOI: 10.1016/j.chb.2023.107760

Kooli, C., Kooli, Y., & Kooli, E. (2025). Generative artificial intelligence addiction syndrome: A new behavioral disorder? *Asian Journal of Psychiatry*, *107*, 104476. DOI: 10.1016/j.ajp.2025.104476 PMID: 40174516

Matsiola, M., Lappas, G., & Yannacopoulou, A. (2024). Generative AI in education: Assessing usability, ethical implications, and communication effectiveness. *Societies (Basel, Switzerland)*, *14*(12), 267. DOI: 10.3390/soc14120267

Shahzad, M. F., Xu, S., Liu, H., & Zahid, H. (2024). Generative Artificial Intelligence (ChatGPT-4) and social media impact on academic performance and psychological well-being in China's higher education. *European Journal of Education*. Advance online publication. DOI: 10.1111/ejed.12716

KEY TERMS AND DEFINITIONS

Artificial Intelligence (AI): A technology that enables computers to perform tasks such as thinking or learning, which are normally carried out by humans.

Generative Artificial Intelligence (GENAI): A type of AI capable of producing new content such as text, images, or audio.

AI Addiction: AI addiction is a behavioral addiction marked by compulsive AI use, loss of control, and disruption of daily life.

Generative Artificial Intelligence Addiction Syndrome (GAID): GAID is a new form of digital addiction characterized by excessive reliance on generative AI tools.

Tendencies Toward AI Addiction: Tendencies toward AI addiction are a pattern of excessive and hard-to-control AI use.

AI in Education: The use of AI in education is the integration of intelligent systems that personalize learning and adapt instruction through data-driven approaches.

AI in everyday life: AI in everyday life is the use of artificial intelligence applications in daily life practices.

Chapter 6
Smartphone Addiction Psychological Drivers, FOMO, and Nomophobia in the Digital Age

Dhruv Khatri
http://orcid.org/0009-0004-8406-5967
Christ University, India

Ramji Nagariya
http://orcid.org/0000-0002-2739-9838
Christ University, India

ABSTRACT

The digital era has become the era of Smartphone addiction, manifesting as an increasing psychological and behavioral phenomenon among young adults and teenagers. Even though the terms like Fear of Missing out (FoMO) and nomophobia have been analyzed extensively, they have been frequently considered as separate entities, which reduces the opinion of their interaction to perpetuate problematic smartphone usage. This chapter summarizes the research of the current times and suggests the Integrative Digital Dysregulation (IDD) model to account for smartphone addiction as a dynamic self-stigmatizing cycle with identity extension, information vigilance, and psychophysical strain. In this context, FoMO and nomophobia serve as the major psychological processes transforming the vulnerability of the identity into the constant surveillance and anxiety-inducing activity. The chapter focuses on how the norms of constant availability and platform design characteristics aggravate digital dysregulation and solution-directed interventions based on resilience, mindfulness and adaptive self regulation.

DOI: 10.4018/979-8-3373-6665-4.ch006

INTRODUCTION

The smartphones are critical to communication, learning and socialization in the modern society. The multifunctionality of mobile devices, which includes connectivity, entertainment, productivity, and access to information, has contributed to extensive use among the different population groups, particularly the adolescent and young adult groups (De-Sola Gutiérrez et al., 2016). Even though their usefulness is absolutely indisputable, the growing addiction to smartphones has raised even more and more concerns about the tendencies of excessive and compulsive usage. Researchers have termed this new behavioural issue as smartphone addiction, which involves uncontrollable use habits that disrupt normal functioning, relationships with other individuals, the efficiency of study, and mental health (Duke & Montag, 2017).

Smartphone addiction is viewed as a subtype of behavioural addiction, which presents itself with such characteristics as tolerance, withdrawal, loss of control, and continued use despite adverse effects (De-Sola Gutiérrez et al., 2016).The groups of university students seem to be especially susceptible, with their school life, socialization, and behavior often relying on the Internet (Abuhamdah & Naser, 2023). In a cross-sectional study involving university students in Jordan, researchers have found significant mental health outcomes in high levels of smartphone dependency, such as high chances of psychological distress and lower wellbeing (Abuhamdah and Naser, 2023). On the same note, Duke and Montak (Duke & Montak, 2017) discovered that overuse of the smartphone augmented daily distractions and reduced self-perceived productivity, which reflected the disruptive nature of cognitive and working activities, though in small yet noticeable ways.

There is growing evidence that smartphone addiction is commonly comorbid with a network of psychosocial variables, in particular, the Fear of Missing Out (FOMO). FOMO is a widespread emotional issue that other people might be having more satisfying activities than one is and is closely related to the heightened use of mobile phones and compulsive checking behaviour(Patani, n.d.). Results of meta-analysis by (Zhang et al., 2011)verified the positivity of FOMO with mobile phone addiction, in terms of cultural conditions and age groups. Those who have a greater degree of FOMO place more significance on the internet, are incessantly connected, and feel increased anxiety whenever they are not connected (Zhang et al., 2011).

The problematic use of mobile phones is also partly due to FOMO since it is linked with low self-control, low social support, and low future orientation (Sun et al., 2022). According to their results, FOMO is both a predictive and a sustaining factor of problematic use that strengthens addictive cycles. The interaction between FOMO and online connectivity can also determine the results of social connectedness. Indicatively, Patani and Babu (2023) identified that, contrary to claims of (Sun et al. 2022) that enduring smartphone connectivity strengthens perceived social connection, it can also cause the experience of inadequacy when peers seem to have more active lives or be more satisfied (Patani, n.d.).

Nomophobia is closely related to smartphone addiction; that is the fear or anxiety of being without his/her mobile phone or not being able to access its functions. Being a new digital anxiety phenomenon, nomophobia is a manifestation of the psychological addiction of people to the accessibility of smartphones, the presence of the Internet and the possibility of social interaction. The initial conceptualisations placed the nomophobia as a growing social health issue, especially in adolescents and young adults who spend their lives being overly dependent on smartphones as their primary means of social engagement and emotional control

The more recent research has focused on the wider mental health and behavioural nomophobia correlates. It was indicated in (Ramos-Soler et al., 2021) that the severity of nomophobia in teens was significantly predicted by digital lifestyles with a high level of social networking. Their results show that the more youths are involved in ongoing digital self-presentation and socialisation, the more dependent on the smart-phone they become emotionally which strengthens the compulsive behaviours and discourages the offline life. Associations between nomophobia and poor mental health outcomes which included depression, anxiety, and stress symptoms, existed in an additional study (Vagka et al., 2024), indicating that nomophobia could be a cause and an effect of poor mental health. Their paper also found that the nomophobia and self-esteem were negatively related, which implies that a person with the lower self-confidence might turn to digital connectivity as a means of assurance.

Nomophobia is a phobia of modern age, a byproduct of the interaction of people with mobile information and communication technologies and smartphones in particular (Yildirim & Correia, 2015). This research aimed at adding to the nomophobia research literature by defining and describing the dimensions of nomophobia and coming up with a questionnaire to measure nomophobia. This study thus took a two phase, exploratory, sequential mixed methods design. The initial step involved qualitative research on the nomophobia by using semi-structured interviews with 9 undergraduate students in a big University located in the Midwest of the United States. Consequently, four dimensions of nomophobia were found due to the first phase: the inability to communicate, the inability to remain connected, the inability to access information and to forego convenience. Results of this qualitative pre-exploration were then built up into a 20-item nomophobia questionnaire (NMP-Q). The NMP-Q was tested in the second phase using a 301 sample of undergraduate students. The analysis of the exploratory factor analysis showed the four-factor pattern of the NMP-Q, which relates to the dimensions of nomophobia. It was demonstrated that the NMP-Q generates valid and reliable scores; and therefore, can be applied in determining the severity of nomophobia(Yildirim & Correia, 2015). Smartphone addiction, FOMO, and nomophobia are different constructs even though they are related. Smartphone addiction includes behavioural dependencies and compulsive use; FOMO reflects the psychological fear of being sidelined; and nomophobia involves fears pertaining to being out of touch or inability to operate his or her phone. However, the ideas are synergistically related. High FOMO forces us to be constantly connected, fosters compulsive use of the smartphone, and nomophobia worsens anxiety linked to being disconnected, which strengthens smartphone addiction (Ramos-Soler et al., 2021). Such a cyclical movement highlights the importance of analysing these phenomena collectively.

LITERATURE REVIEW

Smartphone Addiction: Concept and Evolution

The idea of smartphone addiction has emerged alongside with rapid increase in mobile technologies and the fact that these devices are becoming an integral part of the life. Initial scholarly research conceptualised excessive mobile phone use as a discussion of overuse or dependence and tended to focus more on behavioural frequency as opposed to psychological processes (Alwazzeh et al., 2024). Nevertheless, with the development of smartphones as not only a means to communicate more actively but also as a multifunctional device with unlimited opportunities to connect to the internet, social networks, entertainment, and work-related connectivity, the field of scholarship began to focus on the understanding of smartphone addiction as a type of behavioural addiction instead of excessive use (Billieux et al., 2015).

Modern studies are starting to think of smartphone addiction as a condition marked by compulsive behavior, loss of control, tolerance, and psychological discomfort in the event of limited access to the device.("Examining the Correlation between Excessive Recreational Smartphone Use and Academic Performance Outcomes," 2019; Tateno et al., 2022) These closely resemble other behavioural non-substance-related such as gambling or an internet addiction (Lin et al., 2016; Urfa & Görgülü, 2025). Researchers believe that smartphone addiction should not be defined only by the number of hours spent on the phone, but by the operative inefficiency it creates in personal life, including failure to fulfill academic or occupational tasks, disruption of social connections and mood (Alhassan et al., 2018, 2018; Matar Boumosleh & Jaalouk, 2017).

Recent research in this area has also highlighted upon the significance of the psychological processes behind the addiction to smartphones (Busch & McCarthy, 2021). Instead of regarding the device as addictive, recent research highlights the contributions of applications and digital spaces, especially those based on social media, that are created to be addictive by rewarding intermittently, getting social attention, and giving users personalized content (Chen et al., 2019; Taylor et al., 2024). Such a shift has prompted researchers to argue that they should not just rely on surface measures, such as screen time, but rather motivational, emotional, and cognitive variables that perpetuate compulsive smartphone use (Busch & McCarthy, 2021; Yang et al., 2022).

Psychological factors that cause Smartphone Addiction.

Frequency of use and technological availability alone are inadequate to explain smartphone addiction. Modern research is increasingly shifting toward the focus on psychological motivational factors, internal motivation, emotional, and cognitive mechanisms that predispose the person to compulsive use of a smartphone (Jimenez et al., 2024)(Mostyn Sullivan et al., 2025a). These motives operate beneath observable behavior and determine why the use of smartphones tends to persist even when individuals recognize the adverse effects of this behavior (Busch & McCarthy, 2021; Han et al., 2025) . Instead of considering addiction as a device-specific characteristic, recent literature tends to view it as a product of mental incoherence within virtualized spaces (Sende et al., 2024).

Anxiety-based motivation has been consistently identified as a key driver of problematic smartphone use(Cheng et al., 2024; Cho & Kim, 2025). Smartphones often functions as tools for reassurance, social control, and emotional control tools, specifically when there is uncertainty (Mostyn Sullivan et al., 2025a). Fear of disconnectedness, lack of information or exclusion contributed to an persistent background anxiety, which promotes checking behaviours (Leclercq-Vandelannoitte, 2019; Throuvala et al., 2019). This anxiety is not necessarily triggered by immediate external stimuli but is instead sustained by perceived risks of loss-of-information, linkage, or relevance, and is thus a proactive and not a reactionary engagement with smartphones (Conradie et al., 2023;(Gui et al., 2023).

Reward-based reinforcement represents a second critical driving force. Digital platforms integrated with smartphones are designed around intermittent and variable reward schedules, such as notifications, likes, messages, and updates (Oulasvirta et al., 2012; Taylor et al., 2024). Psychological literature suggests that such reward systems are particularly effective in reinforcing habitual behaviours, where users are conditioned to look at their devices hoping to receive some unpredictable gratification (Veissière & Stendel, 2018). Over time, this positive feedback loop may undermine volitional control and contribute to the automatization of smartphone use (Ayaburi et al., 2019; Jo & Baek, 2023).

These processes are further reinforced by social and identity-related drivers. Smartphones enable social visibility, peer validation, and self-presentation, especially on the Internet (Veissiere and Stendel, 2018). As individuals become more reliant on digital communication to reinforce social identity and personal relevance, smartphones increasingly become psychologically integrated into their sense of self.

Lastly, cognitive drivers (attentional fragmentation and habit formation) are important)(Fabio et al., 2022). The continuous presence of notifications and flows of information trains users to be in a hyper-vigilant state, and they are less tolerant of passivity or not being connected to the world (Berger et al., 2018; Fabio et al., 2022; Markowitz et al., 2019; Ward et al., 2017). With time, this attentional training dies away the self-regulatory ability, and the cognitive discomfort grows around not using the smartphone (Fabio et al., 2022).

Fear of Missing Out

Fear of Missing Out has emerged as an important psychological construct for understanding problematic smartphone use in the digital era(Freytag et al., 2021). Problematic smartphone use (PSU) is particularly prevalent among young people and refers to patterns of uncontrolled smartphone use that results in harm or functional impairment. The pathway model suggests that PSU may manifest distinct patterns including addictive, antisocial, and risky smartphone use. Motivational factors have been proposed as key contributors to the aetiology of PSU. However, much of the research investigating which motives influence PSU has measured smartphone use motives by adapting items designed to assess motives for other forms of media. This approach represents a limitation, as it may overlook motives specific to the context of smartphone use. Addressing this, recent research has employed qualitative approaches to examine motives associated with distinct patterns of PSU. Reflexive thematic analysis of focus group data (N = 25 participants aged 18–25 years) indicated that smartphone use to cope with discomfort (low mood and anxiety, social awkwardness, boredom, safety), obtain rewards (validation, pleasure), conform to perceived social norms, and for their instrumental value differentially motivated addictive, antisocial, and risky patterns of PSU. Some of these motives (including social awkwardness, feel safe, and conform) are not well represented by current measures of smartphone use motives. Accordingly, the development of more comprehensive measure of smartphone use motives may be needed (Mostyn Sullivan et al., 2025b). FOMO is usually characterized by a persistent concern that others may be engaging in rewardable experiences without one's involvement, accompanied by a desire to remain continually informed about others' activities (Alutaybi et al., 2018; Gao et al., 2023). In the modern digital world, this fear is only enhanced by their continual exposure to curated social content, real-time feeds, and visible social metrics, which make users more sensitive to the likelihood of being excluded or lagging behind in terms of information (Syahputra et al., 2023; Tang et al., 2024).

Psychologically, FOMO is an engine instead of a passive emotional condition (Casale et al., 2023; Rozgonjuk et al., 2020). It promotes a state of constant attentional arousal, in which individuals feel compelled to monitor digital environments to see updates, messages, and social cues (Throuvala et al., 2019). This pattern also aligns with the concept of information vigilance, whereby individuals remain cognitively attuned to the possibility of missing socially or informationally relevant content (Freytag et al., 2021). Significantly, FOMO does not presuppose being excluded in real life, just a feeling of missing out is enough to perpetuate the checking habit (Matias et al., 2021).

Empirical studies have demonstrated a strong association between FOMO and compulsive smartphone use, particularly on social media platforms emphasizing immediacy, visibility, and social comparison (Elhai et al., 2016). The vulnerable nature of digital platforms due to their time-related content, notifications, stories, and disappearing content categories of content supports the assumption that disengagement can lead to irreversible social loss (Casale et al., 2023). Consequently, the usage of smartphones becomes less about making a conscious interaction and more about making a regular check-up and surveillance among the users, who check their devices over and over again even without being explicitly encouraged to do so(Dora et al., 2021).

There are also significant developmental and situational differences in FOMO. In adolescents, peer approval, self-identification, and social presence tend to be the backgrounds of FOMO (Throuvala et al., 2019). Online inclusion and exclusion are known to be especially sensitive to adolescents, which makes them particularly susceptible to socially motivated vigilance practices (Yue et al., 2022). FOMO in the adult population is more likely to be associated with work-related significance, social connectivity, and being mindful in highly changing informative contexts (Wallinheimo & Evans, 2025; Zhu et al., 2025). In spite of these differences, the two groups have FOMO as a stimulator of increased alertness of the mind and lowered disconnection.

It turns the issues of identity and social doubt into persistent behavioral surveillance, which keeps the cycle of smartphone addiction in place (Arrivillaga et al., 2023;Brailovskaia et al., 2021). Such vigilance, as time goes by, leads to cognitive load and physiological stress and preconditions the somatic effects that will be described later (Casale et al., 2023). Therefore, FOMO is not an incidental consequence of using smartphones but a crucial process by which digital spaces transform psychological weakness in a compulsive attempt.

Nomophobia

Nomophobia is a term derived from the phrase "no mobile phone phobia" and describes the fear or the hatred that people feel having when they cannot access their smartphones or when they cannot stay connected digitally (Al-Mamun et al., 2025; Navas-Echazarreta et al., 2023). In contrast to general technology-related anxiety, nomophobia is centered on the fear of disconnection, which includes fear of losing contact, being able to access information, and the feeling of being safe with constant connectivity (Sapmaz, 2023; Vagka et al., 2024). With smartphones being regarded as a versatile continuation of everyday existence, the concept of nomophobia has become an acknowledged element of psychological aspects of smartphone addiction (Medrano-Sánchez et al., 2024; Oraison & Wilson, 2024).

Conceptually, it is possible to understand nomophobia in terms of identity extension (Balcioğlu & Artar Biyiklar, 2025; Gui et al., 2023). Mobile phones are becoming more and more archives of personal identity containing social networks, memories, work, navigation, and support networks (Strong & Bakhshi, 2023) . Consequently, disconnection with the device is not taken as a mere inconvenience but interruption with the self (Gui et al., 2023; Saidon et al., 2023). This is the psychological amalgamation of a user and a machine that is why nomophobia is commonly revealed through panic, irritability, or uneasiness even when disconnected over a brief period of time (Aarestad et al., 2023).

Nomophobia is oriented and emotionally detailed as compared to FOMO. Whereas FOMO is motivated by fear of missing external social experiences (Przybylski et al., 2013; Rifkin et al., n.d.), nomophobia is motivated by internal insecurity by feeling that one is unconnected with his or her extended self (Sapmaz, 2023). The suffering is not the result of what another person may be doing, but rather the perceived loss of control, safety and continuity in the individual (Hussien, 2022). This difference is essential as it puts nomophobia in the frontline as a susceptibility and not a behaviour-initiated condition (Safaria et al., 2024).

The use of age patterns also demonstrates the influence of nomophobia in smartphone addiction (León-Mejía et al., 2021). Nomophobia among adolescents is associated with social reassurance and identity validation because smartphones mediate peer interactions and self-presentations (Agüero-Espinoza et al., 2025; Pérez-Torres, 2024). In adults, nomophobia is often based on functional dependence, such as functional access in the workplace, family coordination, orientation, and emergency communication (Gonçalves et al., 2023; Hessari et al., 2024). Even with these differences in context, nomophobia is to be feared in both groups as a form of psychological instability, which confirms the importance of the smartphone being within easy reach (Vagka et al., 2024).

It is the mental state, which turns the smartphone into a need. The disconnection fear triggers attention mechanism that drives people into constant surveillance and verification behaviors thus directly leading into information vigilance on, through this, nomophobia grounds the cycle of addiction to smartphones at the plane of mind, which makes the addiction loop self-reinforcing even without compelling forces (Safaria et al., 2024).

FOMO and Nomophobia Among Adolescents and Adults

Smartphone addiction does not have a standard psychological experience simply depending on age, but instead it is based on the developmental stage, social role and demands of the situation (Jiménez et al., 2024; Wen et al., 2023). According to existing sources, the Fear-of-Missing-Out and Nomophobia tend to behave differently in teenagers and adults despite the possibility that both groups share common outward tendencies of compulsive smartphone use. These differences are likely to be crucial in explaining why the same digital environment generates different addiction pathways across the lifespan (Güzel, 2020) .

FOMO is always perceived as a prevailing psychological motivator among teenagers (Szawłoga et al., 2024). Adolescence is the stage of development characterized by exploration of identity, the increase in the sensitivity to peer assessment, and the necessity of belonging to society (Lestari & Suratmini, 2024; Ngo et al., 2024). These vulnerabilities are enhanced by the social media platforms which make the interactions between peers extremely visible and constantly available (Sequeira et al., 2025) . Therefore, adolescents have higher chances of becoming anxious due to social exclusion, slow reaction, or lack of interaction online (Einstein et al., 2023). This socially driven FOMO is a form of endless information vigilance, periodic checking is an act to keep socially relevant and emotionally safe.

This social dependence goes hand in hand with nomophobia among teenagers but is commonly manifested in the form of fears of not being connected with peers, losing their touch, and being disturbed in their online identity (Balcioğlu & Artar Biyiklar, 2025; Pérez-Torres, 2024). The mobile phone serves as a major access point to social life, and being out of touch with the phone is psychologically dangerous. In this respect, nomophobia strengthens the extension of identity in its early years and puts the device in the core of teenagers identity and aggravates their prone to addictive loops(Agüero-Espinoza et al., 2025).

However, adults, on the contrary, perceive the phenomenon of FOMO and nomophobia in a more functional and responsibility-oriented way (Jaworska, 2025). The phenomenon of adult FOMO is frequently associated with professional relevance, informational awareness, and social and occupational connectedness as opposed to peer validation only (Sapmaz, 2023; Tang et al., 2024). It is possible that on the one hand, adults are pressured by the demands at the workplace, the organization of the family, or the need to meet social requirements that cause one to be constantly available even when off the job(Marsh et al., 2024). This type of FOMO perpetuates obsessive use due to perceived need and not an explicit social anxiety.

Adult nomophobia often has its roots in apprehension of loss of control, efficiency and security (Hessari et al., 2024). Smartphones are necessary in terms of navigation and communicate

THE INTEGRATIVE DIGITAL DYSREGULATION (IDD) FRAMEWORK

The Integrative Digital Dysregulation (IDD) model is presented in Figure 1.

Figure 1. IDD model

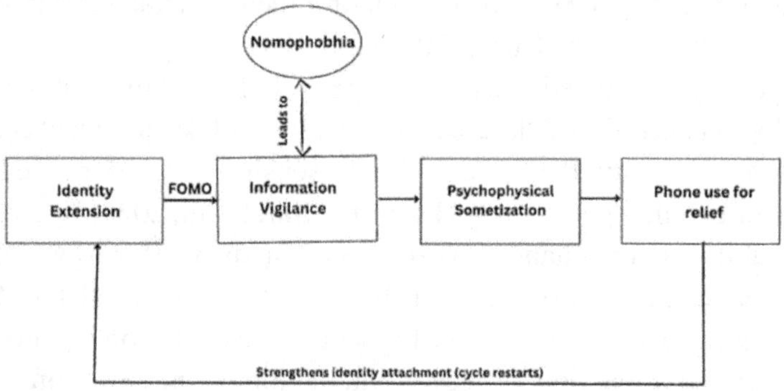

Introduction to the Integrative Digital Dysregulation (IDD) Framework.

Integrative Digital Dysregulation (IDD) framework is suggested to model the concept of smartphone addiction as a self-reinforcing cycle, which is self-reinforcing rather than as a direct consequence of overusing a various device. Instead of the conventional screen-time or usability-intensity descriptions, the IDD model describes the one issue of problematic smartphone use as the escalation of dysregulation that develops through the psychological identity, cognitive-behavioral vigilance, and the embodied psychophysical consequences (Belk, 2013; Brand et al., 2019). In this respect, smartphone addiction can be perceived not as dependence on the device, but a more global violation in how people control their affairs with the digital connectivity and self-concept (Przybylski et al., 2013).

Conceptually the IDD framework divides this process into three stages which are interrelated; Identity Extension (mind), Information Vigilance (behavior), and Psychophysical Somatization (body). These steps are not independent and sequential terminuses, but are instead components of a closed feedback loop in which one stage exacerbates and strengthens the others. The model thus reflects the dynamism of digital dependence, and this is why the distress associated with smartphones can be so perverse and adds to distress regardless of the awareness of the adverse effects of smartphone use among users.

The main assumption of the IDD model is that the constructs that are often examined, including Fear of Missing Out (FoMO) and nomophobia, cannot be addressed as separate psychological issues. Rather, following the integrative views in the literature (Elhai et al., 2021), FoMO and nomophobia are understood as the mechanism of connection between the vulnerability related to identity and the continuous vigilance and the eventual psychophysical burden (Yildirim & Correia, 2015). FoMO is similar to a driving force that maintains attention to digital space, and nomophobia is a manifestation of anxiety that arises when one loses this attention. They work together as the psychological connective tissue of the dysregulation cycle.

With FoMO and nomophobia put in a wider identity-behaviour-body context, the IDD model is able to overcome the weaknesses of previous models that are excessively narrow in terms of anxiety or frequency of use. It also emphasizes the way in which digital dependence is formed as a consequence of interacting self-concept, cognitive control, and physiological stress, and why digital dependence efforts frequently make a person feel uncomfortable, but not relieved (Drouin et al., 2012). Notably, the framework also defines particular components of this cycle, in which regulatory mechanisms like resilience and mindfulness can be applied to undermine or interrupt the processes of dysregulation(Arpaci, 2021).

Overall, the IDD framework offers an integrative perspective according to which smartphone addiction can be viewed as a digital dysregulation, which serves as a unified framework in order to arrange the available empirical data, as well as provides the framework in which the specific object under the focus of the particular model can be analyzed in greater detail in the following sections. FoMO and nomophobia are not realized in the IDD as two autonomous disorders, but as the functional processes of the process of dysregulation. The FoMO is a type of stimulus that starts the process of information vigilance by causing anxiety of the fear of missing something socially or informationally important. Nomophobia plays a preservation mechanism that maintains the vigilance by creating anxiety when the disengagement or disconnection is expected to take place. The combination of these processes controls the development and maintenance of the dysregulation cycle.

Positioning the IDD Framework in Relation to Existing Models

A number of theoretical models have been put forward to address problematic digital and internet-related behaviors, the most notable is Interaction of Person-Affect-Cognition-Execution (I-PACE) model and Compensatory Internet Use (CIU) framework. These models have served significant purposes to explain the functions of impulse control, affective vulnerability, and coping motivations in problematic technology use. Nevertheless, there are critical conceptual gaps of accounting the identity-based, embodied, and self-reinforcing character of smartphone addiction.

The concept of I-PACE model also conceptualizes the appearance of addictive behaviors in the interactions between predispositions, affective reactions, cognitive biases, and processes of executive control (Brand et al., 2019). This model has had a profound effect especially in the elucidation of the role of impulsivity, craving, and the lack of inhibitory control in problematic use. Nevertheless, I-PACE largely views dysregulation as an impulse and affect control failure at the personal level without directly touching upon the concept of identity integration or the cyclical reinforcement according to which digital dependence becomes increasingly integrated into daily self-regulation.

In a like manner, the concept of Compensatory Internet Use (CIU) framework views problematic use of technologies as a coping mechanism that is chosen in reaction to negative affect and psychosocial stressors (Kardefelt-Winther, 2014). Although CIU works well in describing the role of compensatory motivation and negative reinforcement, it is still very much linear in nature and outcome based focusing on the reduction of stress by using other than the internal reorganization of self-regulatory processes that can maintain dependence over time.

The Integrative Digital Dysregulation (IDD) model builds upon these conceptualizations by returning to the definition of smartphone addiction as a vicious cycle of digital self-regulation failure comprising of identity extension, information vigilance, and psychophysical somatization. In contrast to I-PACE, which concentrates more on impulse control and affective vulnerability, IDD makes identity extension the focus of dysregulation in which the smartphone can be viewed as a part of the extended self that changes regulatory limits. As opposed to CIU, which uses compensatory coping as the response to distress, IDD explains distress as the cause and consequence of smartphone use in a self-reinforcing feedback loop.

The IDD framework offers a process-based explanation of smartphone addiction through the combination of identity, vigilance, and embodied strain into a cyclical regulatory framework, which helps to understand its dynamic, embodied, and self-perpetuating nature. By so doing, it builds on the current models by placing the emphasis on the chronic digital dysregulation that occurs within the context of identity construction and normal cognitive-somatic operations.

Identity Extension (The Root of Digital Dysregulation): Node 1.

This model is named the Integrative Digital Dysregulation (IDD) and the initial node is that of Identity Extension which is the initial psychological state in which later dysregulation develops. Based on the extended self-theories, this step demonstrates the reasons why smartphones are viewed not only as the external means of doing things, but as the inseparable part of the personal identity, cognition, and social life. In the IDD model, the issue of identity extension is placed to be the foundation upon which individuals are susceptible to anxiety and distress following the failure of digital connectivity.

The idea of identity extension is based on the theory of extended self-introduced by Belk (2013) yet extended by the one of Attachment to Objects that states that digital items can be so deeply embedded in the self-concept of an individual. In the modern digital environment, smartphones are considered to be the storage of individual memory, relationships, everyday life, and self-representation. Contacts, photographs, messages, calendars, social media profiles, and others create a distributed representation of the self, making the device psychologically inseparable with personal identity. This leads to not having a sense of loss in becoming disconnected with the smartphone but rather as a disturbance in the continuity of the self (Carter & Gilovich, 2012).

This identity-related integration gives the psychological background to nomophobia, which is the fear or anxiety of missing the chance to use or access their mobile phones (Yildirim and Correia, 2015). Empirical studies have proven that nomophobia is a multi-dimensional concept, and fear of disconnection and inability to access information are just some of the dimensions, as they demonstrate threats to the digital self-schema and not the attribute of being threatened by technology. In the IDD model, nomophobia, then, is not to be understood as an independent phobia, but as a symptom of threatened identity extension.

Notably, identity extension changes the affective sense of smartphone availability. Where the self is seen as a component of the device, the disconnection is construed as ego-depletion or loss of self, which leads to the development of separation anxiety and emotional responsiveness. According to recent studies, the dependency leads to a transactive memory system (Wegner & Ward, 2013), in which the smartphone becomes an external cognitive force; therefore, disconnection is experienced as a dysfunctional cognitive impairment. That is why people can feel uncomfortable, nervous, or even scared even under the conditions of short-term failures in the network, like low battery warnings or the loss of access to the network.

In the IDD model, identity extension does not directly cause compulsive smartphone behaviors. Rather, it makes the person sensitive to perceived threat of disconnection, and thus it triggers the following aspect of dysregulation- Information

Vigilance. After the smartphone is integrated into the self-concept, it becomes psychologically vital to have a continued access to retain Identity Stability that establishes the circumstances of continued monitoring and attentional vigilance.

The Digital Dysregulation Engine: Psychological Motivations of FoMO and Nomophobia.

The conceptualization of Fear of Missing Out (FoMO) and nomophobia in the context of the Integrative Digital Dysregulation (IDD) paradigm is not presented as a result of smartphone use but as a combination of interacting psychological processes that transform a vulnerability based on identity in the persistent patterns of digital vigilance. These constructs serve as motivational and anxiety-provoking processes as instead of discrete emotional experience, one that energizes and keeps the attentional focus constantly oriented to digital environments (Elhai et al., 2021).

FoMO functions as a motivational pressure to remain attentive to digital spaces. Whenever people think that their social relevance, access to information, or personal importance depends on their continued connectedness, It becomes a driver of increased sensitivity to possible lapses in awareness. It is not a motivated state that is necessitated by real exclusion or loss but a feeling of a potential loss of socially or informationally desirable experiences. Due to its effect, FoMO enables unremitting surveillance practices that coincide with the idea of information vigilance set out in the framework.

Nomophobia, in its turn, is an anxiety-driven mechanism that strengthens such vigilance in the event of the threat or interference with the access to the smartphone. In the IDD framework, nomophobia becomes apparent in a situation whereby the smartphone has already become a part of his or her self-concept by extending the self-identity. Disconnection is thus not only inconveniencing but a psychologically salient incongruity, which ups the vigilance and drives its speedy restoration of access. Creating such a feeling, nomophobia enhances the sense of urgency involved in keeping constant communication instead of starting watchfulness alone.

Notably, FoMO and nomophobia are perceived in the context of the IDD as complementary processes, not as causal. FoMO increases the motivational salience of staying connected and nomophobia increases the anxiety of losing connectivity. The two components make up a self-reinforcing motivational-anxiety cycle that stabilizes information vigilance patterns in the long term. This interaction can be used to explain why people can still stay in a repetitive cycle of checking even when these behaviors or actions no longer provide satisfaction or any conscious benefit. Self-regulationally, the IDD framework is in agreement with other models like the I-PACE (Brand et al., 2019) on the theory that repetitive vigilance responses might increase in automaticity with the taxation of executive control. Since vigilance turns into a routine and not a thoughtful process, it opens the doors to the accumulation of cognitive and emotional tension, which predetermines the onset of the psychophysical effects, which the next section will examine.

Node 3: Psychophysical Somatization (The Result of Digital Dysregulation)

Psychophysical Somatization is the third step of the Integrative Digital Dysregulation (IDD) model, and this is the point where chronic psychological and behavioral disregulation is manifested. Under the IDD model, the emotional unease or cognitive burden is not the only manifestation of smartphone addiction; instead, the overall health issue caused by chronic information vigilance related to FoMO and nomophobia can be measured (Elhai et al., 2021).This step assumes how digital over-engagement shifts the mental habit to a larger-scale health problem.

Psychophysical somatization, is whereby the chronic psychological stress is developed into physical symptoms. When applied to smartphone use, it is the continual attention or vigilance, which is defined by attentional fragmentation and frequent checking, that puts the constant pressure on the cognitive and emotional control mechanisms(Akgul, n.d.). With time these demands surpass the recovery capability of the individual hence leading to a continued state of stress activation. This conceptualizes IDD model as persistent dysregulation, with the body persisting to be in the state of low-level physiological arousal of the body in the state of Predictive Urgency.

There are a number of physical symptoms that have been reported through empirical studies that are related to compulsive use of smartphones. These are phantom vibration or ringing or numbing sensation, whereby people receive an illusion of a notification that it has not (Drouin et al., 2012), and musculoskeletal tension or text neck, eye fatigue and headaches. The outcome of sleep disruption is important because the disturbances of sleeping patterns and late-night inspections disrupt the circadian cycles and the quality of sleep(Demirci et al., 2015). In addition, recent clinical evidence indicates how the need to be available all the time is a continual stressor, which increases the level of cortisol (Alwazzeh et al., 2024).

Psychophysical somatization, together with physical symptoms, includes emotional and psychological consequences, such as increased irritability, emotional burnout, and burnout (Tandon et al., 2021). These are the immediate consequences of the persistent vigilance and impaired self-regulation, within the context of the IDD. The necessity to be responsive does not allow proper Psychological Detachment, leaving no chances to recover cognitively and regulate emotions.

One of the most essential observations of the IDD model is the fact that psychophysical somatization does not end the cycle of smartphone addiction. Rather, it is physical pain that tends to strengthen digital interaction by the Mood Management Theory (Zillmann, 1988). People who are stressed or feel uncomfortable pick up their smart phones to get their minds off or to get a temporary reprieve. This is a comfort in the short term however, enhances identity attachment and vigilance patterns and therefore the dysregulation cycle intensifies. This interaction preconditions a Feedback Loop which is discussed in the next section.

Feedback Loop and Reinforcement of Digital Dysregulation.

An important characteristic of the Integrative Digital Dysregulation (IDD) model is that it is a self-reinforcing and cyclical model. The processes that are outlined in the model do not move in the usual cause and effect pattern, but rather come back in circles to enhance their own conditions. This process of feedback is why Smartphone depends endure over time and why the effort to disengage the devices usually fails despite the knowledge of the negative outcomes (Brand et al., 2019).

In the IDD framework, psychophysical somatization is not an endpoint. The attendant psychological pressure and bodily distress that arises out of the continued vigilance of information i.e. fatigue, irritability, sleep disturbance or cognitive overload makes one vulnerable. People in this state tend to find a quick reprieve or distraction. Smartphones, which are already a part and parcel of the user and their daily workflow, become the most accessible and familiar way of managing this unease, which is explained by the Compensatory Internet Use (CIU) theory (Kardefelt-Winther, 2014).

The use of the smartphone as a way to cope with stress can be short-term emotional regulation, including distraction, reassurance, or a feeling of connectedness. This temporary fix however, comes at a price that is very serious in an unintended manner; it strengthens identity extension by adding another layer of identity with comfort, control and psychological security (Belk, 2013). This process is occasioned by Negative Reinforcement (Koob, 2013) as the elimination of a bad experience (stress) during phone use promotes the habit, making people more dependent and the need to access it always.

This reinforcer increases FoMO-induced vigilance, as such, the person is more motivated to be on-demand and responsive to prevent the recurrence of negative affect(Tandon et al., 2021).Prone to nomophobia-related anxiety, the circumstance where the access is at stake is even more psychologically salient. All these processes taken together restart and maintain the loop of vigilance and again results in psychophysical strain and Maladaptive Coping (Billieux et al., 2015).

The IDD model, through this process, shows how smartphone addiction is perpetuated not through unremitting pleasure or utility, but through a dysregulation-compensation feedback loop. Digital engagement leads to stress that stimulates more interaction to cope with it, becoming increasingly dependent, and returning to the loop. The given feedback loop explains why the reduction-based strategies, like restricting the time spent on the screen, tend to be ineffective without the intervention that allows addressing the underlying vulnerability of the emotions (Elhai et al., 2021).

Overall, the feedback loop completes the IDD cycle, as the psychophysical results are connected to identity-based attachment and FoMO-induced vigilance. This reinforcement loop is the main key to the concept of smartphone addiction being a long-term phenomenon of digital dysregulation and not a temporary behavioral practice.

Moderating Factors: Breaking the IDD Cycle.

Integrative Digital Dysregulation (IDD) model does not attempt to imply that smartphone addiction is unavoidable or permanent. It instead determines definite psychological points where the dysregulation cycle might be undermined. These arguments are conceptualized as moderating factors, which serve as protective buffers in order to weaken the cycle instead of abolishing the use of smartphones. In the IDD system, resilience and mindfulness control the process of digital dysregulation (Arpaci, 2021).

The association between identity extension and FoMO-induced vigilance is mediated by resilience. The higher the psychological robustness of people, the less reliant their self-image and emotional state are on the continual connection to the Internet (Kwon et al., 2013). Consequently, disconnection or lower availability will not be explained as a danger to identity or social status as much. This undermines FoMO activation and makes it less likely that identity extension will develop into chronic monitoring.

Mindfulness is an intermediary between information vigilance and psychophysical somatization. Mindfulness helps one to be sensitive to habitual checking urges and not act on them automatically. Mindfulness reduces the automatic and prolonged vigilance that is identified to cause cognitive overload and physiological stress by paying more attention to the patterns of attention (Arpaci, 2021). In the IDD model, mindfulness serves as a Decoupling Mechanism (Vanden Abeele, 2021); it does not stop smartphone use but makes the level of digital vigilance to embodied strain and chronic autonomic arousal smaller.

Notably, it is the psychological processes that maintain dysregulation that these moderating factors affect rather than the technology itself. Undermining these connections, the two moderators' lower chances of the psychophysical discomfort being returned to the revived identity attachment and additional vigilance (Tandon et al., 2021).

Overall, resilience and mindfulness can act as control valves in the IDD cycle and prevent its rampage and strengthening instead of preventing digital interaction. Their role in the model is to underline that the innovative approaches to smartphone addiction should shift towards Self-Regulatory Restoration (Alwazzeh et al., 2024) to touch upon the psychological mechanisms underlying the problem and not merely decrease the frequency of its application or screen time.

IMPLICATIONS OF THE IDD FRAMEWORK IN CONTEMPORARY DIGITAL CONTEXTS

Constant Availability as a Psychological Demand within the IDD Model

According to the Integrative Digital Dysregulation (IDD) model, the ubiquitous presence is a contextual stimulus maintaining FoMO-vigilance. The model does not presuppose that FoMO arises only due to personal insecurity, but rather it assumes that the modern online standards keep causing this psychological force to take effect by turning availability into a unspoken need of daily operations The anticipation of fast responses, sustained visibility and immediate responsiveness are external pressure which are internalised over time at the psychological level. These availability norms are viewed through the lenses of the IDD framework to have a direct interaction with identity extension which is the originating condition of the cycle. Under the conditions when smartphones are used as primary interfaces to social interactions, coordinate of work and access to information, responsiveness is correlated with self-evaluation. This correspondence between digital self presence and self concept reduces the activation bar of FoMO. This framework explains the way environmental needs are converted into psychological forces by locating constant availability in the IDD cycle. Availability norms support FoMO, FoMO supports vigilance and vigilance supports the larger dysregulation process described in the model. According to this, the process of the digital age does not simply coincide with smartphone addiction or does not simply precondition the recruitment of its psychological motivators, but actively conditions the mobilization of its psychological drivers, Structural Availability with the psychological processes of the IDD cycle.

Platform design as a Vigilance Amplifier of FoMO in the IDD Model.

The digital platforms are not found only as neutral communication tools in the Integrative Digital Dysregulation (IDD) model but serve as structural reinforcers of

FoMO-inspired vigilance. It explains how the platform design can cause an escalation and maintenance of the pressure by highlighting and focusing attention on the possibilities of social or informational relevance. In the view of IDD, the means of push notifications, read receipts, algorithmic prioritization, and infinite scrolling do not produce new psychological needs, but instead serve to harness and amplify existing drivers. When identity extension and FoMO are in place, these elements of design are used to sustain heighten states of attentional preparedness, which are cues of urgency, novelty, or social significance. Every notification, badge, or signal notification will strengthen the idea that something important can be urgently needed. Importantly, the IDD model places this process on the stage of vigilance of the cycle, during which the behavior becomes more automatic. The design of platforms alleviates the stress on the conscious decision-making process by making cues to engagement externalised, and responding to prompts generated by the system. Such change disempowering the executive control and internalizing vigilance to become a part of the everyday routine enables FoMO to become a round-the-clock phenomenon and cannot be aroused intentionally, which is a condition of the I-PACE model (Brand et al., 2019) that the inhibitory control is broken. In this context, platform design never operates outside the principle of psychological drivers, but subjugates them in recurring cycles of behavior. With time, such interaction stabilizes vigilance as a default state of cognition, and makes more likely the occurrence of disruptions in access subsequently becoming psychologically salient, and hence preconditions the occurrence of nomophobia in critical situations. The new study on the G-DEEG framework (Akgul, n.d.) proves that this trend in the growth of the technological amplification is not a coincidence; it is a radical change in which the Predictive Urgency of the device starts dictating the neurochemical state of the user. It identifies platform design as a part of the vigilance phase of the IDD cycle by placing it explicitly, which shows how technological environments actively contribute to digital dysregulation. The digital era, though, increases smartphone addiction not just due to the enhanced access, but by means of incorporating the psychological motivation in the very design of the daily digital interaction.

Situation Dependence and Nomophobia Development of the IDD Model.

In the Integrative Digital Dysregulation (IDD) model, nomophobia is not a permanent or categorical condition, but a it's an continegent anxiety reaction, which occurs when the availability of smartphones is endangered in contexts of personal relevance. Continuing on the FoMO-stimulated vigilance described above, this subsection describes how the current digital space can establish the conditions according to which the disturbances in access obtain a new psychological meaning (Yildirim and Correia, 2015).

Within the IDD framework, smartphone has become an operational gateway to routine tasks like navigation, authentication, work coordination and information access in the digital age. Consequently, smartphone has ceased to be a simple medium of communication but is now a Infrastructural Tool of involvement in everyday life. The loss of access to this tool can have more than inconvenience effects, especially in situations where connectivity is viewed as a requirement when using Transactive Memory (Wegner and Ward, 2013) when it is interrupted by low battery, network outage, or physical distance.

In this case, the anxiety of lack of communication or control of functioning can be provoked by moments of disconnection in socially-, professionally-, emotionally-significant situations. The IDD model thus frames the occurrence of nomophobia as context-specific accumulation of psychological dependence, and not the generalized fear response (Akgul, n.d.)

Notably, this framing does not attempt to pathologize daily digital distress.The IDD model draws the distinction between routine inconvenience and nomophobia by putting focus on perceived consequence. It is influenced by the previous attachment to the identity and vigilance patterns, which predisposes nomophobia in people whose self-control is already undermined by the previous phases of the cycle (Brand et al., 2019).

This subsection elucidates the role of nomophobia as an anxiety-related reinforcer, and not a driving force, since it is explicitly placed in the later stage of the IDD cycle. The attachment to regaining connectivity is increased by situational anxiety linked to access loss, which reinforces vigilance and recycles the identity-based attachment (Elhai et al., 2021). This way, nomophobia plays into continuing digital dysregulation due to its Fear-Driven Anchor (Alwazzeh et al., 2024) that helps avoid disengagement in cases where the user is consciously aware of the adverse effects.

RE-REGULATING DIGITAL DYSREGULATION: SOLUTIONS IN AN IDP FRAMEWORK.

When applied as digital dysregulation, smartphone addiction needs to be addressed using solutions that target the psychological processes in place to perpetuate dependence instead of behavioral manifestations. Integrative Digital Dysregulation (IDD) model suggests that the persistence of problematic smartphone use occurs due to the breakdown of self-regulatory mechanisms at particular levels of transition in the cycle (Brand et al., 2019). What is needed, then, is a strategic undermining of these transitions, but not the elimination of digital engagement as such.

This section states the main solution architecture that is entrenched in the IDD framework. These solutions work as regulatory breakers, which is aimed to restore psychological control by breaking the development of dysregulation in the most important points of the cycle.

The Resilience Breaker: Re-Anchoring Identity Boundaries by using Psychological Re-Anchoring.

The identity extension is the basis of the digital dysregulation where smart phones get psychologically integrated into the self-concept (Belk, 2013). In low-resilience situations, such kind of identity integration makes people very vulnerable to feelings of disconnection, invisibility and unresponsiveness in society. The IDD framework suggests the existence of the main regulatory breaker, resilience, that is located between identity extension and information vigilance.

Resilience works as a cognitive buffer that maintains a consistent vision of self without ongoing digital affirmation. The more resilient people can be more emotionally stable and self-esteemed even when they are temporarily disconnected (Kwon et al., 2013). Consequently, attachment to the smartphone does not necessarily result in monitoring fear and obsessive checking. Extending identity in itself is thus not enough to trigger dysregulation in the presence of resilience.

This resilience is supported by psychological re-anchoring which consolidates non-digital sources of identity, including personal values, competencies, offline roles, and embodied experiences. As the self is anchored to more than one identity, digital presence is not the main stabilizer of identity, but one of its dimensions (Alwazzeh et al., 2024). This lowers the chances that the temporary unavailability will be viewed as a source of threat to the continuation of self or social irrelevance.

More importantly, the resilience breaker does not eradicate the identity extension rather it controls its impact. Smartphones can continue to be useful connection and self-expression devices, yet their ability to disrupt the self in instances of disconnection grows significantly less. Through this, the first IDD cycle escalation point is undermined, and identity attachment is not allowed to transform into chronic vigilance.

The Mindfulness breaker: Severing Vigilance and Automatic engagement.

Information vigilance is a behavioural expression of digital dysregulation, which is increased monitoring, anticipatory attention, and reactive checking. In the IDD conceptualization, mindfulness acts as a regulatory breaker in the interval between vigilance and psychophysical somatization (Arpaci, 2021). It is not its purpose to render vigilance completely inactive, but simply to separate awareness and automatic response.

Mindfulness helps one to become aware of the temptations to look at their smartphones without following through with them. This pause creates a separation of psychological distance between the stimulus and response and enables attentional impulses to be viewed and not acted (Vanden Abeele, 2021). Consequently, vigilance ceases to be automatic and is placed under the conscious regulation.

This dissociation is essential since it allows the avoidance of vigilance-related anxiety to build up into physiological stress. Lack of mindfulness is where repetitive checking urges will increase cognitive load, sustain a high level of arousal, and ultimately result in somatic symptoms like tension, fatigue, or sleep disturbance. Mindfulness interferes with this process by reinstating agency on the attentional involvement.

Notably, the mindfulness breaker does not involve leaving digital worlds. Rather, it changes the quality of engagement since it becomes reflective instead of reactive in use. Vigilance no longer occupies the cognition resources and determines behavior. In a process of repeated decoupling, the individual restores the attentional autonomy and the vigilance is less likely to result in embodied dysregulation.

Diluting the Reinforcement Loop by Adaptive Emotional Regulation.

The hallmark of digital dysregulation is that the compensatory use of smartphones is driven by psychological or physical discomfort, which is supported by a feedback loop. This type of involvement can be determined as a temporary reprieve but can strengthen the reliance on the device as a general coping strategy The IDD framework determines adaptive emotional regulation as the way to undermine the loop.

Adaptive regulation entails trying to use other ways of coping with stress, boredom, uncertainty and emotional discomfort without resorting to digital distraction. In case people have good non-digital coping strategies, discomfort does not necessarily create smartphone interaction (Koob, 2013). This minimizes the negative reinforcement which reinforces dependence with time.

When one learns to tolerate and do without the immediate discomfort, he or she eventually regains self-confidence in his or her internal controlling capabilities. This change undermines the conditioned relationship between distress and engagement with the digital world, and emotional control can take place without the smartphone. This minimizes compulsive dependency over time, and disrupts the self-supportive processes of dysregulation.

In the IDD model, recovery should involve disruption of the loop of reinforcement since the somatic discomfort will not re-trigger the identity attachment and vigilance, which would lead to re-activation of identity. When compensation use decreases, the momentum of the cycle ceases and the regulatory restoration can be maintained instead of relapse (Elhai et al., 2021).

Maintaining Recovery with Regulatory Resilience and Digital Agency.

Although resilience and mindfulness can be described as targeted breakers in the IDD cycle, long-term control involves developing more general psychological capabilities that can aid in longer-lasting control. Regulatory strength and digital agency act as balancing influences, which do not allow returning to dysregulation after the cycle has been disrupted.

Regulatory resilience increases the tolerance to uncertainty, slowness to response and disconnection. It makes people less sensitive to the perceived pressures of availability and allows people to stay emotionally stable in high-load digital space. Digital agency fills this gap by creating a mindful interaction enabling one to create digital actions that support personal ambitions and goals instead of impulsive actions.

A combination of these capabilities will make digital interaction not a reactionary need but a voluntary one. Smartphones are still an integral part of life, except that they are no longer at the center of the attentional or emotional control mechanism. This change is conducive to sustainable digital health as it ensures psychological flexibility against continuing connectivity pressures.

The IDD model puts recovery as a self-regulatory practice by focusing on restoration instead of restriction. Sustainable engagement is not created out of avoidance of technology, but through the enhancement of the psychological systems that are controlling the application of technology.

CONCLUSION AND FUTURE RESEARCH DIRECTION

This chapter analyzed smartphone addiction as a multidimensional phenomenon that is influenced by psychological vulnerability, behavioral vigilance, and some embodied effects. In a shift out of reductionist discourse, which relied on screen time or technological affordances, the discussion incorporated modern literature on smartphone addiction, Fear of Missing out (FoMO), and nomophobia to show that problematic smartphone use would be best conceptualized as a type of digital dysregulation rather than the specific behavioral excessive use.

The review found out that smartphone addiction is not just a matter of the availability or the frequency of use of the phone, but is an issue of more psychologically deeper processes, such as anxiety regulation, reward-based reinforcement, identity extension, and attentional fragmentation. FoMO was seen as a highly motivating element that perpetuates the perpetual state of surveillance and responsiveness, whereas nomophobia was established as an anxiety-related reaction to endangered connectivity and the feeling of loss of control. These constructs may be conceptually different but they were evidenced to transact in a mutually reinforcing manner, forming a vicious cycle of compulsive engagement.

To put these together, the chapter has proposed the Integrative Digital Dysregulation (IDD) framework that conceptualizes smartphone addiction as a closed feedback loop that includes three mutually dependent steps: Identity Extension (mind), Information Vigilance (behavior) and Psychophysical Somatization (body). According to this model FoMO and nomophobia represent bridging mechanisms of the psyche that transform identity-associated vulnerability into chronic vigilance and, finally, into mental, emotional, and physical tension. Notably, the IDD framework justifies the reason why the awareness of harm is not enough to interrupt the smartphone dependence, as the distress, in turn, is a stimulus of further digital interaction under the pretext of compensatory coping.

The chapter also showed that the digital dysregulation does not affect people and situations in the same way. The stages of development, social roles, and situational requirements define the ways in which FoMO and nomophobia are manifested in adolescents and adults and influences the ways in which smartphone addiction is acquired and maintained. Locating such variations in the IDD cycle, the framework embraces individual differences as well as structural strains, like the constant availability norms and features of platform design.

Last of all, the chapter presented regulation-based solutions based on the IDD framework with an emphasis on resilience, mindfulness, and adaptive emotional regulation as processes of disrupting dysregulation without promoting the technological abstinence policy. Instead of focusing on the behavioral manifestations of the cycle, these interventions aim at addressing the psychological transformations in the latter, which is a more sustainable approach to digital well-being.

To sum up, the chapter adds a theoretically unified understanding of smartphone addiction since it reformulates it into a systemic dynamic of digital dysregulation. The IDD framework offers a common set of glasses through which the existing empirical results can be structured and explained and it also provides the basis of future research and intervention development. Knowledge of smartphone addiction via this integrative model will allow the transition of approaches toward reactive control to psychologically sensitive regulation that is necessary in the age of continuous digital interconnectedness.

Future Research Directions

The next wave of research would be concerned with the empirical testing of the Integrative Digital Dysregulation (IDD) model by a variety of populations and situations to determine the strength of the suggested mechanisms. The longitudinal research designs would especially be helpful in investigating the temporal development of identity extension, information vigilance and psychophysical somatization, and thus enable the researcher to establish cyclic nature of the model other than the cross-sectional relationships. The experimental research manipulating the degree of digital availability, suspected disconnection, or exposure to notification might also contribute to proving the causal mechanisms in the IDD cycle. Besides this, the moderating effect of resilience, mindfulness, and self-regulatory capacity can also be empirically analyzed in future studies by hypothesizing that the relationship between identity extension and vigilance, or that between vigilance and psychophysical outcomes, are weakened by the factors. It would also be helpful to do comparative studies on age groups, occupational background, and cultural contexts so that the occurrence of digital dysregulation under various social needs and technological standards could be determined. Lastly, the IDD framework offers a groundwork to intervention-based research. Further research might consider psychologically informed interventions based on the model, i.e., identity-oriented strategy, mindfulness-based strategy, or self-regulation-enhancing strategy, and contrast their effectiveness with the traditional usage-reduction approaches. These studies would assist in establishing the answer to whether there is a more sustainable enhancement of digital well-being with the focus on underlying psychological mechanisms or screen time restriction itself.

REFERENCES

Aarestad, S. H., Flaa, T. A., Griffiths, M. D., & Pallesen, S. (2023). Smartphone Addiction and Subjective Withdrawal Effects: A Three-Day Experimental Study. *SAGE Open*, *13*(4), 21582440231219538. DOI: 10.1177/21582440231219538

Abuhamdah, S. M. A., & Naser, A. Y. (2023). Smart phone addiction and its mental health risks among university students in Jordan: A cross-sectional study. *BMC Psychiatry*, *23*(1), 812. DOI: 10.1186/s12888-023-05322-6

Agüero-Espinoza, F. A., Neyra-Agama, M., Tasilla-Guayamis, L., Valencia-Acosta, L., Vega-Agurto, G. M., & Morales, J. (2025). Nomophobia and Self-esteem: The Influence of Digital Media on the Leisure Activities of Peruvian Adolescents. *The Open Public Health Journal*, *18*(1), e18749445360319. DOI: 10.2174/011874944 5360319241226120427

Akgul, I. (n.d.). *Smartphone Addiction and the G-DEEG Model: An Interdisciplinary Framework for Psychiatric Rehabilitation. 8*(7).

Alhassan, A. A., Alqadhib, E. M., Taha, N. W., Alahmari, R. A., Salam, M., & Almutairi, A. F. (2018). The relationship between addiction to smartphone usage and depression among adults: A cross sectional study. *BMC Psychiatry*, *18*(1), 148. DOI: 10.1186/s12888-018-1745-4

Alutaybi, A., McAlaney, J., Stefanidis, A., Phalp, K., & Ali, R. (2018, July). *Designing Social Networks to Combat Fear of Missing Out. Proceedings of the 32nd International BCS Human Computer Interaction Conference*. DOI: 10.14236/ewic/ HCI2018.80

Alwazzeh, M., Harfouch, M., Hasan, M. A., Alqatari, S., AlSaid, A. H., & Alwazzeh, M. J. (2024). Clinical Manifestations' Spectrum of Smartphone Addiction: Moving from an Addiction toward a Clinical Syndrome. *Clinical Practice and Epidemiology in Mental Health*, *20*(1), e17450179295575. DOI: 10.2174/01174501792955752 40520064919

Arpaci, I. (2021). Relationships Between Early Maladaptive Schemas and Smartphone Addiction: The Moderating Role of Mindfulness. *International Journal of Mental Health and Addiction*, *19*(3), 778–792. DOI: 10.1007/s11469-019-00186-y

Arrivillaga, C., Hallauer, C. J., Montag, C., & Elhai, J. D. Emotion dysregulation factors associated with problematic smartphone use severity: The mediating role of fear of missing out, Addictive Behaviours, Volume 143,2023,107708, ISSN 0306-4603, https://doi.org/DOI: 10.1016/j.addbeh.2023.107708

Ayaburi, E. W., Wairimu, J., & Andoh-Baidoo, F. K. (2019). Antecedents and Outcome of Deficient Self-Regulation in Unknown Wireless Networks Use Context: An Exploratory Study. *Information Systems Frontiers*, *21*(6), 1213–1229. DOI: 10.1007/s10796-019-09942-w

Balcioğlu, Y. S., & Artar Biyiklar, M. (2025). Analyzing nomophobia among TikTok users: A data mining and text analysis approach. *Current Psychology (New Brunswick, N.J.)*, *44*(23), 18220–18242. DOI: 10.1007/s12144-025-08416-4

Belk, R. W. (2013). Extended Self in a Digital World: Table 1. *The Journal of Consumer Research*, *40*(3), 477–500. DOI: 10.1086/671052

Berger, S., Wyss, A. M., & Knoch, D. (2018). Low self-control capacity is associated with immediate responses to smartphone signals. *Computers in Human Behavior*, *86*, 45–51. DOI: 10.1016/j.chb.2018.04.031

Billieux, J., Maurage, P., Lopez-Fernandez, O., Kuss, D. J., & Griffiths, M. D. (2015). Can Disordered Mobile Phone Use Be Considered a Behavioral Addiction? An Update on Current Evidence and a Comprehensive Model for Future Research. *Current Addiction Reports*, *2*(2), 156–162. DOI: 10.1007/s40429-015-0054-y

Brailovskaia, J., Stirnberg, J., Rozgonjuk, D., Margraf, J., & Elhai, J. D. (2021). From low sense of control to problematic smartphone use severity during Covid-19 outbreak: The mediating role of fear of missing out and the moderating role of repetitive negative thinking. *PLoS One*, *16*(12), e0261023. DOI: 10.1371/journal.pone.0261023

Brand, M., Wegmann, E., Stark, R., Müller, A., Wölfling, K., Robbins, T. W., & Potenza, M. N. (2019). The Interaction of Person-Affect-Cognition-Execution (I-PACE) model for addictive behaviors: Update, generalization to addictive behaviors beyond internet-use disorders, and specification of the process character of addictive behaviors. *Neuroscience and Biobehavioral Reviews*, *104*, 1–10. DOI: 10.1016/j.neubiorev.2019.06.032

Busch, P. A., & McCarthy, S. (2021). Antecedents and consequences of problematic smartphone use: A systematic literature review of an emerging research area. *Computers in Human Behavior*, *114*, 106414. DOI: 10.1016/j.chb.2020.106414

Carter, T. J., & Gilovich, T. (2012). I am what I do, not what I have: The differential centrality of experiential and material purchases to the self. *Journal of Personality and Social Psychology*, *102*(6), 1304–1317. DOI: 10.1037/a0027407

Casale, S., Fioravanti, G., Gioia, F., Redditi, E., & Spada, M. (2023). Fear of missing out and fear of not being up to date: Investigating different pathways towards social and process problematic smartphone use. *Current Psychology (New Brunswick, N.J.)*, *42*(26), 22847–22856. DOI: 10.1007/s12144-022-03368-5

Chen, C., Zhang, K. Z. K., Gong, X., & Lee, M. (2019). Dual mechanisms of reinforcement reward and habit in driving smartphone addiction: The role of smartphone features. *Internet Research*, *29*(6), 1551–1570. DOI: 10.1108/INTR-11-2018-0489

Cheng, Q., Zhou, Y., Zhu, H., Wang, Q., & Peng, W. (2024). Relationships between daily emotional experiences and smartphone addiction among college students: Moderated mediating role of gender and mental health problems. *Frontiers in Psychology*, *15*, 1490338. DOI: 10.3389/fpsyg.2024.1490338

Cho, J., & Kim, H. (2025). The role of impulsivity and emotional dysregulation in smartphone overdependence explored through network analysis. *Scientific Reports*, *15*(1), 1852. DOI: 10.1038/s41598-025-85680-1

Conradie, L., le Roux, D. B., & Parry, D. A. (2023). Cross-domain online vigilance, boundary management and stress among knowledge workers. *South African Journal of Business Management*, *54*(1), a2937. Advance online publication. DOI: 10.4102/sajbm.v54i1.3896

De-Sola Gutiérrez, J., Rodríguez De Fonseca, F., & Rubio, G. (2016). Cell-Phone Addiction: A Review. *Frontiers in Psychiatry*, *7*. Advance online publication. DOI: 10.3389/fpsyt.2016.00175

Demirci, K., Akgönül, M., & Akpinar, A. (2015). Relationship of smartphone use severity with sleep quality, depression, and anxiety in university students. *Journal of Behavioral Addictions*, *4*(2), 85–92. DOI: 10.1556/2006.4.2015.010

Dora, J., Van Hooff, M., Geurts, S., Kompier, M., & Bijleveld, E. (2021). Labor/leisure decisions in their natural context: The case of the smartphone. *Psychonomic Bulletin & Review*, *28*(2), 676–685. DOI: 10.3758/s13423-020-01844-2

Drouin, M., Kaiser, D. H., & Miller, D. A. (2012). Phantom vibrations among undergraduates: Prevalence and associated psychological characteristics. *Computers in Human Behavior*, *28*(4), 1490–1496. DOI: 10.1016/j.chb.2012.03.013

Duke, É., & Montag, C. (2017). Smartphone addiction, daily interruptions and self-reported productivity. *Addictive Behaviors Reports*, *6*, 90–95. DOI: 10.1016/j.abrep.2017.07.002

Einstein, D. A., Dabb, C., & Fraser, M. (2023). FoMO, but not self-compassion, moderates the link between social media use and anxiety in adolescence. *Australian Journal of Psychology*, *75*(1), 2217961. DOI: 10.1080/00049530.2023.2217961

Elhai, J. D., Levine, J. C., Dvorak, R. D., & Hall, B. J. (2016). Fear of missing out, need for touch, anxiety and depression are related to problematic smartphone use. *Computers in Human Behavior*, *63*, 509–516. DOI: 10.1016/j.chb.2016.05.079

Elhai, J. D., Yang, H., & Montag, C. (2021). Fear of missing out (FOMO): Overview, theoretical underpinnings, and literature review on relations with severity of negative affectivity and problematic technology use. *The British Journal of Psychiatry*, *43*(2), 203–209. DOI: 10.1590/1516-4446-2020-0870

Examining the Correlation between Excessive Recreational Smartphone Use and Academic Performance Outcomes. (2019). *Journal of Higher Education Theory and Practice, 19*(5). DOI: 10.33423/jhetp.v19i5.2279

Fabio, R. A., Stracuzzi, A., & Lo Faro, R. (2022). Problematic Smartphone Use Leads to Behavioral and Cognitive Self-Control Deficits. *International Journal of Environmental Research and Public Health, 19*(12), 7445. DOI: 10.3390/ijerph19127445

Freytag, A., Knop-Huelss, K., Meier, A., Reinecke, L., Hefner, D., Klimmt, C., & Vorderer, P. (2021). Permanently Online—Always Stressed Out? The Effects of Permanent Connectedness on Stress Experiences. *Human Communication Research*, *47*(2), 132–165. DOI: 10.1093/hcr/hqaa014

Gao, B., Shen, Q., Luo, G., & Xu, Y. (2023). Why mobile social media-related fear of missing out promotes depressive symptoms? The roles of phubbing and social exclusion. *BMC Psychology*, *11*(1), 189. DOI: 10.1186/s40359-023-01231-1

Gonçalves, L. L., Nardi, A. E., & King, A. L. S. (2023). Digital Dependence in Organizations: Impacts on the Physical and Mental Health of Employees. *Clinical Practice and Epidemiology in Mental Health*, *19*(1), e174501792212300. DOI: 10.2174/17450179-v19-e230109-2022-17

Gui, D.-Y., Dai, Y., Zheng, Z., & Liu, S. (2023). Losing control without your smartphone: Anxiety affects the dynamic choice process of impulsive decision-making and purchase. *Frontiers in Neuroscience*, *17*, 998017. DOI: 10.3389/fnins.2023.998017

Guzel, Halime. (2020). The ınvestigation of the relationship between smartphone addiction, and problem-solving skills and ways of coping with stress. Dusunen Adam:The Journal of Psychiatry and Neurological Sciences. .DOI: 10.14744/DAJPNS.2020.00088

Han, Y., Qiu, J., Shi, C., Huang, S., Huang, H., Wang, X., Zhu, S., Lu, D., Lu, P., & Zeng, F. (2025). Factors Associated With Digital Addiction: Umbrella Review. *JMIR Mental Health*, *12*, e66950–e66950. DOI: 10.2196/66950

Hessari, H., Daneshmandi, F., Busch, P., & Smith, S. (2024). Workplace nomophobia: A systematic literature review. *Current Psychology (New Brunswick, N.J.)*, *43*(31), 25934–25954. DOI: 10.1007/s12144-024-06222-y

Hussien, R. M. (2022). The association between nomophobia and loneliness among the general population in the Kingdom of Saudi Arabia. *Middle East Current Psychiatry, Ain Shams University*, *29*(1), 68. DOI: 10.1186/s43045-022-00235-8

Jaworska, D. (2025). Many faces of FoMO: A qualitative in-depth investigation of context-specific experiences, emotions, and coping strategies. *PLoS One*, *20*(9), e0330978. DOI: 10.1371/journal.pone.0330978

Jimenez, N., San Martin, S., & Rodríguez-Torrico, P. (2024). Effect of smartphone addiction on compulsive app downloading tendency: Protective factors for generation Z consumers. *Young Consumers*, *25*(6), 665–686. DOI: 10.1108/YC-09-2023-1870

Jo, H., & Baek, E.-M. (2023). Exploring the dynamics of mobile app addiction: The interplay of communication, affective factors, flow, perceived enjoyment, and habit. *BMC Psychology*, *11*(1), 404. DOI: 10.1186/s40359-023-01440-8

Kardefelt-Winther, D. (2014). A conceptual and methodological critique of internet addiction research: Towards a model of compensatory internet use. *Computers in Human Behavior*, *31*, 351–354. DOI: 10.1016/j.chb.2013.10.059

Koob, G. F. (2013). Negative reinforcement in drug addiction: The darkness within. *Current Opinion in Neurobiology*, *23*(4), 559–563. DOI: 10.1016/j.conb.2013.03.011

Kwon, M., Kim, D.-J., Cho, H., & Yang, S. (2013). The Smartphone Addiction Scale: Development and Validation of a Short Version for Adolescents. *PLoS One*, *8*(12), e83558. DOI: 10.1371/journal.pone.0083558

Leclercq-Vandelannoitte, A. (2019). Is Employee Technological "Ill-Being" Missing from Corporate Responsibility? The Foucauldian Ethics of Ubiquitous IT Uses in Organizations. *Journal of Business Ethics*, *160*(2), 339–361. DOI: 10.1007/s10551-019-04202-y

León-Mejía, A. C., Gutiérrez-Ortega, M., Serrano-Pintado, I., & González-Cabrera, J. (2021). A systematic review on nomophobia prevalence: Surfacing results and standard guidelines for future research. *PLoS One*, *16*(5), e0250509. DOI: 10.1371/journal.pone.0250509

Lestari, B., & Suratmini, D. (2024). The Relationship FoMO (Fear of Missing Out) and Nomophobia with Phubbing Behavior among Adolescent Instagram Users. [ICON Journal]. *Indonesian Contemporary Nursing Journal*, *8*(2), 82–89. DOI: 10.20956/icon.v8i2.30750

Lin, Y.-H., Chiang, C.-L., Lin, P.-H., Chang, L.-R., Ko, C.-H., Lee, Y.-H., & Lin, S.-H. (2016). Proposed Diagnostic Criteria for Smartphone Addiction. *PLoS One*, *11*(11), e0163010. DOI: 10.1371/journal.pone.0163010

Markowitz, D. M., Hancock, J. T., Bailenson, J. N., & Reeves, B. (2019). Psychological and physiological effects of applying self-control to the mobile phone. *PLoS One*, *14*(11), e0224464. DOI: 10.1371/journal.pone.0224464

Marsh, E., Perez Vallejos, E., & Spence, A. (2024). Overloaded by Information or Worried About Missing Out on It: A Quantitative Study of Stress, Burnout, and Mental Health Implications in the Digital Workplace. *SAGE Open*, *14*(3), 21582440241268830. DOI: 10.1177/21582440241268830

Matar Boumosleh, J., & Jaalouk, D. (2017). Depression, anxiety, and smartphone addiction in university students- A cross sectional study. *PLoS One*, *12*(8), e0182239. DOI: 10.1371/journal.pone.0182239

Matias, J., Quinton, J.-C., Colomb, M., Normand, A., Izaute, M., & Silvert, L. (2021). Fear of Missing Out Predicts Distraction by Social Reward Signals Displayed on a Smartphone in Difficult Driving Situations. *Frontiers in Psychology*, *12*, 688157. DOI: 10.3389/fpsyg.2021.688157

Medrano-Sánchez, E. J., Cuenca Silva, L. S., & Medrano-Sánchez, G. M. (2024). Towards Understanding Nomophobia: A Systematic Review of Its Prevalence, Causes, and Effects in Educational Settings. *Academic Journal of Interdisciplinary Studies*, *13*(6), 306. DOI: 10.36941/ajis-2024-0196

Mostyn Sullivan, B., George, A. M., & Rickwood, D. (2025a). An exploration of motives that influence problematic smartphone use in young adults. *Behaviour & Information Technology*, *44*(9), 1886–1900. DOI: 10.1080/0144929X.2024.2380102

Mostyn Sullivan, B., George, A. M., & Rickwood, D. (2025b). An exploration of motives that influence problematic smartphone use in young adults. *Behaviour & Information Technology*, *44*(9), 1886–1900. DOI: 10.1080/0144929X.2024.2380102

Navas-Echazarreta, N., Juárez-Vela, R., Subirón-Valera, A. B., Rodríguez-Roca, B., Antón-Solanas, I., Fernández-Rodrigo, M. T., De Viñaspre-Hernandez, R. R., Sabater, A. M., Echániz-Serrano, E., Saus-Ortega, C., Santolalla-Arnedo, I., & Satústegui-Dordá, P. J. (2023). Nomophobia in university students during COVID-19 outbreak: A cross-sectional study. *Frontiers in Public Health, 11*, 1242092. DOI: 10.3389/fpubh.2023.1242092

Ngo, T. T. A., Nguyen, N. T. A., La, U. N., Truong, D. N., & Nguyen, H. Q. B. (2024). Impacts of Social Media Experiences on Academically Related Peer Influence and Fear of Missing Out of Secondary and High School Students. [iJEP]. *International Journal of Engineering Pedagogy, 14*(2), 112–129. DOI: 10.3991/ijep.v14i2.43567

Oraison, H., & Wilson, B. (2024). The Relationship Between Nomophobia, Addiction, and Distraction. *Journal of Technology in Behavioral Science, 9*(4), 745–751. DOI: 10.1007/s41347-024-00392-z

Oulasvirta, A., Rattenbury, T., Ma, L., & Raita, E. (2012). Habits make smartphone use more pervasive. *Personal and Ubiquitous Computing, 16*(1), 105–114. DOI: 10.1007/s00779-011-0412-2

Patani, N. S. (n.d.). *Smartphone Use, Fear of Missing Out (FOMO) and Social Connectedness among College Students.*

Pérez-Torres, V. (2024). Problematic use of social media in adolescents or excessive social gratification? The mediating role of nomophobia. *Cyberpsychology (Brno), 18*(4). Advance online publication. DOI: 10.5817/CP2024-4-2

Przybylski, A. K., Murayama, K., DeHaan, C. R., & Gladwell, V. (2013). Motivational, emotional, and behavioral correlates of fear of missing out. *Computers in Human Behavior, 29*(4), 1841–1848. DOI: 10.1016/j.chb.2013.02.014

Ramos-Soler, I., López-Sánchez, C., & Quiles-Soler, C. (2021). Nomophobia in teenagers: Digital lifestyle, social networking and smartphone abuse. *Communicatio Socialis, 34*(4), 17–32. DOI: 10.15581/003.34.4.17-32

Rifkin, J. R., Chan, C., & Kahn, B. E. (n.d.). *Anxiety About the Social Consequences of Missed Group Experiences Intensifies Fear of Missing Out.* FOMO. DOI: 10.1037/pspa0000418

Rozgonjuk, D., Sindermann, C., Elhai, J. D., & Montag, C. (2020). Fear of Missing Out (FoMO) and social media's impact on daily-life and productivity at work: Do WhatsApp, Facebook, Instagram, and Snapchat Use Disorders mediate that association? *Addictive Behaviors, 110*, 106487. DOI: 10.1016/j.addbeh.2020.106487

Safaria, T., Saputra, N.E. & Arini, D.P. (2024). The Impact of Nomophobia: Exploring the Interplay Between Loneliness, Smartphone Usage, Self-control, Emotion Regulation, and Spiritual Meaningfulness in an Indonesian Context. *J. technol. behav. sci.* 10, 382–401 (2025). https://doi.org/DOI: 10.1007/s41347-024-00438-2

Saidon, J., Musa, R., Hashim, H., Atory, N. A. A., Md Sohid, F., Mohd Yusof, N., & Syed Omar, S. A. (2023). Device Features and/or Personality Traits? Disentangling the Determinants of Smartphone Nomophobia and Pathology among Urban Millennials. *Information Management and Business Review, 15*(4(SI)I), 447–455. DOI: 10.22610/imbr.v15i4(SI)I.3619

Sapmaz, F. (2023). The direct and indirect effects of workplace loneliness on FoMO: Nomophobia and general belongingness. *Journal of Educational Technology and Online Learning*, *6*(4), 947–965. DOI: 10.31681/jetol.1369184

Sende, C. C., Ebner, K., & Soucek, R. (2024). *Development and Test of a Conceptual Model on the Emergence of Digital Stress: A Training Intervention Study. SSRN.* DOI: 10.2139/ssrn.4966638

Sequeira, S. L., Rodman, A. M., Nesi, J., & Silk, J. S. (2025). Social threat and adolescent mental health. *Nature Reviews Psychology*, *4*(10), 639–653. DOI: 10.1038/s44159-025-00484-4

Strong, C., & Bakhshi, S. (2023). S. B. (2023). Smartphones and the Future of Remembering: Frictions, Problems, and Pathways. *Conference Proceedings. Ethnographic Praxis in Industry Conference*, *2023*(1), 89–102. DOI: 10.1111/epic.12154

Sun, C., Sun, B., Lin, Y., & Zhou, H. (2022). Problematic Mobile Phone Use Increases with the Fear of Missing Out Among College Students: The Effects of Self-Control, Perceived Social Support and Future Orientation. *Psychology Research and Behavior Management, 15*, 1–8. DOI: 10.2147/PRBM.S345650

Syahputra, Y., Miswanto, M., & Hafni, M. (2023). Exploration of the fear of missing out internet based on demography. [IJERE]. *International Journal of Evaluation and Research in Education, 12*(4), 2186. DOI: 10.11591/ijere.v12i4.25353

Szawłoga, T., Soroka, K., & Śliwińska, M. (2024). Relationship between fear of missing-out and adolescents mental health. *Medycyna Srodowiskowa*, *27*(1), 18–22. DOI: 10.26444/ms/187716

Tandon, A., Dhir, A., Talwar, S., Kaur, P., & Mäntymäki, M. (2021). Dark consequences of social media-induced fear of missing out (FoMO): Social media stalking, comparisons, and fatigue. *Technological Forecasting and Social Change*, *171*, 120931. DOI: 10.1016/j.techfore.2021.120931

Tang, T.-C., Chi, L.-C., & Tang, E. (2024). Office islands: Exploring the uncharted waters of workplace loneliness, social media addiction, and the fear of missing out. *Current Psychology (New Brunswick, N.J.)*, *43*(17), 15160–15175. DOI: 10.1007/s12144-023-05445-9

Tateno, M., Kato, T. A., Shirasaka, T., Kanazawa, J., Ukai, W., & Hirota, T. (2022). A network analysis of problematic smartphone use in Japanese young adults. *PLoS One*, *17*(8), e0272803. DOI: 10.1371/journal.pone.0272803

Taylor, A., Hook, M., Carlson, J., Gudergan, S., & Falk, T. (2024). Appetite for distraction? A systematic literature review on customer smartphone distraction. *International Journal of Information Management*, *75*, 102722. DOI: 10.1016/j.ijinfomgt.2023.102722

Throuvala, M. A., Griffiths, M. D., Rennoldson, M., & Kuss, D. J. (2019). Motivational processes and dysfunctional mechanisms of social media use among adolescents: A qualitative focus group study. *Computers in Human Behavior*, *93*, 164–175. DOI: 10.1016/j.chb.2018.12.012

Urfa, O., & Görgülü, R. (2025). From addiction to pervasiveness: Validation of the Smartphone Pervasiveness Scale in Turkish adolescents. *International Journal of Assessment Tools in Education*, *12*(4), 926–941. DOI: 10.21449/ijate.1579992

Vagka, E., Gnardellis, C., Lagiou, A., & Notara, V. (2024). Smartphone Use and Social Media Involvement in Young Adults: Association with Nomophobia, Depression Anxiety Stress Scales (DASS) and Self-Esteem. *International Journal of Environmental Research and Public Health*, *21*(7), 920. DOI: 10.3390/ijerph21070920

Vanden Abeele, M. M. P. (2021). Digital Wellbeing as a Dynamic Construct. *Communication Theory*, *31*(4), 932–955. DOI: 10.1093/ct/qtaa024

Veissière, S. P. L., & Stendel, M. (2018). Hypernatural Monitoring: A Social Rehearsal Account of Smartphone Addiction. *Frontiers in Psychology*, *9*, 141. DOI: 10.3389/fpsyg.2018.00141

Wallinheimo, A.-S., & Evans, S. L. (2025). Mechanisms that link circadian preference to problematic smartphone and social media use in young adults. *PLoS One*, *20*(9), e0331961. DOI: 10.1371/journal.pone.0331961

Ward, A. F., Duke, K., Gneezy, A., & Bos, M. W. (2017). Brain Drain: The Mere Presence of One's Own Smartphone Reduces Available Cognitive Capacity. *Journal of the Association for Consumer Research*, *2*(2), 140–154. DOI: 10.1086/691462

Wegner, D. M., & Ward, A. F. (2013). How Google Is Changing Your Brain. *Scientific American*, *309*(6), 58–61. DOI: 10.1038/scientificamerican1213-58

Wen, F., Ding, Y., Yang, C., Ma, S., Zhu, J., Xiao, H., & Zuo, B. (2023). Influence of smartphone use motives on smartphone addiction during the COVID-19 epidemic in China: The moderating effect of age. *Current Psychology (New Brunswick, N.J.)*, *42*(22), 19316–19325. DOI: 10.1007/s12144-022-03355-w

Yang, H., Tng, G. Y. Q., Khoo, S. S., & Yang, S. (2022). Multidimensional Profiles of Addictive Smartphone Use: A Latent Profile Analysis. *Current Psychology (New Brunswick, N.J.)*, *41*(12), 8410–8423. DOI: 10.1007/s12144-022-02881-x

Yildirim, C., & Correia, A.-P. (2015). Exploring the dimensions of nomophobia: Development and validation of a self-reported questionnaire. *Computers in Human Behavior*, *49*, 130–137. DOI: 10.1016/j.chb.2015.02.059

Yue, H., Yue, X., Zhang, X., Liu, B., & Bao, H. (2022). Exploring the relationship between social exclusion and smartphone addiction: The mediating roles of loneliness and self-control. *Frontiers in Psychology*, *13*, 945631. DOI: 10.3389/fpsyg.2022.945631

Zhang, Y., Fang, Y., Wei, K.-K., Ramsey, E., McCole, P., & Chen, H. (2011). Repurchase intention in B2C e-commerce—A relationship quality perspective. *Information & Management*, *48*(6), 192–200. DOI: 10.1016/j.im.2011.05.003

Zhu, C., Li, S., & Zhang, L. (2025). The impact of smartphone addiction on mental health and its relationship with life satisfaction in the post-COVID-19 era. *Frontiers in Psychiatry*, *16*, 1542040. DOI: 10.3389/fpsyt.2025.1542040

Zillmann, D. (1988). Mood management through communication choices. *The American Behavioral Scientist*, *31*(3), 327–340. DOI: 10.1177/000276488031003005

ADDITIONAL READINGS

Bayer, J. B., Ellison, N. B., Schoenebeck, S. Y., & Falk, E. B. (2016). Sharing the small moments: Ephemeral social interaction on Snapchat. *Information Communication and Society*, *19*(7), 956–977. DOI: 10.1080/1369118X.2015.1084349

Deci, E. L., & Ryan, R. M. (2000). The "what" and "why" of goal pursuits: Human needs and the self-determination of behavior. *Psychological Inquiry*, *11*(4), 227–268. DOI: 10.1207/S15327965PLI1104_01

Fogg, B. J. (2009). A behavior model for persuasive design. In *Proceedings of the 4th International Conference on Persuasive Technology* (Article 40). Association for Computing Machinery. https://doi.org/DOI: 10.1145/1541948.1541999

Gazzaley, A., & Rosen, L. D. (2016). *The distracted mind: Ancient brains in a high-tech world.* MIT Press.

Goffman, E. (1959). *The presentation of self in everyday life*. Doubleday.

Hofmann, W., Baumeister, R. F., Förster, G., & Vohs, K. D. (2012). Everyday temptations: An experience sampling study of desire, conflict, and self-control. *Journal of Personality and Social Psychology, 102*(6), 1318–1335. DOI: 10.1037/a0026545

Kahneman, D. (2011). *Thinking, fast and slow*. Farrar, Straus and Giroux.

Rosen, L. D., Carrier, L. M., & Cheever, N. A. (2013). Facebook and texting made me do it: Media-induced task-switching while studying. *Computers in Human Behavior, 29*(3), 948–958. DOI: 10.1016/j.chb.2012.12.001

Sherry, J. L. (2004). Flow and media enjoyment. *Communication Theory*, *14*(4), 328–347. DOI: 10.1111/j.1468-2885.2004.tb00318.x

Turel, O., Serenko, A., & Giles, P. (2011). Integrating technology addiction and use: An empirical investigation of online auction users. *Management Information Systems Quarterly*, *35*(4), 1043–1061. DOI: 10.2307/41409972

KEY TERMS AND DEFINITIONS

Fear of Missing Out (FoMO): Fear of missing something significant in either social or informational experiences causes anxiety-induced need to remain up to date.

Identity Extension: The psychological imprint of the smartphone into the personal conceptualization, daily habits, and continuity.

Information Vigilance: Constant habit of checking notifications and computer indicators with repeated checks.

Nomophobia: Phobia or anxiety that someone feels when he or she cannot use his or her smartphone or be digitally connected.

Problematic Smartphone Usage (PSU): Intolerable smartphone use that interferes with normal day to day operations, though may not necessarily be addictive in nature.

Psychophysical Somatization: Individuals develop physical and emotional symptoms (e.g. fatigue, sleeping disturbance) because of persistent digital stress and vigilance.

Smartphone Addiction: Repeated use of smartphone with a loss of control and despite adverse effects.

Chapter 7
Social Media Addiction and the FOMO-Fuelled Economy: A Psychological Perspective

Sumit Kumar Pandey
http://orcid.org/0000-0002-6306-5069
Manipal University Jaipur, India

Utsav Krishan Murari
http://orcid.org/0009-0007-1606-6775
Manipal University Jaipur, India

ABSTRACT

Social media addiction (SMA) is an urgent behavioral emergency, as social platforms take advantage of mental weakness and dopamine as an input to rewards through systemic functionality. This chapter combines neurobiology, addiction theory, and political economy in order to discuss Fear of Missing Out (FOMO) as a psychological motivation and economic force that drives profitability. Based on recent research in psychology, neuroscience, ethics in technology it examines the origins of SMA, brain-based sustainers and its negative effects including depression, anxiety, loneliness, sleep disorders, and suicidality. Presenting the FOMO-driven economy, it states that FOMO is not a by-product of doing business—it is fostered deliberately. The chapter critiques surveillance capitalism and attention economies because they promote addictive designs and suggests evidence-based interventions and regulations to make users wellness-focused, rather than profit-driven.

DOI: 10.4018/979-8-3373-6665-4.ch007

INTRODUCTION

The digital revolution has fundamentally transformed the nature of human interaction, social communication, and information exchange. Social media platforms, such as Facebook, Instagram, Twitter (X), TikTok, Snapchat, and YouTube, have become ubiquitous features of contemporary daily life. With over 5.3 billion users globally, these platforms now represent approximately two-thirds of the world's population (Statista, 2025). While these digital environments offer unprecedented opportunities for connection, community building, and information dissemination, they have simultaneously precipitated a crisis of psychological well-being characterized by rising levels of anxiety, depression, loneliness, and behavioral dependence (Abi-Jaoude et al., 2020).

The problem of social media addiction represents a significant deviation from traditional substance use disorders. Researchers categorize it as a behavioral addiction, a compulsive involvement in pleasurable activities that occurs despite the absence of psychotropic substances, yet induces profound psychological and neurobiological alterations (Griffiths, 2005). Compared to conventional addictions, social media dependency operates through intermittent reinforcement mechanisms designed specifically to optimize user interaction and time-on-platform indicators (Montag et al., 2015).

A central psychological construct in this phenomenon is the "Fear of Missing Out" (FOMO), defined as the persistent worry or apprehension that others are having rewarding experiences from which one is absent (Przybylski et al., 2013). Within the modern digital landscape, FOMO is not merely a transient emotional state but a psychological process inherent to an economic system where platform profitability is based on the stabilization and verification of user anxiety (Harris & Sandoval, 2020).

Systematic Methodological Framework: An Integrative Review Protocol

In response to the need for a systematic and robust academic framework, this study takes the Integrative Review method as updated by (Whittemore & Knafl, 2005) and (Liimatainen, et al., 2016). This particular approach is chosen because it is the only method that enables the incorporation of different methodological approaches (including experimental, cross-sectional, qualitative interviews, and theoretical studies) to develop a comprehensive overview of a complex health and socio-economic issue (Whittemore & Knafl, 2005) and (Liimatainen, et al., 2016). The approach is applied in five steps for transparency and replicability.

The first stage, Problem Identification, defines the conceptual framework of the study by conceptualising social media addiction as a multi-level outcome of the interaction between individual neurobiology and systemic algorithmic logic (Whittemore & Knafl, 2005) and (Liimatainen, et al., 2016). This stage defines the key variables: individual vulnerability (e.g., neuroticism), neuroadaptive mechanisms (dopaminergic reward system), design elements (e.g., infinite scroll) and political-economic forces underpinning surveillance capitalism.

The second stage, Literature Search, included a systematic and focused search of electronic databases (PsycINFO, PubMed, Google Scholar, ACM Digital Library) for literature published from 2013 to 2025. The search terms used a combination of controlled vocabulary and keywords such as "social media addiction," "Fear of Missing Out" (FoMO), "I-PACE model", "Surveillance Capitalism", and "algorithmic personalization". We sought to avoid publication bias (Whittemore & Knafl, 2005) and (Liimatainen, et al., 2016) by considering both published peer-reviewed journals and relevant grey literature (Liimatainen, et al., 2016), such as corporate design patent documents and government health warnings.

The third step, Data Evaluation, involved the use of critical appraisal instruments. The Joanna Briggs Institute (JBI) Critical Appraisal Tools for Analytical Cross-Sectional Studies and Randomized Controlled Trials were applied to empirical studies to assess the risks of bias, especially related to self-reporting validity and confounds (JBI, 2026). Theoretical work was assessed based on constitutive assumptions, coherence and explanatory capacity in the field of behavioral addiction (Battistone et al., 2023).

Table 1. Methodological Synthesis and Quality Appraisal Criteria

Stage	Process Activity	Criteria for Rigor and Validity
Problem Identification	Delineation of research question and scope.	Clarity of variables; alignment with PICOTS/SPIDER templates (Dhollande et al., 2021).
Literature Search	Multi-database, targeted search of empirical and theoretical sources.	Documented search strategy; inclusion of 2013-2025 studies (Whittemore & Knafl, 2005) and (Liimatainen, et al., 2016).
Data Evaluation	Quality assessment using JBI appraisal checklists (JBI, (2026).	Analysis of authenticity, relevance, and methodological quality (Whittemore & Knafl, 2005) and (Liimatainen, et al., 2016).
Data Analysis	Constant comparison and thematic categorization of findings.	Data reduction and display; identification of patterns across sources (Devitt et al., 2017).
Presentation	Synthesis of findings into a coherent theoretical framework.	Explicit linking of evidence to conclusions; identification of gaps (Devitt et al., 2017).

In the fourth stage, Data Analysis, a constant comparison approach was used to identify themes, patterns and causal links (Devitt et al., 2017). This includes grouping data into themes: individual predisposing factors, neurobiological reward systems and macro-economic incentive structures. The final stage, Presentation, synthesises these themes into the narrative below, and in turn, a new theory (Whittemore & Knafl, 2005).

Original Contribution: The Instrumentarian-Neuro-Affective (IINA) Framework

This chapter builds on existing literature in offering the Instrumentarian-Neuro-Affective (IINA) Framework. Unlike current models such as I-PACE, the IINA framework is a closed-loop model, which activates "Instrumentarian Power" (a term used in surveillance capitalism literature) at a macro-economic scale to exploit micro-scale neurobiological vulnerabilities (Laidler, 2019). This integration of the five points of analysis (individual diversity (psychology), dopaminergic exploitation (neuroscience), design strategies (engineering), surveillance capitalism (political economy) and systemic intervention (policy) offers a unique theoretical perspective on why individual action is not always enough to escape platform dependency.

BACKGROUND / THEORETICAL FRAMEWORK

Theoretical Foundations: Understanding Behavioral Addiction

The idea of social media addiction is rooted in the basis of behavioral addiction models, a relatively recent development in the field of addiction. Traditionally, addiction science had a somewhat strong focus on substance use disorders that involve the ingestion, inhalation or injection of psychoactive substances having an impact on the process of the neural activity. Yet, contemporary addiction science has been accepting that the defining features of addiction processes (compulsion to be involved, loss of control, continuation despite adverse consequences, tolerance, and withdrawal) can be expressed in procedural (behavioral) terms without the use of substances.

From Substance Addiction to Behavioral Addiction

Traditionally, addiction studies placed a rather strong emphasis on substance use diseases that involve the consumption, inhalation, or injection of psychoactive drugs that have a direct impact on the processes of neural activity (Nutt et al., 2010).

Nonetheless, modern-day addiction science has been acknowledging the reality that the characteristic aspects of addiction known as compulsive involvement, a loss of control, the persistence of engagement despite the adverse effects, tolerance, and withdrawal can be manifested in behavioral aspects without the involvement of substances (Shaffer et al., 2005).

Gambling Disorder was officially recognized by Diagnostic and Statistical Manual of Mental Disorders (DSM-5) as the initial type of behavioral addiction and was conceptualized as the persistence and repeated problematic gambling events resulting in clinically significant impairment or distress (American Psychiatric Association, 2013).

Behavioral addictions have been described to possess a few major features: (1) preoccupation with the behavior, (2) increase in the levels of behavior with time, (3) failure of attempts to reduce or control behavior, (4) dysphoric mood when denied to engage in behavior and (5) persistent excess use of behavior regardless of being aware of its bad effects (Beard and Wolf, 2001).

Critical Evaluation of the I-PACE Model

The concept of social media addiction could be viewed through the I-PACE model (Interaction of Person-Affect-Cognition-Execution): according to this model, behavioral addictions are acquired by interactions between individual predisposing factors and affective states, cognitive processes and execution of the addictive behavior (Brand et al., 2016). The I-PACE model offers a robust descriptive approach but must be carefully applied to social media. First, it tends to view "Person" and "Affect" as fixed, rather than the dynamic influence of algorithmic personalisation on these factors (Brand et al., 2025). For example, an individual high in neuroticism (Person) may feel socially anxious (Affect), but the recommender system actively reinforces this by feeding them social content that affirms their social anxieties and thus forms a "feedback loop" not captured by the original model (Meynadier et al., 2025).

Additionally, recent analysis points to a "terminological ambiguity" between habit, dependence and addiction (Singer & Omary, 2026). It has been suggested that the I-PACE model may over-pathologize everyday digital media use (such as scrolling through a feed while waiting for an appointment) that may not be wise but does not necessarily constitute a life-threatening disease (Singer & Omary, 2026). A more accurate interpretation of the I-PACE model in 2025 is that the shift into addiction specifically occurs when "reward expectancies" (Cognition) become skewed, such that using the platform is perceived as the only effective mood regulation strategy, resulting in diminished "executive control" (Execution) (Meynadier et al., 2025).

Table 2. Critical Evaluation of I-PACE Components in Social Media Contexts

I-PACE Component	Theoretical Premise	Social Media Reality	Critical Evaluation of Evidence
Person (P)	Genetic and personality predispositions.	Targeted recruitment of those with high neuroticism/social anxiety.	Strong correlation, but direction of causality is often bidirectional (Moretta & Wegmann, 2025).
Affect (A)	Mood states (loneliness, boredom).	Algorithmic "actuation" of outrage or FOMO to drive engagement.	Most studies use self-reports, which may under-report transient affective states (Yang et al., 2025).
Cognition (C)	Biases and reward expectancies.	Cognitive bias in favor of digital validation over real-world intimacy.	Reward expectancies are often the strongest mediators of addiction (Meynadier et al., 2025).
Execution (E)	Reduced inhibitory control.	Infinite scrolling and autoplay bypass conscious decision-making.	EEG data shows a 22% reduction in prefrontal Beta power during use (Satani et al., 2025).

The Self-Determination Theory Perspective

Self-Determination Theory (SDT) by (Ryan and Deci, 2000), offers essential knowledge about the reasons why some people become too addicted to social media. The SDT assumes that human beings have three basic psychological needs, including **autonomy** (the belief that one has a choice and control over their own behaviour), **competence** (the sense of efficiency and ability in their field of desire), and **relatedness** (the sense of belonging to others and connection with them) (Deci and Ryan, 1985). However, the use of SDT in relation to engagement with digital platforms has been criticised for focusing only on the "light side" (need satisfaction) and not the "dark side" (need frustration) (Trigueros et al., 2019). While platforms may appear to be "autonomy supportive" contexts, they engage in "need-thwarting" through the strategic use of coercive design features that negatively influence initiative (Hindman et al., 2025).

Furthermore, research on Behavior Change Technologies (BCTs) shows that designers often use SDT to increase the engagement with the technology itself, rather than the desired positive behaviour (Alberts et al., 2024). This creates a "behavioral backlash" as users report their autonomy is undermined by time restrictions and "nudges", leading to psychological reactance and a relapse into addiction (Alberts et al., 2024). A more refined understanding of SDT in 2025 highlights that social media addiction occurs when a "superficial illusion" of competence and relatedness is offered by a social media platform, which does not satisfy the underlying needs of the user, resulting in a state of "chronic need frustration" and over-compensatory use (Hindman et al., 2025).

THE NEUROBIOLOGY OF SOCIAL MEDIA ADDICTION: THE DOPAMINE PATHWAY

Dopamine is a neurotransmitter made in the ventral tegmental region and deposited all over the brain, which is at the center of solving reward, motivation, learning and habit formation (Schultz, 2007). As opposed to common mass media prejudice, dopamine does not produce pleasure or a sense of reward; instead, it forms motivation and a desire which encodes the motivational salience of the stimuli and approach behavior (Berridge and Robinson, 2016).

The Reward-Motivation Loop in Social Media Engagement

This dopaminergic property is premeditatedly exploited by social media by applying a schedule of variable ratios known as "variable ratio reinforcement schedules". Granular neurocognitive data from 2025 provides evidence for these mechanisms through brainwave activity analysis. Electroencephalography (EEG) research shows that use of social media leads to profound changes in Alpha waves, which decrease during social media use and suggest that users experience a high amount of cognitive processing during interactions with emotionally provocative content (Satani et al., 2025). In contrast, Beta and Gamma waves, which reflect active information processing and emotional arousal, are elevated during social media use, and remain so after use, suggesting prolonged cognitive arousal that impairs emotion regulation (Satani et al., 2025).

Table 3. Neurobiological Indicators of Digital Addiction (EEG Patterns)

Brainwave Type	Associated State	Impact of Social Media Use	Functional Consequence
Alpha (8–12 Hz)	Relaxation and reflection.	Significant decline during active engagement.	Loss of introspective capacity; increased cognitive fatigue (Satani et al., 2025).
Beta (12–30 Hz)	Focused concentration.	Elevated power; 35% drop in variability for heavy users.	Weakened inhibitory control in the prefrontal cortex (Satani et al., 2025).
Gamma (30–100 Hz)	High-level info processing.	62% increase when viewing "high-reward" content (e.g., likes).	Dopaminergic spiking; reinforcement of habit loops (Satani et al., 2025).
Delta (0.5–4 Hz)	Deep sleep and exhaustion.	Increased activity correlated with 2+ hours of use (r=0.45).	Chronic mental exhaustion and disrupted sleep architecture (Satani et al., 2025).

Neuroadaptation, Tolerance, and Structural Degradation

Repeated exposure to unpredictable schedules of reward results in **neuroadaptive changes** of dopaminergic circuitry, which form true neurobiological adaptations similar to those in substance addiction (Kuss & Griffiths, 2017). With repeated dopaminergic stimulation, there are decreases in dopamine receptor density in regions of the brain in which reward generating behaviors take place and a degradation of the **post-synaptic receptors**, so that increasing doses of dopaminergic stimulation are needed to produce similar motivational, or reward-generating, states (Volkow et al., 2006). Structural analyses have verified that subjects with problematic social media use have considerably lower volume of gray matter in the anterior cingulate cortex (ACC) and orbitofrontal cortex (OFC), regions involved in decision-making, self-control and emotional processes. This atrophy validates the subjective complaints about lack of control: people are not simply "weak willed" but have neurobiologically compromised inhibitory systems.

Moreover, the neurobiology often follows a tripartite cycle: (1) binge/intoxication, associated with acute reward; (2) withdrawal/negative affect, associated with reward deficits and increased stress; and (3) preoccupation/anticipation, where impaired executive function makes it difficult to resist (Uhi et al., 2019). This cycle is sustained through an "allostatic load", whereby the baseline state of the brain is reset to a stressed state that is only alleviated by using the apps.

Critical Evaluation of Neurobiological Evidence

Despite the fascinating convergence of neurobiological evidence with clinical and behavioural data, the neuroimaging findings summarised in this section are subject to several limitations that place limits on causal inference and must be acknowledged. Most neuroimaging research in this area is cross-sectional, and relies on small non-representative convenience samples (usually undergraduate students) for statistical power and generalizability. We are still faced with the problem of reverse causality: the neurobiological differences documented between heavy and light social media users may be explained by pre-existing neurobiological differences that predispose to addictive use, rather than neuroadaptation as a result of social media use. Participants with lower baseline gray matter volume in anterior cingulate cortex and orbitofrontal cortex may be predisposed to impulsivity and reward-seeking, and self-select into greater social media use, rather than having these structural changes induced by their social media use.

Moreover, most neuroimaging studies categorise individuals as "addicted" or "non-addicted" based on psychometric self-report measures in the absence of diagnostic guidelines, which may lead to misclassification. Neuroimaging patterns of brain activation related to social media may be compared with those of substance addiction, as a heuristic device, but this approach may inflate the neurobiological equivalence of the two phenomena; reward processes are implicated in many human activities, and the specificity of dopaminergic activation to "true" addictive processes needs to be more carefully distinguished from other types of behaviour than current research enables. These limitations aside, the combination of brain imaging data with behavioural evidence, clinical case studies and the known neurobiology of variable ratio reinforcement provides cumulative evidence to support the broad assertion that high-frequency social media use is associated with neurobiological adaptation of the dopaminergic reward system, with obvious implications for clinical practice and regulatory policy.

FEAR OF MISSING OUT: PSYCHOLOGICAL CONSTRUCTION AND ECONOMIC FUNCTION

The Fear of Missing Out (FOMO) is a social phenomenon in which researchers assume a widespread fear that one is missing out on gratifying moments in the social life (Przybylski et al., 2013). FOMO involves both cognitive and emotional aspects: the cognitive one entails rumination and preoccupation with activity or experience that other people are enjoying or with things that they have not participated in, and the emotional one implies fear, regret, dissatisfaction, and threatening feelings about the social status and belongingness (Alt, 2015).

Individual Differences and Developmental Susceptibility

Individuals are not all equally susceptible to FOMO; there are extensive individual differences in susceptibility to this mental condition (Ellison et al., 2014). Some personality and psychological correlates include neuroticism (prone to negative emotional state), low self-esteem, anxiety about social situations, narcissism (especially vulnerable narcissism), insecure attachment patterns, and dissatisfaction with the foundations of basic psychological needs (Alshowkan et al., 2025).

Fragile narcissism, for example, is an important predictor of FOMO; such persons use social media and its feedback as a means to avoid the experience of inherent insecurity. Attachment insecurity also plays an important role, as people with high attachment anxiety rely on social media as a "digital security blanket" to maintain social connection, resulting in constant vigilance and addiction.

The vulnerability of adolescents is of particular concern. Neuroplasticity of the adolescent brain increases vulnerability to habit formation.1 Adolescents are most susceptible to the "reflexive" (rather than "reflective") system of decision-making, given an immature prefrontal cortex that is responsible for future thinking and impulse control, does not mature until their mid-20s. This occurs in a context of heightened social sensitivity during identity development, which means the fear of missing out (FOMO) is a critical part of development.

FOMO as an Economic Mechanism in Surveillance Capitalism

The most significant shortcoming of existing behavioural models is the lack of recognition of FOMO as an efficient economic tool. The "FOMO-fuelled economy" is a model of economic activity where profits are made by promoting and exploiting social anxiety. In the view of (Zuboff, 2019), social media companies are "Instrumentarian Power" that uses ambient digital instrumentation to control subliminal cues and induce social comparison (Laidler, 2019).

The business model of surveillance capitalism operates through a sequence of (1) extraction of "behavioral surplus" (data not needed for service provision) (2) production of "prediction products" (anticipating users' reactions) (3) sale of predictions into "behavioral futures markets" (Laidler, 2019). FOMO is the "engine" that fuels interaction time and data collection in this system. These social networks don't just "facilitate" connection; they "actuate" behavior by "herding" users toward profitable outcomes such as clicking on an advertisement or scroll-through, through the use of rewards and punishments (e.g., public "likes" vs. the fear of being "unfollowed") (Laidler, 2019).

Table 4. The Economic Value of FOMO-Driven Design

Design Feature	Psychological Mechanism	Economic Outcome (Surveillance Capital)
Ephemeral Content	Regret anticipation; time-bound pressure.	Increased daily active usage (DAU) and data extraction frequency.
Algorithmic Personalization	Reinforcing spirals; echo chambers.	Higher engagement through emotional "actuation" and confirmation bias (Ahmmad et al., 2025).
Gamified Metrics (Streaks)	Need for social competence/validation.	Habit formation and resistance to platform exit (churn reduction).
"Nudges" (Notifications)	Attentional capture; classical conditioning.	Maximization of "behavioral surplus" available for predictive modeling (Laidler, 2019).

PLATFORM DESIGN AND THE MECHANICS OF ENGAGEMENT MAXIMIZATION

Modern social networks integrate a number of architectural features that are explicitly designed to engage users and create addiction. These Attention-Capture Damaging Patterns (ACDPs) or "dark patterns" are deliberate applications of psychology (Backman, 2025).

Architectural Elements of Entrapment

1. **Infinite Scrolling:** Eliminating page breaks creates an open-ended platform with low cost of engagement and a loss of perception of time (Harris, 2019).
2. **Push Notifications:** Creating Pavlovian connections between the sound of notifications and rewards; their purpose is to create a sense of urgency regardless of attention (Thaler and Sunstein, 2008).
3. **Social Proof:** Social proof (likes, shares) measures social approval, driving competition and envy (Cialdini, 2009).
4. **Emotional Prioritisation:** Algorithms prioritise emotional content; content that incenses users receives more user time and data than the same content without incensing (Rosen et al., 2013).

This entrapment leads to "algorithmic ambivalence" whereby users feel both drawn to and repelled by algorithms (Jiang, 2026). An analysis in 2025 found that users who were most motivated to reduce their use were the least successful, due to the pressure to be "seen" and "relevant" by their social network. This trap is a psychological equivalent of "sunk-cost reasoning", where the cost of quitting an activity for which one has committed time and effort creates a sense of loss (Brand et al., 2025).

MENTAL HEALTH CONSEQUENCES OF SOCIAL MEDIA ADDICTION AND FOMO

Huge body of empirical evidence that demonstrates a high degree of correlation between problematic social media use and depression, anxiety and other mood disorders (Twenge et al., 2018). A systematic review and meta-analysis of 23 studies found a high level of correlation between social media addiction and anxiety ($r = 0.47$), depression ($r = 0.53$) and low self-esteem ($r = -0.54$) (Lin et al., 2016).

Critical Evaluation of the Evidence: From Correlation to Causation

The causal nature of the links between social media use and mental health problems outlined in this section requires critical evaluation and cannot be taken as a given simply on the basis of correlation. Most studies in this field are correlational and establish statistical associations but do not address the critical issue of causal direction: that the selection hypothesis, which states that people with pre-existing depression, anxiety or loneliness are more likely to engage in heavy social media use as a form of mood regulation, is indeed plausible and cannot be eliminated on the basis of correlational designs. This issue is compounded by common-method bias in studies that solely rely on self-reported data on social media use and mental health, and the conflation of "problematic" and "heavy" social media use with clinically relevant mental health dysfunction in some of the studies. Despite these concerns, a number of experimental and quasi-experimental studies considerably bolster the causal claim.

Randomised experimental designs featuring social media reduction interventions have shown substantial decreases in depression and loneliness after two to four weeks (Hunt et al., 2018), and quasi-experimental studies leveraging staggered Facebook roll-outs across university campuses have shown significant declines in mental health indices following Facebook's roll-out (Braghieri et al., 2022). Ecological momentary assessment studies also demonstrate within-person effects of social media engagement episodes on negative affect, while controlling for baseline mood, thus addressing within-person selection confounding. Overall, the weight of correlational, experimental and quasi-experimental findings provides a solid body of evidence to conclude that problematic social media use and depression, anxiety, and loneliness are bidirectionally associated, have causally relevant effects in both directions, and are of sufficient magnitude to be of clinical and policy concern - albeit with effect sizes and moderating factors still actively explored within the scientific community.

Causal Mechanisms and Paradoxes

1. **Social Comparison:** Interacting with well-edited online portrayals produces "relative deprivation," where users feel their lives are inferior to their peers (Ihde, 2021).
2. **Loneliness Paradox:** longitudinal studies found that high usage is linked with increased loneliness, contrary to the platform's "connection" mission (Vannucci et al., 2017). This is explained by the "displacement hypothesis," where digital interaction replaces deep face-to-face intimacy (Hunt et al., 2018).

3. **Sleep Disruption:** Blue light inhibits melatonin, while cognitive activation from outrage-inducing content postpones sleep onset (Czeisler and Gooley, 2007); (Chang et al., 2015); (Riemann et al., 2019).
4. **Suicidal Ideation:** High FOMO and problematic use are linked to self-harm content loops, where algorithms recommend increasingly severe content to vulnerable users (Twenge and Campbell, 2019); (Barry et al., 2017).

Table 5. Synthesis of Mental Health Outcomes and Causal Evidence (2024-2025)

Outcome	Causal Mechanism identified	Evidence Quality and Limitations
Anxiety/Depression	Chain mediation: addiction reduced self-efficacy negative coping (Chen et al., 2025).	High; verified through longitudinal multi-wave designs (Dolan, 2026).
Social Isolation	Displacement of real-world interactions and peer support (Dolan, 2026).	Moderate; depends on active vs. passive usage patterns (Vannucci et al., 2017); (Hunt et al., 2018).
Academic Decline	loss of efficiency (20%) and drop in GPA (0.3) due to multitasking (Duc, 2025).	High; significant in higher education populations (Deshmukh et al., 2025)
Suicidality/Self-Harm	exposure to modeling effects and "doomscrolling" cycles (Chen et al., 2025).	Emergent; relies on ethical qualitative data and survey reporting (Haidt & Rausch, 2026).

A critical methodological limitation in these findings is the over-reliance on self-reported data (Yang et al., 2025). Studies using "data donations" of actual digital traces suggest that users often underestimate or overestimate their usage, making it difficult to define "addiction" based on screen time alone (Singer & Omary, 2026). The defining feature of addiction must therefore remain "compulsive behavior despite clear harm" rather than a raw quantity of minutes (Singer & Omary, 2026).

ECONOMIC STRUCTURES: THE BUSINESS MODELS OF PLATFORM ADDICTION

The social media works on what the researcher describes as the attention economy, which is an economic system where most of the value lies on concentrated human attention instead of real-life products and services (Davenport and Beck, 2001).

Surveillance Capitalism and Epistemic Inequality

Surveillance capitalism is the term coined by Shoshana Zuboff that characterizes economic regimes in which corporate entities methodically extract human experiences in the form of raw data, predict behavior and psychological profile using the data, and commercialize the predictions by selling them to the firms willing to manipulate behavior (Zuboff, 2019). This creates a state of "epistemic inequality," where platforms know everything about the user's neurobiological triggers, while the user knows little about the platform's operations (Laidler, 2019). This asymmetry is not just a privacy violation but a direct threat to autonomy, as behavioral modification occurs through subtle "economies of action" that shunt users toward profitable behaviors without their full awareness (Laidler, 2019).

Misalignment of Incentives

The economic incentive model of surveillance capitalism is completely antithetical to the well-being of the user: platforms make more revenue both when emotionally engaged on the platform and when emotionally engaged negatively. This constitutes a "market failure," where voluntary corporate self-regulation is impossible because profit-maximizing motives have a direct adverse impact on user health.1 Corporate fiduciary duties to shareholders effectively "code" addictive design into the platform's architecture.

Regulatory Arbitrage and Externalization of Costs

One last economic process that contributes to social media addiction is a **regulatory arbitrage and externalization of costs** (Lutz and Tamo-Larrieux, 2020). The social media sites exist in countries with highly inconsistent regulatory regimes, which allow them to engage in minimum-protection policies on countries with weak privacy policies and emphasize maximally-protective policies in highly-regulated statuses. A depressed teenager who is suffering from a lack of sleep because of social media overuse pays both real personal costs and social costs and racks in positive engagement data and ad revenue on the platform.

Cost-benefit misalignment: Under the economic bilateral of the society, the societal ills of addiction are a zero cost, in fact, to the degree that harm produces emotional appeal and time involved, the platforms will earn profit. This chronic maladjustment of personal profit and individual health is the root cause of market failure in which voluntary corporate regulation can not be anticipated since profit maximizing motives have a direct adverse impact on the wellbeing of users.

Overall, Social media sites exist in economic frameworks -attention economy and surveillance capitalism- where profitability is pegged on the ability to maximize the time spent on a site and the volume of behavioral data gathered. This economic discussion shows that consumer-level behavior change and voluntary administering corporate self-regulation is not a solution to the issue of social media addiction; the system needs to be ready to intervene systemically through regulatory frameworks to redesign systemic platform incentive systems themselves.

THEORETICAL MODELS OF SOCIAL MEDIA ADDICTION DEVELOPMENT

Needs-Based Models: Compensatory and Frustration Pathways

To understand the reason why certain people will develop problematic social media use and others develop healthy engagement patterns will necessitate an examination of theoretical models of addiction development. There are two models that explain in complementary recognitions that present the needs under framework.

The Compensatory Internet Use Theory

The Compensatory Internet Use Theory assumes problem Internet use forms when the users of the internet use online communication to control the bad emotional conditions they find difficult to cope with offline (Kardefelt-Winther, 2014). This theory states that those suffering chronic negative affect (depression, anxiety, loneliness, social anxiety) find that use of the internet gives them instant and ready emotion regulation, which forms a reinforcing loop of such emotional distress leading them to use the internet which then in turn gives them a short-term emotion rush, thus failing to help them solve the underlying distress, they suffer again so they use the internet and so on (Spada, 2014).

The Social Needs Frustration Model

The other yet complementary theoretical approach highlights the fact that social media addiction is formed in particular cases when fundamental psychological needs (autonomy, competence, relatedness) are not met in interpersonal situations and the platforms provide an illusion of their satisfaction (Baker and White, 2010). In contrast to the compensatory model, which is focused on the regulation of the mood, this model is focused on the need satisfaction: people with low offline autonomy, competence, or relatedness find themselves more vulnerable to social media addiction because these platforms provide an apparent internal fulfillment of these unmet needs.

The Reinforcement Sensitivity Theory Integration

The Reinforcement Sensitivity Theory (RST) is a theory that suggests that people should be sensitive to rewards and punishment cues, and this sensitivity to these stimuli results in the fact that people vary in the underlying neural systems that govern the approach and avoidance motivation (Gray, 1970). The implication of the use of RST in social media addiction implies that people with increased sensitivity to reward would be more prone to social media addiction due to variable reward response to platform use (Brand et al., 2016).

Theoretical model integration: The theoretical models are not exclusive as they are simply the various causal routes to addiction. The realization of these various pathways is why various individuals become addicted in different ways and that any intervention needs to be specifically different based on the causal pathway.

Overall, there are several approaches to explaining the development of addiction: Compensatory Internet Use Theory focuses on mood regulation caused by engagement, Social Needs Frustration Model focuses on platform satisfaction of unfulfilled psychological needs, and Refreezing Sensitivity Theory focuses on differences in reward sensitivity between individuals.

INTERVENTION STRATEGIES AND DIGITAL WELLNESS APPROACHES

Individual-Level Interventions

There are a number of evidence-based intervention programs to deal with problematic social media use at an individual level that are structured according to clinical approach:

Cognitive-Behavioral Therapy (CBT)

Adapted cognitive-behavioral therapy that targets internet addiction has already proved effective and is able to reduce excessive forms of internet use through the conflict of maladaptive cognitions and the development of alternative ways to cope. The use of specific CBT techniques is:

Cognitive restructuring: Recognizing and disputing terrible thoughts regarding missing social data (e.g., Oh, if I do not check Instagram right now, I will be deprived of the essential information and my friends will think that I am not interested in anything)

Behavioral experiments: Trial of feared consequences of non-engaging (purposeful avoiding platforms due to set time intervals to prove that rejection by the social environment does not happen)

Activity scheduling: To compete with platform engagement, more offline rewarding activities should be increased.

Stimulus control: When removing, deleting, or disabling applications, to unfocus activities that instigate engagement, the removal of stimuli by the app icons is reduced.

Mindfulness-Based Interventions

Mindfulness interventions that teach people to be more aware of emotions and automatic behavioral impulses are also effective; participants who underwent training in mindfulness are more able to notice impulses to check social media without directly responding to them and breaking the stimulusresponse habit cycle (Ivanova and Papadaki, 2019). One of the practices is the "**urge surfing:**" an experience of urgency to view some notifications, the user not only notices the urge but in matters like the intensity, its position in the body, and accompanying thoughts, and refrains from the behavioral response; the desire usually cresses in 20-30 seconds and fades.

Motivation Enhancement/Motivational Interviewing

Motivation enhancement technics based on motivational interviewing postulates are effective as they combat ambivalence regarding any change of behavior; most of the individuals who use social media in an abusive manner at the same time have a desire to reduce their use but feel that they cannot do this thus generating ambivalence which is predictive of low intervention success (Miller and Rollnick, 2012).

Neurobiological justification of interventions: It is known that dopamine withdrawal can lead to actual dysphoria and anhedonia, which last between 3-8 weeks to validate the difficulty of users and plan in the most adequate way. The transition gradually with replacement with other rewarding activities is often more likely to be sustained than a sudden removal as it is neurobiologically easier to adjust to, as well as preserves hedonic tone via the alternative sources of reward.

Collective and Policy Interventions

Policy interventions at societal levels are promising to help deal with social media addiction on how incentive systems within the platforms can be restructured:

Regulatory Approaches

The proposed regulatory mechanisms are:

- Algorithmic Restrictions and Transparency - Restrictions on content personalization by algorithm allowed due to psychological vulnerabilities.
- Data Protection and Limitation - Bans on data gathering and retention time-button on micro-targeting adverts based on vulnerabilities to psychological persuasion.
- Engagement Metrics and Disclosure - Required disclosure of time engaged a day to the user.
- Age-Based Protections - Minimum age checks to access content - Children requirement to access content consent through their parents.
- Corporate Liability- Corporate liability of addiction-related harms equivalent to tobacco cases.

Educational Interventions

Interventions based on media literacy and critical awareness that educate users on the principles of platform design and business models can greatly help to become resistant to addiction since users knowing the methods by which likes-based metrics purposefully create a social comparison opportunity and the real purpose of the notifications demonstrate reduced consumption and increased control of engagement (Livingstone, 2008).

Organizational and Clinical Approaches

There is a lack of clinical and treatment recognition and treatment of social media addiction in mental health service systems and lack of treatment programs. The creation of standardized diagnostic criteria, treatment regimens, and clinical education on how to treat social media addiction is a gap of the crucial importance (Kuss et al., 2014). Preliminary care programs that are based on CBT, motivational enhancement, and social media addiction peer support display encouraging initial results, but extensive studies are required (Tsitsika et al., 2014).

Recommendations to the organization: - Universities and schools ought to identify problematic use of social media - Mental health ought to devise specialized assessment and treatment guidelines.

Overall, evidence-based intervention can take the form of individual (CBT, mindfulness, ACT, motivational interviewing), design (structural changes, provisions of the algorithm, which is transparent), policy (regulation, data protection, liability), and organizational (clinical protocols, educational programs) intervention.Lasting changes demand a multi-level intervention that involves structural factors.

FUTURE RESEARCH DIRECTIONS AND CRITICAL PERSPECTIVE

The Social Justice Dimensions of Social Media Addiction

Most research on addiction has focused on individual psychology and behavior change, though, critical accounts highlight that social media addiction has a disproportionately negative impact on vulnerable groups: teenagers who are young and therefore with insufficiently developed prefrontal cortices controlling impulsivity tend to be more vulnerable, those with pre-existing mental illness issues, social outcasts, and disadvantaged populations with fewer social opportunities in the offline world (Duffy et al., 2019). This unequal effect brings deep social justice issues.

Developmental vulnerability: Adolescents who have underdeveloped impulse control and are more socially sensitive are more prone to addiction - Mental health vulnerability: People with depression, anxiety, or ADHD, are more vulnerable to addiction - Social vulnerability: There are people with limited offline social options or social anxiety; these individuals are more threatened by such an addiction - Marginalization: LGBTQ+ youths, racial/ethnic minorities, and other disadvantaged groups are at risk of experiencing such an addiction.

The Role of Regulatory Frameworks

The future development of solving social media addiction seems to be much more regulated on the national and international levels. The failure of voluntary self-regulation of the corporate has been very evident, documents related to platform internal operations show that they are conscious of the addictive design effects, but they are still optimized to attract the greatest number of engagements due to the fiduciary obligation to the shareholders to increase profits. Nonetheless, stricter regulatory structures with specific focus on the addiction-maximizing structure are still needed.

Possible regulatory solutions are:

- Prohibitions on psychological susceptibility of content personalization by algorithms.
- Obligations on open API that guarantees the option of using algorithmic feeds by the user.

- Time disclosed compulsory daily interaction labels such as nutrition labels.
- Limitations on psychological manipulation (notifications pre-emption) Poised to engage, displayed as metrics).
- User verification on age and permission by parents below 16.
- Litigation on addiction-related evils of corporations just like tobacco.
- Duty of care standards demanding a reduction in addictive design attributes in the platform.
- Compulsory addiction-impact evaluations as condition of business operation.

Whether such regulatory methods are effective or not is yet to be established empirically as it is implemented in the EU and other jurisdictions perhaps.

Future Research Directions and Methodological Priorities

Although the social media addiction research has made considerable grounds in recent years, there are still uncovered knowledge gaps that need to be addressed through research investment:

Priorities 1: The Longitudinal Research of Developmental Trajectories

Longitudinal studies considering consumption patterns since first platform use until possible development of addiction and recovery are scant; the majority of literature is available in cross-sectional correlational studies, which are incapable of explaining causal processes and developmental processes. **Research required:** - Multi-wave longitudinal designs that follow individuals since initial adoption to possible problematic use - Experience sampling methods (ecological momentary assessment) which measures real time patterns of engagement, affective states and mood fluctuations.

Priority 2: Cross Cultural and Global Research

Most of the available studies look at the population of Western/Global North; it is crucial to know cultural differences in FOMO, susceptibility to addiction, and intervention benefits. **Research required: -** Comparative studies on the patterns of FOMO and addiction between individualist and collectivist cultures - Studies on the variation in platform design between different parts of the world (WeChat, LINE vs. Instagram, Tik Tok) and how the differences in the two impact the rates of addiction.

Toward Digital Humanism: A Vision for Systemic Change

To deal with the problem of social media addiction it is necessary to shift the individual responsibility approach into a more systematic approach involving the understanding that addiction is the result of a combination of platform design, monetary incentives as well as individual susceptibility.

Systemic change entails a vision of:

- **Regulatory frameworks** overhauling system of platform incentives to emphasize user welfare, not user engagement maximisation.
- **Reform in design** with safety and well-being as the aims and not as the by products.
- **Accountability and transparency** that mandate platforms open up about addiction risks, engagement optimization methods as well as harm measurements.
- **Philanthropic health solutions** that manage social media addiction as a social health crisis that requires research support, professional education, and prevention interventions should be funded.
- **cultural transformations** develop a movement in which consumption is replaced by purposeful and values-oriented utilization.

This systematic method is aware of the significance of individual interventions but these interventions are not sufficient and deep enough to deal with phenomena as a result of carefully designed systems within economic systems oriented at profit maximization.

Overall, there is a disproportionate sample of vulnerable populations impacted by social media addiction as it poses a social justice issue. The solution to this needs to be systematic change that involves regulatory, design, educational, and clinical reforms.

CONCLUSION

Social media addiction and FOMO are complex phenomena residing at the intersection of psychological, neurobiological, and economic systems. This integrative synthesis has demonstrated that addiction results from the predatory exploitation of underlying vulnerabilities by a "FOMO-fuelled economy" that monetizes human distress.

FOMO serves as both a psychological state of social exclusion anxiety and a financialized tool developed strategically to drive platform engagement. Depression, anxiety, loneliness, sleep disturbance, and in extreme events even suicidal ideation, constitutes the human cost of the economic systems that are based on the generation of psychological harm through the use of social media as a tool. A multi-level psychological framework of understanding social media addiction shows that individual intervention in changing behavior is not only potentially beneficial but also targets what is on the surface and not the structure. Platforms create an addictive experience by purposeful design, serving as an economic system getting off on the growth of addiction instead of a deterrent to its growth.

The **FOMO-fuelled economy** is a severe threat to modern psychology, the well-being of people, and the democratic society. To move forward, it demands various fields of action: regulatory policies to introduce legal provisions of human-centered design; technology development of alternative platforms and governance models; clinical research of treatment with evidence; educational activities to develop digital literacy; and culture adjusting values to consumption to careful living.

The remedies to addiction to social media cannot also be through platforms since platforms have economic interests that are in direct contradiction to the well-being of the users. Instead, they need solutions that are provided outside, and they include regulation, community action, technology alternatives, clinical systems and personal consciousness. Such systemic intervention through such levels is all that can help the society move beyond technologies that merely take advantage of the vulnerability of humans to the ones that actually contribute to the flourishing of the human.

REFERENCES

Abi-Jaoude, E., Naylor, K. T., & Pignatiello, A. (2020). Smartphones, social media use and youth mental health. *Canadian Medical Association Journal, 192*(6), E136–E141. DOI: 10.1503/cmaj.190434 PMID: 32041697

Ahmmad, M., Shahzad, K., Iqbal, A., & Latif, M. (2025). Trap of social media algorithms: A systematic review of research on filter bubbles, echo chambers, and their impact on youth. *Societies (Basel, Switzerland), 15*(11), 301. DOI: 10.3390/soc15110301

Alberts, L., Lyngs, U., & Lukoff, K. (2024). Designing for sustained motivation: A review of Self-Determination Theory in behaviour change technologies. *Interacting with Computers, 38*(3), 447–468. DOI: 10.1093/iwc/iwae040

Alshowkan, A., Alsalem, A., Alsulaim, R., Almakki, S., Alqahtani, D., Alsalem, F., & Alshahrani, H. (2025). Fear of missing out, social media addiction, and personality traits among Saudi Arabia university students. *Journal of Education. Health and Community Psychology, 14*(1), 1–15.

Alt, D. (2015). College students' academic motivation, media engagement and fear of missing out. *Computers in Human Behavior, 49*, 111–119. DOI: 10.1016/j.chb.2015.02.057

American Psychiatric Association. (2013). *Diagnostic and statistical manual of mental disorders* (5th ed.)., DOI: 10.1176/appi.books.9780890425596

Backman, N. (2025). *Design against deception: Shifting towards wellbeing-supportive social media platforms* [Master's thesis, Aalto University]. Aalto University Repository. https://aaltodoc.aalto.fi/bitstreams/9b2e932d-ac84-4a9a-9c65-d5a3ada23c87/download

Baker, R. K., & White, K. M. (2010). Predicting adolescents' use of social networking sites from an extended theory of planned behaviour perspective. *Computers in Human Behavior, 26*(6), 1591–1597. DOI: 10.1016/j.chb.2010.06.006

Barry, C. T., Sidoti, C. L., Briggs, S. M., Reiter, S. R., & Lindsey, R. A. (2017). Adolescent social media use and mental health from adolescent and parent perspectives. *Journal of Adolescence, 61*(1), 1–11. DOI: 10.1016/j.adolescence.2017.08.005 PMID: 28886571

Battistone, M. J., Kemeyou, L., & Varpio, L. (2023). The theoretical integrative review: A reader's guide. *Journal of Graduate Medical Education, 15*(4), 449–452. DOI: 10.4300/JGME-D-23-00265.1 PMID: 37637333

Beard, K. W., & Wolf, E. M. (2001). Modification of the proposed diagnostic criteria for internet addiction. *Cyberpsychology & Behavior*, *4*(3), 377–383. DOI: 10.1089/109493101300210286 PMID: 11710263

Berridge, K. C., & Robinson, T. E. (2016). Liking, wanting, and the incentive-sensitization theory of addiction. *The American Psychologist*, *71*(8), 670–679. DOI: 10.1037/amp0000059 PMID: 27977239

Brand, M., Müller, A., Wegmann, E., Antons, S., Brandtner, A., Müller, S. M., Stark, R., Steins-Loeber, S., & Potenza, M. N. (2025). Current interpretations of the I-PACE model of behavioral addictions. *Journal of Behavioral Addictions*, *14*(1), 1–17. DOI: 10.1556/2006.2025.00020 PMID: 40063161

Brand, M., Young, K. S., Laier, C., Wölfling, K., & Potenza, M. N. (2016). Integrating psychological and neurobiological considerations regarding the development and maintenance of specific Internet-use disorders: An Interaction of Person-Affect-Cognition-Execution (I-PACE) model. *Neuroscience and Biobehavioral Reviews*, *71*, 252–266. DOI: 10.1016/j.neubiorev.2016.08.033 PMID: 27590829

Chang, A. M., Aeschbach, D., Duffy, J. F., & Czeisler, C. A. (2015). Evening use of light-emitting eReaders negatively affects sleep, circadian timing, and next-morning alertness. *Proceedings of the National Academy of Sciences of the United States of America*, *112*(4), 1232–1237. DOI: 10.1073/pnas.1418490112 PMID: 25535358

Chen, J., Yu, Z., Ni, R., Zhou, J., & Qu, J. (2025). The effects of social media addiction on college students' psychological anxiety: The mediating role of self-efficacy and coping styles. *Frontiers in Psychology*, *16*, 1676899. DOI: 10.3389/fpsyg.2025.1676899 PMID: 41229591

Cialdini, R. B. (2009). *Influence: Science and practice* (5th ed.). Pearson Education.

Czeisler, C. A., & Gooley, J. J. (2007). Sleep and circadian rhythms in humans. *Cold Spring Harbor Symposia on Quantitative Biology*, *72*(1), 579–597. DOI: 10.1101/sqb.2007.72.064 PMID: 18419318

Davenport, T. H., & Beck, J. C. (2001). *The attention economy: Understanding the new currency of business*. Harvard Business School Press.

Deci, E. L., & Ryan, R. M. (1985). *Intrinsic motivation and self-determination in human behavior*. Plenum Press., DOI: 10.1007/978-1-4899-2271-7

Deshmukh, V., Dange, N., Dhangond, A., Samrit, K., & Pawar, R. (2025). Social media addiction: Causes & effects. *International Journal of Advanced Research in Computer and Communication Engineering*, *8*(11). Advance online publication. DOI: 10.17148/IJARCCE.2025.1411133

Devitt, S. J., Austen, L., & Parkin, H. J. (2017). Integrative reviewing for exploring complex phenomena. *Social Research Update*, (66). https://sru.soc.surrey.ac.uk/SRU66.pdf

Dhollande, S., Taylor, A., Meyer, S., & Scott, M. (2021). Conducting integrative reviews: A guide for novice nursing researchers. *Journal of Research in Nursing : JRN*, *26*(5), 427–438. DOI: 10.1177/1744987121997907 PMID: 35251272

Dolan, E. W. (2026, April 21). Short video addiction is linked to lower life satisfaction through loneliness and anxiety. *PsyPost*. https://www.psypost.org/short-video-addiction-is-linked-to-lower-life-satisfaction-through-loneliness-and-anxiety/

Duc, T. M. (2025). Excessive social media use and its impact on psychological well-being and academic performance of Vietnamese university students. *International Journal of Adolescence and Youth*, *31*(1), 2608766. Advance online publication. DOI: 10.1080/02673843.2025.2608766

Duffy, A., Saunders, K. E. A., Malhi, G. S., Patten, S., Cipriani, A., McNevin, S. H., MacDonald, E., & Geddes, J. (2019). Mental health care for university students: A way forward? *The Lancet. Psychiatry*, *6*(11), 885–887. DOI: 10.1016/S2215-0366(19)30275-5 PMID: 31324561

Ellison, N. B., Vitak, J., Gray, R., & Lampe, C. (2014). Cultivating social resources on social network sites: Facebook relationship maintenance behaviors and their role in social capital processes. *Journal of Computer-Mediated Communication*, *19*(4), 855–870. DOI: 10.1111/jcc4.12078

Gray, J. A. (1970). The psychophysiological basis of introversion-extraversion. *Behaviour Research and Therapy*, *8*(3), 249–266. DOI: 10.1016/0005-7967(70)90069-0 PMID: 5470377

Griffiths, M. (2005). A 'components' model of addiction within a biopsychosocial framework. *Journal of Substance Use*, *10*(4), 191–197. DOI: 10.1080/14659890500114359

Haidt, J., & Rausch, Z. (2026). Social media is harming adolescents at a scale large enough to cause changes at the population level. In *The World Happiness Report*. DOI: 10.18724/WHR-G490-BG86

Harris, B. (2019). *When to put the scroll down: How infinite scroll affects user experience and engagement*. UX Planet. https://uxplanet.org/infinite-scroll-design-patterns-9b5b6c0e7e47

Harris, B., & Sandoval, M. (2020). Datafication and commodification of the self: From digital labor to digital asset. In *The SAGE handbook of digital society* (pp. 227–244). SAGE Publications.

Hindman, J., Zugai, J., Foster, K., & Raeburn, T. (2025). Self-Determination Theory as a framework for research and design of digital applications for nurses' well-being. *Journal of Advanced Nursing*, *82*(1), 897–906. DOI: 10.1111/jan.16895 PMID: 40098227

Hunt, M. G., Marx, R., Lipson, C., & Young, J. (2018). No more FOMO: Limiting social media decreases loneliness and depression. *Journal of Social and Clinical Psychology*, *37*(10), 751–768. DOI: 10.1521/jscp.2018.37.10.751

Ihde, S. (2021). Algorithmic serendipity and the paradox of exposure: Evaluating the role of recommendation algorithms in online harm. *Media and Communication*, *9*(1), 194–206. DOI: 10.17645/mac.v9i1.3501

Ivanova, V., & Papadaki, M. (2019). The effects of mindfulness-based interventions on physical pain: A systematic review. *International Journal of Environmental Research and Public Health*, *16*(23), 4719. DOI: 10.3390/ijerph16234719 PMID: 31779281

JBI. (2026). *JBI critical appraisal tools*. https://jbi.global/critical-appraisal-tools

Jiang, Y. (2026). Surveillance capitalism and social media addiction. *Information, Medium, and Society: Journal of Publishing Studies*. DOI: 10.18848/2691-1507/CGP/A35

Kardefelt-Winther, D. (2014). A conceptual and methodological critique of internet addiction research: Towards a model of compensatory internet use. *Computers in Human Behavior*, *31*, 351–354. DOI: 10.1016/j.chb.2013.10.059

Kuss, D. J., & Griffiths, M. D. (2017). Social media addiction—An overview of prevalence, etiology and consequences. *Journal of Behavioral Addictions*, *6*(4), 529–543. DOI: 10.1556/2006.6.2017.069

Kuss, D. J., Griffiths, M. D., Karila, L., & Billieux, J. (2014). Internet addiction: A systematic review of epidemiological research for the last decade. *Current Pharmaceutical Design*, *20*(25), 4026–4052. DOI: 10.2174/13816128113199990617 PMID: 24001297

Laidler, J. (2019, March 4). Harvard professor says surveillance capitalism is undermining democracy. *Harvard Gazette*. https://news.harvard.edu/gazette/story/2019/03/harvard-professor-says-surveillance-capitalism-is-undermining-democracy/

Liimatainen, L., Latvala, E., & Hopia, H. (2016). Reviewing the methodology of an integrative review. *Scandinavian Journal of Caring Sciences*, *30*(4), 662–669. DOI: 10.1111/scs.12327 PMID: 27074869

Lin, L. Y., Sidani, J. E., Shensa, A., Radovic, A., Miller, E., Colditz, J. B., Hoffman, B. L., Giles, L. M., & Primack, B. A. (2016). Association between social media use and depression among U.S. young adults. *Depression and Anxiety*, *33*(4), 323–331. DOI: 10.1002/da.22466 PMID: 26783723

Livingstone, S. (2008). Taking risky opportunities in youthful content creation: Teenagers' use of social networking sites for intimacy, privacy and self-expression. *New Media & Society*, *10*(3), 393–411. DOI: 10.1177/1461444808089415

Lutz, C., & Tamó-Larrieux, A. (2020). The robot privacy paradox: Understanding how privacy concerns shape intentions to use social robots. *Human-Machine Communication*, *1*, 87–111. DOI: 10.30658/hmc.1.6

Meynadier, J., Malouff, J. M., Schutte, N. S., & Loi, N. M. (2025). Using social media to cope with psychological distress and fear of missing out: The role of social media reward expectancies in social media addiction. *International Journal of Human-Computer Interaction*, *41*(20), 12687–12696. DOI: 10.1080/10447318.2025.2464894

Miller, W. R., & Rollnick, S. (2012). *Motivational interviewing: Helping people change*. Guilford Press.

Montag, C., Błaszkiewicz, K., Sariyska, R., Lachmann, B., Andone, I., Trendafilov, B., & Markowetz, A. (2015). Smartphone usage patterns and personality: The context of cultural differences. *Frontiers in Psychology*, *6*, 33. DOI: 10.3389/fpsyg.2015.00033

Moretta, T., & Wegmann, E. (2025). Toward the classification of social media use disorder: Clinical characterization and proposed diagnostic criteria. *Addictive Behaviors Reports*, *21*, 100603. DOI: 10.1016/j.abrep.2025.100603 PMID: 40256627

Nutt, D., King, L. A., Saulsbury, W., & Blakemore, C. (2010). Development of a rational scale to assess the harm of drugs of potential misuse. *Lancet*, *369*(9566), 1047–1053. DOI: 10.1016/S0140-6736(07)60464-4 PMID: 17382831

Przybylski, A. K., Murayama, K., DeHaan, C. R., & Gladwell, V. (2013). Motivational, emotional, and behavioral correlates of fear of missing out. *Computers in Human Behavior*, *29*(4), 1841–1848. DOI: 10.1016/j.chb.2013.02.014

Riemann, D., Krone, L. B., Wulff, K., & Nissen, C. (2019). Sleep, insomnia, and depression. *Neuropsychopharmacology : Official Publication of the American College of Neuropsychopharmacology*, *45*(1), 74–89. DOI: 10.1038/s41386-019-0411-y PMID: 31071719

Rosen, L. D., Carrier, L. M., & Cheever, N. A. (2013). Facebook and texting made me do it: Media-induced task-switching while studying. *Computers in Human Behavior*, *29*(3), 948–958. DOI: 10.1016/j.chb.2012.12.001

Ryan, R. M., & Deci, E. L. (2000). Self-determination theory and the facilitation of intrinsic motivation, social development, and well-being. *The American Psychologist*, *55*(1), 68–78. DOI: 10.1037/0003-066X.55.1.68 PMID: 11392867

Satani, A., Satani, K. K., Barodia, P., & Joshi, H. (2025). Modern day high: The neurocognitive impact of social media usage. *Cureus*, *17*(7), e87496. DOI: 10.7759/cureus.87496 PMID: 40777702

Schultz, W. (2007). Behavioral dopamine signals. *Trends in Neurosciences*, *30*(5), 203–210. DOI: 10.1016/j.tins.2007.03.007 PMID: 17400301

Shaffer, H. J., LaPlante, D. A., LaBrie, R. A., Kidman, R. C., Donato, A. N., & Stanton, M. V. (2005). Toward a syndrome model of addiction: Multiple expressions, common etiology. *Harvard Review of Psychiatry*, *12*(6), 367–374. DOI: 10.1080/10673220490905705 PMID: 15764471

Singer, J. A., & Omary, A. (2026, April 16). *The case against social media "addiction."* Cato Institute. https://www.cato.org/blog/case-against-social-media-addiction

Spada, M. M. (2014). An overview of problematic internet use. *Addictive Behaviors*, *39*(1), 3–6. DOI: 10.1016/j.addbeh.2013.09.007 PMID: 24126206

Statista. (2025). *Number of social media users worldwide 2018–2025*. https://www.statista.com/forecasts/277694/number-of-internet-users-in-the-world

Thaler, R. H., & Sunstein, C. R. (2008). *Nudge: Improving decisions about health, wealth, and happiness*. Yale University Press.

Trigueros, R., Aguilar-Parra, J. M., López-Liria, R., & Rocamora, P. (2019). The dark side of the Self-Determination Theory and its influence on the emotional and cognitive processes of students in physical education. *International Journal of Environmental Research and Public Health*, *16*(22), 4444. DOI: 10.3390/ijerph16224444 PMID: 31726790

Tsitsika, A. K., Janikian, M., Schoenmakers, T. M., Tzavela, E., Olafsson, K., Iordache, A., & Richardson, C. (2014). Internet addictive behavior in adolescence: A cross-sectional study in seven European countries. *Cyberpsychology, Behavior, and Social Networking, 17*(8), 518–525. DOI: 10.1089/cyber.2013.0382 PMID: 24853789

Twenge, J. M., & Campbell, W. K. (2019). Media use is linked to lower psychological well-being: Evidence from three datasets. *The Psychiatric Quarterly, 90*(2), 311–331. DOI: 10.1007/s11126-019-09630-7 PMID: 30859387

Twenge, J. M., Martin, G. N., & Campbell, W. K. (2018). Decreases in psychological well-being among American adolescents after 2012 and links to screen time during the rise of smartphone technology. *Emotion (Washington, D.C.), 18*(6), 765–780. DOI: 10.1037/emo0000403 PMID: 29355336

Vannucci, A., Flannery, K. M., & Ohannessian, C. M. (2017). Social media use and anxiety in emerging adults. *Journal of Affective Disorders, 207*, 163–166. DOI: 10.1016/j.jad.2016.08.040 PMID: 27723539

Volkow, N. D., Wang, G. J., Begleiter, H., Porjesz, B., Fowler, J. S., Telang, F., & Logan, J. (2006). High levels of dopamine D2 receptors in unaffected members of alcoholic families: Possible protective factors. *Archives of General Psychiatry, 63*(9), 999–1008. DOI: 10.1001/archpsyc.63.9.999 PMID: 16953002

Whittemore, R., & Knafl, K. (2005). The integrative review: Updated methodology. *Journal of Advanced Nursing, 52*(5), 546–553. DOI: 10.1111/j.1365-2648.2005.03621.x PMID: 16268861

Yang, C., Mousavi, S., Dash, A., Gummadi, K. P., & Weber, I. (2025). *Studying behavioral addiction by combining surveys and digital traces: A case study of TikTok*. arXiv. https://arxiv.org/pdf/2501.15539

Zuboff, S. (2019). *The age of surveillance capitalism: The fight for a human future at the new frontier of power*. PublicAffairs.

ADDITIONAL READINGS

Allcott, H., Braghieri, L., Eichmeyer, S., & Gentzkow, M. (2020). The welfare effects of social media. *The American Economic Review, 110*(3), 629–676. DOI: 10.1257/aer.20190658

Cano-Gillis, S. (2023). *Subjective Well-being Among Adolescents Who Engage in Social Media*. Michigan School of Psychology.

Haidt, J., & Allen, N. (2020). Scrutinizing the effects of digital technology on mental health.

Nasr, S. A., Sunitiyoso, Y., & Suhaimi, H. (2023). The effect of fear of missing out on buying and post-purchasing behaviour toward Indonesia's Generation Z online shoppers (Case study: E-commerce Indonesia). *International Journal of Current Science Research and Review*, *6*(09), 6246–6262. DOI: 10.47191/ijcsrr/V6-i9-15

Pranesh, S., & Gupta, S. (2024). The impact of social media on polarization in the society. *arXiv preprint arXiv:2408.12877.*

Tullett-Prado, D., Doley, J. R., Zarate, D., Gomez, R., & Stavropoulos, V. (2023). Conceptualising social media addiction: A longitudinal network analysis of social media addiction symptoms and their relationships with psychological distress in a community sample of adults. *BMC Psychiatry*, *23*(1), 509. DOI: 10.1186/s12888-023-04985-5 PMID: 37442974

KEY TERMS AND DEFINITIONS

Dark Patterns (ACDPs): User interface design choices, specifically Attention-Capture Damaging Patterns, engineered to manipulate cognitive biases and psychological susceptibilities to maximize user interaction time and data extraction.

Epistemic Inequality: A structural knowledge imbalance where digital platforms possess comprehensive predictive insights into user behavior while users remain uninformed about the algorithmic processes shaping their digital experiences.

IINA Framework: The Instrumentarian-Neuro-Affective Framework, a theoretical synthesis proposing that digital addiction is a closed-loop system where macro-economic platform incentives intentionally exploit individual neurobiological and psychological vulnerabilities.

Instrumentarian Power: A form of digital authority that operates through ubiquitous digital instrumentation to manipulate subliminal cues and choice architectures, aimed at remotely tuning and modifying human behavior for economic gain.

Social Media Addiction: A behavioral disorder characterized by a compulsive and uncontrollable urge to engage with social networking platforms, leading to functional impairment in personal, occupational, and social spheres despite awareness of detrimental consequences. **Fear of Missing Out (FOMO):** A pervasive psychological state involving apprehension that others are having rewarding experiences from which one is absent, typically accompanied by a desire to remain digitally connected to monitor social dynamics.

Surveillance Capitalism: An economic logic where human experience is extracted as free raw material for translation into behavioral data, which is then processed into prediction products and sold in dedicated behavioral futures markets.

Chapter 8
An Examination of Online Shopping Addiction in the Context of FOMO (Fear Of Missing Out)

Asena Irmak Kuş
http://orcid.org/0009-0007-4562-8001
Marmara University, Turkey

ABSTRACT

This study examines the construction of online shopping addiction within the context of Fear of Missing Out (FOMO) in digital consumption environments. With the rise of digitalization, consumption has shifted from a need-based activity to a continuous, emotionally driven practice. The study adopts a qualitative research design and applies critical discourse analysis to textual elements from an e-commerce platform. Findings reveal that discursive strategies such as scarcity, urgency, social proof, and emotional persuasion systematically trigger FOMO and accelerate impulsive purchasing behavior. These mechanisms operate together to weaken rational decision-making and reinforce repetitive consumption patterns. As a result, online shopping behavior evolves into a cyclical process associated with temporary satisfaction and long-term loss of control. The study highlights the role of digital platforms in shaping consumer behavior and contributes to understanding the psychological and structural dynamics underlying online shopping addiction.

DOI: 10.4018/979-8-3373-6665-4.ch008

INTRODUCTION

Today, people live in constant interaction with technology. As technology advances, the number of phenomena integrated into our lives continues to grow. With the acceleration of digitalization, individuals' daily life practices have entered a process of profound transformation. This transformation has not only affected communication methods and ways of accessing information but has also reshaped the relationship individuals have with consumption. With the rapid development of technology and the increasing speed, widespread availability, and uninterrupted nature of internet access, the time individuals spend on platforms in their daily lives has significantly increased, leading to a growing interest in and attachment to digitalization (Çopuroğlu, 2021). With the widespread adoption of the internet and the advancement of mobile technologies, consumption has become independent of time and place constraints. As a result, the act of shopping has evolved from a planned behavior into a continuous and accessible practice integrated into the flow of daily life. This new form of consumption provides individuals with speed and convenience while also significantly transforming decision-making processes. The personalized content, instant notifications, limited-time campaigns, and visibility-focused structures offered by digital platforms shape an individual's consumption behavior not only through rational evaluations but also through emotional and psychological processes. In this context, consumption no longer represents merely the fulfillment of a need. Consumption has evolved into a multi-layered phenomenon that carries meanings such as belonging, being up-to-date, and social positioning. Particularly in online environments, individuals' constant exposure to others' experiences further intertwines consumption behavior with social comparison mechanisms.

One of the key concepts emerging during this transformation process is FOMO (Fear of Missing Out). FOMO increases an individual's motivation to stay constantly up-to-date and avoid being left out of these experiences, driven by the anxiety they feel about missing out on opportunities others are experiencing. In digital consumption environments, this situation drives individuals to act impulsively. Consequently, consumption behavior shifts away from being need-based and often takes on a structure rooted in momentary, impulsive, and emotional reactions. On the other hand, the design features and marketing strategies of digital platforms are among the key dynamics that support the emergence and perpetuation of FOMO. Discursive strategies such as emphasizing scarcity, creating a sense of urgency, using social proof, and emotional manipulation accelerate the individual's decision-making process, thereby encouraging consumption. In this process, the individual may engage in purchasing behavior without questioning their needs, simply to avoid missing out on an opportunity. This repeatedly occurring behavioral pattern can, over time, lay the groundwork for online shopping addiction, characterized by a loss of control, recurring urges to purchase, and feelings of regret.

This study aims to examine how online shopping addiction is constructed and reproduced within the context of FOMO in digital consumption environments. In this regard, by examining the impact of discursive strategies employed on digital platforms on individuals' perceptions and behaviors, the study reveals how consumption is shaped through emotional, psychological, and social dynamics. In this regard, the study aims to contribute to the understanding of contemporary consumption practices and to evaluate consumption behaviors that are becoming increasingly visible in the digital environment from a multidimensional perspective.

LITERATURE REVIEW

Digital Consumption and Online Shopping

With the advancement of technology, traditional consumption habits have largely given way to digital consumption habits. Digitalization has fundamentally transformed not only forms of communication but also the relationship individuals have with consumption. Digital technologies, which have permeated nearly every aspect of daily life, have freed consumption from the constraints of time and place while simultaneously making it a faster, more visible, and continuous practice. Consumption is no longer limited to merely fulfilling a need; it is often reproduced as a symbol of belonging, relevance, and individual identity. One of the most visible areas of this transformation is online shopping. Online shopping is a form of commerce that refers to individuals conducting processes such as obtaining information, comparing, and purchasing products or services through internet-based digital platforms (Armağan & Temel, 2018). As physical stores increasingly give way to digital platforms, the shopping experience has been transformed into a seamless and instantaneous one. E-commerce platforms, as key sites where digital capitalism becomes visible, provide significant examples for understanding the transformation of consumption behaviors. The rapid expansion of e-commerce and the increasing pressure on traditional retail formats to digitalize are largely driven by shifts in consumers' shopping practices and preferences (Demirkaya & Koyuncu, 2021). The ability to access products with a single click accelerates the consumption process while significantly shortening the decision-making phase. As a result, individuals often engage in consumption behavior guided by digital prompts without even questioning their needs. Digital consumption culture has a structure that constantly calls the individual to the present moment. Campaigns, discounts, and recommendations offered on online shopping platforms do not merely promote a product; they also create a perception focused on the individual's fear of missing out. Phrases like "limited time," "last items," and "best sellers" transform consumption from a rational choice into an emotional reaction. At this point, consumption ceases to be a planned action and becomes an impulsive, often thoughtless behavior. Algorithms and personalized content further reinforce this aspect of digital consumption. Online shopping sites and social media platforms analyze individuals' past behaviors to offer recommendations. This makes it difficult for the individual to distinguish what they truly need, while constantly encouraging consumption. These "personalized" recommendations actually enable the pressure of digital consumption to operate in a more invisible and effective manner. This structure of online shopping transforms consumption from a purely economic activity into a multi-layered process with cultural and psychological dimensions. Through their purchasing behavior in the online environment, individuals aim not merely to acquire a product, but to be part of a specific trend, participate in a simultaneous consumption practice with others, and avoid the feeling of being left behind. In this regard, online shopping transcends a simple purchasing experience to become part of social comparison mechanisms and the pursuit of digital visibility. Consequently, digital consumption functions as one of the ways individuals position themselves relative to others and express their identity. Within this framework, digital consumption and online shopping are not merely practices that save time and space in modern society. Digital consumption and online shopping emerge as dynamics that guide individuals' decision-making processes and transform consumption into a continuous structure. Built on the principles of speed, accessibility, and visibility, this system often unconsciously directs individuals toward greater consumption while simultaneously redefining the meaning and social function of consumption.

As digitalization has gained momentum, significant transformations have occurred in many aspects of individuals' daily lives, and these transformations have affected not only forms of communication or ways of accessing information but also the relationship individuals have with consumption (Ökten, 2025). In particular, consumption preferences, habits, and decision-making processes at both the individual and societal levels have begun to be reshaped in line with the opportunities offered by digital technologies. The act of shopping, which was once tied to a specific time frame, location, and often a preparation process, has today transformed into an action embedded within the flow of daily life. A brief screen scroll while waiting for a bus, just before going to sleep at night, or simply to pass the time can result in a purchase without the user even realizing it. In this sense, online shopping has become a natural part of daily routine rather than a planned act of necessity. When all these elements are considered together, it becomes clear that digital consumption and online shopping are not merely tools that provide convenience. This structure operates as a system that transforms an individual's perception of time, decision-making process, and definition of need. At this very point, it becomes evident that online shopping can evolve into a behavioral pattern associated with a cycle of repeated pleasure-seeking, loss of control, and regret. The limitless and stimulating environment offered by digital consumption provides a crucial foundation for understanding the phenomenon of online shopping addiction, which will be addressed in the next section. This transformative process has also fundamentally altered the temporal structure of consumption. While traditional consumption practices were tied to specific time frames and moments of need, these boundaries have largely dissolved in the digital consumption environment. The act of consumption has become a continuous practice, extending to every moment of the day. This situation, in turn, leads to a more intense reshaping of the individual's relationship with consumption. Particularly with the widespread adoption of mobile technologies, shopping has moved beyond being an activity confined to a specific location and has become possible in any environment where the individual is present. Digital environments have significantly transformed consumers' purchasing behaviors by offering time savings, increased transaction speed, and the ability to compare prices and features across products (Karakuş, 2022). Another key feature of digital consumption environments is their capacity to continuously generate stimuli. Through social media platforms, e-commerce sites, and mobile applications, individuals are systematically exposed to new products, campaigns, and recommendations. This constant exposure directs the individual's attention toward consumption and blurs the boundaries of the concept of need. In this context, consumption transforms into a process where it is not merely about fulfilling a lack but also about the continuous reproduction of desire, with the individual actively positioned within this cycle. This dynamic structure lays the groundwork for consumption behavior to become continuous and, over time, evolve into a state that is difficult to control. Indeed, the conditions offered by the digital consumption environment provide a critical framework for understanding the phenomenon of online shopping addiction.

Online Shopping Addiction

Online shopping has become a routine part of daily life thanks to the speed and accessibility it offers. However, for some individuals, this convenience can go beyond simply being a tool to meet their needs and turn into a difficult-to-control behavior. Online shopping helps consumers find the best price for the products they want by providing the opportunity to research and compare prices, thereby simplifying the decision-making process (Häubl & Trifts, 2000, cited in Demirel & Tapan, 2023). In particular, the digital environment's constant production of stimuli creates the conditions for purchasing behavior to occur within a repetitive cycle. Shopping addiction can be considered a significant dimension of consumer buying behavior, as it is closely associated with the emergence of compulsive purchasing tendencies and repetitive consumption patterns driven by psychological and emotional factors (Nash, 2019). At this point, the act of shopping is no longer merely a process of acquiring a product; it begins to function as a means of temporary relief, pleasure, or filling emotional voids. Online shopping addiction is characterized by the individual partially or completely losing control over their purchasing behavior, maintaining a constant mental focus on shopping, and continuing this behavior despite its negative impact on daily life. The intense desire felt before a purchase, the brief pleasure experienced during the act of shopping, and the subsequent feelings of regret form the core components of this cycle. Over time, shopping can become one of the individual's methods for coping with stress, escaping negative emotions, or feeling better.

Online shopping addiction is defined as a condition characterized by the individual's loss of control over their motivation to shop, the behavior causing intense anxiety, and the excessive allocation of time and energy to shopping activities; it is also a condition that negatively impacts other important areas of the individual's life (Andreassen et al., 2015). In this context, online shopping addiction is not a condition that can be explained solely by the individual's lack of control. Online shopping addiction should also be evaluated as a result of the constant stream of stimuli provided by the digital ecosystem in which the individual is embedded. While digital platforms are designed to enhance the user experience, the underlying goal of this design is to keep the individual on the platform for longer periods and encourage interaction. This creates a mechanism that sustains shopping behavior, transforming the act of purchasing from a routine practice into a repetitive habit. In particular, personalized content delivered through algorithms directly appeals to the individual's interests, keeping the desire to purchase constantly alive and laying the groundwork for the uninterrupted reproduction of consumption behavior. Furthermore, the anonymity and ease of access offered by the digital environment are also key factors supporting this process. Although social media plays a beneficial role in this context, its excessive use has been associated with an increased likelihood of individuals developing a stronger dependence on social media platforms (Zhao & Zhou, 2021). Social constraints or time limitations that might be encountered in physical stores are largely eliminated in the online shopping environment. This allows individuals to engage in purchasing behavior with less self-control and to shop more frequently. Shopping behaviors, particularly those occurring late at night or during emotionally vulnerable moments, can be shaped by the individual's fleeting emotions and may subsequently lead to feelings of regret. Another notable aspect of online shopping addiction is how this behavior becomes linked over time to an individual's identity formation and self-expression. Purchasing behaviors on digital platforms go beyond being merely a personal choice and are associated with social visibility and acceptance. An individual may aim to reflect a certain lifestyle, taste, and sense of belonging through the products they purchase. This transforms consumption from merely an economic activity into a social and cultural practice. Thus, shopping can become one of the tools for self-realization and adapting to one's social environment. Another notable aspect of this process is the increasing automation of shopping behavior. Constant exposure to stimuli, repetitive purchasing behaviors, and rapid decision-making processes can transform the individual's shopping action from a conscious choice into a habit-based behavior. This situation leads to a weakening of critical thinking skills during the purchasing process and results in decisions being made more impulsively. Over time, this cycle can lead the individual to feel restless when unable to shop and to view shopping as a form of coping mechanism. In this context, to understand an individual's consumption behaviors, it is necessary to comprehensively examine and evaluate not only their personal motivations but also the digital cues they are exposed to, social comparison processes, and emotional triggers.

FOMO (Fear of Missing Out) and Consumption

The concept of FOMO (Fear of Missing Out) was first used in the literature by Patrick J. McGinnis. McGinnis introduced this concept in his 2004 article titled "Social Theory at HBS: McGinnis." However, the concept was not addressed in the academic literature until later years. In particular, the scientific measurement and theoretical framework of FOMO in the field of psychology were systematically examined in a study published by Andrew K. Przybylski et al. (2013), and the concept began to gain a broader place in academic research. The Cambridge Dictionary (n.d.), defines the concept as a feeling that you might miss out on exciting events others are attending because of what you see on social media. However, in academic literature, fear of missing out (FOMO) is defined as a pervasive and persistent form of anxiety arising from the belief that others are experiencing rewarding and meaningful experiences while the individual is absent from them, and it can be understood within the framework of Self-Determination Theory as resulting from the frustration of individuals' basic psychological needs for autonomy, competence, and relatedness (Przybylski et al., 2013).

FOMO is not merely a simple anxiety about missing out on something; it operates at a deeper level. It causes individuals to define themselves through the experiences of others. This phenomenon has become increasingly visible, particularly with the widespread use of social media platforms. FOMO refers to the anxiety arising from the possibility of missing out on valuable opportunities or experiences, a condition that is further intensified and continuously reinforced through individual's interactions on social media platforms (Nurmalasari et al., 2024). This process is not merely a result of passive exposure; rather, it is shaped by the ways individuals actively engage with digital platforms and the purposes these platforms serve in their daily lives. From the perspective of Uses and Gratifications Theory, individuals actively engage with digital platforms to fulfill various needs such as information seeking, social interaction, and participation in marketplace activities, which increases their exposure to others' experiences and contributes to the intensification of FOMO (Maignan & Lukas, 1997). In this context, individuals no longer merely experience their own lives; they also constantly witness the lives of others. Although this state of witnessing often appears to be a passive viewing process, it actually directly influences the individual's perception of their own life. Being exposed to others' experiences that seem more fun, more fulfilling, or more meaningful can lead the individual to feel that their own experiences are inadequate, and this is where FOMO emerges. FOMO, the anxiety stemming from the thought that others might be experiencing pleasurable moments while one is deprived of them stirs a desire to stay connected online (Aktaş, 2025). This emotion not only increases the individual's desire to participate in social activities but also significantly influences their consumption behaviors. Okazaki et al. (2021) argue that FOMO, when combined with a strong passion for a brand, can significantly reinforce compulsive buying behavior, which may, over time evolve into a broader and more serious social issue. This is because experiences in the digital environment often become visible through consumption. A purchased product, a visited location, or an owned object is no longer merely a personal choice but transforms into a social indicator; thus, the issue shifts from meeting needs to becoming a desire not to fall behind. This relationship between FOMO and consumption becomes particularly evident in online shopping environments. Technological changes and advancements, the primary triggers of FOMO, are significantly transforming consumption practices and individuals' decision-making processes (Alat & Filizöz, 2021). Digital platforms do not merely present products to consumers; they also create the possibility of missing out. Constantly updated campaigns, limited-time discounts, and flash sales directly influence an individual's decision-making process. Whether a product is truly necessary takes a backseat; what matters is not missing out on that opportunity. This situation removes consumption from a rational evaluation process, turning it into behavior driven by emotional reactions. Phrases such as "limited stock," "final hours," or "X people are currently viewing this product" are among the elements that trigger an individual's existing FOMO (Fear of Missing Out) levels. Calls to action such as "limited production" or "last day," along with discount campaigns, coupons, and similar tactics, are deliberately employed by marketers to create a perception of scarcity, as scarcity is one of the potential triggers of FOMO (Hodkinson, 2019). Such messages create a sense of urgency in the individual's mind; this sense of urgency conveys the message that time is running out and accelerates the decision-making process. Since the time allotted for thinking is reduced, the individual often ends up purchasing a product they do not actually need simply to avoid missing out. While this process may feel like a satisfying experience in the short term, it can lead to different outcomes in the long term.

Another important aspect of FOMO is its relationship with social comparison. Social comparison, or social comparison theory, is a psychological theory developed by Leon Festinger in 1954. This theory posits that every individual possesses unique talents and skills; it describes a cognitive framework that enables individuals to position and make sense of themselves by both evaluating these traits internally and comparing them with the qualities possessed by others (Festinger, 1954). As individuals observe others' consumption practices online, they begin to shape their own preferences accordingly. The products others own, the brands they use, and the trends they follow become decisive factors in an individual's own consumption behavior. This situation pushes the individual's unique preferences into the background, and thus consumption increasingly takes on a more homogeneous structure. Similar products are preferred, and similar trends are becoming widespread because avoiding being left behind has become more decisive than standing out. However, FOMO is not merely a factor that triggers purchasing behavior. FOMO also functions as a mechanism that sustains this behavior. When an individual purchases a product, they experience a brief sense of relief; by making the purchase, they feel they haven't missed out and have become part of the trend. However, this feeling is not permanent because the digital environment is constantly evolving. New products, new campaigns, and new trends emerge. Thus, the individual re-enters the same cycle. This cycle creates a structure that oscillates between pleasure and regret. It is precisely at this point that the relationship between FOMO and online shopping addiction becomes clearer. The compulsive purchasing behaviors which individuals struggle to control, are impulsive in nature, and recur repeatedly are conceptualized in the literature as online shopping addiction or online compulsive purchasing behavior when carried out through e-commerce sites operating in the digital environment (Kerse & Yüce, 2022). An individual who is constantly stimulated, guided, and subjected to comparisons may eventually lose control over their consumption behavior. Shopping ceases to be merely an act of fulfilling a need and becomes a tool for emotional regulation. The individual shops to feel good, but since this positive emotion is short-lived, the behavior repeats. This repetition can, over time, turn into a habit, and in some cases, even into an addiction. Therefore, FOMO should not be viewed merely as an individual anxiety condition within the digital consumption culture. Rather, it should be considered a significant psychological mechanism that encourages, accelerates, and sustains consumption. According to Gottberg, FOMO can lead to numerous negative outcomes that negatively impact an individual's life; as a result, individuals fail to appreciate the value of what they possess and thus cannot derive pleasure from these actions (Gottberg, 2017, cited in Tanhan et al., 2022). Especially when considered in the context of online shopping, it is observed that FOMO weakens an individual's decision-making processes, brings emotional reactions to the forefront, and makes consumption behavior more intense and uncontrolled. In this regard, FOMO emerges as one of the key concepts in understanding contemporary consumption practices and explaining online shopping addiction.

Another key concept in understanding the relationship between FOMO and consumption is the perception of scarcity. Scarcity simply refers to the feeling that a product or opportunity is limited; however, what matters here is not whether this limitation is real, but rather how it is perceived. In digital environments, this perception is often deliberately created. Research in the literature demonstrates that perceiving a product as scarce increases consumers' fear of missing out, and this, in turn, triggers impulsive purchasing behavior, thereby reinforcing the reciprocal interaction and cyclical relationship between the perception of scarcity and FOMO (Özer Canarslan, 2025). Phrases like "limited stock," "last 3 items," or "valid only today" create a sense of urgency in the individual's mind. When combined with FOMO, this urgency becomes a powerful motivator. Because the individual no longer merely wants the product; they also want to avoid missing out on it. This situation quietly alters the nature of consumption behavior. Normally, the considerations before purchasing a product are clear: is there a need for it, is the price reasonable, what are the alternatives? However, when the perception of scarcity comes into play, these questions take a backseat, and the individual may purchase a product often without fully understanding why they want it simply because of the thought, "If I don't buy it now, I might never find it again." Marketing strategies come into play precisely at this point. Today's digital marketing approach doesn't just try to understand what the consumer wants; it also analyzes how the consumer makes decisions. The campaigns created as a result of these analyses are often designed to consciously trigger FOMO and the perception of scarcity. For example, the Starbucks brand releases cups designed to match the theme of specific periods (seasons, special days, religious holidays, etc.) to a limited number of consumers each year. Another example is the "flash sale" promotions frequently used on e-commerce platforms. Short-term high discounts catch the individual's attention, but what is truly effective is not the discount rate itself, but the limited timeframe. As the timeframe becomes more restricted, the risk of missing out becomes more real, which directly fuels FOMO; consequently, what matters most to the individual is no longer what they gain, but the possibility of what they might miss out on. Another effect of the perception of scarcity is that it makes the product's value seem higher than it actually is. Cialdini (2021) explains this phenomenon by noting that the rarer a desired product is—or the harder it is to obtain—the more consumers base its perceived reasonable price on its scarcity rather than its perceived quality. Limited items are often perceived as more valuable. This is a psychologically widespread tendency; therefore, presenting a product as scarce or quickly selling out makes it appear more appealing. Here, the individual is not just purchasing the product but also the exclusivity it represents. Owning something that not everyone can have can make a person feel different and special. However, this process does not always lead to such positive outcomes. Moreover, the structure of digital environments as continuously accessible and interaction-driven marketplaces exposes individuals to an ongoing flow of products and opportunities, thereby reinforcing the persistent nature of FOMO and sustaining repetitive consumption tendencies (Ko et al., 2005; Siekpe & Kamssu, 2005). Therefore, FOMO should not be viewed merely as an individual anxiety condition within the digital consumption culture. In this context, in situations where the perception of scarcity and FOMO work together, purchasing behavior often occurs quickly but is not questioned at the same pace. After the product is purchased, the sense of relief the individual initially felt may soon give way to doubt. These doubts typically emerge after the purchase has taken place, creating a cycle that oscillates between consumption, pleasure, and regret. The striking aspect of this cycle is its ability to constantly reproduce itself. Because in the digital environment, scarcity never ends; there is always a new campaign, a new discount, or a new "last chance." Even if an individual doesn't miss one, they encounter the next, and this situation ensures the continuity of consumption while creating a constant state of vigilance in the individual's mind. Therefore, when FOMO and the perception of scarcity are considered together, it is insufficient to speak of them merely as individual emotional states. This situation is also a systematic form of manipulation because while the individual believes they are making a decision, they are being guided unconsciously. As a result, FOMO and the perception of scarcity emerge as two key dynamics at the heart of digital consumption culture. When these two key elements work together, consumption ceases to be merely a practice that meets needs; it transforms into a behavior driven by emotions, accelerating and becoming continuous. This situation provides a critical framework for understanding an individual's purchasing behavior, particularly in the context of online shopping.

METHODOLOGY

This study aims to examine how online shopping addiction is constructed and reproduced in the context of FOMO (Fear of Missing Out) within digital consumption environments. To this end, a qualitative research design was adopted, and discourse analysis was employed as the primary method. This approach offers the opportunity to deeply examine how language shapes consumer perception and behavior, particularly in the context of motivations based on urgency, scarcity, and fear. The study's dataset consists of textual elements obtained from the Trendyolmilla e-commerce platform. This platform was selected because of its widespread use in Turkey and its intensive use of marketing language emphasizing urgency and scarcity. These characteristics provide a suitable context for examining the relationship between FOMO and online shopping behavior. Purposive sampling was employed in the study. Within this scope, a total of 20 product pages were selected from the "best-selling" and "most-visited" categories. These categories were chosen because they contain a higher concentration of expressions that trigger FOMO, such as limited-time offers, stock scarcity, and indicators of high demand. During the data collection process, product descriptions, campaign texts, statements on the user interface, and system-generated notifications were examined. The data collection process was conducted between March 10 and March 20, 2026. During this period, the selected product pages were systematically reviewed and archived in order to ensure consistency throughout the analysis process. The analysis focused particularly on phrases that create a sense of urgency and scarcity, such as "X people have added this to their cart—don't miss out," "last X items," "X items sold in 3 days," and "X people visited in the last 1 day." In the analysis phase, Teun A. Van Dijk's critical discourse analysis approach was utilized to uncover the underlying meanings and persuasion strategies in the texts. This approach focuses not only on explicit meanings but also on the forms of guidance, desire production, and the normalization of consumption present in the background of the discourse. The analysis process was conducted within the framework of thematic categories such as scarcity discourse, the construction of urgency, the use of social proof, and emotional manipulation. These categories were evaluated to determine how FOMO is produced and how it can be linked to online shopping addiction. The coding process was carried out in multiple stages. During the coding process, the data were examined repeatedly and coded according to recurring patterns and discursive strategies identified within the texts. The thematic categories were derived inductively from the data while also being informed by the theoretical framework of the study. To enhance the reliability and consistency of the analysis, a second researcher independently reviewed portions of the coded data and the emerging thematic structure. Any discrepancies in coding and interpretation were discussed and resolved collaboratively in order to strengthen analytical validity and minimize subjective bias. First, an open coding approach was adopted to identify recurring expressions and patterns within the dataset. In this stage, phrases related to urgency, scarcity, emotional appeal, and social influence were marked and categorized. In the second stage, these initial codes were grouped into broader thematic categories through axial coding. Themes such as scarcity discourse, urgency construction, social proof, and emotional guidance were derived based on the frequency and functional role of these expressions within the texts. Finally, in the selective coding phase, relationships between these themes were analyzed to understand how they collectively contribute to the construction of FOMO and its connection to online shopping addiction. This step enabled a more structured and theory-driven interpretation of the data.

FINDINGS

The Discourse of Scarcity

One of the most striking elements on the analyzed product pages is the heavy use of scarcity messaging. In particular, phrases such as "grab it before it's gone," "only 1 item left," and "hurry—only a few items left" were frequently repeated. Such messaging creates the perception that the product's availability is limited, thereby raising awareness among consumers about the risk of missing out. What matters here is not whether the scarcity is real, but how it is perceived by the individual. The emphasis on scarcity shortens the individual's evaluation process regarding the product and accelerates the decision-making process. Often, the individual may make a purchase simply to avoid missing out, without even questioning whether they truly need the product. This creates a scenario where FOMO directly comes into play. The fear of missing out triggered by the scarcity narrative pushes the individual's rational evaluation process into the background while bringing emotional reactions to the forefront. This mechanism also reinforces a tendency toward repeated consumption in similar situations rather than a one-time purchase.

Building a Sense of Urgency

Another notable element on the analyzed product pages is the systematic creation of a sense of urgency. In particular, phrases such as "1 flash sale every 24 hours," "buy now," and "don't miss out" are frequently used. Such messaging accelerates the individual's decision-making process by creating the perception that time is limited. At this point, the message presented to the individual is not merely the existence of an opportunity; it is that this opportunity will disappear shortly. The sense of time running out limits the individual's time for thinking and evaluating alternatives, leading to a need to make a decision immediately because waiting could mean missing out. In this regard, the urgency message functions as one of the most direct triggers of FOMO. The individual comes to aim not only at purchasing the product but also at not missing out on that opportunity. This situation causes purchasing behavior to drift away from a rational evaluation process and rely more on immediate reactions. On the other hand, the sense of urgency is not limited to generating a one-time purchasing behavior. Constantly updated campaigns and time-limited offers lead the individual to repeatedly face similar decision-making processes. Each new "last chance" follows the previous one, so the individual becomes accustomed to acting under constant time pressure. This situation is also transforming the role of online shopping in daily life. Shopping ceases to be a planned action and becomes a behavior shaped by impulsive decisions. This repetitive structure can, over time, weaken the individual's control over their purchasing behavior. Consequently, the language of urgency is not merely a factor that triggers FOMO; it emerges as a significant mechanism supporting the formation and maintenance of online shopping addiction.

The Use of Social Proof

Another prominent rhetorical element on the analyzed product pages is the frequent use of social proof. In particular, phrases such as "X people visited in the last 1 day," "X people have it in their cart," and "X units sold in 3 days" appear frequently. Such indicators provide a framework that makes the individual feel they are not alone in the decision-making process. At this point, the individual no longer evaluates the product solely based on their own needs, and what others are doing begins to matter. This information, suggesting high interest in the product, creates a perception that the product is valuable and desirable. As a result, the individual tends to reference the behavior of other consumers when forming their own decisions. The use of social proof operates as a mechanism directly linked to FOMO. This is because when an individual sees others gravitating toward a product, they begin to feel the possibility of being left out of that experience in a more tangible way. It is not just about missing out on the product itself, but also about being excluded from an experience others are part of—this becomes a source of anxiety. This situation creates a significant effect that accelerates purchasing behavior. On the other hand, this phenomenon is not limited to influencing individual decisions but generates a broader consumption dynamic. As others' preferences become visible, the preference for similar products becomes more widespread. This leads to consumption behavior taking on an increasingly homogeneous structure, where the desire not to fall behind becomes the determining factor rather than diverse preferences. The constant reproduction of social proof can trap an individual in a repetitive cycle of shopping behavior. Every new product and every new campaign is presented through the lens of others' preferences. This can lead the individual to constantly compare themselves to others, push their own needs to the background, and struggle to control their purchasing behavior. Therefore, the use of social proof is not merely an element that encourages consumption; it can also be viewed as a significant rhetorical strategy that reinforces FOMO and lays the groundwork for the development of online shopping addiction.

Emotional Guidance

Another key element that stands out in the analyzed content is the extensive use of language that directly appeals to consumers' emotions. Phrases found on product pages such as "an opportunity not to be missed," "inspired by what you've viewed," and "tailored to the products you've looked at/tailored just for you" do more than simply highlight the product's features; they aim to trigger the individual's emotional responses. Such language removes consumption from a rational evaluation process, transforming it into a decision-making process based more on emotions. An individual may be inclined to purchase not because they truly need the product, but based on the emotion they are feeling at that moment. Sometimes this is a sense of reward. Other times, it is the desire to alleviate a feeling of lack. The decision is often made unconsciously through emotions. When emotional guidance combines with FOMO, it creates an even more powerful effect. This is because the individual faces not only the possibility of missing out on a product but also the possibility of missing out on the emotional experience that product promises. Purchasing the product does not merely mean owning an object; it also carries the meaning of feeling good, belonging, or not falling behind. This supports purchasing behavior with a stronger motivation. On the other hand, while this process may offer a satisfying experience in the short term, it can lead to different outcomes in the long term. The pleasure felt at the moment of purchase is usually temporary. This feeling may give way to a neutral or, at times, negative emotion shortly thereafter. In this case, the individual may show a tendency to shop again in order to regain that same feeling. Thus, consumption behavior becomes a tool for emotional regulation. This relationship built on emotions creates a recurring cycle over time. The individual buys to feel good, experiences short-term relief, and repeats the same behavior when that feeling fades. This cycle can cause online shopping to evolve beyond merely a practice of fulfilling needs and transform into a more emotional coping mechanism. In this context, emotional guidance can be viewed not only as a factor that triggers FOMO but also as one of the fundamental discursive strategies supporting the formation and maintenance of online shopping addiction.

Future Research Directions

This study makes a significant conceptual contribution by examining the relationship between FOMO and online shopping addiction in digital consumption environments from a discursive perspective. However, the findings point to various areas for future research.

First and foremost, the fact that this study was conducted using a qualitative design and a limited sample necessitates that it be supported by quantitative research in the future. In particular, large-scale studies conducted across different age groups, sociodemographic characteristics, and cultural contexts will enhance the generalizability of the relationship between FOMO and online shopping addiction. In this regard, the use of advanced analytical techniques such as structural equation modeling (SEM) could help clarify the causal relationships among variables.

Second, a comparative analysis of different digital platforms presents an important area of research. While this study was limited to a single e-commerce platform, examining the dynamics of interaction between social media platforms (such as Instagram and TikTok) and e-commerce sites would facilitate the development of a more comprehensive understanding of how FOMO is generated and how it shapes consumer behavior.

Third, there is a need for experimental research designs. In particular, testing the effects of rhetorical strategies—such as scarcity, urgency, and social proof—on individuals in controlled experimental settings will provide an opportunity to observe the behavioral outcomes of these mechanisms more directly. Such studies can also contribute to the evaluation of the ethical dimensions of marketing practices.

Furthermore, studies utilizing neuromarketing methods (eye tracking, galvanic skin response, facial expression analysis, etc.) will enable a deeper understanding of the cognitive and emotional responses individuals exhibit to FOMO-triggering messages. As a result, it will become possible to support the understanding of consumer behavior not only through self-reports but also through biophysiological indicators.

Another important aspect of future research is the examination of individual differences. In particular, the role of psychological variables such as self-control, impulsivity, loneliness, self-esteem, and the tendency toward social comparison in the relationship between FOMO and online shopping addiction should be explored in greater detail. Such studies will contribute to the identification of user profiles at risk.

Finally, the development of intervention models designed to promote more mindful and controlled consumption behaviors in digital environments has emerged as a significant area of research. In particular, examining the impact of digital literacy, awareness-based education, and ethical regulations regarding platform design could offer important contributions to both the academic literature and practical applications.

Discussion

The findings of this study indicate that, in digital consumption environments, FOMO functions not merely as an individual psychological tendency but also as a mechanism systematically generated and reinforced by platform design and marketing strategies. The discursive structures analyzed reveal that consumption behavior is increasingly shaped by emotional, impulsive, and guided decisions, moving away from rational evaluation processes. Particularly in situations where scarcity discourse and the construction of urgency work in tandem, it is observed that the individual's decision-making process accelerates significantly, and the likelihood of evaluating alternatives decreases. This finding aligns with studies in the literature indicating that time pressure limits cognitive processes. Additionally, it is understood that the use of social proof leads the individual to establish a connection not only with the product but also with the collective behavior directed toward that product. This situation contributes to consumption shifting from an individual preference to a practice of social conformity and keeping up with the Joneses. Findings regarding emotional regulation, meanwhile, indicate that consumption is now directly linked not only to external stimuli but also to the individual's internal emotional needs. The fact that individuals sometimes use purchasing behavior as a means of reward, relaxation, or alleviating a sense of deficiency suggests that online shopping can evolve into a form of emotional regulation mechanism. In this context, shopping behavior, while producing short-term pleasure, can create a recurring cycle in the long term, thereby laying the groundwork for the emergence of addiction-like patterns.

The findings also indicate that these discursive strategies do not operate in isolation but within a complementary framework. While the perception of scarcity reinforces a sense of urgency, social proof legitimizes this process, and emotional appeal makes purchasing behavior internally meaningful. This multi-layered structure reveals that FOMO functions not merely as a trigger but as a cyclical mechanism that sustains the continuity of consumption behavior. This study emphasizes the need to consider both individual psychological processes and structural digital dynamics together when understanding digital consumption practices. This study contributes to the existing literature in several ways. First, it conceptualizes FOMO not only as an individual psychological tendency but also as a discursively constructed mechanism embedded in digital platform design. Second, by adopting a critical discourse analysis approach, it provides a deeper understanding of how marketing language particularly through scarcity, urgency, social proof, and emotional persuasion systematically shapes and reinforces online shopping behaviors. Finally, the study offers an integrated perspective by linking FOMO directly to online shopping addiction, highlighting how these processes operate as a continuous and self-reinforcing cycle within digital consumption environments. However, the fact that the study was conducted on a specific platform and with a limited number of samples constitutes a limitation regarding the generalizability of the findings. Expanding future research to include different platforms, user groups, and quantitative datasets will contribute to a more comprehensive understanding of these relationships.

CONCLUSION

The findings of this study indicate that, in digital consumption environments, FOMO operates not merely as an individual psychological tendency but also as a mechanism systematically generated and reinforced by platform design and marketing strategies. The discursive structures analyzed reveal that consumption behavior is increasingly shaped by emotional, impulsive, and guided decisions, moving away from rational evaluation processes. Particularly in situations where scarcity discourse and the construction of urgency work in tandem, it is observed that the individual's decision-making process accelerates significantly, and the likelihood of evaluating alternatives decreases. This finding aligns with studies in the literature indicating that time pressure limits cognitive processes. Additionally, it is understood that the use of social proof leads the individual to establish a connection not only with the product but also with the collective behavior directed toward that product. This situation contributes to consumption shifting from an individual preference to a practice of social conformity and keeping up with the Joneses. Findings regarding emotional regulation, meanwhile, indicate that consumption has become directly linked not only to external stimuli but also to the individual's internal emotional needs. The fact that individuals sometimes use purchasing behavior as a means of reward, relaxation, or alleviating a sense of deficiency suggests that online shopping can evolve into a form of emotional regulation mechanism. In this context, shopping behavior, while producing short-term pleasure, can create a recurring cycle in the long term, thereby laying the groundwork for the emergence of addiction-like patterns.

The findings also indicate that these discursive strategies do not operate in isolation but within a complementary framework. While the perception of scarcity reinforces a sense of urgency, social proof legitimizes this process, and emotional appeal makes purchasing behavior internally meaningful. This multi-layered structure reveals that FOMO functions not merely as a trigger but as a cyclical mechanism that sustains the continuity of consumption behavior. This study emphasizes the need to consider both individual psychological processes and structural digital dynamics together when understanding digital consumption practices. However, the fact that the study was conducted on a specific platform and with a limited number of samples constitutes a limitation regarding the generalizability of the findings. Expanding future research to include different platforms, user groups, and quantitative datasets will contribute to a more comprehensive understanding of these relationships.

REFERENCES

Aktaş, Ö. (2025). Çevrimiçi alışverişte hedonik tüketim eğilimi ve fomo'nun içgüdüsel satın alma davranışı üzerindeki etkisi. *Gümüşhane Üniversitesi Sosyal Bilimler Dergisi, 16*(3), 1141–1158.

Alat, H., & Filizöz, B. (2021). Örgütsel destek algısının, çalışanların gelişmeleri kaçırma korkusu ve içsel işten ayrılma niyeti üzerine etkisi. *Çağ University. Journal of Social Sciences, 18*(2), 64–78.

Andreassen, C. S., Griffiths, M. D., Paleesen, S., & Bilder, R. M. (2015). The Bergen Shopping Addiction Scale: Reliability and Validity of a Brief Screening Test. *Frontiers in Psychology, 6*, 1–11. DOI: 10.3389/fpsyg.2015.01374 PMID: 26441749

Armağan, E., & Temel, E. (2018). Türkiye'de online kompulsif alışveriş davranışı üzerine ampirik bir çalışma. *Dokuz Eylül Üniversitesi Sosyal Bilimler Enstitüsü Dergisi, 20*(4), 621–653.

Cambridge Dictionary. (n.d.) *FOMO*. https://dictionary.cambridge.org/dictionary/english/fomo

Cialdini, R. B. (2021). *Influence, New and Expanded.* Harper Business.

Çopuroğlu, F. (2021). Tüketicilerin Sosyal Medya Kullanımı, FoMO ve Hedonik Tüketim Arasındaki İlişki. *OPUS International Journal of Society Researches, 17*(37), 4298–4326. DOI: 10.26466/opus.845545

Demirel, A. C., & Tapan, M. G. (2023). Üniversite Öğrencilerinin Sosyal Medya ve Kompulsif Çevrimiçi Alışveriş Bağımlılığı Arasındaki İlişkinin İncelenmesi. *İnsan ve Toplum Bilimleri Araştırmaları Dergisi, 12*(1), 60-78. https://doi.org/DOI: 10.15869/itobiad.1147669

Demirkaya, İ., & Koyuncu, E. (2021). Dijital Kapitalizm, Tüketim Kültürü ve Y Kuşağının Değişen Tüketim Davranışları. *Intermedia International E-journal, 8*(15), 174–196. DOI: 10.21645/intermedia.2021.107

Festinger, L. (1954). A Theory of Social Comparison Processes. *Human Relations, 7*(2), 117–140. DOI: 10.1177/001872675400700202

Gupta, M., & Sharma, A. (2021). Fear of missing out: A brief overview of origin, theoretical underpinnings and relationship with mental health. *World Journal of Clinical Cases, 9*(19), 4881–4889. DOI: 10.12998/wjcc.v9.i19.4881 PMID: 34307542

Hodkinson, C. (2019). Fear of missing out (FOMO) marketing appeals: A conceptual model. *Journal of Marketing Communications*, *25*(1), 65–88. DOI: 10.1080/13527266.2016.1234504

Karakuş, M. (2022). Sosyal Medyanın ve Online Alışveriş Sitelerinin Tüketici Davranışlarına Etkisi Üzerine Nitel Bir Araştırma. *Atatürk İletişim Dergisi*, *23*, 1–8. DOI: 10.54614/communicata.2022.1020911

Kerse, Y., & Yüce, A. (2022). FOMO ve Online Kompulsif Satın Alma: Sosyal Medya Fenomenleri Tüketicilerin Kaygılarını ve Takıntılarını Tetikliyor Mu? *KMÜ Sosyal ve Ekonomik Araştırmalar Dergisi*, *24*(43), 704–716.

Ko, H., Cho, C. H., & Roberts, M. S. (2005). Internet uses and grafitications: A structural equation model of interactive advertising. *Journal of Advertising*, *34*(2), 57–70. DOI: 10.1080/00913367.2005.10639191

Maignan, I., & Lukas, B. A. (1997). The nature & social uses of the Internet: A qualitative investigation. *The Journal of Consumer Affairs*, *31*(2), 346–37. DOI: 10.1111/j.1745-6606.1997.tb00395.x

Nash, J. (2019). Exploring how social media platforms influence fashion consumer decisions in the UK retail sector. *Journal of Fashion Marketing and Management*, *23*(1), 82–103. DOI: 10.1108/JFMM-01-2018-0012

Nurmalasari, E., Hartini, I., Putri, R. A., & Soesilo, P. K. M. (2024). Effect of FOMO and Hedonic Value on Impulsive Buying and Post Purchase Regret for Purchasing Skincare Products at the Online Shop. [Andalas Management Review]. *AMAR*, *8*(1), 1–21. DOI: 10.25077/amar.8.1.1-21.2024

Okazaki, S., Schuberth, F., Tagashira, T., & Andrade, V. (2021). Sneaking the dark side of brand engagement into Instagram: The dual theory of passion. *Journal of Business Research*, *130*, 493–505. DOI: 10.1016/j.jbusres.2019.11.028

Ökten, B. (2025). X,Y ve Z kuşağının dijital tüketim eğilimleri: Sosyal medya ve bilinçli harcama perspektifi. *Journal of Internet Applications and Management*, *16*(1), 31–53. DOI: 10.34231/iuyd.1615441

Özer Canarslan, N. (2025). Online alışverişte kıtlık etkisi, FOMO ve sürü davranışının anlık satın alma üzerindeki rolü. *bmij 13*(1): 243-262 DOI: 10.15295/bmij.v13i1.2521

Przybylski, A. K., Murayama, K., Dehaan, C. R., & Galdwell, V. (2013). Motivational, emotional, and behavioral correlates of fear of missing out. *Computers in Human Behavior*, *29*(4), 1841–1848. DOI: 10.1016/j.chb.2013.02.014

Sayan, N., & Uslu, A. (2025). Online Yeniden Satın Alma Niyetinde FOMO, Algılanan Kıtlık ve Online Anlık Satın Alma Davranışının Etkisi. *Journal of Research in Business, 10*(1), 1–29. DOI: 10.54452/jrb.1510782

Siekpe, J. S., & Kamssu, A. A. (2005). The effect of culture & uses and gratifications in online shopping. *Southwest Decision Sciences Institute 2005: Proceedings of the 36th Southwest Decision Sciences Institute Annual Conference*, Southwest DSI, Dallas, USA, 370-378.

Tanhan, F., Özok, H. İ., & Tayiz, V. (2022). Gelişmeleri Kaçırma Korkusu (FoMO): Güncel Bir Derleme. *Psikiyatride Güncel Yaklasimlar, 14*(1), 74–85. DOI: 10.18863/pgy.942431

Zhao, N., & Zhou, G. (2021). Covid-19 stress and addictive social media use (SMU): Mediating role of active use and social media flow. *Frontiers in Psychiatry, 12*, 12–85. DOI: 10.3389/fpsyt.2021.635546 PMID: 33633616

ADDITIONAL READINGS

Argan, M. ve Argan, M. T. (2019). Toward a New Understanding of Fomo: 'Fomsumerism'. *Pazarlama Teorisi ve Uygulamaları Dergisi, 5*(2), 277–302.

Bakır, U. (2020). *Pazarlama İletişimi Odağında Tüketim Psikolojisi*. Nobel Akademik Yayıncılık.

Baudrillard, J. (1998). *The consumer society: Myths and structures*. Sage Publications. DOI: 10.4135/9781526401502

Kazankaya, K. (2019). *E-Ticaret ve Dijital Pazarlama*. Sokak Kitapları Yayınları.

Kotler, P., Kartajaya, H., & Setiawan, I. (2021). *Marketing 5.0: Technology for humanity*. Wiley.

Lindstrom, M. (2008). *Buyology: Truth and lies about why we buy*. Doubleday.

Metin, B., Pehlivan, R., & Tarhan, N. (2017). Realiability and validity of Uskudar fear of missing out scale. *The Journal of Neurobehavioral Sciences, 4*(2), 43–46.

Oktavia, D. Y. (2024). The Effect Of Fear Of Missing Out (FoMo), Hedonic Shopping, And Online Shopping Anxiety On Purchasing Decissions. *International Conference of Business and Social Sciences, 4*(1), 1233–1241.

Şahin, C., & Günüç, S. (2020). *Teknoloji Bağımlılıkları*. Nobel Akademik Yayıncılık.

Widyastuti, P. (2022). Shopping Anxiety And "Fear Of Missing Out" (FOMO) For Purchase Intention Of E-Commerce During Pandemic Covid-19. *Jurnal Ekonomi*, *11*(02), 1116–1123.

KEY TERMS AND DEFINITIONS

Emotional Persuasion: A form of influence in which consumers are guided toward purchasing behavior through messages that appeal to their emotions rather than their rational decision-making processes, and in which decisions are shaped more by momentary feelings than by actual needs.

FOMO (Fear of Missing Out): A psychological state of anxiety that arises from the fear of missing out on opportunities, events, or consumption habits experienced by others, driving individuals to constantly stay up-to-date, keep track of what others are doing, and ensure they are not left out of these experiences.

Online Shopping Addiction: A behavioral pattern characterized by an individual's partial or complete loss of control over their online shopping behavior, their persistence in a repetitive cycle of purchasing, and their continued engagement in this behavior despite its negative impact on their daily life.

Perception of Scarcity: A psychological phenomenon in which an individual perceives a product or opportunity as limited—regardless of whether that limitation actually exists—leading to an increased perceived value of the product and a faster purchasing decision.

Social Proof: The tendency to use the actions of others as a source of validation and guidance, leading individuals to shape their own choices by referencing the behaviors, preferences, and interests of other consumers during the decision-making process.

Urgency: A situation in which the perceived time pressure—arising from the belief that an opportunity or product will soon disappear—shortens an individual's time for reflection and evaluation, leading them to make quick and often impulsive decisions.

Chapter 9
Binge-Watching:
Psychological Impact and Social Effects in the Digital Age

Deeksha Ranga
http://orcid.org/0009-0001-3042-3720
Lovely Professional University, India

ABSTRACT

Continuous content consumption has become an important part of entertainment in the digital era, especially with the widespread availability of on-demand streaming platforms, easy accessibility to high-speed internet and mobiles etc. Viewers increasingly engage in watching multiple episodes of series or online content in a single sitting, which results in making binge-watching a common media viewing habit. This chapter focuses on examining marathon-viewing as a contemporary viewing practice by reviewing existing literature, with particular attention to its prevalence, psychological mechanisms, associated mental health and social outcomes and differentiating unhealthy binge-watching from healthy viewing habits. Lastly, this chapter highlights the importance of practical intervention approaches, cultural considerations, and key research gaps.

INTRODUCTION

Entertainment has been an integral aspect of human life for centuries and has evolved over time through storytelling, art, theatre, festivals, cinema, and television. While earlier audiences engaged with entertainment occasionally, the digital era has transformed consumption patterns, with individuals now spending extended periods engaging with online content and binge-watching television series. In today's hyper-connected world, binge-watching is commonly defined as viewing multiple

DOI: 10.4018/979-8-3373-6665-4.ch009

episodes of a television series or online content in a single, continuous session (Alimoradi et al., 2022). This practice has become increasingly widespread and has reshaped contemporary leisure habits across global populations (Kandola, 2022).

Research suggests that the rapid growth of streaming platforms such as Netflix, Disney Hotstar, and Amazon MiniTV has accelerated this shift by enabling uninterrupted access to entire seasons of content (Flayelle et al., 2019). As a result, marathon viewing is increasingly prioritized over other daily activities, raising important questions regarding its psychological and social implications. Furthermore, evidence from studies conducted during the COVID-19 pandemic further indicates that increased binge-watching was associated with higher levels of anxiety and depressive symptoms among users of streaming platforms (Raza et al., 2021).

Background and Context

Research on binge-watching expanded significantly in the early 2010s, largely due to the rise of streaming services that release complete seasons simultaneously, thereby encouraging prolonged viewing sessions (Alimoradi et al., 2022). Industry reports from PwC (2025) and Statista (2025) indicate that streaming platforms now dominate global entertainment consumption, with worldwide subscriptions reaching unprecedented levels by 2025. This growth reflects a broader cultural shift from traditional broadcast viewing to on-demand digital media (Flayelle et al., 2019).

Early studies largely framed binge-watching as a pleasurable leisure activity, commonly defining it as watching three or more episodes of a series consecutively in one sitting. However, subsequent research has highlighted potential concerns associated with excessive viewing. Although binge-watching may provide short-term enjoyment and relaxation, it can become problematic when viewing behaviour intensifies during periods of heightened stress, such as public health crises (Flayelle et al., 2019; Alimoradi et al., 2022). Empirical evidence further suggests that binge-watching occurs across all age groups, with young adults showing stronger associations with stress, anxiety, and sleep-related difficulties (Alimoradi et al., 2022).

From a theoretical perspective, binge-watching has been linked to established media-use frameworks that emphasise emotional regulation, escapism, and parasocial engagement with on-screen characters. Studies indicate that viewers may experience short-term emotional gratification through narrative immersion; however, prolonged or excessive engagement has been associated with adverse psychological outcomes (Sil et al., 2025). Research conducted in South Asian contexts similarly reports that binge-watching is frequently used as a coping strategy for academic and daily stress among young adults (Subramanian & Das, 2024). Comparable findings have also been reported in other non-Western contexts. For example, Tolba and Zoghaib (2022) found significant associations between binge-watching, depression, and loneliness among Egyptian adults, while Özkent and Akdoğan (2025) observed higher engagement levels during evenings and weekends.

Taken together, these findings suggest that binge-watching represents a complex behavioural process shaped by individual motivations, emotional regulation mechanisms, and platform-driven affordances, which collectively influence psychological and social outcomes.

Problem and Research Gap

Despite its widespread popularity, binge-watching still presents significant but under-explored risks to mental health and social functioning. Prior research has linked heavy or problematic binge-watching to increased anxiety, depressive symptoms, sleep disturbances, and social withdrawal (Flayelle et al., 2019; Alimoradi et al., 2022). During periods of restricted mobility, such as pandemic-related lockdowns, individuals engaging in excessive content consumption reported significantly higher psychological distress compared to moderate viewers (Raza et al., 2021). Additionally, marathon-watching has been associated with weaker offline social relationships and heightened feelings of isolation, with some studies reporting gender-based differences in these effects (Tse et al., 2025).

Critical Research Gaps

Western bias in samples: As expressed in the study conducted by Sil et al. (2025), existing literature predominantly relies on convenience samples drawn from Western populations, limiting generalizability to non-Western societies with distinct cultural and family structures.

Lack of causal evidence: Current research is largely cross-sectional; therefore it cannot determine whether binge-watching can cause mental health problems or whether individuals experiencing distress are more likely associated with heavy marathon-viewing (Alimoradi et al., 2022).

Gap in theoretical integration: Previous studies have largely explored motivational, emotional, cognitive, and platform-based factors separately, with limited effort to bring them together into one unified explanatory framework of binge-watching behaviour.

Limited intervention studies: A systematic review and meta-analysis by Alimoradi et al. (2022) concluded that more strategies, interventions and programs to reduce marathon-viewing should be developed and tested. This indicates the limited availability of rigorous interventions.

Global South underrepresentation: Few studies focus on South Asian or other developing regions, resulting in limited understanding of culturally specific patterns and implications of binge-watching (Subramanian & Das, 2024).

This chapter seeks to address these gaps by analysing recent data from diverse global contexts, exploring demographic variations, and proposing evidence-based strategies for healthier viewing habits and platform design improvements.

Chapter Objectives

The aim of this chapter is to examine the psychological and social impacts of binge-watching in the digital era, with attention to both individual and societal dimensions. The specific objectives are as follows:

To examine prevalence rates and demographic patterns of binge-watching across different global populations, highlighting variations by age, gender, and cultural context.

To identify key risk factors that distinguish healthy, recreational viewing habits from excessive or problematic content consumption.

To analyse the psychological mechanisms linking binge-watching to mental health outcomes such as stress, anxiety, depression, and loneliness.

To evaluate social and functional consequences of marathon-viewing, including effects on relationships, sleep quality, and overall well-being.

To review current and emerging intervention strategies while highlighting critical gaps in research to guide future studies.

Chapter Roadmap

This chapter is organized to provide a systematic understanding of binge-watching and its consequences. Following the introduction, the prevalence and demographics section examines patterns of marathon-viewing across populations. The psychological mechanisms section explores motivations, emotional regulation processes, and coping strategies associated with heavy and continuous content consumption. Furthermore, the chapter addresses social and health-related effects, including disruptions to daily functioning and interpersonal relationships. The distinction between healthy and problematic binge-watching is then discussed, followed by an examination of intervention strategies. The chapter concludes by synthesizing key insights and outlining priorities for future research, with implications for researchers, mental health professionals, and platform designers.

Chapter Contribution

This chapter contributes to the growing binge-watching literature by addressing a key conceptual gap. While prior studies and reviews have primarily focused on prevalence rates and psychological associations (Flayelle et al., 2019; Alimoradi et al., 2022), limited attention has been given to integrating motivational, emotional, cognitive, and platform-driven mechanisms within a single explanatory structure. Existing research often examines these components independently, resulting in fragmented interpretations of binge-watching behaviour.

The present chapter advances the field by proposing a continuum-based conceptual framework that distinguishes between adaptive and problematic binge-watching. By synthesising evidence from diverse cultural contexts, including emerging findings beyond Western samples (Subramanian & Das, 2024; Sil et al., 2025), the chapter provides clearer theoretical organisation of how binge-watching behaviours develop, are reinforced, and lead to varied psychological and social outcomes. In doing so, it moves beyond descriptive narrative review and offers a structured explanatory perspective to guide future empirical and intervention-based research.

METHODOLOGY

Research Design

The present chapter is based on a structured and comprehensive review of existing literature to examine binge-watching behaviour and its psychological, social, and health-related implications. A systematic and organised approach was adopted to identify, analyse, and synthesise findings from previously published peer-reviewed studies. As the chapter does not involve primary data collection, it draws entirely upon existing empirical research to explore behavioural patterns, theoretical perspectives, associated outcomes, and emerging gaps within binge-watching scholarship. This approach allows for an integrative understanding of the phenomenon while maintaining clarity and conceptual coherence.

A narrative synthesis approach was adopted because studies on binge-watching differ considerably in design, population groups, and measurement tools. Many investigations include cross-sectional surveys (Dixit et al., 2020; Sil et al., 2025), qualitative explorations (Flayelle et al., 2017), cluster analyses (Flayelle et al., 2019), and systematic reviews (Joseph & Varghese, 2025). Given this methodological diversity, statistical aggregation was not appropriate. Therefore, thematic integration was selected to allow conceptual interpretation of psychological mechanisms, behavioural patterns, and contextual influences.

Search Strategy

A comprehensive literature search was conducted to identify relevant peer-reviewed studies examining binge-watching behaviour and its associated outcomes. Electronic academic databases commonly used in psychological and behavioural research were systematically searched, including PubMed, Scopus, Web of Science, and Google Scholar. These databases were selected because the majority of included studies, such as Alimoradi et al. (2022), Özkent and Akdoğan (2025), Tse et al. (2025), and Yu and Alizadeh (2024), are indexed within these platforms.

The search focused on studies published between 2010 and 2025, reflecting the rapid expansion of streaming platforms and the emergence of binge-watching as a distinct behavioural phenomenon during this period. Keywords were developed based on recurring terminology in the literature and included combinations of: binge-watching behaviour, marathon viewing, problematic binge-watching, streaming media consumption, mental health outcomes, loneliness, sleep disturbance, emotional regulation, and behavioural addiction. Boolean operators (AND, OR) were used to refine search results and improve retrieval accuracy.

Additionally, industry and global media reports (e.g., PwC, 2025; Statista, 2025) were consulted to contextualise prevalence trends in the digital entertainment environment.

Inclusion and Exclusion Criteria

Studies were included in this review if they were published in peer-reviewed academic journals and focused primarily on binge-watching behaviour in relation to psychological, behavioural, or social outcomes. Empirical quantitative, qualitative, and mixed-method studies were considered to ensure comprehensive coverage of the phenomenon. Articles examining motivations, emotional regulation, problematic viewing patterns, mental health correlates, or digital platform influences were included. Only studies published in English were considered. Given the rapid expansion of streaming platforms, preference was given to studies published between 2010 and 2025 to ensure conceptual and contextual relevance.

Studies were excluded if they did not directly examine binge-watching as a primary construct or if they focused solely on general television consumption without distinguishing binge-viewing patterns. Editorials, commentaries, dissertations, conference abstracts without full texts, and non-peer-reviewed sources were excluded to maintain methodological rigor. Studies lacking clear methodological description or empirical data were also omitted. Duplicate records identified during the screening process were removed.

Study Selection Process

The selection process followed a structured screening approach. Initially, database searches generated a broad pool of potentially relevant studies. After removing duplicates, titles and abstracts were screened to determine relevance to binge-watching behaviour and associated psychological or social outcomes. Articles meeting preliminary criteria were then reviewed in full text to confirm eligibility based on the inclusion criteria.

This multi-stage screening ensured that selected studies were both conceptually relevant and methodologically appropriate for synthesis.

Data Extraction and Synthesis

After final selection, relevant information was systematically extracted from each study. Extracted data included:

Author(s) and year of publication
Research design
Sample characteristics
Cultural or geographic context
Measurement tools used
Key psychological or behavioural findings

A thematic narrative synthesis approach was then applied. Studies were grouped based on recurring themes such as emotional regulation, loneliness, sleep disturbances (Jindal, 2020), parasocial attachment (Ferchaud et al., 2022), problematic patterns (Joseph & Varghese, 2025), and gender-specific academic outcomes (Tse et al., 2025). Patterns, similarities, and differences across cultural contexts were critically compared.

This approach enabled integration of diverse research findings while maintaining conceptual coherence and methodological transparency.

Quality Considerations

Although formal meta-analytic quality scoring was not conducted, methodological clarity, sampling procedures, and research design robustness were considered when interpreting findings. Systematic reviews and meta-analyses (Alimoradi et al., 2022) were given particular attention due to their broader evidence synthesis, while cross-sectional studies were interpreted with caution due to limitations in causal inference.

Ethical Considerations

Since this chapter is based entirely on previously published peer-reviewed research, no direct involvement of human participants was required. Ethical standards were maintained by accurately representing findings, avoiding misinterpretation, and properly acknowledging all original sources.

PREVALENCE AND DEMOGRAPHICS OF BINGE-WATCHING

As discussed in the previous section, binge-watching has emerged as a dominant mode of contemporary media consumption, characterized by the continuous viewing of multiple episodes of a television series in a single sitting. The rapid expansion of digital streaming platforms, widespread smartphone accessibility, and algorithm-driven content recommendations have substantially transformed how audiences engage with entertainment. With the growth of marathon viewing, increased scholarly attention has been observed between 2020 and 2025, focusing on the prevalence of binge-watching across age groups, cultural contexts, and socioeconomic backgrounds. While early research primarily focused on Western populations, recent studies from Asian countries have significantly expanded the empirical base. This section reviews current evidence on prevalence and demographic patterns, with particular emphasis on age, gender, regional variations, and pandemic-related shifts.

Global Patterns of Prevalence

Research consistently indicates that binge-watching is widespread among young adults, particularly students. A systematic review and meta-analysis by Alimoradi et al. (2022) concluded that binge-watching is highly prevalent across diverse populations and frequently associated with psychological factors such as stress, emotional dysregulation, and loneliness. The review further identified young adults as the group most likely to engage in heavy marathon viewing, reflecting their high digital engagement and rapid adoption of streaming technologies.

During periods of restricted mobility, binge-watching increased globally. Dixit et al. (2020), in a cross-national online survey from India and Indonesia, reported sharp increases in streaming consumption during lockdowns. Participants frequently described extended viewing sessions as a coping response to isolation, boredom, and uncertainty. Similar patterns were observed across regions, suggesting that binge-watching functioned as a commonly adopted adaptive behavior during prolonged home confinement.

Although prevalence rates vary due to differences in measurement and operational definitions, evidence indicates that binge-watching is a normative activity among young people. Studies such as Özkent and Akdoğan (2025) distinguish between casual, recreational binge-watching and problematic binge-watching, which is characterized by loss of control, prolonged viewing despite negative consequences, and psychological distress.

Asian Context: High Engagement and Rapid Growth

Even though previous studies were more focused on the data gathered from western population, recent studies highlight Asia as a key region for understanding current marathon-viewing patterns, particularly among urban youth and students. Some of these studies are discussed as follows:

India

In India, increased access to smartphones and affordable mobile data has contributed to the normalization of binge-watching as a leisure activity. Subramanian and Das (2024) reported that a substantial proportion of late adolescents and young adults engaged in frequent binge-watching, often using Binge-watching to manage academic stress and emotional discomfort. Their findings further indicated strong associations between binge-watching and mental health outcomes, particularly anxiety and mood disturbances.

Similarly, Sil et al. (2025) examined the prevalence of binge-watching among Indian youth and found significant links between extended screen time, digital dependence, and stress-related motivations. Their findings suggest that binge-watching often functions as a coping mechanism rather than solely a form of entertainment, particularly in urban contexts where internet access is constant. Furthermore, this study also highlighted the role of low-cost data plans and platform algorithms in sustaining prolonged viewing behavior.

China

Yu and Alizadeh (2024) investigated marathon-viewing among Chinese college students and reported high levels of regular engagement. Their findings demonstrated significant associations between frequent binge-watching and loneliness, anxiety, and depressive symptoms. Consistent with psychological models of media use, Binge-watching was found to function as an emotional regulation strategy among students experiencing academic and social stress.

Indonesia and Transnational Media Consumption

Bonny-Noach et al. (2024) examined problematic series watching among international audiences of Korean dramas in Israel and Indonesia. Although not designed as a national prevalence study, their findings revealed that a considerable proportion of Indonesian youth exhibited problematic binge-watching patterns, particularly when combined with other risk behaviours such as alcohol consumption. This study illustrates how global streaming platforms contribute to intensive viewing patterns across non-Western contexts.

Collectively, studies from Asian regions demonstrate high engagement in binge-watching alongside strong associations with emotional well-being.

Age-Based Demographic Patterns

Emerging Adults (18–24 Years)

Across studies, emerging adults consistently represent the demographic group with the highest prevalence of binge-watching. Alimoradi et al. (2022) identified this age group as the most frequently represented in empirical research, reflecting high digital exposure and lifestyle flexibility. University students and early-career adults commonly report multiple binge-watching sessions per week, facilitated by on-demand access and social normalization of streaming culture.

Sil et al. (2025) similarly observed that Indian college students integrate binge-watching into daily routines, particularly during evenings and periods of academic stress. The authors noted that binge-watching serves both recreational and coping-related functions within student life.

Adolescents

In a study, Tse et al. (2025) examined adolescents and reported associations between binge-watching and reduced academic self-efficacy, as well as poorer social and mental well-being. Gender-specific patterns were observed, with male adolescents reporting poorer sleep quality and female adolescents reporting lower perceived social support. However, this study focused primarily on outcomes rather than prevalence differences across age groups.

Older Adults

Although younger populations dominate prevalence statistics, older adults tend to engage more frequently in traditional television viewing rather than intensive binge-watching. Fingerman et al. (2022) found that older adults were more likely to view content in shared or social contexts, suggesting that media consumption in later life may serve a social rather than coping-related function.

Gender Differences in Binge-Watching

Findings regarding gender differences in binge-watching remain mixed and culturally contingent. While Collectively engagement rates are often similar, differences emerge in motivations and psychological outcomes. Tse et al. (2025) reported stronger associations between marathon-watching and loneliness and anxiety among female students, whereas male participants demonstrated greater vulnerability to sleep-related consequences.

Lim et al. (2023) further suggested that while frequency differences are minimal, males are more likely to be motivated by excitement and genre-specific appeal. In contrast, female viewers tend to engage more with emotionally driven and socially oriented content, potentially influenced by social expectations and fear of missing out (FOMO). These patterns, however, are not universal and vary across cultural contexts.

Socioeconomic and Educational Influences

Access to digital infrastructure plays a significant role in binge-watching behavior. Studies consistently report higher engagement among urban youth and students with stable internet access and personal digital devices (Sil et al., 2025; Yu & Alizadeh, 2024). Sil et al. (2025) noted that affordable mobile data in India has expanded access to streaming services across socioeconomic groups, contributing to frequent binge-watching.

Yu and Alizadeh (2024) similarly observed that Chinese college students enrolled in higher education exhibited heavier content consumption, likely due to flexible schedules and consistent device access. However, binge-watching patterns among rural populations and individuals with limited connectivity remain underexplored.

Lastly, Singh and Thomas (2025) found that Indian undergraduate students demonstrated awareness of the risks associated with excessive binge-watching and reported using self-regulatory strategies such as time management, content limits, and periodic digital detox practices. These findings indicate increasing awareness among educated youth regarding the potential negative consequences of habitual binge-watching.

Impact of the COVID-19 Pandemic

The COVID-19 pandemic represents a major turning point in global binge-watching behaviour. Lockdowns, remote learning, and social isolation led to substantial increases in time spent on streaming platforms. Dixit et al. (2020) reported marked increases in prolonged viewing sessions during lockdowns, with boredom, loneliness, and stress identified as primary motivators.

Raza et al. (2021) further demonstrated that young adults reported near-regular binge-watching during the pandemic, alongside intensified mental health concerns linked to extended screen time. Boursier et al. (2020), although focusing primarily on social media use, similarly found heightened digital reliance associated with loneliness and anxiety, reinforcing the broader impact of pandemic conditions on excessive screen engagement.

In conclusion, evidence indicates that the prevalence of binge-watching has expanded globally, with young adults and students emerging as the most engaged demographic groups. Asian countries such as India, China, and Indonesia now contribute substantial empirical evidence, highlighting the influence of age, gender, socioeconomic status, and educational context. The pandemic further accelerated and normalized Binge-watching, reinforcing binge-watching as a dominant media behavior.

PSYCHOLOGICAL MECHANISMS OF BINGE-WATCHING

Binge-watching refers to the consecutive viewing of multiple episodes of a television series in a single sitting and has become a dominant form of media consumption with the expansion of on-demand streaming platforms. Rather than representing a simple leisure activity, marathon-viewing reflects a complex psychological process shaped by motivational factors, emotional regulation strategies, cognitive immersion, individual vulnerabilities, and platform-level reinforcements. Contemporary research increasingly emphasizes that Binge-watching emerges from several interconnected factors, such as the pursuit of enjoyment, emotional management, deep narrative absorption, addiction-like tendencies, and individual personality traits. These factors explain why binge-watching may range from normal recreational viewing to problematic behavior associated with psychological distress and impairments in daily functioning (Alimoradi et al., 2022; Joseph & K Varghese, 2025). This section presents empirical evidence explaining the key psychological mechanisms underlying marathon-watching, with particular emphasis on Asian and Indian contexts, where mobile and internet accessibility is widespread and academic pressures intensify heavy media engagement.

Motivational Drivers and Uses-and-Gratifications

The uses-and-gratifications framework provides a foundational explanation for binge-watching behavior. According to this framework, audiences actively select media to satisfy specific psychological needs. Research consistently identifies entertainment, relaxation, information-seeking, and escapism as primary motivations for extended viewing (Pittman & Sheehan, 2015). Streaming platforms further enhance these gratifications by allowing viewers to control viewing pace, eliminate advertisements through paid subscriptions, and access entire seasons instantly.

In addition to these motivations, narrative-related factors further strengthen marathon-viewin tendencies. Ferchaud et al. (2022) demonstrated that emotional investment in storylines and attachment to characters significantly predict prolonged viewing, particularly when episodes conclude with unexpected plot twists. This narrative immersion encourages viewers to continue watching beyond their initial intentions, as psychological closure is repeatedly delayed.

Studies conducted in Indian settings highlight context-specific motivational patterns. Subramanian and Das (2024) found that adolescents and young adults frequently conceptualize binge-watching as a coping strategy for academic pressure and emotional fatigue rather than mere entertainment. Similarly, Karmakar (2024) described marathon-watching among Indian youth as an ambivalent practice, where marathon viewing serves both as a source of relaxation and potential overuse. Social motivations also play a role, as Sil et al. (2025) reported that fear of missing out (FOMO) encourages students to consume trending content to participate in peer discussions, transforming binge-watching into a socially driven behavior.

Parasocial Relationships and Emotional Attachment

Research has demonstrated that parasocial relationships, defined as one-sided emotional bonds with fictional characters, act as a central psychological mechanism sustaining heavy content consumption. Ferchaud et al. (2022) showed that binge-watchers often experience heightened emotional involvement with on-screen characters, leading to stronger narrative engagement and intensified emotional responses. These parasocial attachments increase the desire to continue viewing content to maintain emotional connection.

Furthermore, Shaker and Bukhari (2025) found that early adults who formed strong parasocial relationships reported short-term psychosocial benefits, including reduced loneliness and improved mood. However, these benefits were conditional on moderation. As marathon-viewing became excessive, individuals demonstrated increased reliance on fictional relationships, which was associated with reduced real-world social interaction.

Within the Indian context, Karmakar (2024) observed that youth, particularly those with limited offline social opportunities, were more vulnerable to parasocial engagement, often perceiving characters as emotional companions. These findings suggest that binge-watching may function as a substitute for social interaction, especially under conditions of academic stress, urban isolation, or restricted social networks.

Emotional Regulation and Coping Functions

Emotional regulation is one of the most consistently documented mechanisms underlying binge-watching. Flayelle et al. (2019), through qualitative and quantitative studies, indicated that viewers frequently use serial content to manage stress, boredom, loneliness, and negative affect. Immersive narratives provide temporary psychological relief by facilitating emotional detachment from daily stressors. However, this coping function is not uniformly adaptive. Alimoradi et al. (2022), in their systematic review and meta-analysis, found that psychological distress predicts longer binge-watching sessions, while excessive viewing is associated with guilt, fatigue, sleep disruption, and reduced well-being. This bidirectional relationship suggests that Binge-watching may initially alleviate distress but subsequently contribute to emotional difficulties when excessive.

During the COVID-19 pandemic, these dynamics intensified. Dixit et al. (2020) and Raza et al. (2021) reported significant increases in marathon viewing during lockdown periods, with prolonged screen time showing strong associations with stress, anxiety, and emotional exhaustion. Joseph and K Varghese (2025) further emphasized that individuals with flexible coping strategies experienced fewer negative outcomes, whereas those who relied predominantly on binge-watching for emotional regulation were more likely to develop problematic viewing patterns.

Additionally, Tse et al. (2025) found that female adolescents were more likely to engage with emotionally driven content for relational coping, whereas male viewers more commonly used binge-watching as a distraction-oriented strategy.

Cognitive Engagement, Flow, and Narrative Absorption

Flayelle et al. (2019) described binge-watching as a state of deep cognitive absorption characterized by reduced time awareness, diminished self-monitoring, and intense narrative focus. This experience closely resembles flow, wherein viewers become fully immersed in a rewarding activity. Such cognitive immersion plays a critical role in sustaining binge-watching behavior.

Pittman and Sheehan (2015) argued that auto play features, immediate episode availability, and narrative continuity facilitate prolonged engagement. Cliff-hangers and episodic storytelling maintain anticipation, making disengagement psychologically challenging. Özkent and Akdoğan (2025) identified sunk-cost thinking and impaired self-regulation as predictors of problematic excessive viewing, wherein viewers continue watching to justify prior time investment despite awareness of negative consequences. Supporting these findings, Karmakar (2024) reported that Indian students frequently entered heightened absorption states, using binge-watching as a form of cognitive escape during periods of academic stress or anxiety.

Addiction-Like Features and Problematic Binge-Watching

Although marathon-viewing is not formally classified as a behavioral addiction, an emerging body of literature documents addiction-like characteristics among some viewers. Joseph and K Varghese (2025) identified features such as loss of control, tolerance, withdrawal-related discomfort, and functional impairment in academic and social domains associated with Binge-watching. Flayelle et al. (2019) similarly reported that compulsive viewing patterns are often accompanied by post-viewing regret.

Additional studies align with this perspective. Sil et al. (2025) observed that youth with high impulsivity and low self-regulation were more likely to exhibit problematic binge-watching behaviors. Özkent and Akdoğan (2025) further demonstrated associations between problematic viewing, negative emotional states, and impaired social functioning. Thus, these findings underscore the importance of distinguishing recreational binge-watching from maladaptive use.

Individual Differences and Vulnerability Factors

According to Özkent and Akdoğan (2025), personality traits such as high neuroticism and low conscientiousness are associated with emotional escape motives and weaker self-regulation. Karmakar (2024) reported similar patterns among Indian students, linking excessive viewing to emotional instability and impulsivity.

Mental health history further moderates engagement patterns. Subramanian and Das (2024) found that individuals with anxiety symptoms tended to engage in longer viewing sessions, using narrative content as an emotional coping mechanism. Attachment styles also shape vulnerability, as Shaker and Bukhari (2025) demonstrated that individuals with insecure attachment styles reported stronger parasocial bonds and greater reliance on binge-watching for emotional support.

Cultural and Platform-Level Reinforcements

Karmakar (2024) explained that in India, competitive educational systems and high academic pressure make easily accessible digital content particularly appealing as a form of escapism. The rapid expansion of OTT platforms has further intensified FOMO-driven engagement, as algorithmic recommendations and trending indicators encourage immediate content consumption (Sil et al., 2025). These findings indicate that cultural and technological contexts shape how psychological mechanisms underlying binge-watching operate.

Platform architecture further reinforces these tendencies. Umesh and Bose (2019) highlighted how auto play, personalization, and minimal stopping prompts reduce self-regulatory barriers, thereby reinforcing prolonged viewing behavior.

In conclusion, the psychological mechanisms of binge-watching operate in combination rather than isolation, with motivations initiating viewing, cognitive immersion sustaining engagement, and emotional outcomes influencing repeated consumption (Joseph & K Varghese, 2025). Whether binge-watching remains recreational or becomes problematic is shaped by individual vulnerability, cultural context, and platform design. Understanding these processes highlights the importance of multi-level interventions, including strengthening emotional regulation and self-awareness, as well as utilizing platform-based features such as usage reminders, particularly for youth in rapidly digitalizing Asian societies (Alimoradi et al., 2022; Özkent & Akdoğan, 2025).

SOCIAL AND HEALTH EFFECTS OF BINGE-WATCHING

Social Relationships and Interpersonal Functioning

In a study conducted on Indian young adults, Garg and Singh (2023) found that higher levels of binge-watching were associated with increased loneliness, lower interpersonal competence, and greater social anxiety. Furthermore, participants who reported regular binge-watching also experienced difficulty initiating conversations and maintaining social confidence. This suggests that prolonged content consumption may weaken everyday social skills, as extended viewing sessions often occur in isolation and may shift individuals' focus from social interaction to solitary media use.

Subramanian and Das (2024) supported this view by reporting similar findings that linked higher levels of marathon viewing with poorer mental health and reduced social connections among late adolescents and young adults. Although participants initially described binge-watching as a means of relaxation or boredom relief, excessive binge-watching showed strong associations with withdrawal from peer interaction and decreased participation in academic and extracurricular activities. These findings suggest that binge-watching may function as an avoidant coping strategy, offering short-term emotional comfort but potentially limiting access to social support in the long run, thereby contributing to isolating behaviors.

Tse et al. (2025) reported similar findings, demonstrating that binge-watching was negatively associated with social functioning, academic engagement, and psychological well-being. Their gender-specific analysis indicated that girls were more likely to experience declines in emotional and social well-being, whereas boys demonstrated lower academic engagement. These findings suggest that marathon viewing may influence social and developmental outcomes differently across demographic groups.

Raj and Ida (2022) noted that shared viewing experiences, such as watching series with friends or family, can occasionally promote bonding and provide common topics for social interaction. However, these benefits appear to depend on moderation and shared viewing contexts, as excessive or solitary marathon-watching may lead to social displacement that outweighs potential social benefits.

Loneliness, Stress, and Psychological Well-Being

Alimoradi et al. (2022), in their systematic review and meta-analysis, concluded that binge-watching is significantly associated with poorer mental health outcomes across diverse cultural contexts.

Raza et al. (2021) found that during lockdown periods, binge-watching was associated with increased psychological distress. Participants reported that prolonged exposure to Binge-watching and increased screen time contributed to negative mental health outcomes.

Similarly, Sahar Abdul Gafoor (2024) and Sil et al. (2025) reported a positive association between perceived stress and binge-watching among Indian populations. Their findings demonstrated that frequent binge-watching among young adults was associated with higher stress levels, emotional exhaustion, and reduced psychological well-being.

To address these outcomes, Özkent and Akdoğan (2025) emphasized the importance of distinguishing between casual and problematic binge-watching. Their study demonstrated that individuals exhibiting problematic binge-watching patterns, characterized by loss of control and continued viewing despite awareness of negative consequences, reported significantly poorer psychological and social functioning. In contrast, moderate binge-watchers did not show similar levels of negative impact, underscoring the importance of viewing patterns rather than binge-watching itself.

Sleep Disruption and Fatigue

Jindal (2020) highlighted that binge-watching frequently delays bedtime, leading to shortened sleep duration and compromised sleep quality. The immersive nature of serialized narratives and the availability of entire seasons encourage viewers to extend viewing late into the night, often at the expense of sleep.

Subramanian and Das (2024) reported similar findings among late adolescents and emerging adults, showing that habitual binge-watching was associated with irregular sleep schedules and daytime fatigue. These disruptions are particularly concerning for students, as inadequate sleep impairs attention, emotional regulation, and academic performance. Additionally, Alimoradi et al. (2022) suggested that poor sleep quality may partially mediate the relationship between binge-watching and mental health problems, including anxiety and depressive symptoms.

Physical Health

Devi and Singh (2023) examined the risks associated with excessive screen time, including musculoskeletal discomfort, visual strain, fatigue, and reduced physical activity. Although their study focused on general screen use rather than binge-watching specifically, its relevance lies in the fact that binge-watching also involves prolonged immobility and continuous screen exposure.

Academic, Developmental, and Youth-Specific Impacts

Tse et al. (2025) demonstrated that binge-watching among children and adolescents was associated with poorer academic engagement, reduced social well-being, and heightened psychological distress.

Similar trends have been observed among university students. Sil et al. (2025) reported that frequent marathon viewing was linked to increased stress, decreased academic focus, and emotional exhaustion. Sahar Abdul Gafoor (2024), through an online survey, found a positive association between academic stress and binge-watching behaviour, which further impaired academic functioning and psychological resilience.

Paulus et al. (2023) emphasized that adolescence is a critical developmental period during which habits related to attention, reward sensitivity, and self-regulation are established, making excessive media consumption particularly impactful during this stage.

Cumulative Effects on Well-Being

Garg and Singh (2023) demonstrated that heavy binge-watching leads to increased loneliness and interaction anxiety, while Subramanian and Das (2024) linked excessive content consumption to poorer mental health among emerging adults. Alimoradi et al. (2022) further confirmed these patterns across cultural contexts, highlighting consistent associations between problematic binge-watching and emotional distress.

Özkent and Akdoğan (2025) emphasized that most harmful outcomes are concentrated among individuals who exhibit loss of control, preoccupation with marathon viewing, and continued use despite awareness of negative consequences. Thus, while not all binge-watching is harmful, excessive and uncontrolled patterns pose meaningful risks to Collectively well-being.

In conclusion, these empirical findings indicate that although binge-watching is a normalized and technologically facilitated practice, its excessive forms are associated with significant social and health consequences. Therefore, distinguishing maladaptive binge-watching from healthy prolonged viewing habits is essential.

HEALTHY VS. PROBLEMATIC BINGE-WATCHING

Contemporary research increasingly emphasizes the importance of distinguishing between healthy (non-problematic) and problematic patterns of binge-watching, demonstrating that marathon viewing is not inherently harmful. Rather than conceptualizing binge-watching as a uniformly negative behavior, scholars describe Binge-watching as existing along a continuum, ranging from controlled and enjoyable engagement to compulsive and distressing behavior (Flayelle et al., 2017; Alimoradi et al., 2022). This distinction is essential for understanding when binge-watching functions as adaptive leisure and when it becomes psychologically maladaptive.

Healthy Binge-Watching

Healthy prolonged viewing refers to intentional, time-limited, and self-regulated watching that does not interfere with daily functioning or psychological well-being. According to Pittman and Sheehan (2015), viewers often engage in extended viewing for entertainment, relaxation, or social connection, such as unwinding after academic or work-related stress. It is important to note that, individuals who engage in healthy binge-watching retain control over when to start and stop viewing, ensuring that their habits do not significantly disrupt sleep, academic responsibilities, physical activity, or interpersonal relationships.

Research further suggests that, for some viewers, binge-watching can serve adaptive functions, including temporary mood regulation and leisure satisfaction (Sil et al., 2025). During planned leisure periods, such as weekends or holidays, extended viewing may function as recreational activity rather than emotional avoidance. Evidence from studies among adolescents and young adults indicates that when prolonged content consumption is balanced with offline responsibilities and self-regulation, it does not necessarily predict adverse mental health outcomes (Subramanian & Das, 2024). Therefore, viewing frequency alone is insufficient to classify binge-watching as harmful; contextual factors and self-regulatory capacity play a critical role.

Problematic Binge-Watching

In contrast, problematic binge-watching is characterized by loss of control, emotional dependence on media content or characters, and functional impairment. Individuals may continue watching despite awareness of negative consequences, such as sleep deprivation, academic disruption, social withdrawal, or psychological distress (Özkent & Akdoğan, 2025). This pattern closely resembles behavioral addiction mechanisms, including compulsive engagement, tolerance, and difficulty disengaging from viewing (Joseph & Varghese, 2025).

Empirical evidence consistently links problematic binge-watching with higher levels of loneliness, anxiety, depression, and perceived stress, particularly among students and young adults (Yu & Alizadeh, 2024; Raza et al., 2021). In many cases, binge-watching is used as an avoidant coping strategy to manage negative emotions. Although it may provide short-term emotional relief, prolonged reliance on this behavior can reinforce maladaptive coping patterns over time. Sleep disruption is one of the most frequently reported consequences, as late-night and uncontrolled viewing contributes to fatigue and impaired daytime functioning (Jindal, 2020).

Cross-cultural research conducted during and after the COVID-19 pandemic further indicates that stressful environments and increased screen accessibility intensified problematic viewing behaviors (Dixit et al., 2020; Sil et al., 2025). Additionally, maladaptive binge-watching has been associated with other risk behaviors, such as increased alcohol consumption, suggesting broader psychosocial vulnerability rather than an isolated media habit (Bonny-Noach et al., 2024).

Key Indicators Differentiating Healthy and Problematic Patterns

Several indicators help differentiate healthy from problematic binge-watching, including viewing motivation, degree of self-control, emotional reliance, and functional impact. Healthy marathon viewing is typically driven by enjoyment and choice, whereas problematic viewing is more often motivated by emotional escape, compulsion, and distress regulation. Functional impairment, such as declining academic performance, social isolation, or continuous feeling of guilt after marathon-watching, is a central marker of problematic engagement (Alimoradi et al., 2022). Recognizing this distinction is crucial for developing accurate interventions and prevention strategies that emphasize self-regulation, media literacy, and adaptive coping mechanisms, rather than pathologizing all forms of prolonged media consumption.

CONCEPTUAL FRAMEWORK AND INTEGRATIVE MODEL

This chapter is guided by an integrative conceptual framework that views binge-watching as a behavioural continuum rather than a uniformly problematic activity. Existing research has associated binge-watching with emotional regulation, escapism, and platform-driven reinforcement mechanisms (Flayelle et al., 2019; Alimoradi et al., 2022). However, these elements are often examined separately. The present chapter brings them together within a structured explanatory framework.

Within this model, binge-watching behaviour is shaped by the interaction between individual motivations (such as entertainment and stress relief), emotional and cognitive processes (including emotional coping and narrative immersion), and platform-level affordances such as autoplay and continuous content availability. These interacting factors influence whether viewing remains controlled and recreational or develops into a problematic pattern associated with psychological, social, and health-related outcomes.

Integrative Conceptual Model of Binge-Watching Behaviour

To illustrate these relationships clearly, Figure 1 presents the conceptual model proposed in this chapter.

Figure 1.

INDIVIDUAL MOTIVATIONS

(Entertainment | Stress Relief | Emotional Escape | Social Connection)

↓

EMOTIONAL & COGNITIVE PROCESSES

(Emotional Regulation | Narrative Immersion | Character Attachment)

↓

PLATFORM AFFORDANCES

(Autoplay | Easy Accessibility | On-Demand Streaming | Algorithmic Recommendations)

↓

BINGE-WATCHING BEHAVIOUR

(Prolonged / Continuous Viewing)

↓

↓	↓
HEALTHY ENGAGEMENT	**PROBLEMATIC ENGAGEMENT**
(Self-Controlled Viewing)	(Loss of Control & Compulsive Viewing)
↓	↓
Positive Leisure Outcome	Psychological & Social Outcomes
(Relaxation, Enjoyment)	(Stress, Sleep Problems, Isolation, Academic Decline)

↑

MODERATING FACTORS

(Self-Regulation | Coping Style | Social Support | Cultural Context)

This model demonstrates that individual motivations activate emotional and cognitive engagement, which are further reinforced by streaming platform features. Furthermore, depending on moderating factors such as self-regulation and coping style, binge-watching may result in positive leisure outcomes or problematic consequences including stress, sleep disturbance, and social withdrawal (Flayelle et al., 2019; Alimoradi et al., 2022).

INTERVENTIONS AND STRATEGIES

As discussed earlier in this chapter, binge-watching exists on a continuum ranging from intentional leisure use to problematic patterns marked by loss of control and functional impairment. Therefore, interventions should not aim to eliminate binge-watching entirely, but rather focus on reducing its negative psychological, social, and behavioral consequences when it becomes excessive. Addressing problematic binge-watching requires a multi-level approach that considers individual self-regulation, psychological vulnerability, educational awareness, and broader public health perspectives (Alimoradi et al., 2022).

Individual Self-Regulation and Behavioral Approaches

Empirical evidence consistently links problematic binge-watching with deficits in self-control, emotional regulation, and time management (Alimoradi et al., 2022; Özkent & Akdoğan, 2025). Accordingly, interventions at the individual level should prioritize awareness and intentional viewing practices. Self-monitoring strategies, such as tracking viewing duration and recognizing emotional triggers, are often identified as a foundational step in reducing maladaptive media use.

Research further suggests that problematic binge-watching frequently functions as a coping mechanism for stress, emotional discomfort, or avoidance of negative affect (Alimoradi et al., 2022; Subramanian & Das, 2024). In this context, substitution strategies, such as engaging in physical activity, social interaction, or structured leisure, may help disrupt excessive viewing cycles while still addressing underlying emotional needs. Stress-management and time-structuring techniques are particularly relevant, as higher stress levels are consistently associated with heavier content consumption.

Psychological and Therapeutic Interventions

Although problematic binge-watching shares characteristics with behavioral addictions, such as loss of control and continued use despite negative outcomes, there are currently no disorder-specific treatment models for this behavior (Alimoradi et al., 2022; Özkent & Akdoğan, 2025). Nevertheless, therapeutic approaches commonly applied to related behavioural concerns may be cautiously relevant. Cognitive-behavioural strategies that focus on identifying maladaptive viewing patterns, modifying cognitive justifications, and strengthening alternative coping responses may support behavioural change.

Motivational approaches may also be useful, particularly because binge-watching often provides immediate enjoyment and emotional relief. Goal-setting strategies that emphasize well-being, academic functioning, or sleep regulation may help individuals reassess their viewing habits without framing binge-watching as inherently pathological. This is especially relevant among young adults, where excessive viewing has been associated with poorer mental health and functional disruption (Subramanian & Das, 2024).

Educational and Preventive Strategies

Given the strong association between problematic binge-watching and psychological distress, educational institutions represent an important context for prevention efforts. Awareness-based programs that promote healthy digital habits, emotional regulation, and time management may help reduce reliance on prolonged viewing as a coping strategy. Research among Indian college students highlights that higher perceived stress is linked to stronger binge-watching tendencies, further supporting the value of preventive education (Sahar Abdul Gafoor, 2024).

Encouraging open discussions around binge-watching within student wellness initiatives may also reduce stigma and support self-reflection, without portraying the behavior as uniformly harmful.

Technological and Environmental Considerations

Problematic binge-watching is frequently associated with uninterrupted viewing and reduced opportunities for behavioral reflection (Özkent & Akdoğan, 2025). From a behavioral perspective, introducing structured pauses and limiting continuous screen exposure may help support healthier viewing patterns. Screen-management approaches used in broader public health contexts, including recommendations to reduce sedentary behavior and promote physical activity, are relevant to binge-watching practices as well (Devi & Singh, 2023; World Health Organization, 2024).

Cultural and Population-Specific Adaptations

Evidence from Indian and South Asian contexts indicates that binge-watching among young adults is closely linked to stress, loneliness, and emotional vulnerability (Garg & Singh, 2023; Subramanian & Das, 2024). These findings emphasize the importance of culturally sensitive interventions that prioritize social reconnection and collective support. Adolescents represent another high-risk group, as marathon viewing in this population has been associated with poorer academic outcomes and reduced social well-being (Tse et al., 2025). Addressing underlying emotional and social difficulties remains essential for achieving sustainable behavioral change (Özkent & Akdoğan, 2025).

RESEARCH GAPS AND FUTURE DIRECTIONS

Despite the rapid expansion of binge-watching research, the literature remains methodologically and conceptually constrained. A central limitation across studies is the reliance on cross-sectional and self-report designs. For instance, Alimoradi et al. (2022) report significant associations between binge-watching and depression, anxiety, stress, emotional dysregulation, and sleep problems; however, most included studies are correlational, limiting causal interpretation. Similarly, Subramanian and Das (2024) identify links between binge-watching and reduced psychological well-being among late adolescents and young adults, yet their cross-sectional design restricts understanding of behavioral changes over time. Even studies examining problematic binge-watching, such as Özkent and Akdoğan (2025), rely primarily on subjective self-reports rather than objective usage data.

Future research should prioritize longitudinal designs to clarify directionality between psychological distress and binge-watching behavior. The integration of objective indicators, such as digital usage records or screen-time tracking, alongside validated self-report measures would strengthen methodological rigor.

Another significant gap concerns limited demographic and cultural representation. Much of the existing literature focuses on adolescents and emerging adults, often within academic settings. While studies such as Subramanian and Das (2024) and Tse et al. (2025) highlight developmental vulnerabilities, broader age groups, occupational populations, and diverse socioeconomic contexts remain underexplored. Although research from India and Türkiye (Sil et al., 2025; Özkent & Akdoğan, 2025) demonstrates expanding geographical coverage, representation from Africa, Latin America, and several Asian regions is still limited. Gender- and subgroup-based analyses are also insufficiently examined.

Future studies should adopt cross-cultural and cross-national approaches using standardized measures to better understand contextual influences on binge-watching patterns.

Conceptually, inconsistency in defining and measuring binge-watching continues to hinder theoretical clarity. Studies differ in operational criteria, ranging from number of episodes viewed to subjective loss of control, making comparison difficult (Alimoradi et al., 2022). Furthermore, there is limited consensus regarding when high engagement transitions into problematic behavior. Greater emphasis on theoretically grounded definitions and cross-cultural validation of measurement tools is necessary to advance the field.

CONCLUSION

Binge-watching has emerged as a central feature of contemporary digital media consumption, shaped by on-demand streaming platforms and changing viewing habits. This chapter examined binge-watching as both a normative leisure activity and a behavior that may carry psychological and social risks when it becomes excessive or compensatory.

A key contribution of this chapter lies in its clear conceptual distinction between healthy and problematic binge-watching. While extended viewing may function as intentional entertainment and social engagement, problematic patterns are associated with psychological distress, including stress, anxiety, depressive symptoms, and sleep disruption (Alimoradi et al., 2022). The chapter further highlights emotional regulation and coping motives as important mechanisms underlying excessive engagement (Subramanian & Das, 2024).

By synthesizing findings across psychological, social, and health domains, and by incorporating evidence from non-Western contexts, this chapter provides greater conceptual clarity within a fragmented body of research. Rather than framing binge-watching as inherently harmful, it situates the behavior along a continuum shaped by self-regulation, motivation, and contextual factors.

Collectively, this integrative perspective advances existing literature by organizing empirical findings into a structured framework that distinguishes normative engagement from risk-oriented patterns. Such clarity has implications for future research, preventive strategies, and responsible digital media use.

REFERENCES

Alimoradi, Z., Jafari, E., Potenza, M. N., Lin, C. Y., Wu, C. Y., & Pakpour, A. H. (2022). Binge-Watching and Mental Health Problems: A Systematic Review and Meta-Analysis. *International Journal of Environmental Research and Public Health, 19*(15), 9707. DOI: 10.3390/ijerph19159707 PMID: 35955069

Bonny-Noach, H., Sinambela, Y., Hanafi, E., Shina, C., & Siste, K. (2024). Problematic series watching and alcohol consumption among global audiences of Korean Drama in Israel and Indonesia. *Scientific Reports, 14*(1), 17624. DOI: 10.1038/s41598-024-68700-4 PMID: 39085323

Boursier, V., Gioia, F., Musetti, A., & Schimmenti, A. (2020). Facing Loneliness and Anxiety During the COVID-19 Isolation: The Role of Excessive Social Media Use in a Sample of Italian Adults. *Frontiers in Psychiatry, 11*, 586222. DOI: 10.3389/fpsyt.2020.586222 PMID: 33363484

Devi, K. A., & Singh, S. K. (2023). The hazards of excessive screen time: Impacts on physical health, mental health, and Collectively well-being. *Journal of Education and Health Promotion, 12*(1), 413. DOI: 10.4103/jehp.jehp_447_23 PMID: 38333167

Dixit, A., Marthoenis, M., Arafat, S. M. Y., Sharma, P., & Kar, S. K. (2020). Binge watching behavior during COVID 19 pandemic: A cross-sectional, cross-national online survey. *Psychiatry Research, 289*, 113089. DOI: 10.1016/j.psychres.2020.113089

Ferchaud, A., Yan, Z., & Daniel, E. S. (2022). Binging on the heartbreak: The effect of binge-watching on narrative engagement and parasocial breakups. *Psychology of Popular Media, 11*(4), 402–412. DOI: 10.1037/ppm0000414

Fingerman, K. L., Kim, Y. K., Ng, Y. T., Zhang, S., Huo, M., & Birditt, K. S. (2022). Television Viewing, Physical Activity, and Loneliness in Late Life. *The Gerontologist, 62*(7), 1006–1017. DOI: 10.1093/geront/gnab120 PMID: 34379115

Flayelle, M., Maurage, P., & Billieux, J. (2017). Toward a qualitative understanding of binge-watching behaviors: A focus group approach. *Journal of Behavioral Addictions, 6*(4), 457–471. DOI: 10.1556/2006.6.2017.060 PMID: 29025269

Flayelle, M., Maurage, P., Karila, L., Vögele, C., & Billieux, J. (2019). Overcoming the unitary exploration of binge-watching: A cluster analytical approach. *Journal of Behavioral Addictions, 8*(3), 586–602. DOI: 10.1556/2006.8.2019.53 PMID: 31537085

Gafoor, S. A. (2024). Perceived Stress And Binge-Watching Behavior Among Indian College Students, Educational Administration. *Theory into Practice*, *30*(5), 117–126. DOI: 10.53555/kuey.v30i5.2787

Garg, S. & Singh, A.K. (2023). Binge Watching, Loneliness, Interpersonal Competence and Interaction Anxiety in Young Adults. International Journal of Indian Psychology, 11(3), 541-553. DIP:18.01.051.20231103, DOI:DOI: 10.25215/1103.051

Jindal, R. D. (2020). Is binge-watching competing with sleep? And winning? *Journal of Clinical Sleep Medicine : JCSM : Official Publication of the American Academy of Sleep Medicine*, *16*(S1), 31–32. DOI: 10.5664/jcsm.8898 PMID: 33054964

Joseph, D., & Varghese, K. (2025). Binge-watching as a behavioural addiction: A systematic review of causes, consequences, and potential for mental health intervention. *Indian Journal of Psychiatric Social Work*, *16*(1), 36–47. DOI: 10.29120/ijpsw.2025.v16.i1.637

Kandola, A. (2022, November 29). What is binge watching? Definition, health effects, and more. Medical News Today. https://www.medicalnewstoday.com/articles/what-is-binge-watching

Karmakar, A. (2024). Era of binge-watching: An 'asset' or an 'abyss'? *International Journal of Indian Psychology*, *12*(2), 4408–4416. https://ijip.in/wp-content/uploads/2024/07/18.01.393.20241202.pdf

Özkent, Y., & Akdoğan, Y. (2025). Relationships between problematic binge-watching behavior with psychological and social states. *BMC Public Health*, *25*(1), 2309. DOI: 10.1186/s12889-025-23422-8 PMID: 40611062

Paulus, M. P., Zhao, Y., Potenza, M. N., Aupperle, R. L., Bagot, K. S., & Tapert, S. F. (2023). Screen media activity in youth: A critical review of mental health and neuroscience findings. *Journal of Mood and Anxiety Disorders*, *3*, 100018. DOI: 10.1016/j.xjmad.2023.100018 PMID: 37927536

Pittman, M., & Sheehan, K. (2015). Sprinting a media marathon: Uses and gratifications of binge-watching television through Netflix. *First Monday*, *20*(10). Advance online publication. DOI: 10.5210/fm.v20i10.6138

PwC. (2025). Global entertainment & media outlook 2025-2029. https://www.pwc.com/gx/en/issues/business-model-reinvention/outlook.html

Raj, N., & Ida, S. (2022). A new era of viewing, binge watching: Review article. *International Journal of Health Sciences*, *6*(S6), 7831–7840. DOI: 10.53730/ijhs.v6nS6.11099

Syed Hassan Raza, Muhammad Yousaf, Faryal Sohail, Rehana Munawar, Emenyeonu C Ogadimma & Jenny Marisa Lim Dao Siang (2021) Investigating Binge-Watching Adverse Mental Health Outcomes During Covid-19 Pandemic: Moderating Role of Screen Time For Web Series Using Online Streaming, Psychology Research and Behavior Management,, 1615-1629, DOI: To link to this article: https://doi.org/ DOI: 10.2147/PRBM.S328416

Raza, S. H., Yousaf, M., Sohail, F., Munawar, R., Ogadimma, E. C., & Siang, J. M. L. D. (2021). Investigating Binge-Watching Adverse Mental Health Outcomes During Covid-19 Pandemic: Moderating Role of Screen Time for Web Series Using Online Streaming. *Psychology Research and Behavior Management*, *14*, 1615–1629. DOI: 10.2147/PRBM.S328416 PMID: 34675702

Shaker, K. S., & Bukhari, S. R. (2025). Binge Watching, Para Social Relationships and Psycho Social well-Being in Early Adults. *Journal of Development and Social Sciences*, *6*(2), 53–67. DOI: 10.47205/jdss.2025(6-II)06

Sil, M., Mondal, A., & Kumar, M. (2025). Prevalence and psychological correlates of binge-watching: The digital era of entertainment. *Industrial Psychiatry Journal*, *34*(2), 215–220. DOI: 10.4103/ipj.ipj_36_25 PMID: 40861144

Singh, P., & Thomas, R. (2025). Binge-watching behavior and the strategies adopted to overcome this among undergraduate students. *Journal of Health and Society*, *7*(2). https://jhas-nu.in/binge-watching-behavior-and-the-strategies-adopted-to-overcome-this-among-the-undergraduate-students/

Statista. (2025). Video streaming – worldwide. https://www.statista.com/outlook/dmo/digital-media/video-on-demand/worldwide

Subramanian, P.S. & Das, K. (2024). Binge Watching and Mental Health Among Late Adolescence and Early Adulthood. International Journal of Indian Psychology, 12(1), 1002-1030. DIP:18.01.095.20241201, DOI:DOI: 10.25215/1201.095

Tolba, A. A., & Zoghaib, S. Z. (2022). Understanding the Binge-watching Phenomenon on Netflix and Its Association with Depression and Loneliness in Egyptian Adults. *Media Watch*, *13*(3), 264–279. DOI: 10.1177/09760911221117339

Tse, N., Pang, N. S., Wang, X., Li, Y., Lo, C. K., & Yang, X. (2025). Binge-watching and gender-specific effects on academic, social, and mental well-being in children and adolescents. *PLoS One*, *20*(8), e0329655. DOI: 10.1371/journal.pone.0329655 PMID: 40845080

Umesh, S., & Bose, S. (2019). Binge-Watching: A Matter of Concern? *Indian Journal of Psychological Medicine*, *41*(2), 182–184. DOI: 10.4103/IJPSYM.IJPSYM_279_18 PMID: 30983669

Yu, H., & Alizadeh, F. (2024). Online Binge-Watching Among Chinese College Students: Implications for Loneliness, Anxiety, and Depression. *Psychology Research and Behavior Management*, *17*, 295–303. DOI: 10.2147/PRBM.S447311 PMID: 38292254

ADDITIONAL READING

Alfonsi, V., Varallo, G., Scarpelli, S., Gorgoni, M., Filosa, M., De Gennaro, L., Musetti, A., & Franceschini, C. (2023). 'This is the last episode': The association between problematic binge-watching and loneliness, emotion regulation, and sleep-related factors in poor sleepers. *Journal of Sleep Research*, *32*(1), e13747. DOI: 10.1111/jsr.13747 PMID: 36254098

Bastos, M., Naranjo-Zolotov, M., & Aparício, M. (2024). Binge-watching uncovered: Examining the interplay of perceived usefulness, habit, and regret in continuous viewing. *Heliyon*, *10*(6), e27848. DOI: 10.1016/j.heliyon.2024.e27848 PMID: 38515690

Billaux, P., Billieux, J., Gärtner, L., Maurage, P., & Flayelle, M. (2022). Negative affect and problematic binge-watching: The mediating role of unconstructive ruminative thinking style. *Psychologica Belgica*, *62*(1), 272–285. DOI: 10.5334/pb.1163 PMID: 36246519

Exelmans, L., & Van den Bulck, J. (2017). Binge viewing, sleep, and the role of pre-sleep arousal. *Journal of Clinical Sleep Medicine : JCSM : Official Publication of the American Academy of Sleep Medicine*, *13*(8), 1001–1008. DOI: 10.5664/jcsm.6704 PMID: 28728618

Forte, G., Favieri, F., Tedeschi, D., & Casagrande, M. (2021). Binge-watching: Development and validation of the binge-watching addiction questionnaire. *Behavioral Sciences (Basel, Switzerland)*, *11*(2), 27. DOI: 10.3390/bs11020027 PMID: 33672253

Ort, A., Wirz, D. S., & Fahr, A. (2020). Is binge-watching addictive? Effects of motives for TV series use on the relationship between excessive media consumption and problematic viewing habits. *Addictive Behaviors Reports*, *13*, 100325. DOI: 10.1016/j.abrep.2020.100325 PMID: 33457488

Riddle, K., Peebles, A., Davis, C., Xu, F., & Schroeder, E. (2018). The addictive potential of television binge watching: Comparing intentional and unintentional binges. *Psychology of Popular Media Culture, 7*(4), 589–604. DOI: 10.1037/ppm0000167

Starosta, J., Izydorczyk, B., Sitnik-Warchulska, K., & Lizińczyk, S. (2021). Impulsivity and difficulties in emotional regulation as predictors of binge-watching behaviours. *Frontiers in Psychiatry, 12*, 743870. DOI: 10.3389/fpsyt.2021.743870 PMID: 34858225

Starosta, J. A., & Izydorczyk, B. (2020). Understanding the phenomenon of binge-watching—A systematic review. *International Journal of Environmental Research and Public Health, 17*(12), 4469. DOI: 10.3390/ijerph17124469 PMID: 32580289

Wingralek, Z. J., Banaszek, A., Giermasiński, A., Czarnecki, A., Goliszek, K., Kajka, N., Juchnowicz, D., Kohn, P. M., & Karakuła-Juchnowicz, H. (2024). Turn on the screen, turn off the loneliness: Analysis of risk factors for binge-watching among Polish medical and non-medical students: A web-based cross-sectional study. *Annals of Agricultural and Environmental Medicine, 31*(2), 264–271. DOI: 10.26444/aaem/183779 PMID: 38940111

KEY TERMS AND DEFINITIONS

Binge-Watching: Marathon viewing can be defined as the practice of watching multiple episodes or seasons of a television series or online content continuously in a single sitting, usually through rapidly growing streaming platforms.

Digital Dependence: Digital dependence can be defined as a pattern of heavy reliance on digital devices and online platforms for entertainment, relaxation, or emotional support, which may result in prolonged screen engagement.

Mood Management: Mood management can be defined as a process to regulate negative emotions, associated with distress or anxiety etc., by immersing in heavy use of media consumption, such as binge-watching.

Problematic Binge-Watching: Problematic binge-watching refers to a maladaptive pattern of content consumption in which viewing becomes excessive, leads to difficulty in self-control, and begins to interfere with daily responsibilities, sleep, or collectively well-being.

Screen Time: A record on the amount of time an individual spends using digital devices with screens, including smartphones, tablets, computers, and televisions.

Self-Regulation: Self- regulation can be defined as, an ability of individuals to be able to control their viewing habits by setting limits, managing time effectively, and maintaining balance between entertainment and other life activities.

Streaming Platforms: Streaming platforms are online services, such as Netflix, Amazon Prime Video, and HiTV, that provide on-demand access to television shows, movies, and other digital content, enabling continuous and flexible viewing.

Chapter 10
Attracting Attention in the Age of Digital Addiction:
Content Analysis of Short-Form Video in the Attention Economy

Neslihan Bulur Demirel
http://orcid.org/0000-0001-6148-5556
Üsküdar University, Turkey

ABSTRACT

Digital platforms like TikTok are known to shorten attention spans and foster addiction symptoms such as FOMO and doomscrolling. This study investigates the interplay between digital content, the attention economy, and digital addiction. Employing content analysis, the research examines 300 TikTok videos tagged #beforeafter (#öncesisonrası), systematically collected via data scraping on August 20, 2025. This specific hashtag was selected as the contrast between initial "chaos" and final "order" offers high visual satisfaction, encouraging viewer retention. By analyzing both metadata and qualitative structures, the study deconstructs the mechanisms behind the "doomscroll" experience. Findings are discussed through a techno-political lens, revealing the visual dynamics underpinning the attention economy. Ultimately, this research provides a theoretical and empirical foundation for understanding "digital malaise," including cognitive fatigue and screen dependency.

DOI: 10.4018/979-8-3373-6665-4.ch010

INTRODUCTION

The evolution of the digital ecosystem represents a transition from an era of information scarcity to one where human attention has become the scarcest resource. Herbert Simon's early thesis—that a wealth of information creates a poverty of attention—constitutes the fundamental economic model of contemporary digital platforms. However, within current critical literature, this situation is defined not merely as a resource management issue, but as "Surveillance Capitalism," where human experience is converted into behavioral data and commodified. In this context, attention has ceased to be an act directed by the user's free will; instead, it has transformed into a tool of capital accumulation that is "harvested" by platform architectures and shaped through tools of algorithmic governmentality.

In this process, which Yves Citton interprets through "The Ecology of Attention," digital platforms emerge as a new form of governance that fragments individual subjectivity and "enchants" the collective mind. Consequently, the attention economy is a techno-political sphere of power that restructures the masses' perception of time and capacity for focus, beyond being a mere commercial activity. The rise of short-form video platforms—particularly TikTok, YouTube Shorts, and Instagram Reels—points to a paradigm shift in media consumption habits termed "TikTokification". By integrating "variable ratio reward" mechanisms and "doomscrolling" features into their interfaces, these platforms create a slot-machine-like dopaminergic loop in users. This mechanism, which Johann Hari characterizes as the "theft of attention," targets users' biological vulnerabilities, such as impulsivity and the search for novelty.

It is widely acknowledged that this new media ecology, shaped by constant notifications and rapid content flow, leads to symptoms of digital addiction such as distractibility, FOMO (Fear of Missing Out), and doomscrolling. Current debates in the literature demonstrate that digital addiction stems not only from the technical structure of the platform but also from the qualitative structure of the content. Specifically, the "curiosity gap" and the "need for closure" in visual content are among the most powerful psychological triggers compelling the user to watch a video to the end. In this regard, the "before/after" concept holds a special place in the attention economy literature. The contrast between the initial chaos and the final order offers high visual satisfaction, encouraging the viewer to continue watching to see the result.

This study primarily aims to discuss the relationship between content on digital platforms, the attention economy, and digital addictions. The research is based on an examination of the content that contributes to the addictive "doomscrolling" experience through both its metadata (e.g., video duration, interaction counts) and its qualitative structure (e.g., attention-grabbing elements, narrative structure). Within this scope, 300 videos featuring the hashtag #öncesisonrası (#beforeafter) on the popular video platform TikTok were analyzed using the content analysis method. By revealing the practical visual dynamics upon which the attention economy is based, this study aims to shed light on the formation mechanisms of digital addictions. Furthermore, the research will provide a theoretical and empirical foundation for phenomena that can be evaluated as "digital malaise," such as attention deficit, screen addiction, and cognitive fatigue.

SHORT-FORM VIDEOS AND THE ECOLOGY OF ATTENTİON: A CRITICAL ANALYSIS OF TIKTOK #BEFOREAFTER CONTENT

The evolution of the digital ecosystem represents a transition from an era of information scarcity to one where human attention has become the scarcest resource. Herbert Simon's (1971) early prediction that "a wealth of information creates a poverty of attention" now constitutes the fundamental economic model of digital platforms (Simon, 1971: 40). However, in current critical literature, this situation is defined not merely as a resource management issue, but as "Surveillance Capitalism," a system where human experience is converted into behavioral data and commodified (Zuboff, 2019). In this context, attention has ceased to be an act directed by the user's free will; instead, it has transformed into a tool of capital accumulation that is "harvested" by platform architectures and shaped through tools of "algorithmic governmentality." Yves Citton (2017) interprets this process through the lens of the "Ecology of Attention," arguing that digital platforms represent a new form of governance that fragments individual subjectivity and "enchants" the collective mind (Citton 2017: 7-19). Similarly, Dominic Pettman (2017) underscores that social media traps the user not only through technical means but also by enveloping them in a mechanism of affective and perceptual capture, thereby confining them within a form of 'infinite distraction' (Pettman, 2018).

Consequently, the attention economy is not merely a commercial activity, but a techno-political sphere of power that restructures the masses' perception of time and capacity for focus.

The rise of short-form video platforms such as TikTok, YouTube Shorts, and Instagram Reels points to a paradigm shift in media consumption habits termed "TikTokification" (Vizcaíno-Verdú & Abidin, 2022: 884-885; Gerbaudo, 2024: 2-16). By integrating "variable ratio schedule" mechanisms derived from B.F. Skinner's behavioral psychology into digital interfaces (e.g., "doomscrolling"), these platforms create a slot-machine-like dopaminergic loop in users (Alter, 2017: 100). Johann Hari (2022) characterizes this mechanism as the "theft of attention," noting that platforms deliberately target users' biological vulnerabilities, such as impulsivity, the need for validation, and novelty seeking. The rapid flow generated by short-form videos also aligns with Byung-Chul Han's (2021) critique of the "aesthetics of smoothness." According to Han, digital content excludes all forms of intellectual resistance and negativity, becoming "objects of instant gratification" that transform the consumer into a passive viewer (Han, 2021: 79-82; Han, 2020: 3-11). This situation results in a "fragmented mind" structure that is trapped in a constant "now," has lost its perception of past and future, and has forfeited the capacity for deep reading (Carr, 2010: 45-60).

Current debates in the literature demonstrate that digital addiction stems not only from the technical structure of the platform (algorithms) but also from the qualitative structure of the content (Zhang et al., 2019: 12-13). Specifically, the "curiosity gap" and the "need for closure" in visual content are among the most powerful psychological triggers compelling the user to watch a video to the end (Loewenstein, 1994: 85-95; Kruglanski, 2004: 9-11). In this regard, the #beforeafter concept holds a special place in the attention economy literature. The human brain possesses an evolutionary predisposition to process visual contrasts and the transition from chaos to order. The clutter, dirt, or imperfection (chaos) in the "Before" stage creates cognitive tension in the viewer, while the cleanliness, aesthetic appeal, or order in the "After" stage offers high "visual satisfaction" that resolves this tension. This structure can be explained by the "principle of closure" in Gestalt psychology; the viewer is unable to abandon the video in order to see the narrative's conclusion and achieve mental "wholeness" (Lang, 2000: 59-64). Such content provides "digital satisfaction" (similar to ASMR or cleaning videos), immersing the viewer in a hypnotic "flow" and causing a loss of time perception. This mechanism not only satisfies curiosity but also sustains a constant impulse to "see more," fueling pathological behaviors such as Doomscrolling or FOMO (Fear of Missing Out).

This new media ecology, shaped by constant notifications and rapid content flow, leads to symptoms defined in the literature as "digital obesity" or "cognitive fatigue" (Lorenz-Spreen et al., 2019: 1-2). The narrowing of the attention span is not merely an individual efficiency issue but an "epistemological crisis" that hinders the analysis of complex societal problems. Although Newport (2019) discusses this situation through the need for "digital minimalism," the core problem lies less in individual will than in business models based on the "engineering of attention." This study, which analyzes how short-form video content published with the #beforeafter hashtag on TikTok reflects the dynamics of the attention economy and digital addiction theories, aims to discuss the relationship between content on digital platforms, the attention economy, and digital addictions. The study primarily seeks to answer the question of how short-form video content published with the #beforeafter hashtag on TikTok reflects—at both the content and metadata levels—the attention-grabbing dynamics and addiction mechanisms predicted by the attention economy and digital addiction theories. Therefore, the analysis of the content addressed in this study is critical for understanding not merely what the videos depict, but how these visual strategies lock the user to the screen and reproduce mechanisms of digital addiction.

RESEARCH MODEL

In this study, a content analysis method incorporating mixed data approaches was adopted to empirically ground the relationship between short-form video content on digital platforms, the attention economy, and digital addiction mechanisms. Defined as a research technique for the objective, systematic, and quantitative description of communication content (Berelson, 1952), content analysis in this study enabled the examination of both structural/quantitative metadata and content-related/qualitative indicators. The research design was constructed within a descriptive framework to reveal how digital content commodifies user attention and constructs the "doom-scrolling" experience. The population of the research consists of content on the TikTok platform, one of the most popular venues for the short-form video format. The study's sample comprises 300 video contents tagged with the #öncesisonrası (#beforeafter) hashtag, selected using the purposive sampling method.

The primary rationale for selecting this hashtag is that, by its very nature, the content offers high visual satisfaction and utilizes the contrast between "chaos and order" to increase the viewer's tendency to watch until the end (retention) through the anticipation of seeing the result. This mechanism provides an ideal basis for the empirical examination of attention-grabbing strategies that trigger reward anticipation at a cognitive level, thereby leading to symptoms of digital addiction. Data were systematically collected on August 20, 2025, using the TikTok Scraper data scraping tool to obtain an objective and replicable dataset independent of algorithmic bias and the researcher's personal viewing history.

The collected dataset of 300 videos was analyzed across two fundamental dimensions using a coding scheme[1] derived from indicators in attention economy and digital addiction theories. The first dimension includes quantitative indicators comprising metadata such as video duration, view/like/share counts, and interaction calls in the video description. The second dimension includes qualitative indicators related to content features, such as topic type, presence of verbal narrative, attention-grabbing elements, and effects. Data analysis was performed using frequency and percentage distributions alongside descriptive statistics. The findings were discussed from a critical perspective in light of the empirical foundations of phenomena such as distractibility, cognitive fatigue, and screen addiction.

Development of the Coding Scheme

The coding scheme was developed through a multi-stage iterative process to ensure both theoretical relevance and empirical accuracy. Initially, a deductive framework was established based on the attention economy and digital addiction literature (e.g., Simon, 1971; Alter, 2017; Han, 2021), focusing on standardized interaction metrics and theorized psychological triggers such as "reward mechanisms" and "aesthetics of smoothness".

Following this, an exploratory analysis was conducted on a pilot sample of 50 videos to identify platform-specific features. During this stage, inductive categories emerged from the data, specifically regarding the "Topic Types" (e.g., Personal Transformation, Decoration) and specific "Narrative Forms" (e.g., Fast-Paced Montage) unique to TikTok's visual culture. These categories were then integrated into the final coding scheme, ensuring a comprehensive analytical framework that captures both overarching economic logics and nuanced content dynamics.

To ensure analytical rigor and transparency, the codes, their definitions, and their theoretical or empirical origins are systematically presented in Table 1.

Table 1. Analytical Categories and Coding Scheme

Category	Definition	Origin
Metadata Metrics	Quantitative data including view, like, share, and comment counts.	**Deductive:** Attention economy metrics (Simon, 1971).
Video Duration	Length of the video in seconds.	**Deductive:** Attention span and "TikTokification" literature.
Topic Type	The thematic focus of the content (e.g., Personal Transformation, Decoration).	**Inductive:** Emerged from exploratory data immersion.
Narrative Form	The structural delivery of content (e.g., Montage vs. Vlog type).	**Inductive:** Refined through exploratory analysis of visual styles.
Dramatic Introduction	Presence of an expositional/teasing start to build tension.	**Deductive:** Narrative theory and curiosity gap (Loewenstein, 1994).
Emphasis on Perfection	Visual focus on idealized, flawless final results.	**Deductive:** Aesthetics of smoothness (Han, 2021).
Contrast Intensity	The degree of visual difference between "before" and "after" states.	**Inductive:** Developed based on observed variance in content.
Interaction Call	Explicit requests for user engagement (e.g., "follow for more").	**Deductive:** Marketing and "Call to Action" (CTA) theories.
Presence of Effects	Use of digital filters or artificial enhancements.	**Inductive:** Categorized based on empirical observation of TikTok features.

Reliability and Application

To ensure the reliability of the findings, two researchers independently coded a sub-sample of 90 videos, representing 30% of the total dataset. Inter-coder reliability was assessed using Cohen's Kappa, and a high level of agreement (above 0.80) was achieved across all categories. This rigorous pre-testing process confirmed that the analytical framework was robust and replicable for the main study. Furthermore, as previously noted, data were systematically collected on August 20, 2025, using the TikTok Scraper tool to obtain an objective and replicable dataset independent of algorithmic bias and the researcher's personal viewing history.

FINDINGS

In this study, the operational mechanisms of the attention economy and the dynamics of digital addiction were examined through videos shared with the #öncesisonrası (#beforeafter) hashtag on the TikTok platform. The findings reveal that digital platforms are not merely tools for entertainment; on the contrary, they constitute sophisticated spheres of power that harvest human attention at speeds measured in milliseconds, break down cognitive resistance, and engender addiction. The descriptive analysis based on the metadata of the 300 videos examined within the scope of the research and shared with the #beforeafter hashtag reveals the speed of consumption and the hierarchy of interaction on digital platforms. The data presented in Table 2 quantitatively substantiate the platform's capacity for the "harvesting of attention" and users' content consumption habits.

Table 2. Descriptive Statistics Regarding Metadata

Meta Data	Total	Average
Share Count	527915	1759,71667
Comment Count	70014	233,38
Like Count	7574802	25249,34
View Count	162155241	540517,47
Video Duration	6742	22,4733333

The most striking data point in the table is that the videos constituting the sample reached a total of 162,155,241 views, with an average of approximately 540,517 views per video. This massive volume of reach transcends Herbert Simon's thesis that "a wealth of information creates a poverty of attention," serving as proof that attention has transformed into a resource that is processed and commodified on an industrial scale. The average duration of the analyzed videos was determined to be 22.47 seconds. This duration is a typical indicator of the "short-form video" format and the phenomenon of "TikTokification" described in the literature. This 22-second duration represents an ideal interval optimized to keep the "curiosity gap" alive without boring the user and to lead them to the "order/aesthetic" result at the end of the video. This brevity supports constant notifications and a rapid flow of content, breaking down the user's cognitive resistance and creating a "smooth" perception of time that feeds the "doomscrolling" loop.

A comparative analysis of the interaction types in the data reveals a dramatic disparity between the Like Count (AVG: 25,249) and the Comment Count (AVG: 233). Viewers demonstrate a marked preference for low-effort, rapid reactions such as "liking" (impulsive validation) over actions requiring cognitive effort, such as "commenting." Rather than prompting the viewer toward intellectual deliberation (commenting), the content is consumed as objects of instant gratification, thereby creating a passive audience. However, the average share count of 1,759 indicates that these videos are not merely objects of individual consumption; they are also circulated within the network, generating a viral effect. The visual satisfaction derived from the contrast between the "chaos" of the "before" and the "order" of the "after" incentivizes repeated viewing and sharing by inducing a hypnotic "flow" in the viewer. Consequently, the data in Table 2 quantitatively confirms that #beforeafter videos are not merely popular content, but powerful "attention traps" compressed into 22-second micro-timeframes that are viewed millions of times and serve to pacify the audience.

A fundamental and striking finding of the research is that the use of music constitutes an "indispensable backdrop" within the auditory universe of TikTok. The most overwhelming statistic in Table 3 is the presence of "Use of Music" in 288 videos (96%) out of the 300-video sample. In contrast, music was absent in only 12 videos. This situation constitutes the most concrete technical equivalent of the concept of "enchantment" discussed by Yves Citton (2017) in "The Ecology of Attention." Music on TikTok is not merely a background element; it is the fundamental binding agent that rhythmically synchronizes the "chaos-order" transitions in the imagery and immerses the viewer in a state of "flow." Silence is systematically excluded from the platform architecture, as it could lead the viewer to think and ask, "Why am I watching this?"—potentially triggering a cognitive awakening. Constant music transforms the infinite scroll experience into a rhythmic ritual, obliterating the perception of time.

Table 3. Distribution of Music Usage and Interaction Calls

	Use of Music	Interaction Call
Yes	288	29
No	12	271
Grand Total	300	300

Conversely, Table 3 reveals a starkly different situation regarding user engagement: In 271 of the videos (90.3%), no "Interaction Call" (e.g., like, comment, follow) was made. An explicit request is present in only 29 videos. While traditional marketing theories mandate the inclusion of a "Call to Action" (CTA), these data point to a new paradox within the attention economy. To "ask" something of the user (to make a call) is to force them out of the position of a passive viewer and into that of an active decision-maker. Content creators render the viewer addicted by rewarding them solely with visual and auditory pleasure (dopamine), effectively bypassing the need to explicitly ask for a "like." The absence of an interaction call conceals the commercial/artificial nature of the video, thereby disabling the viewer's defense mechanisms. Consequently, this structure—predicated on the combination of high auditory stimulation (music) and low cognitive demand (absence of calls)—constitutes the ideal consumption model of "surveillance capitalism," transforming the viewer from a "thinking subject" into a "sensory object" that merely reacts to rhythmic stimuli.

Table 4. Distribution of Narrative Forms by Topic

Narrative Form	Decoration	Aesthetic	Other	Personal Transformation	Cleaning /Order	Grand Total
Fast-Paced Montage	25	12	9	36	11	93
Text Overlay	41	41	8	61	30	181
Verbal Narrative/Vlog Type	4	10	2	7	3	26
Grand Total	**70**	**63**	**19**	**104**	**44**	**300**

The data presented in Table 4 clearly demonstrates that content creators, operating under the "speed" and "consumability" pressures of the attention economy, gravitate towards narrative forms that demand minimum cognitive effort from the viewer. The most distinct finding in the Table 4 is the overwhelming predominance of "Text Overlay" (181 videos) and "Fast-Paced Montage" (93 videos) techniques over "Verbal Narrative/Vlog Type" (26 videos). While verbal narrative demands a certain cognitive "resistance" from the viewer—such as listening, comprehending, and following a storyline—fast-paced visuals with text overlays are consumed as "objects of instant gratification" without creating any intellectual barrier. The platform architecture encourages flow (via text/montage) by remaining on the surface rather than fostering depth (via verbal narrative). An examination of the topic distribution reveals that the "Personal Transformation" category (104 videos) has the highest frequency, with "Text Overlay" (61 videos) being the most preferred narrative form within this category. The contrast between the flawed state in the "before" phase and the ideal self in the "after" phase is the element that most potently triggers the viewer's "need for closure". The presentation of personal transformation videos through visual evidence and brief text, rather than through verbal storytelling, demonstrates that the body and self are transformed into rapidly consumed data points within the context of "surveillance capitalism".

The "Fast-Paced Montage" technique, which is particularly concentrated in the "Decoration" (25 videos) and "Personal Transformation" (36 videos) categories, prevents the viewer from reaching the boredom threshold by optimizing the video's duration. This technique is a reflection of the "TikTokification" phenomenon described in the literature. Edited with jump cuts, these videos manipulate the viewer's perception of time, compressing the process between "initial chaos" and "final order" to provide high visual satisfaction. Although this situation induces "cognitive fatigue" by immersing the viewer in a hypnotic flow, it sustains the continuity of the action (scrolling) by keeping the dopamine loop alive. Consequently, Table 4 indicates that #beforeafter videos on TikTok exhibit a structure that strips the viewer of the faculty of "listening," conditioning them solely to "see" and "read" (specifically, brief texts). This structure constitutes a significant content strategy that technically enables "doomscrolling" behavior by minimizing cognitive effort.

Table 5. Distribution of Interaction Metrics by Narrative Form

Narrative Form	View Count	Like Count	Comment Count	Share Count	Video Duration
Fast-Paced Montage	41,19%	60,29%	55,98%	69,78%	28,81%
Text Overlay	53,46%	37,93%	40,88%	25,42%	48,90%
Verbal Narrative/Vlog Type	5,34%	1,78%	3,14%	4,80%	22,29%
Grand Total	**100,00%**	**100,00%**	**100,00%**	**100,00%**	**100,00%**

The data in Table 5 supports the previous inferences. Table 5 demonstrates that the interaction hierarchy on digital platforms is inversely proportional to the "cognitive load" of the content. Users' interaction preferences empirically validate Byung-Chul Han's "aesthetics of smoothness" and Skinner's interpretations of "reward mechanisms." The most striking data in the table is that the "Fast-Paced Montage" technique, despite accounting for 41.19% of total views, dominates 69.78% of Share

Counts alone. This indicates that the visual flow created by montage possesses a much higher "virality" coefficient compared to other formats. With a 60.29% like rate, "Fast-Paced Montage" also proves to be the format providing the highest visual satisfaction. This format is the structure that most strongly triggers the dopaminergic loop in the viewer by presenting the transition from chaos to order in the fastest and smoothest manner. This overwhelming dominance in share rate indicates that such videos are not merely watched and bypassed, but are circulated within digital networks as "social capital."

Although the "Text Overlay" category holds the largest share of views at 53.46%, it lags behind its viewership in terms of likes (37.93%) and shares (25.42%). This data suggests that while text-heavy videos are frequently presented to the user by the platform algorithm ("viewing"), the user does not establish as strong an emotional bond ("interaction") with this content as they do with montage videos. Even though the viewer remains on the screen to read the text, thereby increasing "watch time," the impulse to share remains lower because the content does not provide as high a gratification as "fast montage." This situation confirms the platform's success in "harvesting attention" while validating that the effect created by the content remains at a more passive level.

Furthermore, Table 5 clearly reveals that "Verbal Narrative/Vlog Type" content has become marginalized or has collapsed within the digital attention economy. Verbal narrative remained at negligible levels across all metrics (Views: 5.34%; Likes: 1.78%; Shares: 4.80%), especially when considering the scarcity of "verbal narrative" in the category distributions in Table 4. Listening to a story, processing voice, and empathizing with a narrator create a "cognitive cost" for the viewer. Instead of paying this cost, users gravitate towards visual formats that show the result immediately. This data serves as concrete proof of the "fragmented mind" structure in which the faculty of "deep reading/listening" is lost. Consequently, Table 5 demonstrates that the valid "currency of attention" in the TikTok universe is not words or text, but speed and visual rhythm. The faster (montage), smoother, and less cognitively demanding the content is, the more strongly it fuels the addiction loop (likes/shares).

Table 6. Distribution of Interaction Metrics by Topic Type

Topic Type	View Count	Like Count	Comment Count	Share Count	Video Duration
Decoration	17,94%	9,86%	8,59%	10,07%	27,37%
Other	11,99%	11,82%	13,84%	7,30%	25,62%
Aesthetic	4,02%	3,34%	1,52%	2,95%	5,53%

continued on following page

Table 6. Continued

Topic Type	View Count	Like Count	Comment Count	Share Count	Video Duration
Personal Transformation	65,26%	74,80%	75,60%	79,44%	23,78%
Cleaning/Order	0,79%	0,18%	0,44%	0,25%	17,71%
Grand Total	**100,00%**	**100,00%**	**100,00%**	**100,00%**	**100,00%**

Table 6 demonstrates that user attention within #beforeafter tagged content on TikTok is not distributed homogeneously; rather, content constructed around the "human body" and "self-presentation" dominates all other categories. This situation reveals that the attention economy is not merely a matter of visual satisfaction, but also a socio-psychological process of identification. Indeed, the most striking data in Table 6 is that the "Personal Transformation" category has established overwhelming superiority across all interaction metrics. This category alone accounts for 65.26% of the View Count, 74.80% of the Like Count, and 75.60% of the Comment Count. Zuboff's concept of "Surveillance Capitalism," as cited in the literature, transforms here into a concrete reality wherein bodies are converted into digital data packets and commodified. Viewers focus on the transformation of a "human subject" (e.g., weight loss, aesthetics, makeup) rather than the alteration of a room or object. This indicates that "attention" is most concentrated in areas where human biological and aesthetic vulnerabilities are exhibited.

Another striking finding in Table 6 is that the "Decoration" and "Cleaning/Order" categories, which are presented in the literature as strong examples of the "chaos and order" contrast, performed below expectations within this sample group. Although "Decoration" ranked second with a view rate of 17.94%, it experienced a dramatic decline in like (9.86%) and share (10.07%) rates. Even more striking is the fact that "Cleaning/Order" videos remained at a negligible view rate of 0.79%. This finding demonstrates that object-based "visual satisfaction" does not create as potent an "addiction" as dramatic narratives based on human stories. The viewer merely "watches and moves on" from the smoothing of an object, but actively "participates" in the transformation of a human being through likes, comments, or shares. Consequently, Table 6 empirically confirms that the "human body and its story" occupy the apex of the hierarchy within the attention economy. The best-selling "product" under the #beforeafter hashtag is not a clean house, but a "renewed self." This situation reveals that digital addiction is not merely an algorithmic mechanism, but also a deeply narcissistic and human-centric one.

Table 7. Distribution of Qualitative Indicators by Topic Type

Topic Type	Dramatic Introduction		Emphasis on Perfection		Emphasis on Immediate Gratification		Presence of Effects		Interaction Call	
	Yes	No	Yes	No	Yes	No	Yes	No	Yes	No
Decoration	20	50	48	22	54	16	8	62	5	65
Other	7	56	10	53	6	57	4	59	4	59
Aesthetic		19	12	7	11	8		19	1	18
Personal Transformation	27	77	72	32	71	33	15	89	17	87
Cleaning/Order	5	39	29	15	26	18	2	42	2	42
Grand Total	**59**	241	**171**	129	**168**	132	**29**	271	**29**	271

Table 7 demonstrates that #beforeafter videos on TikTok establish an implicit psychological contract with the viewer based on "visual perfection" and "rapid gratification" rather than "verbal communication." The most dominant strategy emerging from the table is the "Emphasis on Perfection," which is particularly concentrated in the "Personal Transformation" (72 Yes) and "Decoration" (48 Yes) categories. In the "after" stage, the content eliminates all manner of flaws, dirt, or incompatibility (negativity), offering the viewer a hygienic and idealized reality. In accordance with the "principle of closure" in Gestalt psychology, the viewer resolves their cognitive tension by observing the transition from chaos to this perfect order, thereby achieving high visual satisfaction.

"Time," the fundamental currency of the attention economy, can be analyzed through the data on "Emphasis on Immediate Gratification" in the table. The high frequency observed in the "Personal Transformation" (71 Yes) and "Decoration" (54 Yes) categories indicates that the primary promise of the content is the "result." The process (labor, time, difficulty) is erased via montage; the transformation is presented as if it occurred "instantly." This phenomenon fuels the "loss of time perception" and "static present time" (nowist culture) described in the literature. The user attains the dopamine reward (the result) within seconds without the need for patience. This "immediate gratification" mechanism acts as the primary fuel that keeps the digital addiction loop constantly active.

The most surprising and paradoxical finding of the table is that the "Interaction Call" (e.g., like, comment, follow) is extremely low (Personal Transformation: 17 Yes, 87 No; Decoration: 5 Yes, 65 No). Contrary to traditional social media marketing, the fact that these videos do not verbally or textually demand an action from the viewer suggests that the strategy is built upon "passive hypnosis." Instead of explicitly saying "like me," the content creator directs the viewer toward interaction solely by utilizing the shocking power of the visual (the before/after contrast). The absence of an interaction call ensures that the "flow" remains uninterrupted and that the viewer forgets the "commercial" or "fictional" nature of the video, focusing exclusively on visual pleasure.

The fact that the "Presence of Effects" generally remains at low levels (Personal Transformation: 15 Yes; Decoration: 8 Yes) suggests that #beforeafter videos derive their power from "provable reality." If the transformation were presented with excessive digital effects (filters, artificial interventions), the viewer's belief that "I can have this too" and their perception of the "reality of the result" could be compromised. Thus, the digital addiction mechanism operates here paradoxically through a claim of "naturalness" or "raw reality." In conclusion, **Table 7** reveals that the success of these videos on TikTok is not coincidental; rather, it is based on sophisticated content engineering that sanctifies perfection, obscures the process to focus on the result (immediate gratification), and immerses the viewer in an undemanding flow.

Table 8. Distribution of Dramatic Introduction by Narrative Form

Narrative Form	Dramatic Introduction	
	Yes	No
Fast-Paced Montage	17	76
Text Overlay	38	143
Verbal Narrative/Vlog Type	4	22
Grand Total	**59**	**241**

Table 8 reveals that employing a "dramatized introduction" to capture the viewer is not a dominant strategy within content production practices on TikTok. On the contrary, the data indicates that content has evolved into a direct, unmediated structure characterized by the absence of an "introductory section." This situation can also be interpreted as the speed-oriented architecture of digital platforms transforming the narrative structure. Indeed, the most striking finding in the table is that the vast majority of the sample (241 videos, 80%) does not feature any "Dramatic Introduction." Introductory sections (exposition), traditionally used in media narratives to arouse curiosity, are encoded as a "waste of time" within the speed of the attention economy, which is measured in milliseconds.

Rather than watching a script or fictional tension (drama) at the beginning of the video, the viewer desires to see the visual proof of the "before" state immediately. In this respect, the absence of a dramatic introduction signifies the removal of obstacles between the viewer and the reward (the result image) and the provision of a "smooth" flow. Even in the "Fast-Paced Montage" category, which represents the most dynamic form of video editing, the fact that "Dramatic Introduction" is limited to only 17 "Yes" responses against 76 "No" responses indicates a shift in the attention-grabbing mechanism. The element that locks the viewer to the video is not a fictional drama, but the visual shock created by the image in a state of "chaos." Loewenstein's "curiosity gap" theory acquires a visual dimension here; what triggers curiosity is not a story, but the immediate visual incongruity. Content creators prefer to trigger the viewer's "desire for completion" by presenting the visual contrast (chaos/order) directly, rather than wasting time with an introduction.

The category where the dramatic introduction is observed at the highest rate is the "Text Overlay" narrative form, with 38 "Yes" responses. However, even here, the "No" (143) response is dominant. Nevertheless, this data indicates that if drama is to be created, it is done not through "verbal" means or "acting," but through short and striking texts written on the screen (e.g., "You won't believe this change," "The end is shocking"). Since text feeds the element of curiosity without interrupting the visual flow of the video (without stealing time like audio narrative), it is positioned as the dramatic tool most suitable for the "speed" imperative of the attention economy. Consequently, Table 8 proves that #beforeafter videos dismantle the classical narrative structure (introduction-development-conclusion), evolving instead into a new visual format that is "Introduction-less and Result-Oriented." This format represents a strategic choice aimed at inserting the viewer directly into the dopamine loop without stalling them with an "introduction," in an ecosystem where attention is the scarcest resource.

Table 9. Distribution of Presence of Effects by Contrast Intensity

Contrast Intensity	**Presence of Effects**	
	Yes	**No**
Low	2	44
Medium	4	68
High	23	159
Grand Total	29	271

The most striking data in Table 9 is that the vast majority of the sample (182 videos) falls within the "High" contrast category. This situation constitutes an overwhelming dominance over the "Low" (46 videos) and "Medium" (72 videos) contrast categories. As indicated in the literature, the human brain possesses an evolutionary predisposition to process visual contrasts and the transition from chaos to order. The higher the contrast (e.g., the transition from an obese body to a fit one, or from a ruined house to a luxurious salon), the deeper the "curiosity gap" becomes for the viewer. "High Contrast" maximizes the viewer's desire to see the end of the video (the completion impulse) by elevating cognitive tension to its peak.

However, what is truly noteworthy here is that 159 of the 182 videos containing "High Contrast" do not feature the "Presence of Effects" (No). In the general total, effects were not used in 271 of the 300 videos. This data indicates that the perception of "beauty," which is generally associated with artificial filters on digital platforms, operates in reverse within the #beforeafter format. If the transformation is too radical (high contrast), the viewer demands "raw footage" to believe that it is "real." The use of effects is consciously rejected as it undermines the credibility of the change. This creates a contract of trust based on the "provability" of the content.

Thus, Table 9 proves that the fundamental formula of attention engineering on TikTok is built upon "High Contrast + Raw Reality." It appears that the element locking the viewer to the screen is not artificial effects, but the width of the gap (contrast) between the "before" and "after." In conclusion, Table 9 demonstrates that the success of #beforeafter videos lies not in "digital embellishments," but in the naked reality of radical change. The best-selling value in the attention economy is not a lie polished with effects, but an illusion of "accessible reality" dramatized by high contrast.

FUTURE RESEARCH DIRECTIONS

Empirical Verification of Cognitive and Behavioral Effects: Future research should move beyond content analysis to utilize experimental designs—such as eye-tracking, EEG, or neuro-imaging technologies—to directly measure the "hypnotic flow," cognitive fatigue, and dopaminergic responses triggered by high-contrast visual transitions.

Comparative Analysis of Short-Form Video Platforms: While this study focuses on TikTok, subsequent investigations should include comparative analyses across different platforms like Instagram Reels and YouTube Shorts to determine if "TikTokification" dynamics and attention-grabbing strategies vary based on specific platform architectures.

Cross-Cultural Dimensions of Digital Consumption: Future studies should explore #beforeafter content across diverse cultural contexts to reveal how varying social norms and values influence the perception of "perfection" and "chaos," as well as how these variables affect susceptibility to digital addiction.

Qualitative Inquiries into User Reception and Self-Perception: Research focusing on the reception of "personal transformation" narratives is needed to gain deeper insights into the psycho-social and narcissistic dimensions of digital addiction, specifically how witnessing idealized transformations impacts the viewer's own body image and self-esteem.

Longitudinal Designs for Tracking Digital Malaise: Future work should adopt longitudinal studies to observe the long-term impact of constant exposure to short-form, introduction-less content on users' capacity for "deep reading" and sustained attention spans.

Isolating and Testing Discrete Content Elements: Experimental studies should manipulate specific variables identified in this study—such as the presence of music, the speed of montage, or the intensity of contrast—to identify their causal effects on user retention and the "loss of time perception".

Examining the Role of Auditory Stimulation in Flow State: Given that 96% of the analyzed videos utilized music, future research should investigate how different auditory rhythms and soundscapes contribute to the "enchantment" of the collective mind and the bypassing of cognitive resistance.

Developing Ethical Standards for Attention Engineering: As digital platforms increasingly utilize "engineering of attention" and "algorithmic governmentality," future studies should prioritize developing ethical guidelines to protect users from manipulative design patterns and "digital obesity".

Impact of "Raw Reality" Claims on Trust and Addiction: Since this study found a low usage of artificial effects (9.7%), future research should explore the paradox of how claims of "raw reality" in high-contrast videos enhance the credibility of the content and thereby strengthen the addiction loop.

CONCLUSION

This study has revealed, in light of empirical data, how "human attention"—regarded as the new oil of digital capitalism—is harvested and commodified through #öncesisonrası (#beforeafter) videos on the TikTok platform. The findings obtained not only confirm Herbert Simon's thesis that "a wealth of information creates a poverty of attention," but also demonstrate how this poverty is transformed into a sustainable model of addiction through algorithmic engineering. The research results indicate that the experience offered by digital platforms is far beyond a mere practice of entertainment; it is a sphere of power that fragments the subject's perception of time and space.

One of the most striking outcomes of the research is the hegemony established by the average 22-second duration of the examined videos and the "fast-paced montage" technique. This content structure—defined in the literature as the "aesthetics of smoothness" and purified of all cognitive friction and resistance—paralyzes the viewer's faculty of "deep reading/listening." The marginalization of verbal narrative in the findings (8.6%) and the dominance of text/visual-oriented narrative serve as proof that digital culture displaces the "thinking subject," substituting it with a "seeing and feeling" passive object. Rather than enduring the effort of listening to a story, the viewer surrenders to immediate dopamine pleasures triggered by visual shocks (the chaos/order contrast).

The findings suggest that this surrender is not merely a technical process, but a hypnotic one. The use of music in 96% of the videos and the surprising absence of any "call to action" (CTA) in 90.3% of them align with Yves Citton's concept of "enchantment." Unlike traditional marketing, the lack of a demand for action from the viewer transforms interaction from a conscious choice into a reflexive impulse. This "absence of calls," synchronized with music and visual rhythm, traps the viewer in an unquestioned "flow," thereby collecting the behavioral data required by surveillance capitalism merely through "viewership," without even seeking the user's consent.

The content analysis results also reveal that the "human body" and the "construction of the self" lie at the center of the attention economy. The fact that "Personal Transformation" videos dominate interaction metrics (Likes: 74.80%) compared to object-oriented videos such as decoration or cleaning points to the narcissistic roots of digital addiction. The transformation of the flawed body in the "before" stage into the ideal form in the "after" stage offers the viewer not only visual satisfaction but also a purchasable "promise of perfection." However, a paradoxical detail in our findings is that this perfection is presented not through "effects," but through a claim of "raw reality" (a 90.3% non-use rate of effects). The individual of the digital age, while drowning in artificiality, paradoxically hungers for the illusion that appears most "real"—that is, change containing high contrast.

In conclusion, although #beforeafter videos on TikTok offer a visual catharsis promising a transition from "chaos" to "order," they actually drag the viewer into cognitive chaos. This "introduction-less/result-oriented" narrative format, in which dramatic introductions are discarded and the result is shown immediately, devalues patience and process, creating a pathological perception of time trapped in the "now." This study argues that the struggle against digital addiction cannot be achieved solely by restricting screen time; the real issue lies in understanding this ontological crisis, in which platforms radically transform the human mind's mode of operation, reward mechanisms, and perception of reality through "attention engineering."

While this study illuminates the structural dynamics of the attention economy through content analysis, future research should aim to empirically verify the cognitive and behavioral effects of these mechanisms on users. In particular, experimental designs utilizing eye-tracking or neuro-imaging technologies could provide direct evidence for the "hypnotic flow" and "cognitive fatigue" theorized in this study. Furthermore, expanding the scope to include comparative analyses across different platforms (e.g., Instagram Reels, YouTube Shorts) and diverse cultural contexts would be instrumental in generalizing the phenomenon of "TikTokification." Finally, qualitative inquiries into the reception of "personal transformation" narratives would offer deeper insights into the psycho-social and narcissistic dimensions of digital addiction.

REFERENCES

Alter, A. (2017). *Irresistible: The Rise of Addictive Technology and the Business of Keeping Us Hooked*. Penguin Press.

Berelson, B. (1952). *Content analysis in communication research*. Free Press.

Carr, N. (2010). *The Shallows: What the Internet Is Doing to Our Brains*. W. W. Norton & Company.

Citton, Y. (2017). *The Ecology of Attention*. Polity Press.

Gerbaudo, P. (2024). TikTok and the algorithmic transformation of social media publics: From social networks to social interest clusters. *New Media & Society*. Advance online publication. DOI: 10.1177/14614448241304106

Han, B.-C. (2020). *Güzeli kurtarmak* [Saving beauty]. (Filiz, K., Trans.). İnsan Yayınları.

Han, B.-C. (2021). *Capitalism and the death drive*. John Wiley & Sons.

Hari, J. (2022). *Stolen Focus: Why You Can't Pay Attention—and How to Think Deeply Again*. Crown.

Kruglanski, A. W. (2004). *The Psychology of Closed Mindedness*. Psychology Press.

Lang, A. (2000). The limited capacity model of mediated message processing. *Journal of Communication, 50*(1), 46–70. DOI: 10.1111/j.1460-2466.2000.tb02833.x

Loewenstein, G. (1994). The psychology of curiosity: A review and reinterpretation. *Psychological Bulletin, 116*(1), 75–98. DOI: 10.1037/0033-2909.116.1.75

Lorenz-Spreen, P., Mønsted, B. M., Hövel, P., & Lehmann, S. (2019). Accelerating dynamics of collective attention. *Nature Communications, 10*(1), 1759. DOI: 10.1038/s41467-019-09311-w PMID: 30988286

Newport, C. (2019). *Digital Minimalism: Choosing a Focused Life in a Noisy World*. Portfolio.

Pettman, D. (2018). *Sonsuz Dikkat Dağınıklığı: Gündelik Yaşamda Sosyal Medyaya Odaklanmak* (Y. Çetin, Trans.). Sel.

Simon, H. A. (1971). Designing Organizations for an Information-Rich World. In Greenberger, M. (Ed.), *Computers, Communications, and the Public Interest* (pp. 37–72). Johns Hopkins Press.

Vizcaíno-Verdú, A., & Abidin, C. (2022). Music challenge memes on TikTok: Media spreadability, iterativity, and user engagement. *New Media & Society, 25*(12), 883–908.

Zhang, X., Wu, Y., & Liu, S. (2019). Exploring short-form video application addiction: Socio-technical framework. *Computers in Human Behavior, 101*, 257–268. DOI: 10.1016/j.chb.2019.07.019

Zuboff, S. (2019). *The Age of Surveillance Capitalism: The Fight for a Human Future at the New Frontier of Power*. PublicAffairs.

ADDITIONAL READING

Bucher, T. (2018). If...*Then: Algorithmic Power and Politics*. Oxford University Press. (This work complements the article's discussion on algorithmic governmentality and how algorithms shape social reality).

Crary, J. (2013). *24/7: Late Capitalism and the Ends of Sleep*. Verso Books. (Essential reading for understanding the temporal dimensions of the attention economy and the destruction of the boundary between time and consumption).

Fuchs, C. (2021). *Social Media: A Critical Introduction*. SAGE Publications. (Provides a broader political economy perspective on digital labor and the commodification of users, aligning with the "Surveillance Capitalism" arguments).

Manovich, L. (2017). *Instagram and Contemporary Image*. (This text is crucial for understanding the visual aesthetics, "smoothness," and filtering culture discussed in the context of #beforeafter videos).

Marwick, A. E. (2013). *Status Update: Celebrity, Publicity, and Branding in the Social Media Age*. Yale University Press. (Offers insight into the "micro-celebrity" and "self-presentation" aspects of the personal transformation videos analyzed in your study).

Schüll, N. D. (2012). *Addiction by Design: Machine Gambling in Las Vegas*. Princeton University Press. (The foundational text linking slot machine mechanics to modern interface design, directly supporting the "variable ratio schedule" argument). DOI: 10.2307/j.ctt12f4d0

Turkle, S. (2011). *Alone Together: Why We Expect More from Technology and Less from Each Other*. Basic Books. (Explores the psychological impact of digital dependency and the loss of deep interpersonal connection/deep reading).

Wu, T. (2016). *The Attention Merchants: The Epic Scramble to Get Inside Our Heads*. Alfred A. Knopf. (A comprehensive history of the attention economy, providing context to Herbert Simon's early theories cited in your paper).

KEY TERMS AND DEFINITIONS

Aesthetics of Smoothness: A concept by Byung-Chul Han describing digital content that is polished, devoid of negativity or friction, and designed for instant gratification and passive consumption.

Algorithmic Governmentality: A form of governance where social control and behavioral management are exercised through algorithmic architectures and data processing rather than traditional laws or direct discipline.

Attention Economy: An economic system where human attention is treated as a scarce commodity to be captured, harvested, and monetized by digital platforms amidst an abundance of information.

Curiosity Gap: A cognitive state of deprivation proposed by George Loewenstein that occurs when an individual perceives a gap between what they know and what they want to know, driving them to consume content to close that gap.

Doomscrolling: A web design technique that loads content continuously as the user scrolls down, eliminating stopping cues and creating a seamless, potentially addictive user experience.

Need for Closure: A psychological motivation to find a definite answer or conclusion, which drives viewers of #beforeafter videos to watch until the end to resolve the tension between visual chaos and order.

Surveillance Capitalism: A term coined by Shoshana Zuboff describing an economic logic that claims human experience as free raw material for translation into behavioral data, which is then sold as prediction products.

TikTokification: A paradigm shift in media consumption characterized by the dominance of short-form, fast-paced, and algorithmically driven video content that alters users' attention spans and viewing habits.

Variable Ratio Schedule: A psychological reinforcement mechanism derived from behavioral psychology, akin to slot machines, where rewards are delivered unpredictably to maximize user engagement and habit formation.

Visual Satisfaction: The gratification derived from witnessing the resolution of visual tension, specifically the transition from a disordered state (chaos) to an ordered state (perfection) in transformation videos.

ENDNOTE

1 Prior to the construction of the coding scheme, an exploratory analysis was conducted on the videos to identify distinct features and categories. Following the development of the scheme, two researchers independently coded 90 data units (corresponding to 30% of the dataset) to assess reliability, resulting in a high level of inter-coder agreement. This demonstrates the reliability of the coding scheme employed for the main study.

Chapter 11
The Infinite Scroll of Vehicle Dreams as a Form of Digital Compulsion on Sahibinden.com

Muhammed Enes Yılmaz
http://orcid.org/0009-0004-1368-8171
Independent Researcher, Turkey

Özgül Dağlı
http://orcid.org/0000-0002-3173-9196
Independent Researcher, Turkey

ABSTRACT

This study examines how the habit of monitoring vehicle listings on Sahibinden.com, Turkey's largest classifieds platform, transforms into a digital compulsion. Using a phenomenological approach, in-depth interviews were conducted with male users who regularly browse automobile ads. Findings reveal that browsing is often used as a tool for escaping daily stress, daydreaming, and leisure, rather than a concrete purchase intent. Specifically, Turkey's inflationary environment and market fluctuations drive users to monitor the platform like a stock market ticker due to the Fear of Missing Out (FOMO). The study demonstrates that platform mechanisms, such as infinite scrolling and notifications, shift users away from rational information-seeking toward a cyclical digital dependency. Ultimately, the act of browsing evolves into a hedonic ritual that surpasses the original goal of purchasing, turning the marketplace into a site of habitual psychological engagement.

DOI: 10.4018/979-8-3373-6665-4.ch011

INTRODUCTION

The explosion of digital technology in the early 21st century has fundamentally changed how we live, shop, and interact. Today, over 5.07 billion people worldwide use the internet, spending an average of more than six hours online each day (Kemp, 2023). What began as a tool for convenience has become deeply woven into the fabric of everyday life.

However, this digital transformation presents a critical socio-technical duality. While the internet has democratized access to information and connected people across the globe, it has also given rise to new psychological maladaptation. Central to current academic discourse is the rise of problematic internet use (PIU) and various manifestations of digital behavioural addictions, which challenge traditional frameworks of consumer well-being and psychological health (Griffiths, 2014; Kuss & Griffiths, 2011; Moretta et al., 2021; Stănculescu & Griffiths, 2024). As digital platforms become increasingly immersive, the boundary between functional utility and compulsive engagement becomes progressively obscured, necessitating a deeper investigation into the underlying drivers of modern online behaviours.

Within developing economies such as Turkey, digitalization has reconfigured the conventional linear consumer journey into a complex, iterative process increasingly mediated by hedonic motivations (Wang & Jia, 2023). Sahibinden.com, Turkey's preeminent online classifieds platform, serves as a quintessential case, reporting 62.9 million unique monthly users and 16.8 billion page views in 2025 (Sahibinden.com, 2025). Diverging from strictly utilitarian e-commerce paradigms, the platform operates as a social-entertainment hybrid where user engagement is frequently sustained by the gratification of leisurely browsing rather than immediate purchase intent (Liu et al., 2023; Chen et al., 2019; Zheng et al., 2019). While such hedonic activity significantly amplifies session duration and page-view metrics, its lack of direct correlation with transactional revenue underscores the rising prominence of non-transactional drivers in contemporary digital marketplaces (Gkikas & Theodoridis, 2024; Roy & Sharma, 2021; Ricci et al., 2023).

Contemporary digital marketplaces increasingly function as experiential mediators, obscuring the traditional boundaries between commercial activity, leisure, and social participation (Liu et al., 2020; Chen et al., 2019; Zheng et al., 2019). A salient behavioural paradox has surfaced within these ecosystems: high-involvement product categories, such as automobiles, are progressively subject to low-involvement, recreational browsing patterns. This shift signifies a structural decoupling of exploratory digital engagement from transactional outcomes, wherein online interaction serves as a vicarious substitute for material ownership (Herzallah et al., 2021). Consequently, these non-transactional interactions generate significant affective value and psychological fulfilment, persisting independently of conventional conversion metrics or purchase intentions (Evelina, 2022; Siregar et al., 2023).

This chapter investigates the relationship between habitual scrolling and hedonic gratification, specifically analysing "hedonic window shopping" within the Turkish automotive sector on Sahibinden.com. The analysis explores the psychological drivers—including economic concerns, fear of missing out (FOMO), and platform design features—that sustain digital compulsion and vicarious consumption, situating these behaviours within frameworks of problematic internet use and behavioural addiction (Mazhar et al., 2023; Griffiths, 2005).

This chapter proceeds as follows: First, we examine how e-commerce features facilitate hedonic browsing and non-transactional engagement. Second, we explore the broader determinants of digital consumption—convenience, trust, and social influence. Third, we establish a comprehensive theoretical framework for digital compulsion, synthesising insights from addiction psychology, behavioural economics, and interface design. After articulating the study's contribution to the literature and research methodology, we present phenomenological findings from five Turkish users who compulsively monitor vehicle listings. The chapter concludes with implications for theory, practice, and future research directions.

Impact of E-commerce Features on Hedonic Browsing

Before examining the specific psychological mechanisms of digital compulsion, it is essential to understand how contemporary e-commerce features have fundamentally transformed the nature of consumer browsing itself. This section explores how digital platforms have amplified hedonic shopping behaviours, creating environments where exploration and identity construction often supersede transactional objectives.

Consumer behaviour research traditionally distinguishes between utilitarian shopping (driven by necessity) and hedonic shopping (pursued for pleasure) (Babin et al., 1994). However, "digital window shopping" represents a third category where the browsing experience itself becomes the primary product. As Kim and Eastin (2011) argue, users navigate "potential futures" through exploratory browsing, transforming interfaces into spaces for identity construction where viewing is decoupled from buying.

In the specific context of Sahibinden.com, this manifests as online window shopping—defined as the examination of products without immediate purchase intent (Bloch et al., 1989)—frequently observed in users scrutinizing luxury assets that exceed their financial reach or perpetually monitoring the market valuation of their current holdings. This practice often evolves into "compulsive browsing," a distinct digital precursor hyper-accelerated by platform design that stands apart from traditional "compulsive buying" literature (Kukar-Kinney et al., 2016). On Sahibinden.com, the "Favourites" (Favorilerim) feature functions as a curated repository of these aspirations. Aligning with Belk's (2013) theory of the "Extended Self in a Digital World," these digital collections facilitate the construction of alternative identities, allowing users to vicariously inhabit the role of luxury asset owners regardless of their objective economic reality. Ultimately, these transformations establish the psychological preconditions that platform features exploit to generate compulsive engagement.

Having established how e-commerce features facilitate hedonic browsing and non-transactional engagement, it is necessary to examine the broader determinants that sustain digital consumption patterns. While platform features create the conditions for extended engagement, the actual persistence of user behaviour depends on a complex interplay of convenience, trust, and social influence. Understanding these determinants provides essential context for comprehending why users continue to engage with platforms like Sahibinden.com even when their browsing does not culminate in purchase transactions.

Determinants of Digital Consumption: Convenience, Trust, and Social Influence

The Experience Economy shift from transactions to immersive experiences has reconfigured consumer engagement while raising concerns about digital compulsion (Pine & Gilmore, 1998). Sahibinden.com exemplifies how marketplace platforms leverage experiential principles to cultivate prolonged engagement, illustrating tensions between high user involvement and problematic consumption patterns.

The contemporary digital landscape is increasingly defined by the convergence of technological ubiquity and heightened consumer expectations. Central to this milieu is the multi-dimensional synergy between convenience—characterized by the erosion of temporal and spatial barriers—and epistemic trust. In this context, perceived platform security and structural transparency function as critical antecedents to transaction finality. While the "anytime, anywhere" utility of mobile ICTs provides the initial impetus for platform entry, the long-term sustainability of the consumer-platform relationship remains contingent upon the equilibrium between competitive pricing architectures and the perceived reliability of the digital environment.

Contemporary consumption has pivoted toward non-linear pathways mediated by the synergy of algorithms and social dynamics. AI-driven recommendation engines leverage granular consumer data to minimize the friction between desire and purchase, systematically catalysing impulsive acquisition (Zhang et al., 2019).

This shift is further intensified within social commerce, where user-generated content and influencer endorsements serve as critical heuristics for quality. This is particularly salient among younger users, who demonstrate a heightened susceptibility to digital stimuli and a structural requirement for social validation (Hajli, 2014). Ultimately, effective e-commerce frameworks must reconcile this automated efficiency with the foundational necessity of maintaining consumer trust.

While the preceding discussion has outlined the general determinants of digital consumption—convenience, trust, and social influence—these factors alone cannot fully explain the intensity and persistence of engagement observed on marketplace platforms. A comprehensive understanding of how routine browsing escalates into compulsive monitoring requires an examination of the specific psychological mechanisms and interface design features that transform functional search behaviour into digital compulsion. The following section establishes a rigorous theoretical framework for this phenomenon, synthesizing insights from addiction psychology, behavioural economics, and interface design.

Digital Compulsion: Psychological Mechanisms and Interface Architecture

To understand the behavioural patterns observed among Sahibinden.com users, it is essential to establish a rigorous conceptual and theoretical framework for digital compulsion. This section synthesizes the psychological drivers, neurobiological mechanisms, and interface design features that collectively transform casual browsing into compulsive engagement—laying the groundwork for interpreting the lived experiences documented in this study.

Defining Digital Compulsion

Digital compulsion refers to repetitive, difficult-to-control online behaviours that persist despite negative consequences, primarily motivated by reward-seeking and emotional regulation needs (Kuss & Griffiths, 2011). Although distinct from substance-based disorders, it aligns with core elements of the addiction syndrome model, encompassing salience, mood modification, tolerance, withdrawal symptoms, conflict, and relapse (Griffiths, 2005). Scholarly work distinguishes problematic use—involving functional impairment—from true compulsive use, marked by complete loss of voluntary control, both increasingly evident in behaviours such as obsessive property searching and vehicle listing monitoring (Fineberg et al., 2018).

This phenomenon arises from a complex, bidirectional interaction between neurobiological predispositions and the persuasive design features embedded within contemporary digital interfaces. Understanding this interplay requires examining both the psychological vulnerabilities that users bring to the platform and the architectural features that exploit these vulnerabilities.

Psychological Drivers of Compulsive Engagement

A central psychological mechanism underpinning digital compulsion is emotional dysregulation. Individuals with diminished interoceptive sensibility—reflecting an impaired capacity to accurately perceive internal physiological states—or those exhibiting alexithymia traits frequently employ digital platforms as external regulatory instruments. In such cases, the platform functions as a maladaptive coping strategy to attenuate or modulate affective states (Elhai et al., 2018).

Additionally, intolerance of uncertainty drives compulsive monitoring. Anxious individuals engage in repetitive information-seeking—checking property markets or prices—to alleviate distress. This cycle is reinforced by social comparison and algorithmic feedback systems that exploit neural reward pathways (Alter, 2017).

Empirical evidence suggests that for a significant cohort of users, routine monitoring of online listings transcends habitual information-seeking and evolves into a distinct compulsive behavioural pattern. The synergistic interaction between smartphone push notifications and the platform's algorithmic architecture systematically triggers curiosity regarding "new entries," thereby inducing a chronic urge to refresh the interface. As users pursue the prospect of identifying an "undervalued" or "exclusive" asset, they enter a dopaminergic feedback loop. This cycle effectively shifts the activity from a deliberate, goal-oriented choice to an automated, non-conscious reflex.

The Neurobiological Reward Loop: Variable Ratio Reinforcement

The architectural design of digital platforms leverages the psychological principle of Variable Ratio Reinforcement—the same mechanism that governs the addictive nature of slot machines in casinos. This behavioural trajectory is sustained by a schedule wherein the user is conditioned to repeatedly access the application under the intermittent hope of encountering a lucrative opportunity (Alter, 2017).

The mechanics of this "slot machine effect" operate through three interconnected processes: (1) uncertainty and intermittent rewards reinforce continued scrolling, (2) dopaminergic release creates a "seeking" impulse rather than satisfaction, and (3) elimination of stopping cues induces flow states that distort time perception and undermine self-regulation.

Through Flow Theory (Csikszentmihalyi, 1975), this manifests as "dark flow"—a state where time perception distorts and engagement duration is maximized over utility (Hoffman & Novak, 1996). The "hunt" for listings eclipses purchase intent, creating perpetual, non-terminating consumption (Starcevic & Berle, 2013) wherein interface-driven dopamine loops triumph over executive control.

Interface Architecture: The Infinite Scroll Mechanism

These psychological vulnerabilities are not merely internal; they are amplified by platform architecture. By leveraging advances in DOM manipulation and data pre-fetching, infinite scroll transitions users from the "Page Paradigm"—defined by natural endpoints—to a continuous, bottomless "Stream Paradigm" (Alter, 2017; Williams, 2018).

From a marketing perspective, infinite scrolling is a strategic interface design that facilitates frictionless content consumption by neutralizing the "stopping rules" inherent in traditional pagination. This dynamic loading architecture transitions users from goal-directed search to hedonic browsing, maintaining a continuous stream of stimuli (Naveed & Al-Madfai, 2022). Within the attention economy, this design optimized to maximize Time on Site (ToS) and expand ad inventory, leveraging variable-ratio reinforcement where the unpredictability of high-value rewards sustains user anticipation (Alter, 2017).

The absence of stopping cues drives compulsive behaviours and anxiety, with research showing negative mental health outcomes from prolonged scrolling without cognitive breaks (Conci & Müller, 2009; Montag et al., 2019). For marketplace platforms like Sahibinden.com, infinite scrolling—or interface designs that produce psychologically similar effects—transforms a functional utility (finding a product) into a ritualistic consumption of digital images. This shift prioritizes the platform's key performance indicator of user engagement over the consumer's objective of task completion, effectively monetizing the user's "property dreams" through an endless feedback loop of search and scroll (Bhargava & Velasquez, 2021).

Platform-Specific Manifestations: The "Infinite Search" on Classifieds Platforms

Platforms like Sahibinden.com, despite utilizing paginated interfaces, often induce behaviours synonymous with the "infinite scroll" psychology, particularly during high stakes searches such as vehicle purchasing. This transition from casual browsing to obsessive monitoring is driven by three primary psychological factors that interact with the platform's design features:

Three psychological factors drive this transition: First, the paradox of choice creates analysis paralysis—users view continuous scrolling as necessary risk-mitigation rather than delay. Second, escalating prices induce "maximiser" behaviour, where users chronically refresh interfaces haunted by the thought "What if a better car appears in five minutes?" transforming the catalogue into a high-anxiety news feed. Third, the endowment effect triggers dopaminergic hits through simulated ownership, but because transactions remain unfinalized, the loop never closes, making scrolling a ritualistic anxiolytic behaviour.

The Mediating Role of Choice Architecture

Behavioural research suggests that while user agency remains a factor, the "choice architecture" of a platform can either mitigate or amplify compulsive tendencies (Kahneman et al., 1990). A critical distinction exists between pagination and infinite scrolling models. Pagination provides inherent "stopping cues"—natural cognitive break points that facilitate decision-making and provide a sense of completion. In contrast, infinite scroll mechanisms promote continuous engagement by eliminating these thresholds, leading to a loss of temporal awareness and heightened fatigue in information-dense environments (Thaler & Sunstein, 2008; Sharma & Murano, 2020; Park & Jung, 2024).

The transition from exploratory browsing to a finalized transaction is, therefore, not a purely functional progression. It is moderated by a complex interplay of trust, platform quality, and the "scroll architecture." These design choices determine whether a platform serves as a tool for functional searching or acts as a catalyst for compulsive consumption cycles (Petcharat & Leelasantitham, 2021).

In the context of Sahibinden.com, these architectural choices intersect with economic pressures to amplify compulsive behaviours. While the platform employs pagination rather than pure infinite scrolling, the high volatility of Turkey's vehicle market creates a psychological imperative for constant monitoring. The fear that a "kelepir" (bargain listing) might appear and disappear within hours transforms each page load into a high-stakes gamble, effectively replicating the compulsive dynamics of infinite scroll interfaces despite the pagination structure. Thus, the platform's design cannot be evaluated in isolation from the economic context in which it operates.

Implications for User Well-being and Future Design

As "user experience" expands to include "user well-being," designers must incorporate stopping cues that facilitate self-regulation (Conci & Müller, 2009). The future of interface design lies not in seamlessness but in creating "brakes" that restore user control.

While the aforementioned mechanisms—variable ratio reinforcement and persuasive architecture—explain digital compulsion at a neurobiological level, a formal diagnostic framework is needed to distinguish habit from addiction in Sahibinden.com users. Griffiths' (2005) Components Model of Addiction provides this lens, offering six empirical criteria to differentiate casual engagement from pathological usage.

The Conceptualization of Digital Addiction: Griffiths' Components Model

While traditional addiction literature has historically focused on chemical dependencies, the proliferation of digital ecosystems has shifted scholarly attention toward behavioural addictions. Digital addiction is conceptualized as the compulsive, maladaptive use of technological interfaces—such as the internet, smartphones, or social media—to the detriment of an individual's psychological, social, and occupational functioning (Kuss & Griffiths, 2011). To understand the theoretical foundations of this pathological usage, the Components Model of Addiction, developed by Mark Griffiths (2005), provides a robust biopsychosocial framework.

According to Griffiths, a behaviour must manifest six core components to be classified as an addiction. Within the context of digital consumption, these components manifest as follows:

- **Salience:** This occurs when the digital activity becomes the most important aspect of an individual's life, dominating their thoughts and behaviours. Even when offline, the user is cognitively preoccupied with the next session or virtual events—for instance, a consumer mentally tracking e-commerce discounts during a professional meeting.
- **Mood Modification:** Technological engagement functions as a coping mechanism. Users retreat to screens to alleviate stress, anxiety, or boredom, or to achieve a state of heightened arousal. This represents the digitized version of "retail therapy."
- **Tolerance:** This refers to the requirement for increasing "dosages" of the activity to achieve the initial mood-altering effects. A gradual shift from one hour of daily screen time to five hours indicates the development of tolerance.
- **Withdrawal Symptoms:** The onset of unpleasant psychological (irritability, depression) or physiological (tremors, palpitations) reactions when digital access is restricted or terminated.
- **Conflict:** This involves the friction caused by digital use between the individual and their social environment (interpersonal conflict), their work/education, or their own internal sense of control (intrapsychic conflict). Disrupting sleep cycles or familial harmony due to shopping applications is a typical manifestation.
- **Relapse:** The tendency for the individual to revert to pathological patterns of use after periods of voluntary control or abstinence (Griffiths, 2005).

This framework demonstrates that digital addiction is not merely a matter of excessive time expenditure but is rooted in complex psychological processes and neurological reward mechanisms.

As we examine the lived experiences of Sahibinden.com users in the empirical section of this chapter, these six components provide a diagnostic lens for assessing whether observed behaviours constitute genuine addiction or merely intensive engagement. The framework allows us to distinguish between users who monitor vehicle listings as a functional economic activity and those for whom the behaviour has become psychologically compulsive and detached from any realistic purchase intention. In the case of marketplace platforms operating within volatile economic environments like Turkey, the manifestation of these components takes on unique characteristics shaped by inflation anxiety, FOMO regarding undervalued listings (kelepir), and the specific affordances of the platform's interface design.

Griffiths' six-component framework provides the diagnostic criteria for identifying addiction. When applied to Sahibinden.com users, these components help distinguish between functional market monitoring and pathological compulsion. For instance, salience manifests when users mentally track car prices during work meetings; mood modification occurs when browsing serves as "digital escapism" from daily stressors; tolerance is evident in the escalation from occasional checks to 20-25 daily logins; withdrawal symptoms appear as discomfort when unable to access the platform; conflict emerges in disrupted sleep patterns and family tensions; and relapse is seen when users return to compulsive checking after brief periods of control. These manifestations are amplified by Turkey's specific economic context and the platform-specific features discussed below.

Aetiology of Obsessive Monitoring and Economic Anxiety

Having established the general psychological mechanisms and interface design features that drive digital compulsion, we now turn to the contextual factors that make marketplace monitoring particularly addictive within Turkey's economic climate. While scholarship has predominantly focused on gaming and social media, the dynamics within real estate and classifieds platforms—exemplified by Sahibinden.com—reveal a parallel aetiology. This phenomenon is characterised by high-frequency monitoring cycles, where users obsessively track price fluctuations and market volatility.

In this volatile market, economic anxiety and FOMO drive behaviour. The unpredictability of finding undervalued listings creates reinforcement loops similar to gambling (Oberst et al., 2017), which gradually erode self-regulation. Consequently, what begins as rational economic monitoring paradoxically yields pathological outcomes, including sleep disruption, reduced productivity, and sustained psychological distress.

This theoretical synthesis demonstrates that digital compulsion on marketplace platforms emerges from a complex intersection of psychological predispositions, neurobiological rewards, and persuasive interface design. By situating these mechanisms within the context of market volatility, this chapter advances existing scholarship. The following section delineates the specific contextual, conceptual, and theoretical contributions this work offers to the discourse on behavioural addictions.

Contribution to the Literature

This chapter provides a comprehensive and multifaceted contribution to the academic discourse surrounding digital consumption and behavioural addictions. By moving beyond conventional e-commerce analysis, the study advances the existing literature in the following three dimensions:

Contextual Contribution: While the majority of digital addiction research focuses on social media platforms or online gaming in Western contexts, this work offers a unique perspective by examining marketplace platforms within the specific socio-economic environment of Turkey. It investigates how high macroeconomic volatility and an inflationary climate transform platforms like Sahibinden.com from simple utility tools into high anxiety "market surveillance" environments. This shift is particularly evident in the automobile sector, where price tracking becomes a perceived necessity rather than a choice.

Conceptual Contribution: This study redefines the boundaries of consumer engagement by focusing on non-transactional interactions. It advances the concept of "digital window shopping" or "hedonic browsing" by illustrating that user engagement is often decoupled from immediate purchase intent. By analysing the "Favourites" list as a "curated museum of aspirations" and a site for identity construction, the chapter offers a new conceptual framework for understanding how consumers derive affective value from digital exploration without a final transaction.

Theoretical Contribution: The chapter synthesizes Griffiths' Components Model of Addiction with the principles of the Experience Economy to explain the "pathological usage" of classifieds platforms. It provides a theoretical bridge between interface architecture (such as infinite scrolling) and neurobiological reward mechanisms, specifically through the "Slot Machine Effect" and variable ratio reinforcement. By adopting a phenomenological lens, the study offers a deep, qualitative exploration of the "lived experience" of digital compulsion, demonstrating how "dark flow" and time distortion (chrono stasis) undermine executive inhibitory control.

Given the contextual uniqueness of Turkey's volatile marketplace environment, the conceptual innovation of analysing non-transactional digital engagement, and the theoretical synthesis of addiction frameworks with interface design principles, this study adopts a phenomenological approach to capture the lived experience of compulsive browsing. The following research questions guide the empirical investigation, each designed to illuminate different facets of how users experience, interpret, and negotiate their relationship with vehicle listing monitoring on Sahibinden.com.

THE AIM OF THE STUDY

The aim of this study is to reveal, through a phenomenological approach, how the practice of following vehicle listings on Sahibinden.com transforms into an experience in individuals' daily lives and the meaning(s) underlying this digital habit. In this context, the research questions developed are as follows:

1. How do participants interpret the act of browsing vehicle listings without a concrete intention to purchase within their own life contexts?
2. How does this digital practice function as a "leisure activity," "daydreaming," or "stress relief" tool for users?
3. Is regular listing tracking perceived by users as a "digital addiction," and how do the impulses experienced during this process shape the experience?
4. How do economic dynamics and car market culture in Turkey influence users' motivations for tracking listings and their "fear of missing out"?

To address these research questions, a qualitative phenomenological approach was deemed most appropriate. Phenomenology allows for deep exploration of how specific phenomena—such as the act of examining listings without concrete purchase intention—are experienced within individuals' lifeworld. The following section details the methodological framework, participant selection criteria, data collection procedures, and the analytical approach employed to ensure rigor and trustworthiness in capturing these subjective experiences.

METHODOLOGY

This research is conducted using a phenomenological approach within the qualitative tradition, aiming to examine in depth the practice of continuously monitoring vehicle listings on Sahibinden.com and the subjective meanings this practice acquires in individuals' daily lives. Phenomenology focuses on how specific phenomena—such as the act of browsing listings without a concrete intention to purchase—are experienced within the individuals' "lifeworld." As Yılmaz et al. (2012) emphasize, phenomenology seeks to illuminate the nature and meaning of lived experiences, providing an ideal foundation for exploratory research that requires deep insights into participants' internal processes. In determining whether this digital habit constitutes a leisure activity or an addiction, the principle established by Hou et al. (2012) was adopted: capturing subjective meanings as expressed by the participants and constructing a structured understanding of lived experiences based on personal narratives rather than external definitions.

Regarding the sample size, this study was conducted with five participants who intensely experience the phenomenon. Within the phenomenological tradition, sample sizes vary significantly, ranging from a single participant (Dukes, 1984) to as many as 325 (Creswell & Poth, 2018). However, methodological scholars such as Kleiman (2004) and Starks and Trinidad (2007) suggest that phenomenological samples typically range from one to ten participants. Similarly, Yıldırım and Şimşek (2016) argue that such studies should ideally not exceed ten participants to maintain analytical depth, while Wilson (2015) notes that while the number often falls between six and twenty, it may decrease to a few individuals depending on the richness of the data.

In this study, the selection of five participants is justified by the high degree of homogeneity within the sample, as all participants share a consistent and long-term pattern of obsessive vehicle listing monitoring. Data saturation was reached at the fifth interview, at which point the narratives began to yield repetitive patterns across all thematic domains—including motivations, emotional responses, and behavioural patterns—and no significant new phenomenological insights emerged. This convergence of experiences among participants sharing similar demographic profiles and behavioural intensities confirmed the adequacy of the sample within the phenomenological tradition. This alignment with established qualitative standards for small, deeply focused samples ensures that the phenomenon is captured with the existential depth required by the phenomenological tradition.

The research process requires examining participants' experiences without abstracting them from specific contexts such as Turkey's economic dynamics and vehicle market culture. In this context, the study shares a similar methodological perspective to that of Pérez-Castejón et al. (2025) interpreting midwives' job satisfaction within specific work environments, or Acosta and Acosta (2016) examined the impact of educational reforms on teachers within their own context; that is, the experience of following vehicle listings is interpreted in a nuanced way, along with the economic and cultural atmosphere in which this experience takes place.

In this regard, data is collected through semi-structured in-depth interviews. During the interview process, the researcher avoids leading questions and adopts an approach that allows participants to express their fear of missing out or daydreaming processes in their own words. Thomas (2020) states that maintaining openness in interviews is critical for discovering participants' experiences in an unfiltered way. In this study, adhering to this principle, the aim was for the experience to emerge organically during data collection. Furthermore, as emphasized by Secrest (2000), phenomenological inquiry focuses on capturing the dynamics of individuals' relationships with a phenomenon and the transformations experienced. Therefore, the interviews were structured to highlight the participants' relational experiences.

When determining the participant group, qualitative depth was prioritized over statistical generalizability. In this context, as Flankegård et al. (2020) presented as a methodological basis in their study on parental experiences, the sample size was kept limited, guided by the principle of "depth rather than breadth." Thus, by working with a small number of participants, the richness and detailed experiences of each participant regarding the practice of following listings on Sahibinden.com could be analysed in accordance with the enriched data promised by phenomenology.

The interview data reveals a complex interplay between the theoretical constructs discussed earlier—particularly variable ratio reinforcement, economic anxiety, identity construction, and platform architecture—and the actual experiences reported by participants. The following section presents these findings organized thematically, illustrating how digital compulsion emerges from the intersection of platform design, market volatility, and psychological needs. Each thematic domain is explored through direct participant quotations, allowing their voices to illuminate the phenomenon in their own words while demonstrating empirical support for the theoretical framework established earlier.

FINDINGS

Interviews were conducted with five participants who regularly browse vehicle listings on Sahibinden.com. The participants' ages were 28, 34, 30, 36, and 32, respectively. Since a large proportion of users posting vehicle listings on the site are male, participants were selected from this demographic. Interview questions were structured around the following themes: general experience and introduction, reasons and motivation, essence and meaning of the experience, behavioural and psychological aspects, social and cultural context, and self-reflection and future perspectives.

General Experience and Introduction

Participants were first asked when they started following vehicle listings on Sahibinden.com and how this habit developed. All participants stated that they had been following the site since its launch. Regarding how the habit developed, Participant 5 stated it stemmed from his love of cars. Participant 4 explained that since he preferred not to use other social media platforms, he used the site to pass time, and the habit grew due to his personal interest in automobiles. Similarly, Participant 2 indicated that curiosity drove the development of this habit. Additionally, Participant 2 mentioned using the application for market tracking purposes, logging in 20-25 times per day. The remaining participants stated their habits developed for similar reasons such as gathering information and market monitoring.

When asked whether they viewed this behaviour as digital addiction, Participants 2 and 3 stated they did not consider it an addiction because they were tracking the market at regular intervals rather than using the application excessively. The remaining participants expressed that they did view it as addictive:

P4: Yes, I do. Especially during the period when I was frequently changing vehicles. At those times, you start thinking: What's the price? Why has it increased? What cars are available? Will it drop to a reasonable price? And then an addiction develops. Also, since I don't spend time on other social media platforms, I use Sahibinden.com to pass time. If I don't check it several times a day, I feel uncomfortable. Like, I go and check: What's happened? What's changed?

P5: I'd say to some extent, yes, because when you're idle, it becomes like scrolling through social media content after a while.

These initial responses reveal the foundational motivations that draw users to Sahibinden.com—ranging from practical market monitoring to pure automotive enthusiasm. Notably, even participants who engage in high-frequency monitoring (20-25 times daily) do not uniformly self-identify as "addicted," suggesting a complex relationship between behavioural intensity and subjective awareness of compulsion.

Reasons and Motivation

Regarding the fundamental reasons for following listings, Participant 4 explained that he was escaping from daily troubles: "In recent years, I've been using it purely to fill spare time. Because when you browse, you actually forget your daily worries." Participant 3 stated he used it to view vehicle features, thereby satisfying both his curiosity and need for exploration, acknowledging that his rational and emotional motivations were intertwined. Participant 2 responded from an economic perspective, saying that tracking was difficult due to inflation, which is why he frequently used the application. Participants 1 and 5 stated they used the application to fantasise about purchasing a vehicle. Participant 5's response is particularly noteworthy: "There's daydreaming. Those dreams that start with 'if only I had the means.' If I had the means, I would buy this. I'd look at this particular brand and model with these specific features, and I use it to track the market. Even if it's a very expensive car, you still look at it and follow it. In fact, if there's a car I really like, I'll even watch videos about it afterwards."

When asked whether the application's features triggered their browsing behaviour, Participant 1 stated that the simple interface encouraged usage. Everyone except Participant 4 agreed that the application's interface triggered their behaviour, while Participant 4 stated that his notifications were turned off, giving him control over when to browse. Regarding satisfaction gained from browsing listings without purchase plans, Participant 4's response was noteworthy, stating that making predictions about vehicle prices and having those predictions prove correct provided cognitive satisfaction. Other participants gave various responses such as feeling happy, daydreaming, getting motivated, killing time, gaining market knowledge, experiencing pleasure, and getting modification ideas for their own vehicles. This demonstrated that Sahibinden.com usage should be considered multidimensional.

Essence and Meaning of the Experience

When asked what this process meant to them, Participant 5 explained that it excited him: "When browsing the site, if I see a car model I've never encountered before, it sparks curiosity. When looking at cars I'm considering buying, it's also exciting. It creates that excitement of 'I've gotten closer to my goal, I can get even closer.'" Participant 2 stated it satisfied his desire to learn, while Participant 3 expressed that the process gave him a sense of relaxation and satisfied his curiosity.

Regarding emotions experienced while browsing, Participant 5 mentioned that misinformation on the platform frustrated him: "It's a bit complicated because even cars in poor condition are described as if they're problem-free in the listings. That's frustrating. I wouldn't say it makes me angry, but it's annoying because the car's actual condition is obvious from the photos, but they've entered the wrong model, wrong engine, wrong mileage." Participant 1 stated that his primary emotion was a desire for control, acknowledging that he might be digitally addicted.

When asked whether the listings represented freedom, status, or other symbolic meanings, four participants indicated they did not view them this way. Participant 3 stated: "I don't think so. Basically, everyone looks at something they like. For example, women might look at certain bags, certain brand watches and shoes. Men also probably look at watches, maybe some look at houses and cars. Sometimes people look at things they can't reach." Participant 5 said: "No, it doesn't carry any such meaning. I approach it more pragmatically because ultimately, a vehicle is just a material asset I'll use to get from point A to point B or to meet a need." However, Participant 4 stated that it did carry status significance: "Technically, yes, it does. As vehicle prices increase, the user demographic also changes. When the demographic changes, you sense a status shift there, or from what people write in their descriptions, you can get a sense of people's income levels or attitudes. As prices increase or brands shift toward European makes, people's profiles change considerably."

Behavioural and Psychological Aspects

Regarding this habit's place in their daily routines and whether it caused stress and fatigue, Participant 5 stated that browsing Sahibinden.com was more enjoyable than social media and took about one hour of his daily routine. Participant 4 explained that thanks to the interface's ease of use, he obtained vehicle information from Sahibinden.com instead of official manufacturer websites, viewing the application as an alternative to official sources. He stated this did not cause stress because spending time on Sahibinden.com satisfied him more than viewing morally questionable content on social media. Participant 5 noted that while it didn't create stress, having a favourite listing sold saddened him and decreased his motivation. Participant 3 stated that when actively searching for or selling a car, he had to constantly monitor the site, and this situation could create a gambling-like addiction. Participant 2 expressed that while browsing listings to buy a car didn't create stress, it could create excitement, and missing a car he was tracking could upset him.

When asked how factors like fear of missing a listing or excitement about new listings affected their behaviour, Participant 3 expressed his dissatisfaction: "It causes stress. It can create frustration at any moment. Because you've saved a certain amount of money. If you delay too much in buying what you're planning to buy and can't reach the seller, you go through a nerve-wracking ordeal." Participant 2 stated that fear of missing a listing would trigger him to purchase the vehicle.

Social and Cultural Context

Participants were asked how people around them interpreted their browsing habits. Participant 3's response illustrates the social dimension: "They can say things like 'you're looking too much now.' Some say, 'enough already, stop looking,' but if I end up in a group that also browses, our communication completely breaks down because we're all on Sahibinden.com. It triggers the addiction. Like a collective addiction party. Even if there's minimal conversation, it's still related to the topic. For example, browsing cars starts with vehicles you can actually afford. Then suddenly you find yourself looking at Audis and BMWs with your friends." Participant 2 stated that his circle advised him to quit in a humorous manner. Participant 1 said his circle approached the situation pragmatically, asking him for advice when they wanted to buy a car.

When asked how Turkey's vehicle market shaped their behaviour, responses highlighted market volatility and platform inadequacies. Participants 4 and 5 expressed concerns about the site's lack of control:

P4: There's a manipulative aspect to it. You can't predict anymore. Browsing listings on Sahibinden or taking those numbers as a reference doesn't seem very logical anymore. Because someone like me who regularly browses can anticipate which car's price is normal, which is cheap, which is expensive, and when I look at Sahibinden.com, I don't really see logical car prices. How does Sahibinden.com allow a car with a market value of 2 million to be posted at 2.5 million? This doesn't make any sense to me.

P5: Turkey's vehicle market is bad. It's bad in terms of both purchasing power and sellers' carelessness, and because of the many incorrect listings. For example, a car has been in an accident, but the owner had it repaired and doesn't mention this. Also, the lack of a mandatory inspection system is a shortcoming for Sahibinden.com, in my opinion.

Participant 3 compared the market to stock trading: "I have to constantly monitor this. Like a stock trader, because you have to track prices. You're selling something yourself. You have to track it at the same time, but something changes every day, every second. For example, if you're looking at 10 listings, typically 2 of them disappear each day. It keeps you constantly on alert and vigilant." Participant 2 expressed that inflation triggered purchasing behaviour: "In a standard market, prices are generally stable or increase gradually. Here, inflation creates an incentive to use the platform. Say, a car worth one million becomes 1.2 million overnight, or conversely, a tax reduction comes and suddenly the secondary market eases up and supply increases."

Self-Reflection and Future Perspectives

In the final section, participants were asked about positive and negative aspects of this behaviour and whether they viewed themselves as digitally addicted. Participant 3 stated: "It becomes very stressful because you constantly experience this anxiety about what you're going to buy or sell. In terms of digital addiction, I can say this: During the period when I need it, I use it excessively. I mean, I use it like an addict. There's really some need-based triggering happening with me, but I don't use it that much during normal times. Maybe it's related to reaching a saturation point." Participant 2 responded: "It can create anxiety sometimes. After all, if the car's price is increasing, other things' prices are probably increasing too, and this increases your anxiety."

When asked whether they considered reducing or quitting the habit, and whether acquiring a vehicle would change their behaviour, Participant 5 stated that he did not define himself as an addict and therefore had not considered reducing the habit, adding that if he bought his dream car, he would never look back at the site again. Participant 4 explained why he did not consider quitting: "I'm also a conservative person, there's that dimension to it as well. Going to Instagram to follow and look at things, and then the advertisements that start appearing bother me. Sahibinden.com provides pleasure at some level and reduces stress. Sometimes you get cognitive pleasure when you realise that a car's price really is what you predicted. When spending time on other platforms or watching movies, I can already predict many things anyway, and at some point, I got tired of that. Predicting the selling prices of cars is more enjoyable." Participant 4 also added that far from quitting, this habit actually reduced his stress. Participant 2 stated that since he bought a vehicle, his habit had decreased: "I don't think it poses a problem for me. If the market stabilises, we'll also stop looking at cars. When I bought the car from Sahibinden.com, during the buying period, I looked very frequently—you could say every day, every minute. After buying the car, it naturally stabilises. Then, if you're just a regular user and not trading vehicles, you just occasionally look out of curiosity."

The phenomenological data reveals complex interplay between theoretical constructs and lived experience. Participants' narratives validate key mechanisms identified in the literature—variable ratio reinforcement manifested in the "hunt" for undervalued listings, dopaminergic reward loops activated by new post notifications, and emotional regulation through escapist browsing. However, the findings also illuminate critical contextual factors: Turkey's inflationary crisis transforms price monitoring from a leisure activity into anxiety-driven surveillance; the cultural significance of automobile ownership intensifies vicarious consumption through fantasy; and the platform's specific affordances (Favourites lists, simple interface, lack of mandatory inspection systems) amplify compulsive behaviours. Notably, participants demonstrate limited self-awareness of addiction, rationalising their behaviour as "market research" despite admitting to discomfort when unable to access the platform. While these phenomenological insights advance understanding of digital compulsion in marketplace platforms, the exploratory nature of this study and its focus on adult males within Turkey's unique socio-economic context limit generalizability.

FUTURE RESEARCH DIRECTIONS

Building upon the phenomenological findings of this study, future research should aim to quantify the relationship between macroeconomic volatility and digital monitoring behaviours through large-scale surveys to validate the patterns observed within the adult male demographic. Since the current participant pool was limited to men due to the cultural nature of the Turkish automobile market, subsequent investigations could explore "digital window shopping" within female-dominated or gender-neutral sectors, such as real estate, fashion, or high-end collectibles, to determine if gender-based differences exist in the motivations for hedonic browsing. Furthermore, comparative studies are needed to analyse how different interface architectures, specifically the "Stream Paradigm" of infinite scrolling versus the traditional "Page Paradigm," influence the loss of temporal awareness across various age groups. Experimental research could also test the efficacy of incorporating "design brakes" or ethical "stopping cues" within marketplace platforms to help users regain executive inhibitory control and mitigate the addictive effects of variable ratio reinforcement. Finally, future scholarly work should investigate the longitudinal impact of chronic market monitoring on mental health, specifically focusing on whether the transition from functional search to habitual scrolling leads to sustained psychological distress or remains a temporary coping mechanism during periods of high inflation.

Having outlined promising directions for extending this research, we now turn to a synthetic interpretation of the study's findings in relation to existing literature. The following discussion situates the empirical results within broader scholarly conversations about digital addiction, evaluating how the observed patterns among Sahibinden.com users both align with and diverge from established understandings of problematic internet use. Particular attention is given to the contextual factors—economic volatility, cultural norms, and platform-specific features—that shape the manifestation of digital compulsion in this particular setting.

CONCLUSION AND DISCUSSION

The findings of this phenomenological study suggest that addictive patterns on Sahibinden.com are not merely functional habits but are deeply intertwined with emotional regulation and cognitive coping mechanisms. While literature frequently associates internet and smartphone-related addictions with sleep disturbances, depression, and self-esteem deficits (Younes et al., 2016; Do & Lee, 2018), this research highlights how such patterns manifest as "market surveillance" and "escapism" in an adult male population. The participants' tendency to use the platform to "forget daily troubles" or "dream of a better life" aligns with the stress and anxiety correlates documented in broader addictive behaviours.

Although adolescence is identified as a particularly vulnerable period for digital addiction due to neurodevelopmental and psychosocial factors (Han et al., 2012; Benedetto et al., 2024), this study demonstrates that adults are equally susceptible when faced with volatile macroeconomic triggers. The participants' constant need to monitor prices—likened to a "stock market"—and their fear of missing out on a listing serve as evidence of what Benedetto et al. (2024) describe as "maladaptive regulation" and "distraction." In this context, the platform provides a digital space for cognitive engagement (e.g., price prediction) that offers a temporary sense of control yet ultimately leads to increased anxiety and compulsive checking behaviours.

Furthermore, the global concern regarding internet-related addictions is heavily influenced by cultural and economic contexts (Younes et al., 2016). In the case of Sahibinden.com, Turkey's inflationary environment creates a unique "addictive loop" where price tracking becomes a perceived necessity rather than a leisure activity. Participants rationalize their behaviour as "market research" or a "safer alternative to social media," yet they admit to feeling discomfort when unable to check the app. Consequently, prevention and intervention strategies should go beyond limiting screen time; they must address the underlying "affective regulation" targets (Benedetto et al., 2024), helping users manage the economic anxieties and psychological triggers that transform a marketplace into a source of digital dependency.

REFERENCES

Acosta, A., & Acosta, I. (2016). Does teacher licensure matter? Basic education reform in the Philippine education system. *International Journal of Education*, *8*(4), 73. DOI: 10.5296/ije.v8i4.10247

Alter, A. (2017). *Irresistible: The rise of addictive technology and the business of keeping us hooked*. Penguin Press.

Babin, B. J., Darden, W. R., & Griffin, M. (1994). Work and/or fun: Measuring hedonic and utilitarian shopping value. *The Journal of Consumer Research*, *20*(4), 644–656. DOI: 10.1086/209376

Belk, R. W. (2013). Extended self in a digital world. *The Journal of Consumer Research*, *40*(3), 477–500. DOI: 10.1086/671052

Benedetto, L., Rollo, S., Cafeo, A., Rosa, G. D., Pino, R., Gagliano, A., & Ingrassia, M. (2024). Emotional and Behavioural Factors Predisposing to Internet Addiction: The Smartphone Distraction among Italian High School Students. https://doi.org/ DOI: 10.20944/preprints202401.2155.v1

Bhargava, V. R., & Velasquez, M. (2021). Ethics of the attention economy: The problem of social media addiction. *Business Ethics Quarterly*, *31*(3), 321–359. DOI: 10.1017/beq.2020.32

Bloch, P. H., Ridgway, N. M., & Sherrell, D. L. (1989). Extending the concept of shopping: An investigation of browsing activity. *Journal of the Academy of Marketing Science*, *17*(1), 13–21. DOI: 10.1007/BF02726349

Chen, A., Lu, Y., & Wang, B. (2019). Enhancing perceived enjoyment through social commerce features: The role of social presence and flow experience. *International Journal of Information Management*, *44*, 131–144. DOI: 10.1016/j.ijinfomgt.2018.10.001

Conci, M., & Müller, H. J. (2009). The role of visual short-term memory in visual search. *Visual Cognition*, *17*(1–2), 173–197. DOI: 10.1080/13506280802283021

Creswell, J. W., & Poth, C. N. (2018). *Qualitative inquiry and research design: Choosing among five approaches* (4th ed.). SAGE Publications.

Csikszentmihalyi, M. (1975). *Beyond boredom and anxiety: Experiencing flow in work and play*. Jossey-Bass.

Do, K., & Lee, K. (2018). Relationship between Problematic Internet Use, Sleep Problems, and Oral Health in Korean Adolescents: A National Survey. *International Journal of Environmental Research and Public Health, 15*(9), 1870. DOI: 10.3390/ijerph15091870 PMID: 30158492

Dukes, S. (1984). Phenomenological methodology in the human sciences. *Journal of Religion and Health, 23*(3), 197–203. DOI: 10.1007/BF00990785 PMID: 24307074

Elhai, J. D., Tiamiyu, M. F., & Weeks, J. W. (2018). Depression and anticipatory anxiety as predictors of problematic smartphone use: The moderating role of emotional reactivity. *Journal of Affective Disorders, 229*, 79–85. DOI: 10.1016/j.jad.2017.12.045

Evelina, L. W. (2022). Digital engagement and consumer behavior: The shift from transactional to emotional value. *Journal of Digital Marketing and Communication, 2*(1), 45–58. DOI: 10.53623/jdmc.v2i1.132

Fineberg, N. A., Demetrovics, Z., Stein, D. J., Ioannidis, K., Potenza, M. N., Billieux, J., & Chamberlain, S. R. (2018). Manifestos for the future of research into problematic usage of the internet. *European Psychiatry : the Journal of the Association of European Psychiatrists, 53*, 24–32. DOI: 10.1016/j.eurpsy.2018.05.004

Flankegård, G., Mörelius, E., Duchén, K., & Rytterström, P. (2020). Experiences of parents who give pharmacological treatment to children with functional constipation at home. *Journal of Advanced Nursing, 76*(12), 3519–3527. DOI: 10.1111/jan.14539 PMID: 33043491

Gkikas, D. C., & Theodoridis, P. K. (2024). Examining the role of non-transactional consumer engagement in e-commerce: A systematic literature review and future research agenda. *Electronic Commerce Research and Applications, 63*, 101344. DOI: 10.1016/j.elerap.2023.101344

Griffiths, M. (2005). A "components" model of addiction within a biopsychosocial framework. *Journal of Substance Use, 10*(4), 191–197. DOI: 10.1080/14659890500114359

Griffiths, M. D. (2014). Behavioral addiction and co-morbidity. *Journal of Behavioral Addictions, 3*(2), 69–71. DOI: 10.1556/JBA.3.2014.015

Hajli, N. (2014). A study of the impact of social media on consumers. *International Journal of Market Research, 56*(3), 387–404. DOI: 10.2501/IJMR-2014-025

Han, D. H., Kim, S. M., Lee, Y. S., & Renshaw, P. F. (2012). The effect of family therapy on the changes in the severity of on-line game play and brain activity in adolescents with on-line game addiction. *Psychiatry Research: Neuroimaging*, *202*(2), 126–131. DOI: 10.1016/j.pscychresns.2012.02.011 PMID: 22698763

Herzallah, A. M., Mukhtar, M., & Al-shami, S. A. (2021). The influence of hedonic browsing and sales promotion on online impulse buying: The mediating role of urgent to buy. *International Journal of Electronic Business*, *16*(4), 324–341. DOI: 10.1504/IJEB.2021.1189457

Hoffman, D. L., & Novak, T. P. (1996). Marketing in hypermedia computer-mediated environments: Conceptual foundations. *Journal of Marketing*, *60*(3), 50–68. DOI: 10.1177/002224299606000304

Hou, W., Ko, N., & Shu, B. (2012). Recovery experiences of Taiwanese women after terminating abusive relationships. *Journal of Interpersonal Violence*, *28*(1), 157–175. DOI: 10.1177/0886260512448851 PMID: 22809818

Kahneman, D., Knetsch, J. L., & Thaler, R. H. (1990). Experimental tests of the endowment effect and the Coase theorem. *Journal of Political Economy*, *98*(6), 1325–1348. DOI: 10.1086/261737

Kemp, S. (2023, January 26). *Digital 2023: Global overview report*. DataReportal. https://datareportal.com/reports/digital-2023-global-overview-report

Kim, S., & Eastin, M. S. (2011). Hedonic tendencies and the online consumer: An investigation of the online shopping process. *Journal of Internet Commerce*, *10*(1), 68–90. DOI: 10.1080/15332861.2011.558458

Kleiman, S. (2004). Phenomenology: To wonder and search for meanings. *Nurse Researcher*, *11*(4), 7–19. DOI: 10.7748/nr2004.07.11.4.7.c6211 PMID: 15227895

Kukar-Kinney, M., Scheinbaum, A. C., & Schaefers, T. (2016). Compulsive buying in online social networking sites: An investigation of the role of social presence and social identification. *Journal of Business Research*, *69*(8), 2717–2723. DOI: 10.1016/j.jbusres.2015.11.005

Kuss, D. J., & Griffiths, M. D. (2011). Online social networking and addiction—A review of the psychological literature. *International Journal of Environmental Research and Public Health*, *8*(9), 3528–3552. DOI: 10.3390/ijerph8093528 PMID: 22016701

Liu, C., Bao, Z., & Zheng, C. (2020). Exploring the factors influencing consumers' social commerce intention: An integrated model. *Information & Management*, *57*(7), 103325. DOI: 10.1016/j.im.2020.103325

Liu, H., Chu, H., Huang, Q., & Chen, X. (2023). How social commerce features influence consumers' browsing behavior and purchase intention: An investigation from the perspective of social capital. *Information & Management*, *60*(3), 103762. DOI: 10.1016/j.im.2023.103762

Mazhar, M., Farhan, M., & Raza, S. A. (2023). Fear of missing out, social media addiction and compulsive buying: The mediating role of digital window shopping. *Information Technology & People*, *36*(7), 2845–2867. DOI: 10.1108/ITP-10-2021-0815

Montag, C., Lachmann, B., Herrlich, M., & Zweig, K. (2019). Addictive features of social media/messenger platforms and freemium games: A design perspective. *Human Behavior and Emerging Technologies*, *1*(1), 23–31. DOI: 10.1002/hbe5.108

Moretta, T., Buodo, G., Demetrovics, Z., & Potenza, M. N. (2021). Tracing the boundaries between problematic Internet use and its specific manifestations: A systematic review. *Comprehensive Psychiatry*, *111*, 152274. DOI: 10.1016/j.comppsych.2021.152274

Naveed, A., & Al-Madfai, S. (2022). Influence of infinite scrolling on consumer browsing behavior: A study of e-commerce platforms. *International Journal of Marketing Studies*, *14*(2), 45–62.

Oberst, U., Wegmann, E., Stodt, B., Brand, M., & Chamarro, A. (2017). Negative consequences from social media use: Body dissatisfaction, self-esteem, and fear of missing out. *Journal of Adolescence*, *55*, 20–28. DOI: 10.1016/j.adolescence.2016.12.008 PMID: 28033503

Park, S., & Jung, Y. (2024). Digital engagement and the loss of temporal awareness: A longitudinal study of interface paradigms. *Computers in Human Behavior*, *151*, 108012. DOI: 10.1016/j.chb.2023.108012

Pérez-Castejón, M., Martínez-Alarcón, L., Molina-Rodríguez, A., & Jiménez-Ruiz, I. (2025). Job satisfaction among midwives in high-intervention birthing rooms: A qualitative phenomenological study. *Health Care*, *13*(11), 1318. DOI: 10.3390/healthcare13111318 PMID: 40508931

Petcharat, N., & Leelasantitham, A. (2021). A retentive consumer behavior model of electronic commerce to influence sustainable purchase intention. *Sustainability*, *13*(16), 8695. DOI: 10.3390/su13168695

Pine, B. J., & Gilmore, J. H. (1998). Welcome to the experience economy. *Harvard Business Review*, *76*, 97–105. PMID: 10181589

Ricci, L., Gnisci, A., & Spagnoli, P. (2023). Digital consumer engagement: A systematic review of its antecedents and consequences. *Journal of Consumer Behaviour*, *22*(4), 841–858. DOI: 10.1002/cb.2141

Roy, G., & Sharma, S. (2021). The roles of utilitarian and hedonic values in enhancing mobile social commerce customer loyalty. *Journal of Retailing and Consumer Services*, *58*, 102298. DOI: 10.1016/j.jretconser.2020.102298

Sahibinden.com. (2025). *Sayılarla sahibinden*. https://www.sahibinden.com/kurumsal/sayilarla-sahibinden

Secrest, J. (2000). Transformation of the relationship: The experience of primary support persons of stroke survivors. *Rehabilitation Nursing*, *25*(3), 93–99. DOI: 10.1002/j.2048-7940.2000.tb01877.x

Sharma, P., & Murano, P. (2020). Infinite scrolling vs. pagination: A comparison of user satisfaction and usability for mobile websites. *Journal of Universal Computer Science*, *26*(2), 237–254. DOI: 10.3897/jucs.2020.014

Siregar, Z. M. E., Syahputra, S., & Ginting, R. (2023). The impact of digital consumer engagement and affective value on social commerce. *International Journal of Data and Network Science*, *7*(2), 855–864. DOI: 10.5267/j.ijdns.2023.1.008

Stănculescu, E., & Griffiths, M. D. (2024). Problematic social media use and its relationship with psychopathology: A systematic review and meta-analysis. *Current Psychology (New Brunswick, N.J.)*, *43*, 1–18. DOI: 10.1007/s12144-023-05534-1

Starcevic, V., & Berle, D. (2013). Cyberchondria: Towards a better understanding of excessive health-related Internet use. *Expert Review of Neurotherapeutics*, *13*(2), 205–213. DOI: 10.1586/ern.12.162 PMID: 23368807

Starks, H., & Trinidad, S. B. (2007). Choose your method: A comparison of phenomenology, discourse analysis, and grounded theory. *Qualitative Health Research*, *17*(10), 1372–1380. DOI: 10.1177/1049732307307031 PMID: 18000076

Thaler, R. H., & Sunstein, C. R. (2008). *Nudge: Improving decisions about health, wealth, and happiness*. Yale University Press.

Thomas, S. (2020). Resolving tensions in phenomenological research interviewing. *Journal of Advanced Nursing*, *77*(1), 484–491. DOI: 10.1111/jan.14597 PMID: 33058245

Wang, Y., & Jia, J. (2023). Understanding the effects of hedonic and utilitarian values on consumer online impulse buying: A meta-analysis. *Frontiers in Psychology*, *14*, 1118671. DOI: 10.3389/fpsyg.2023.1118671

Williams, J. (2018). *Stand Out of Our Light: Freedom and Resistance in the Attention Economy*. Cambridge University Press., DOI: 10.1017/9781108453004

Wilson, A. (2015). A guide to phenomenological research. *Nursing Standard, 29*(34), 38–43. DOI: 10.7748/ns.29.34.38.e8821 PMID: 25902251

Yıldırım, A., & Şimşek, H. (2016). *Sosyal bilimlerde nitel araştırma yöntemleri*. Seçkin Yayıncılık.

Yılmaz, K., Filiz, N., & Yılmaz, A. (2012). Learning social studies via objects in museums: Investigation into Turkish elementary school students' lived experiences. *British Educational Research Journal, 39*(6), 979–1001. DOI: 10.1002/berj.3018

Younes, F., Halawi, G., Jabbour, K., Osta, N. E., Karam, L. B., Hajj, A., & Khabbaz, L. R. (2016). Internet Addiction and Relationships with Insomnia, Anxiety, Depression, Stress and Self-Esteem in University Students: A Cross-Sectional Designed Study. *PLoS One, 11*(9), e0161126. DOI: 10.1371/journal.pone.0161126 PMID: 27618306

Zhang, K. Z., Benyoucef, M., & Zhao, S. J. (2019). Consumer behavior and social commerce: A systematic review of over a decade of research (2008–2018). *International Journal of Information Management, 47*, 1–10. DOI: 10.1016/j.ijinfomgt.2019.01.001

Zheng, X., Men, J., Yang, F., & Gong, X. (2019). Understanding users' satisfaction with social commerce sites from the perspective of social capital. *Computers in Human Behavior, 91*, 217–228. DOI: 10.1016/j.chb.2018.10.011

ADDITIONAL READINGS

Bridges, E., & Florsheim, R. (2008). Hedonic and utilitarian shopping goals: The online experience. *Journal of Business Research, 61*(4), 309–314. DOI: 10.1016/j.jbusres.2007.06.017

Dewi, I., & Mahemba, U. (2024). Utilitarian and Hedonic Shopping Motives and Attitude towards Online Shopping of Generation Z in Indonesia. *Ilomata International Journal of Management, 5*(2), 542–558. DOI: 10.61194/ijjm.v5i2.1135

Hirschman, E., & Holbrook, M. (1982). Hedonic Consumption: Emerging Concepts, Methods and Propositions. *Journal of Marketing, 46*(3), 92–101. DOI: 10.1177/002224298204600314

Kaur, A., & Thakur, P. (2019). Determinants of Tier 2 Indian consumer's online shopping attitude: A SEM approach. *Asia Pacific Journal of Marketing and Logistics, 33*(6), 1309–1338. DOI: 10.1108/APJML-11-2018-0494

Kim, E.-L., Bender, P. K., & Gentile, D. A. 'Digital Media Use: From Problematic Use and Addiction to Healthy Media Engagement', in Karen E. Shackleford, and Nicholas D. Bowman (eds), *The Oxford Handbook of Media Psychology*, 2nd edn, Oxford Library of Psychology (2025; online edn, Oxford Academic, 22 July 2025), https://doi.org/, accessed 4 Jan. 2026.DOI: 10.1093/oxfordhb/9780197689875.013.0013

Liu, X. (2019). Research on Influencing Factors of Consumer Shopping Behavior in Online Shopping Festival. DOI: 10.35532/JSSS.V4.007

O'Brien, H. (2010). The influence of hedonic and utilitarian motivations on user engagement: The case of online shopping experiences. *Interacting with Computers, 22*(5), 344–352. DOI: 10.1016/j.intcom.2010.04.001

Wang, J., & Jia, X. (2023). Click it, and increase hedonic consumption ratio: How does online shopping improve the long-term subjective well-being of consumers? *Journal of Consumer Behaviour, 22*(2), 235–252. DOI: 10.1002/cb.2086

Wulansari, Y., & Wilujeng, I. (2024). *The Effect of Hedonic Consumption Tendency on Online Impulse Buying through Positive Emotion on the Flash Sale Marketplace on Millennial Generation*. Kne Social Sciences., DOI: 10.18502/kss.v9i4.15072

Yulianto, Y., Sisko, A., & Hendriana, E. (2021). The Stimulus of Impulse Buying Behavior on E-Commerce Shopping Festival: A Moderated-Mediated Analysis. *Journal of Business Management Review, 2*(10), 692–714. DOI: 10.47153/jbmr210.2152021

KEY TERMS AND DEFINITIONS

Analysis Paralysis: A cognitive state caused by the fear of missing the "perfect deal" among vast listings, leading the user to perceive continuous scrolling as a necessary labour to mitigate risk.

Endowment Effect: A psychological phenomenon where individuals value items more highly because they have engaged in mental simulations of ownership while viewing them.

Experience Economy: A paradigm shift in market dynamics that prioritizes the provision of memorable, lived experiences over simple transactional exchanges.

Extended Self: A theoretical framework suggesting that digital collections and favourites allow users to construct alternative identities as potential owners of luxury goods.

Infinite Scrolling: An interface design that replaces the "Page Paradigm" with a continuous "Stream Paradigm," removing natural stopping cues to promote non-stop access to visual stimuli.

Variable Ratio Reinforcement: A behavioural principle analogous to slot machines where rewards are delivered at unpredictable intervals, creating a potent and automated seeking impulse.

Compilation of References

Aarestad, S. H., Flaa, T. A., Griffiths, M. D., & Pallesen, S. (2023). Smartphone Addiction and Subjective Withdrawal Effects: A Three-Day Experimental Study. *SAGE Open*, *13*(4), 21582440231219538. DOI: 10.1177/21582440231219538

Abbas, N., Ali, I., Manzoor, R., Hussain, T., & Al Hussaini, M. H. (2023). Role of artificial intelligence tools in enhancing students' educational performance at higher levels. *Journal of Artificial Intelligence Machine Learning and Neural Network*, *3*(5), 36–49. DOI: 10.55529/jaimlnn.35.36.49

Abi-Jaoude, E., Naylor, K. T., & Pignatiello, A. (2020). Smartphones, social media use and youth mental health. *Canadian Medical Association Journal*, *192*(6), E136–E141. DOI: 10.1503/cmaj.190434 PMID: 32041697

Abuhamdah, S. M. A., & Naser, A. Y. (2023). Smart phone addiction and its mental health risks among university students in Jordan: A cross-sectional study. *BMC Psychiatry*, *23*(1), 812. DOI: 10.1186/s12888-023-05322-6

Acosta, A., & Acosta, I. (2016). Does teacher licensure matter? Basic education reform in the Philippine education system. *International Journal of Education*, *8*(4), 73. DOI: 10.5296/ije.v8i4.10247

Agüero-Espinoza, F. A., Neyra-Agama, M., Tasilla-Guayamis, L., Valencia-Acosta, L., Vega-Agurto, G. M., & Morales, J. (2025). Nomophobia and Self-esteem: The Influence of Digital Media on the Leisure Activities of Peruvian Adolescents. *The Open Public Health Journal*, *18*(1), e18749445360319. DOI: 10.2174/0118749445360319241226120427

Ahern, K. (2019). MY SELFIE-IMAGE: AN ARTIST'S MULTIMEDIA PERSPECTIVE TO SELF-DISCOVERY.

Ahmad, S. F., Han, H., Alam, M. M., Rehmat, M., Irshad, M., Arraño-Muñoz, M., & Ariza-Montes, A. (2023). Impact of artificial intelligence on human loss in decision making, laziness and safety in education. *Humanities & Social Sciences Communications*, *10*(1), 1–14. PMID: 37325188

Ahmmad, M., Shahzad, K., Iqbal, A., & Latif, M. (2025). Trap of social media algorithms: A systematic review of research on filter bubbles, echo chambers, and their impact on youth. *Societies (Basel, Switzerland)*, *15*(11), 301. DOI: 10.3390/soc15110301

Akgul, I. (n.d.). *Smartphone Addiction and the G-DEEG Model: An Interdisciplinary Framework for Psychiatric Rehabilitation. 8*(7).

Aktaş, Ö. (2025). Çevrimiçi alışverişte hedonik tüketim eğilimi ve fomo'nun içgüdüsel satın alma davranışı üzerindeki etkisi. *Gümüşhane Üniversitesi Sosyal Bilimler Dergisi*, *16*(3), 1141–1158.

Alat, H., & Filizöz, B. (2021). Örgütsel destek algısının, çalışanların gelişmeleri kaçırma korkusu ve içsel işten ayrılma niyeti üzerine etkisi. *Çağ University. Journal of Social Sciences*, *18*(2), 64–78.

Alberts, L., Lyngs, U., & Lukoff, K. (2024). Designing for sustained motivation: A review of Self-Determination Theory in behaviour change technologies. *Interacting with Computers*, *38*(3), 447–468. DOI: 10.1093/iwc/iwae040

Alhaidry, H. M., Fatani, B., Alrayes, J. O., Almana, A. M., & Alfhaed, N. K. (2023). ChatGPT in dentistry: A comprehensive review. *Cureus*, *15*(4), e38317. DOI: 10.7759/cureus.38317 PMID: 37266053

Alhassan, A. A., Alqadhib, E. M., Taha, N. W., Alahmari, R. A., Salam, M., & Almutairi, A. F. (2018). The relationship between addiction to smartphone usage and depression among adults: A cross sectional study. *BMC Psychiatry*, *18*(1), 148. DOI: 10.1186/s12888-018-1745-4

Alimoradi, Z., Jafari, E., Potenza, M. N., Lin, C. Y., Wu, C. Y., & Pakpour, A. H. (2022). Binge-Watching and Mental Health Problems: A Systematic Review and Meta-Analysis. *International Journal of Environmental Research and Public Health*, *19*(15), 9707. DOI: 10.3390/ijerph19159707 PMID: 35955069

Aljanabi, M., Ghazi, M., Ali, A. H., & Abed, S. A. (2023). ChatGpt: Open possibilities. *Iraqi Journal for Computer Science and Mathematics*, *4*(1), 62–64. DOI: 10.52866/ijcsm.2023.01.01.0018

Al-Obaydi, L. H., & Pikhart, M. (2025). Artificial intelligence addiction: Exploring the emerging phenomenon of addiction in the AI age. *AI & Society*. Advance online publication. DOI: 10.1007/s00146-025-02535-z

Alshowkan, A., Alsalem, A., Alsulaim, R., Almakki, S., Alqahtani, D., Alsalem, F., & Alshahrani, H. (2025). Fear of missing out, social media addiction, and personality traits among Saudi Arabia university students. *Journal of Education. Health and Community Psychology*, *14*(1), 1–15.

Alt, D. (2015). College students' academic motivation, media engagement and fear of missing out. *Computers in Human Behavior*, *49*, 111–119. DOI: 10.1016/j.chb.2015.02.057

Alter, A. (2017). *Irresistible: The rise of addictive technology and the business of keeping us hooked*. Penguin Press.

Alter, A. (2017). *Irresistible: The Rise of Addictive Technology and the Business of Keeping Us Hooked*. Penguin Press.

Alutaybi, A., McAlaney, J., Stefanidis, A., Phalp, K., & Ali, R. (2018, July). *Designing Social Networks to Combat Fear of Missing Out. Proceedings of the 32nd International BCS Human Computer Interaction Conference*. DOI: 10.14236/ewic/HCI2018.80

Alwazzeh, M., Harfouch, M., Hasan, M. A., Alqatari, S., AlSaid, A. H., & Alwazzeh, M. J. (2024). Clinical Manifestations' Spectrum of Smartphone Addiction: Moving from an Addiction toward a Clinical Syndrome. *Clinical Practice and Epidemiology in Mental Health*, *20*(1), e17450179295575. DOI: 10.2174/0117450179295575240520064919

American Psychiatric Association. (2013). *Diagnostic and statistical manual of mental disorders* (5th ed.)., DOI: 10.1176/appi.books.9780890425596

Amnesty International. (2025). Dragged into the rabbit hole: New evidence of TikTok's risks to children's mental health (Index: POL 40/0360/2025). https://www.amnesty.org/en/documents/pol40/0360/2025/en/

Ananny, M., & Crawford, K. (2018). Seeing without knowing: Limitations of the transparency ideal and its application to algorithmic accountability. *New Media & Society*, *20*(3), 973–989. DOI: 10.1177/1461444816676645

Andreassen, C. S. (2015). Online social network site addiction: A comprehensive review. *Current Addiction Reports*, *2*(2), 175–184. DOI: 10.1007/s40429-015-0056-9

Andreassen, C. S., Billieux, J., Griffiths, M. D., Kuss, D. J., Demetrovics, Z., Mazzoni, E., & Pallesen, S. (2016). The relationship between addictive use of social media and video games and symptoms of psychiatric disorders: A large-scale cross-sectional study. *Psychology of Addictive Behaviors*, *30*(2), 252–262. DOI: 10.1037/adb0000160

Andreassen, C. S., Griffiths, M. D., Paleesen, S., & Bilder, R. M. (2015). The Bergen Shopping Addiction Scale: Reliability and Validity of a Brief Screening Test. *Frontiers in Psychology*, *6*, 1–11. DOI: 10.3389/fpsyg.2015.01374 PMID: 26441749

Appel, M., Marker, C., & Gnambs, T. (2020). Are social media ruining our lives? A review of meta-analytic evidence. *Review of General Psychology, 24*(1), 60–74. https://doi.org/DOI: 10.1177/1089268019880891

Armağan, E., & Temel, E. (2018). Türkiye'de online kompulsif alışveriş davranışı üzerine ampirik bir çalışma. *Dokuz Eylül Üniversitesi Sosyal Bilimler Enstitüsü Dergisi*, *20*(4), 621–653.

Arpaci, I. (2021). Relationships Between Early Maladaptive Schemas and Smartphone Addiction: The Moderating Role of Mindfulness. *International Journal of Mental Health and Addiction*, *19*(3), 778–792. DOI: 10.1007/s11469-019-00186-y

Arrivillaga, C., Hallauer, C. J., Montag, C., & Elhai, J. D. Emotion dysregulation factors associated with problematic smartphone use severity: The mediating role of fear of missing out, Addictive Behaviours, Volume 143,2023,107708, ISSN 0306-4603, https://doi.org/DOI: 10.1016/j.addbeh.2023.107708

Aslitdinova, M. S. (2025). How artificial intelligence helps us in our daily life. *International Journal of Artificial Intelligence*, *5*(05), 538–542. https://www.academicpublishers.org/journals/index.php/ijai/article/view/4421

Avcı, Ö. (2025). Yapay zekâ bağımlılığı [Conference presentation]. 4th International Turkic World Congress on Social, Humanities, Administrative, and Educational Sciences, Baku, Azerbaijan.

Ayaburi, E. W., Wairimu, J., & Andoh-Baidoo, F. K. (2019). Antecedents and Outcome of Deficient Self-Regulation in Unknown Wireless Networks Use Context: An Exploratory Study. *Information Systems Frontiers*, *21*(6), 1213–1229. DOI: 10.1007/s10796-019-09942-w

Babin, B. J., Darden, W. R., & Griffin, M. (1994). Work and/or fun: Measuring hedonic and utilitarian shopping value. *The Journal of Consumer Research*, *20*(4), 644–656. DOI: 10.1086/209376

Backman, N. (2025). *Design against deception: Shifting towards wellbeing-supportive social media platforms* [Master's thesis, Aalto University]. Aalto University Repository. https://aaltodoc.aalto.fi/bitstreams/9b2e932d-ac84-4a9a-9c65-d5a3ada23c87/download

Baker, R. K., & White, K. M. (2010). Predicting adolescents' use of social networking sites from an extended theory of planned behaviour perspective. *Computers in Human Behavior, 26*(6), 1591–1597. DOI: 10.1016/j.chb.2010.06.006

Balcioğlu, Y. S., & Artar Biyiklar, M. (2025). Analyzing nomophobia among TikTok users: A data mining and text analysis approach. *Current Psychology (New Brunswick, N.J.), 44*(23), 18220–18242. DOI: 10.1007/s12144-025-08416-4

Barry, C. T., Sidoti, C. L., Briggs, S. M., Reiter, S. R., & Lindsey, R. A. (2017). Adolescent social media use and mental health from adolescent and parent perspectives. *Journal of Adolescence, 61*(1), 1–11. DOI: 10.1016/j.adolescence.2017.08.005 PMID: 28886571

Battistone, M. J., Kemeyou, L., & Varpio, L. (2023). The theoretical integrative review: A reader's guide. *Journal of Graduate Medical Education, 15*(4), 449–452. DOI: 10.4300/JGME-D-23-00265.1 PMID: 37637333

Baumeister, R. F., & Vohs, K. D. (2007). Self-regulation, ego depletion, and motivation. *Social and Personality Psychology Compass, 1*(1), 115–128. DOI: 10.1111/j.1751-9004.2007.00001.x

Baumeister, R. F., Vohs, K. D., & Tice, D. M. (2007). The strength model of self-control. *Current Directions in Psychological Science, 16*(6), 351–355. DOI: 10.1111/j.1467-8721.2007.00534.x

Bayer, J. B., Campbell, S. W., & Ling, R. (2020). Connection cues: Activating norms and habits of social connectedness. *Communication Theory, 30*(2), 173–193.

Baym, N. K. (2015). *Personal connections in the digital age* (2nd ed.). Polity Press.

Beard, K. W., & Wolf, E. M. (2001). Modification of the proposed diagnostic criteria for internet addiction. *Cyberpsychology & Behavior, 4*(3), 377–383. DOI: 10.1089/109493101300210286 PMID: 11710263

Becker, H. S. (1963). *Outsiders: Studies in the sociology of deviance*. Free Press.

Belk, R. W. (2013). Extended Self in a Digital World: Table 1. *The Journal of Consumer Research, 40*(3), 477–500. DOI: 10.1086/671052

Benedetto, L., Rollo, S., Cafeo, A., Rosa, G. D., Pino, R., Gagliano, A., & Ingrassia, M. (2024). Emotional and Behavioural Factors Predisposing to Internet Addiction: The Smartphone Distraction among Italian High School Students. https://doi.org/ DOI: 10.20944/preprints202401.2155.v1

Berelson, B. (1952). *Content analysis in communication research*. Free Press.

Berger, S., Wyss, A. M., & Knoch, D. (2018). Low self-control capacity is associated with immediate responses to smartphone signals. *Computers in Human Behavior*, *86*, 45–51. DOI: 10.1016/j.chb.2018.04.031

Berridge, K. C., & Robinson, T. E. (2016). Liking, wanting, and the incentive-sensitization theory of addiction. *The American Psychologist*, *71*(8), 670–679. DOI: 10.1037/amp0000059 PMID: 27977239

Bhargava, V. R., & Velasquez, M. (2021). Ethics of the attention economy: The problem of social media addiction. *Business Ethics Quarterly*, *31*(3), 321–359. DOI: 10.1017/beq.2020.32

Billieux, J., Maurage, P., Lopez-Fernandez, O., Kuss, D. J., & Griffiths, M. D. (2015a). Can disordered mobile phone use be considered a behavioral addiction? *Current Addiction Reports*, *2*(2), 156–162. DOI: 10.1007/s40429-015-0054-y

Billieux, J., Schimmenti, A., Khazaal, Y., Maurage, P., & Heeren, A. (2015b). Are we overpathologizing everyday life? A tenable blueprint for behavioral addiction research. *Journal of Behavioral Addictions*, *4*(3), 119–123. DOI: 10.1556/2006.4.2015.009

Bloch, P. H., Ridgway, N. M., & Sherrell, D. L. (1989). Extending the concept of shopping: An investigation of browsing activity. *Journal of the Academy of Marketing Science*, *17*(1), 13–21. DOI: 10.1007/BF02726349

Boehmer, N. (2024). The double-edged sword of algorithmic governance: Transparency at stake. Ash Center for Democratic Governance and Innovation, Harvard Kennedy School. https://ash.harvard.edu/wp-content/uploads/2024/02/niclas_boehmer_essay.pdf

Bom, H.-S.-H. (2023). Exploring the opportunities and challenges of ChatGPT in academic writing: A roundtable discussion. *Nuclear Medicine and Molecular Imaging*, *57*(4), 165–167. Advance online publication. DOI: 10.1007/s13139-023-00809-2 PMID: 37483875

Bonny-Noach, H., Sinambela, Y., Hanafi, E., Shina, C., & Siste, K. (2024). Problematic series watching and alcohol consumption among global audiences of Korean Drama in Israel and Indonesia. *Scientific Reports*, *14*(1), 17624. DOI: 10.1038/s41598-024-68700-4 PMID: 39085323

Boursier, V., Gioia, F., Musetti, A., & Schimmenti, A. (2020). Facing Loneliness and Anxiety During the COVID-19 Isolation: The Role of Excessive Social Media Use in a Sample of Italian Adults. *Frontiers in Psychiatry, 11*, 586222. DOI: 10.3389/fpsyt.2020.586222 PMID: 33363484

boyd, d. (2010). Social network sites as networked publics: Affordances, dynamics, and implications. In Z. Papacharissi (Ed.), *A networked self: Identity, community, and culture on social network sites* (pp. 39–58). Routledge.

Brailovskaia, J., Stirnberg, J., Rozgonjuk, D., Margraf, J., & Elhai, J. D. (2021). From low sense of control to problematic smartphone use severity during Covid-19 outbreak: The mediating role of fear of missing out and the moderating role of repetitive negative thinking. *PLoS One, 16*(12), e0261023. DOI: 10.1371/journal.pone.0261023

Brand, M., Müller, A., Wegmann, E., Antons, S., Brandtner, A., Müller, S. M., Stark, R., Steins-Loeber, S., & Potenza, M. N. (2025). Current interpretations of the I-PACE model of behavioral addictions. *Journal of Behavioral Addictions, 14*(1), 1–17. DOI: 10.1556/2006.2025.00020 PMID: 40063161

Brand, M., Wegmann, E., Stark, R., Müller, A., Wölfling, K., Robbins, T. W., & Potenza, M. N. (2019). The Interaction of Person–Affect–Cognition–Execution (I-PACE) model for addictive behaviors: Update, generalization, and specification. *Neuroscience and Biobehavioral Reviews, 104*, 1–10. DOI: 10.1016/j.neubiorev.2019.06.032

Brand, M., Young, K. S., Laier, C., Wölfling, K., & Potenza, M. N. (2016). Integrating psychological and neurobiological considerations regarding the development and maintenance of specific Internet-use disorders: An interaction of person–affect–cognition–execution (I-PACE) model. *Neuroscience and Biobehavioral Reviews, 71*, 252–266. DOI: 10.1016/j.neubiorev.2016.08.033

Braun, V., & Clarke, V. (2006). Using thematic analysis in psychology. *Qualitative Research in Psychology, 3*(2), 77–101. DOI: 10.1191/1478088706qp063oa

Bronfenbrenner, U. (1979). *The ecology of human development: Experiments by nature and design.* Harvard University Press. DOI: 10.4159/9780674028845

Brooker, P., Dutton, W., & Mair, M. D. (2019). The New Ghosts in the Machine: 'Pragmatist' AI and the Conceptual Perils of Anthropomorphic Description.

Browne, D. T., May, S. S., Colucci, L., Gawrilow, C., & Besic, N. (2021). From screen time to digital engagement: A critical review of measures used to assess problematic digital media use. *BMJ Open, 11*(5), e046367. DOI: 10.1136/bmjopen-2020-046367

Bucher, T. (2018). *If… then: Algorithmic power and politics*. Oxford University Press. DOI: 10.1093/oso/9780190493028.001.0001

Budiningsih, I., Oktapiani, M., Rijanto, W., & Masuwd, M. A. (2024). Comparative analysis of creative assignments, participatory collaborative learning, and students' satisfaction in digital & non-digital learning media. *Jurnal Pendidikan Progresif, 14*(3), 1900–1913. DOI: 10.23960/jpp.v14.i3.2024129

Burén, J., van Rooij, A. J., van de Mheen, D., & Schoenmakers, T. M. (2023). Screen time as a proxy for problematic smartphone use: A weak and inconsistent indicator. *Frontiers in Psychology, 14*, 1258784. DOI: 10.3389/fpsyg.2023.1258784

Busch, P. A., & McCarthy, S. (2021). Antecedents and consequences of problematic smartphone use: A systematic literature review of an emerging research area. *Computers in Human Behavior, 114*, 106414. DOI: 10.1016/j.chb.2020.106414

Cambridge Dictionary. (n.d.) *FOMO*. https://dictionary.cambridge.org/dictionary/english/fomo

Caplan, S. E. (2002). Problematic Internet use and psychosocial well-being: Development of a theory-based cognitive–behavioral measurement instrument. *Computers in Human Behavior, 18*(5), 553–575. DOI: 10.1016/S0747-5632(02)00004-3

Carr, N. (2010). *The Shallows: What the Internet Is Doing to Our Brains*. W. W. Norton & Company.

Carr, N. (2020). *The shallows: What the internet is doing to our brains* (2nd ed.). W. W. Norton.

Carter, T. J., & Gilovich, T. (2012). I am what I do, not what I have: The differential centrality of experiential and material purchases to the self. *Journal of Personality and Social Psychology, 102*(6), 1304–1317. DOI: 10.1037/a0027407

Casale, S., Fioravanti, G., Gioia, F., Redditi, E., & Spada, M. (2023). Fear of missing out and fear of not being up to date: Investigating different pathways towards social and process problematic smartphone use. *Current Psychology (New Brunswick, N.J.), 42*(26), 22847–22856. DOI: 10.1007/s12144-022-03368-5

Çeber, B. (2024a). Yapay zekâ etiği bağlamında reklamcılık sektörü üzerine uygulamalı bir araştırma. *Intermedia International E-journal, 11*(20), 63–84. DOI: 10.56133/intermedia.1462312

Çeber, B. (2024b). Yapay zekâyı sorgulamak: Veri etiği ve dijital reklamcılığın kesişimi. In *Yapay zekâ etiği ve iletişim: Sorunlar, sınırlar ve zorluklar*. Nobel Akademik Yayıncılık.

Çeber, B. (2025). Generative artificial intelligence and brain rot from an advertising perspective. *The Turkish Online Journal of Design Art and Communication*, *15*(3), 1162–1177. DOI: 10.7456/tojdac.1674327

Chang, A. M., Aeschbach, D., Duffy, J. F., & Czeisler, C. A. (2015). Evening use of light-emitting eReaders negatively affects sleep, circadian timing, and next-morning alertness. *Proceedings of the National Academy of Sciences of the United States of America*, *112*(4), 1232–1237. DOI: 10.1073/pnas.1418490112 PMID: 25535358

Chen, A., Lu, Y., & Wang, B. (2019). Enhancing perceived enjoyment through social commerce features: The role of social presence and flow experience. *International Journal of Information Management*, *44*, 131–144. DOI: 10.1016/j.ijinfomgt.2018.10.001

Chen, C., Zhang, K. Z. K., Gong, X., & Lee, M. (2019). Dual mechanisms of reinforcement reward and habit in driving smartphone addiction: The role of smartphone features. *Internet Research*, *29*(6), 1551–1570. DOI: 10.1108/INTR-11-2018-0489

Cheng, Q., Zhou, Y., Zhu, H., Wang, Q., & Peng, W. (2024). Relationships between daily emotional experiences and smartphone addiction among college students: Moderated mediating role of gender and mental health problems. *Frontiers in Psychology*, *15*, 1490338. DOI: 10.3389/fpsyg.2024.1490338

Chen, J., Yu, Z., Ni, R., Zhou, J., & Qu, J. (2025). The effects of social media addiction on college students' psychological anxiety: The mediating role of self-efficacy and coping styles. *Frontiers in Psychology*, *16*, 1676899. DOI: 10.3389/fpsyg.2025.1676899 PMID: 41229591

Cho, J., & Kim, H. (2025). The role of impulsivity and emotional dysregulation in smartphone overdependence explored through network analysis. *Scientific Reports*, *15*(1), 1852. DOI: 10.1038/s41598-025-85680-1

Cialdini, R. B. (2009). *Influence: Science and practice* (5th ed.). Pearson Education.

Cialdini, R. B. (2021). *Influence, New and Expanded*. Harper Business.

Cinelli, M., Quattrociocchi, W., Galeazzi, A., Valensise, C. M., Brugnoli, E., Schmidt, A. L., Zola, P., Zollo, F., & Scala, A. (2021). The echo chamber effect on social media. *Proceedings of the National Academy of Sciences of the United States of America*, *118*(9), e2023301118. DOI: 10.1073/pnas.2023301118

Citton, Y. (2017). *The Ecology of Attention*. Polity Press.

Citton, Y. (2017). The ecology of attention. *Polity*.

Conci, M., & Müller, H. J. (2009). The role of visual short-term memory in visual search. *Visual Cognition, 17*(1–2), 173–197. DOI: 10.1080/13506280802283021

Conradie, L., le Roux, D. B., & Parry, D. A. (2023). Cross-domain online vigilance, boundary management and stress among knowledge workers. *South African Journal of Business Management, 54*(1), a2937. Advance online publication. DOI: 10.4102/sajbm.v54i1.3896

Çopuroğlu, F. (2021). Tüketicilerin Sosyal Medya Kullanımı, FoMO ve Hedonik Tüketim Arasındaki İlişki. *OPUS International Journal of Society Researches, 17*(37), 4298–4326. DOI: 10.26466/opus.845545

Couldry, N. (2012). *Media, society, world: Social theory and digital media practice*. Polity Press.

Couldry, N., & Hepp, A. (2017). The mediated construction of reality. *Polity*.

Couldry, N., & Mejias, U. A. (2019). *The costs of connection: How data is colonizing human life and appropriating it for capitalism*. Stanford University Press.

Creswell, J. W., & Poth, C. N. (2018). *Qualitative inquiry and research design: Choosing among five approaches* (4th ed.). SAGE Publications.

Crompton, H., & Burke, D. (2023). Artificial intelligence in higher education: The state of the field. *International Journal of Educational Technology in Higher Education, 20*(1), 1–22. DOI: 10.1186/s41239-023-00392-8

Csikszentmihalyi, M. (1975). *Beyond boredom and anxiety: Experiencing flow in work and play*. Jossey-Bass.

Czeisler, C. A., & Gooley, J. J. (2007). Sleep and circadian rhythms in humans. *Cold Spring Harbor Symposia on Quantitative Biology, 72*(1), 579–597. DOI: 10.1101/sqb.2007.72.064 PMID: 18419318

Davenport, T. H., & Beck, J. C. (2001). *The attention economy: Understanding the new currency of business*. Harvard Business School Press.

Deci, E. L., & Ryan, R. M. (1985). *Intrinsic motivation and self-determination in human behavior*. Plenum Press., DOI: 10.1007/978-1-4899-2271-7

De, D., El Jamal, M., Aydemir, E., & Khera, A. (2025). Social media algorithms and teen addiction: Neurophysiological impact and ethical considerations. *Cureus, 17*(1), e77145. Advance online publication. DOI: 10.7759/cureus.77145

Demir, G. (2025, June). *Digital media addiction and the transformation of everyday practices among young adults*. 13th International Conference on Research in Behavioral and Social Sciences, Vienna, Austria. https://www.dpublication.com/wp-content/uploads/2025/05/04-4387.pdf

Demirci, K., Akgönül, M., & Akpinar, A. (2015). Relationship of smartphone use severity with sleep quality, depression, and anxiety in university students. *Journal of Behavioral Addictions*, *4*(2), 85–92. DOI: 10.1556/2006.4.2015.010

Demirel, A. C., & Tapan, M. G. (2023). Üniversite Öğrencilerinin Sosyal Medya ve Kompulsif Çevrimiçi Alışveriş Bağımlılığı Arasındaki İlişkinin İncelenmesi. *İnsan ve Toplum Bilimleri Araştırmaları Dergisi, 12*(1), 60-78. https://doi.org/DOI: 10.15869/itobiad.1147669

Demirkaya, İ., & Koyuncu, E. (2021). Dijital Kapitalizm, Tüketim Kültürü ve Y Kuşağının Değişen Tüketim Davranışları. *Intermedia International E-journal*, *8*(15), 174–196. DOI: 10.21645/intermedia.2021.107

Deshmukh, V., Dange, N., Dhangond, A., Samrit, K., & Pawar, R. (2025). Social media addiction: Causes & effects. *International Journal of Advanced Research in Computer and Communication Engineering*, *8*(11). Advance online publication. DOI: 10.17148/IJARCCE.2025.1411133

De-Sola Gutiérrez, J., Rodríguez De Fonseca, F., & Rubio, G. (2016). Cell-Phone Addiction: A Review. *Frontiers in Psychiatry*, *7*. Advance online publication. DOI: 10.3389/fpsyt.2016.00175

Deuze, M. (2012). *Media life*. Polity Press.

Devi, K. A., & Singh, S. K. (2023). The hazards of excessive screen time: Impacts on physical health, mental health, and Collectively well-being. *Journal of Education and Health Promotion*, *12*(1), 413. DOI: 10.4103/jehp.jehp_447_23 PMID: 38333167

Devitt, S. J., Austen, L., & Parkin, H. J. (2017). Integrative reviewing for exploring complex phenomena. *Social Research Update*, (66). https://sru.soc.surrey.ac.uk/SRU66.pdf

Dhollande, S., Taylor, A., Meyer, S., & Scott, M. (2021). Conducting integrative reviews: A guide for novice nursing researchers. *Journal of Research in Nursing : JRN*, *26*(5), 427–438. DOI: 10.1177/1744987121997907 PMID: 35251272

Dilmegani, C. (2023). *ChatGpt education use cases, benefits & challenges in 2023*. AI Multiple. https://research.aimultiple.com/chatgpt-education/

Dixit, A., Marthoenis, M., Arafat, S. M. Y., Sharma, P., & Kar, S. K. (2020). Binge watching behavior during COVID 19 pandemic: A cross-sectional, cross-national online survey. *Psychiatry Research, 289*, 113089. DOI: 10.1016/j.psychres.2020.113089

Do, K., & Lee, K. (2018). Relationship between Problematic Internet Use, Sleep Problems, and Oral Health in Korean Adolescents: A National Survey. *International Journal of Environmental Research and Public Health, 15*(9), 1870. DOI: 10.3390/ijerph15091870 PMID: 30158492

Dolan, E. W. (2026, April 21). Short video addiction is linked to lower life satisfaction through loneliness and anxiety. *PsyPost*. https://www.psypost.org/short-video-addiction-is-linked-to-lower-life-satisfaction-through-loneliness-and-anxiety/

Dora, J., Van Hooff, M., Geurts, S., Kompier, M., & Bijleveld, E. (2021). Labor/leisure decisions in their natural context: The case of the smartphone. *Psychonomic Bulletin & Review, 28*(2), 676–685. DOI: 10.3758/s13423-020-01844-2

Douglas, P., Stella, W., & Didi, E. F. (2024). Influence of artificial intelligence (AI) tools on students' learning outcome in adult education postgraduate programme in Rivers State University. *International Journal of Advanced Research and Learning, 3*(4), 132–141.

Drouin, M., Kaiser, D. H., & Miller, D. A. (2012). Phantom vibrations among undergraduates: Prevalence and associated psychological characteristics. *Computers in Human Behavior, 28*(4), 1490–1496. DOI: 10.1016/j.chb.2012.03.013

Duc, T. M. (2025). Excessive social media use and its impact on psychological well-being and academic performance of Vietnamese university students. *International Journal of Adolescence and Youth, 31*(1), 2608766. Advance online publication. DOI: 10.1080/02673843.2025.2608766

Duffy, A., Saunders, K. E. A., Malhi, G. S., Patten, S., Cipriani, A., McNevin, S. H., MacDonald, E., & Geddes, J. (2019). Mental health care for university students: A way forward? *The Lancet. Psychiatry, 6*(11), 885–887. DOI: 10.1016/S2215-0366(19)30275-5 PMID: 31324561

Duke, É., & Montag, C. (2017). Smartphone addiction, daily interruptions and self-reported productivity. *Addictive Behaviors Reports, 6*, 90–95. DOI: 10.1016/j.abrep.2017.07.002

Dukes, S. (1984). Phenomenological methodology in the human sciences. *Journal of Religion and Health, 23*(3), 197–203. DOI: 10.1007/BF00990785 PMID: 24307074

Einstein, D. A., Dabb, C., & Fraser, M. (2023). FoMO, but not self-compassion, moderates the link between social media use and anxiety in adolescence. *Australian Journal of Psychology*, *75*(1), 2217961. DOI: 10.1080/00049530.2023.2217961

Elhai, J. D., Levine, J. C., Dvorak, R. D., & Hall, B. J. (2017). Fear of missing out, need for touch, anxiety and depression are related to problematic smartphone use. *Computers in Human Behavior*, *63*, 509–516. DOI: 10.1016/j.chb.2016.05.079

Elhai, J. D., Levine, J. C., Dvorak, R. D., & Hall, B. J. (2020). Non-social features of smartphone use are most related to depression, anxiety, and problematic smartphone use. *Computers in Human Behavior*, *69*, 75–82. DOI: 10.1016/j.chb.2016.12.023

Elhai, J. D., Tiamiyu, M. F., & Weeks, J. W. (2018). Depression and anticipatory anxiety as predictors of problematic smartphone use: The moderating role of emotional reactivity. *Journal of Affective Disorders*, *229*, 79–85. DOI: 10.1016/j.jad.2017.12.045

Elhai, J. D., Yang, H., & Montag, C. (2021). Fear of missing out (FOMO): Overview, theoretical underpinnings, and literature review on relations with severity of negative affectivity and problematic technology use. *The British Journal of Psychiatry*, *43*(2), 203–209. DOI: 10.1590/1516-4446-2020-0870

Ellison, N. B., Vitak, J., Gray, R., & Lampe, C. (2014). Cultivating social resources on social network sites: Facebook relationship maintenance behaviors and their role in social capital processes. *Journal of Computer-Mediated Communication*, *19*(4), 855–870. DOI: 10.1111/jcc4.12078

El-Sayed, Ahmed Abdelwahab Ibrahim, Alsenany, Samira Ahmed, Asal, Maha Gamal Ramadan, Alasqah, Ibrahim, Development and Validation of Artificial Intelligence Addiction Scale for Researchers: A Methodological Study, Journal of Nursing Management, 2025, 8458533, 15 pages, 2025. DOI: 10.1155/jonm/8458533

Epstein, Z., Hertzmann, A., Herman, L., Mahari, R., Frank, M., Groh, M., Schroeder, H., Smith, A., Akten, M., Fjeld, J., Farid, H., Leach, N., Pentland, A., & Russakovsky, O. (2023). Art and the science of generative AI: A deeper dive. *Science*, *380*(6650), 1110–1111. DOI: 10.1126/science.adh4451 PMID: 37319193

ESPOSITO, E. (2017). Artificial Communication? The Production of Contingency by Algorithms.

Eubanks, V. (2018). *Automating inequality: How high-tech tools profile, police, and punish the poor*. St. Martin's Press.

European Commission. (2022). The Digital Services Act package. https://digital-strategy.ec.europa.eu/en/policies/digital-services-act-package

European, C. (2020). *Libro blanco sobre la inteligencia artificial: un enfoque europeo orientado a la excelencia y la confianza*. Oficina de Publicaciones de la Unión Europea. https://eur-lex.europa.eu/legal-content/ES/TXT/PDF/?uri=CELEX:52020DC0065

Evelina, L. W. (2022). Digital engagement and consumer behavior: The shift from transactional to emotional value. *Journal of Digital Marketing and Communication, 2*(1), 45–58. DOI: 10.53623/jdmc.v2i1.132

Examining the Correlation between Excessive Recreational Smartphone Use and Academic Performance Outcomes. (2019). *Journal of Higher Education Theory and Practice, 19*(5). DOI: 10.33423/jhetp.v19i5.2279

Eyal, N. (2014). *Hooked: How to build habit-forming products*. Portfolio.

Fabio, R. A., Stracuzzi, A., & Lo Faro, R. (2022). Problematic Smartphone Use Leads to Behavioral and Cognitive Self-Control Deficits. *International Journal of Environmental Research and Public Health, 19*(12), 7445. DOI: 10.3390/ijerph19127445

Farghaly Abdelaliem, S. M., Dator, W. L. T., & Sankarapandian, C. (2023). The relationship between nursing students' smart devices addiction and their perception of artificial intelligence. *Health Care, 11*(1), 110. DOI: 10.3390/healthcare11010110 PMID: 36611570

Ferchaud, A., Yan, Z., & Daniel, E. S. (2022). Binging on the heartbreak: The effect of binge-watching on narrative engagement and parasocial breakups. *Psychology of Popular Media, 11*(4), 402–412. DOI: 10.1037/ppm0000414

Festinger, L. (1954). A Theory of Social Comparison Processes. *Human Relations, 7*(2), 117–140. DOI: 10.1177/001872675400700202

Fineberg, N. A., Demetrovics, Z., Stein, D. J., Ioannidis, K., Potenza, M. N., Billieux, J., & Chamberlain, S. R. (2018). Manifestos for the future of research into problematic usage of the internet. *European Psychiatry : the Journal of the Association of European Psychiatrists, 53*, 24–32. DOI: 10.1016/j.eurpsy.2018.05.004

Fingerman, K. L., Kim, Y. K., Ng, Y. T., Zhang, S., Huo, M., & Birditt, K. S. (2022). Television Viewing, Physical Activity, and Loneliness in Late Life. *The Gerontologist, 62*(7), 1006–1017. DOI: 10.1093/geront/gnab120 PMID: 34379115

Flankegård, G., Mörelius, E., Duchén, K., & Rytterström, P. (2020). Experiences of parents who give pharmacological treatment to children with functional constipation at home. *Journal of Advanced Nursing, 76*(12), 3519–3527. DOI: 10.1111/jan.14539 PMID: 33043491

Flayelle, M., Maurage, P., & Billieux, J. (2017). Toward a qualitative understanding of binge-watching behaviors: A focus group approach. *Journal of Behavioral Addictions*, *6*(4), 457–471. DOI: 10.1556/2006.6.2017.060 PMID: 29025269

Flayelle, M., Maurage, P., Karila, L., Vögele, C., & Billieux, J. (2019). Overcoming the unitary exploration of binge-watching: A cluster analytical approach. *Journal of Behavioral Addictions*, *8*(3), 586–602. DOI: 10.1556/2006.8.2019.53 PMID: 31537085

Fogg, B. J. (2003). *Persuasive technology: Using computers to change what we think and do*. Morgan Kaufmann. DOI: 10.1016/B978-155860643-2/50011-1

Freytag, A., Knop-Huelss, K., Meier, A., Reinecke, L., Hefner, D., Klimmt, C., & Vorderer, P. (2021). Permanently Online—Always Stressed Out? The Effects of Permanent Connectedness on Stress Experiences. *Human Communication Research*, *47*(2), 132–165. DOI: 10.1093/hcr/hqaa014

Fuchs, C. (2017). *Social media: A critical introduction* (2nd ed.). Sage.

Gafoor, S. A. (2024). Perceived Stress And Binge-Watching Behavior Among Indian College Students, Educational Administration. *Theory into Practice*, *30*(5), 117–126. DOI: 10.53555/kuey.v30i5.2787

Gao, B., Shen, Q., Luo, G., & Xu, Y. (2023). Why mobile social media-related fear of missing out promotes depressive symptoms? The roles of phubbing and social exclusion. *BMC Psychology*, *11*(1), 189. DOI: 10.1186/s40359-023-01231-1

Garg, S. & Singh, A.K. (2023). Binge Watching, Loneliness, Interpersonal Competence and Interaction Anxiety in Young Adults. International Journal of Indian Psychology, 11(3), 541-553. DIP:18.01.051.20231103, DOI:DOI: 10.25215/1103.051

Gavranović, V., & Veljković Michos, M. (2022). Utilizing Ludic Foreign Language Pedagogy at the Tertiary Level. Paper presented at Sinteza 2022 - *International Scientific Conference on Information Technology and Data Related Research*. Retrieved from: DOI:DOI: 10.15308/Sinteza-2022-353-357

Gerbaudo, P. (2024). TikTok and the algorithmic transformation of social media publics: From social networks to social interest clusters. *New Media & Society*. Advance online publication. DOI: 10.1177/14614448241304106

Gillespie, T. (2014). The relevance of algorithms. In Gillespie, T., Boczkowski, P. J., & Foot, K. A. (Eds.), *Media technologies: Essays on communication, materiality, and society* (pp. 167–193). MIT Press. DOI: 10.7551/mitpress/9042.003.0013

Gillespie, T. (2018). *Custodians of the Internet: Platforms, content moderation, and the hidden decisions that shape social media*. Yale University Press.

Gkikas, D. C., & Theodoridis, P. K. (2024). Examining the role of non-transactional consumer engagement in e-commerce: A systematic literature review and future research agenda. *Electronic Commerce Research and Applications*, *63*, 101344. DOI: 10.1016/j.elerap.2023.101344

Goffman, E. (1959). *The presentation of self in everyday life*. Doubleday.

Gonçalves, L. L., Nardi, A. E., & King, A. L. S. (2023). Digital Dependence in Organizations: Impacts on the Physical and Mental Health of Employees. *Clinical Practice and Epidemiology in Mental Health*, *19*(1), e174501792212300. DOI: 10.2174/17450179-v19-e230109-2022-17

Granovetter, M. (1985). Economic action and social structure: The problem of embeddedness. *American Journal of Sociology*, *91*(3), 481–510. DOI: 10.1086/228311

Grant, J. E., Potenza, M. N., Weinstein, A., & Gorelick, D. A. (2010). Introduction to behavioral addictions. *The American Journal of Drug and Alcohol Abuse*, *36*(5), 233–241. DOI: 10.3109/00952990.2010.491884

Gray, J. A. (1970). The psychophysiological basis of introversion-extraversion. *Behaviour Research and Therapy*, *8*(3), 249–266. DOI: 10.1016/0005-7967(70)90069-0 PMID: 5470377

Griffiths, M. (1995). Technological addictions. *Clinical Psychology Forum*, *76*(76), 14–19. DOI: 10.53841/bpscpf.1995.1.76.14

Griffiths, M. D. (2005). A "components" model of addiction within a biopsychosocial framework. *Journal of Substance Use*, *10*(4), 191–197. DOI: 10.1080/14659890500114359

Griffiths, M. D. (2013). Social networking addiction: Emerging themes and issues. *Journal of Addiction Research & Therapy*, *4*(5), e118. Advance online publication. DOI: 10.4172/2155-6105.1000e118

Griffiths, M. D. (2014). Behavioral addiction and co-morbidity. *Journal of Behavioral Addictions*, *3*(2), 69–71. DOI: 10.1556/JBA.3.2014.015

Gui, D.-Y., Dai, Y., Zheng, Z., & Liu, S. (2023). Losing control without your smartphone: Anxiety affects the dynamic choice process of impulsive decision-making and purchase. *Frontiers in Neuroscience*, *17*, 998017. DOI: 10.3389/fnins.2023.998017

Gupta, M., & Sharma, A. (2021). Fear of missing out: A brief overview of origin, theoretical underpinnings and relationship with mental health. *World Journal of Clinical Cases*, *9*(19), 4881–4889. DOI: 10.12998/wjcc.v9.i19.4881 PMID: 34307542

Guzel, Halime. (2020). The ınvestigation of the relationship between smartphone addiction, and problem-solving skills and ways of coping with stress. Dusunen Adam:The Journal of Psychiatry and Neurological Sciences. .DOI: 10.14744/DAJPNS.2020.00088

Haidt, J., & Rausch, Z. (2026). Social media is harming adolescents at a scale large enough to cause changes at the population level. In *The World Happiness Report*. DOI: 10.18724/WHR-G490-BG86

Hajli, N. (2014). A study of the impact of social media on consumers. *International Journal of Market Research*, *56*(3), 387–404. DOI: 10.2501/IJMR-2014-025

Han, B.-C. (2020). *Güzeli kurtarmak* [Saving beauty]. (Filiz, K., Trans.). İnsan Yayınları.

Han, B.-C. (2021). *Capitalism and the death drive*. John Wiley & Sons.

Han, D. H., Kim, S. M., Lee, Y. S., & Renshaw, P. F. (2012). The effect of family therapy on the changes in the severity of on-line game play and brain activity in adolescents with on-line game addiction. *Psychiatry Research: Neuroimaging*, *202*(2), 126–131. DOI: 10.1016/j.pscychresns.2012.02.011 PMID: 22698763

Han, Y., Qiu, J., Shi, C., Huang, S., Huang, H., Wang, X., Zhu, S., Lu, D., Lu, P., & Zeng, F. (2025). Factors Associated With Digital Addiction: Umbrella Review. *JMIR Mental Health*, *12*, e66950–e66950. DOI: 10.2196/66950

Hargittai, E. (2010). Digital na(t)ives? Variation in internet skills and uses among members of the "net generation.". *Sociological Inquiry*, *80*(1), 92–113. DOI: 10.1111/j.1475-682X.2009.00317.x

Hari, J. (2022). *Stolen Focus: Why You Can't Pay Attention—and How to Think Deeply Again*. Crown.

Harris, B. (2019). *When to put the scroll down: How infinite scroll affects user experience and engagement*. UX Planet. https://uxplanet.org/infinite-scroll-design-patterns-9b5b6c0e7e47

Harris, B., & Sandoval, M. (2020). Datafication and commodification of the self: From digital labor to digital asset. In *The SAGE handbook of digital society* (pp. 227–244). SAGE Publications.

Hepp, A. (2019). *Deep mediatization*. Routledge. DOI: 10.4324/9781351064903

Herzallah, A. M., Mukhtar, M., & Al-shami, S. A. (2021). The influence of hedonic browsing and sales promotion on online impulse buying: The mediating role of urgent to buy. *International Journal of Electronic Business*, *16*(4), 324–341. DOI: 10.1504/IJEB.2021.1189457

Hessari, H., Daneshmandi, F., Busch, P., & Smith, S. (2024). Workplace nomophobia: A systematic literature review. *Current Psychology (New Brunswick, N.J.)*, *43*(31), 25934–25954. DOI: 10.1007/s12144-024-06222-y

Hindman, J., Zugai, J., Foster, K., & Raeburn, T. (2025). Self-Determination Theory as a framework for research and design of digital applications for nurses' well-being. *Journal of Advanced Nursing*, *82*(1), 897–906. DOI: 10.1111/jan.16895 PMID: 40098227

Hodkinson, C. (2019). Fear of missing out (FOMO) marketing appeals: A conceptual model. *Journal of Marketing Communications*, *25*(1), 65–88. DOI: 10.1080/13527266.2016.1234504

Hoffman, D. L., & Novak, T. P. (1996). Marketing in hypermedia computer-mediated environments: Conceptual foundations. *Journal of Marketing*, *60*(3), 50–68. DOI: 10.1177/002224299606000304

Hofmann, W., Schmeichel, B. J., & Baddeley, A. D. (2012). Executive functions and self-regulation. *Trends in Cognitive Sciences*, *16*(3), 174–180. DOI: 10.1016/j.tics.2012.01.006

Holden, C. (2001). 'Behavioral' addictions: Do they exist? *Science*, *294*(5544), 980–982. DOI: 10.1126/science.294.5544.980

Hong, J., & Chen, N. (2024). *Effects of achievement motivation and Chat-GPT self-efficacy on ChatGPT addiction and ChatGPT continuance intention. SSRN.* DOI: 10.2139/ssrn.5064583

Horton, D., & Wohl, R. R. (1956). Mass communication and para-social interaction: Observations on intimacy at a distance. *Psychiatry*, *19*(3), 215–229. DOI: 10.1080/00332747.1956.11023049

Hoşgör, H. K., & Güngördü, H. (2025). Dijital yerlilerde ChatGPT'nin kullanım alanları ve ChatGPT bağımlılığı üzerine bir araştırma: A study on the usage areas of ChatGPT and ChatGPT addiction among digital natives. *Socrates Journal of Interdisciplinary Social Researches*, *11*(57), 12–24. DOI: 10.5281/zenodo.17179422

Hou, W., Ko, N., & Shu, B. (2012). Recovery experiences of Taiwanese women after terminating abusive relationships. *Journal of Interpersonal Violence*, *28*(1), 157–175. DOI: 10.1177/0886260512448851 PMID: 22809818

Hou, Y., Xiong, D., Jiang, T., Song, L., & Wang, Q. (2019). Social media addiction: Its impact, mediation, and intervention. *Cyberpsychology (Brno), 13*(1), 4. Advance online publication. DOI: 10.5817/CP2019-1-4

Huang, S., Lai, X., Ke, L., Li, Y., Wang, H., Zhao, X., Dai, X., & Wang, Y. (2024). Mental health and AI dependence: A cross-lagged panel model and the mediating roles of motivations for AI use among adolescents. *Psychology Research and Behavior Management, 17*(3), 1087–1102. DOI: 10.2147/PRBM.S440889 PMID: 38495087

Huang, Y., & Huang, H. (2024). Exploring the effect of attachment on tech- nology addiction to generative AI chatbots: A structural equation modeling analysis. *International Journal of Human-Computer Interaction*. Advance online publication. DOI: 10.1080/10447318.2024.2426029

Hu, B., Mao, Y., & Kim, K. J. (2023). How social anxiety leads to problematic use of conversational AI: The roles of loneliness, rumination, and mind perception. *Computers in Human Behavior, 143*, 107760. DOI: 10.1016/j.chb.2023.107760

Hunt, M. G., Marx, R., Lipson, C., & Young, J. (2018). No more FOMO: Limiting social media decreases loneliness and depression. *Journal of Social and Clinical Psychology, 37*(10), 751–768. DOI: 10.1521/jscp.2018.37.10.751

Hussien, R. M. (2022). The association between nomophobia and loneliness among the general population in the Kingdom of Saudi Arabia. *Middle East Current Psychiatry, Ain Shams University, 29*(1), 68. DOI: 10.1186/s43045-022-00235-8

Ihde, S. (2021). Algorithmic serendipity and the paradox of exposure: Evaluating the role of recommendation algorithms in online harm. *Media and Communication, 9*(1), 194–206. DOI: 10.17645/mac.v9i1.3501

Illouz, E. (2007). *Cold intimacies: The making of emotional capitalism*. Polity Press.

Ivanova, V., & Papadaki, M. (2019). The effects of mindfulness-based interventions on physical pain: A systematic review. *International Journal of Environmental Research and Public Health, 16*(23), 4719. DOI: 10.3390/ijerph16234719 PMID: 31779281

Jaworska, D. (2025). Many faces of FoMO: A qualitative in-depth investigation of context-specific experiences, emotions, and coping strategies. *PLoS One, 20*(9), e0330978. DOI: 10.1371/journal.pone.0330978

JBI. (2026). *JBI critical appraisal tools*. https://jbi.global/critical-appraisal-tools

Jiang, Y. (2026). Surveillance capitalism and social media addiction. *Information, Medium, and Society: Journal of Publishing Studies*. DOI: 10.18848/2691-1507/CGP/A35

Jimenez, N., San Martin, S., & Rodríguez-Torrico, P. (2024). Effect of smartphone addiction on compulsive app downloading tendency: Protective factors for generation Z consumers. *Young Consumers*, *25*(6), 665–686. DOI: 10.1108/YC-09-2023-1870

Jindal, R. D. (2020). Is binge-watching competing with sleep? And winning? *Journal of Clinical Sleep Medicine : JCSM : Official Publication of the American Academy of Sleep Medicine*, *16*(S1), 31–32. DOI: 10.5664/jcsm.8898 PMID: 33054964

Jo, H., & Baek, E.-M. (2023). Exploring the dynamics of mobile app addiction: The interplay of communication, affective factors, flow, perceived enjoyment, and habit. *BMC Psychology*, *11*(1), 404. DOI: 10.1186/s40359-023-01440-8

John, B., Alsamarra'i, Z., & Panteli, N. (2025). Reconfiguring digital embeddedness in hybrid work: The case of employee experience management platforms. *Information Systems Journal*, *35*(2), 450–479. DOI: 10.1111/isj.12545

Joseph, D., & Varghese, K. (2025). Binge-watching as a behavioural addiction: A systematic review of causes, consequences, and potential for mental health intervention. *Indian Journal of Psychiatric Social Work*, *16*(1), 36–47. DOI: 10.29120/ijpsw.2025.v16.i1.637

Jovanović, M., & Campbell, M. (2022). Generative artificial intelligence: Trends and prospects. *Computer*, *55*(10), 107–112. DOI: 10.1109/MC.2022.3192720

Kahneman, D., Knetsch, J. L., & Thaler, R. H. (1990). Experimental tests of the endowment effect and the Coase theorem. *Journal of Political Economy*, *98*(6), 1325–1348. DOI: 10.1086/261737

Kamalov, F., Calonge, D. S., & Gurrib, I. (2023). A new era of artificial intelligence in education: A multifaceted revolution. *Sustainability*, *15*(16), 12451. DOI: 10.3390/su151612451

Kandola, A. (2022, November 29). What is binge watching? Definition, health effects, and more. Medical News Today. https://www.medicalnewstoday.com/articles/what-is-binge-watching

Karakuş, M. (2022). Sosyal Medyanın ve Online Alışveriş Sitelerinin Tüketici Davranışlarına Etkisi Üzerine Nitel Bir Araştırma. *Atatürk İletişim Dergisi*, *23*, 1–8. DOI: 10.54614/communicata.2022.1020911

Kardefelt-Winther, D. (2014). A conceptual and methodological critique of internet addiction research. *International Journal of Mental Health and Addiction*, *12*(1), 21–34.

Kardefelt-Winther, D. (2014). A conceptual and methodological critique of internet addiction research: Towards a model of compensatory internet use. *Computers in Human Behavior, 31*, 351–354. DOI: 10.1016/j.chb.2013.10.059

Kardefelt-Winther, D., Hebert, V., Heidari, S., Minges, K. E., Brindis, C. D., & Victor, L. (2019). Effects of excessive screen time on neurodevelopment, learning, memory, mental health, and neurodegeneration: A scoping review. *International Journal of Mental Health and Addiction, 17*(5), 1119–1139. DOI: 10.1007/s11469-019-00118-2

Kardefelt-Winther, D., Heeren, A., Schimmenti, A., van Rooij, A., Maurage, P., Carras, M., Edman, J., Blaszczynski, A., Khazaal, Y., & Billieux, J. (2017). How can we conceptualize behavioural addiction without pathologizing common behaviours? *Addiction (Abingdon, England), 112*(10), 1709–1715. DOI: 10.1111/add.13763

Karmakar, A. (2024). Era of binge-watching: An 'asset' or an 'abyss'? *International Journal of Indian Psychology, 12*(2), 4408–4416. https://ijip.in/wp-content/uploads/2024/07/18.01.393.20241202.pdf

Karppi, T. (2022). *Disconnect: Facebook's affective bonds*. University of Minnesota Press.

Kasneci, E., Seßler, K., Küchemann, S., Bannert, M., Dementieva, D., Fischer, F., Gasser, U., Groh, G., Günnemann, S., Hüllermeier, E., Krusche, S., Kutyniok, G., Michaeli, T., Nerdel, C., Pfeffer, J., Poquet, O., Sailer, M., Schmidt, A., Seidel, T., & Kasneci, G. (2023). ChatGPT for good? On opportunities and challenges of large language models for education. *Learning and Individual Differences, 103*, 102274. DOI: 10.1016/j.lindif.2023.102274

Katz, J. E., & Aakhus, M. (Eds.). (2002). *Perpetual contact: Mobile communication, private talk, public performance*. Cambridge University Press. DOI: 10.1017/CBO9780511489471

Kbaiah, A. T., & Nashwan, A. J. (2024). Beyond the image: Artificial intelligence's role in refining and transforming radiology nursing. *Avicenna (Doha), 2024*(1), 3. DOI: 10.5339/avi.2024.3

Kellogg, K. C., Valentine, M. A., & Christin, A. (2020). Algorithms at work. *The Academy of Management Annals, 14*(1), 366–410. DOI: 10.5465/annals.2018.0174

Kemp, S. (2023, January 26). *Digital 2023: Global overview report*. DataReportal. https://datareportal.com/reports/digital-2023-global-overview-report

Kennedy, B., Tyson, A., & Saks, E. (2023). *Public awareness of artificial intelligence in everyday activities: Limited enthusiasm in U.S. over AI's growing influence in daily life*. Pew Research Center. https://www.pewresearch.org/science/2023/02/15/public-awareness-of-artificial-intelligence-in-everyday-activities/

Kerse, Y., & Yüce, A. (2022). FOMO ve Online Kompulsif Satın Alma: Sosyal Medya Fenomenleri Tüketicilerin Kaygılarını ve Takıntılarını Tetikliyor Mu? *KMÜ Sosyal ve Ekonomik Araştırmalar Dergisi*, *24*(43), 704–716.

Kılıç, S., & Koca, F. (2025). Artificial intelligence addiction of university students: The case of Ordu University. *Ordu Üniversitesi Sosyal Bilimler Enstitüsü Sosyal Bilimler Araştırmaları Dergisi, 15*(ISRIS 2025), 352–368. DOI: 10.48146/odusobiad.1725693

Kim, H. C., Park, C. J., Ko, Y. M., Hyun, J. S., & Kim, C. M. (2011). The good and the bad: The effects of excellence in internet and mobile phone usage. In Park, J. J., Jin, H., & Park, M. S. (Eds.), *Advanced software engineering and its applications* (pp. 559–568). Springer., DOI: 10.1007/978-3-642-27207-3_61

Kim, S., & Eastin, M. S. (2011). Hedonic tendencies and the online consumer: An investigation of the online shopping process. *Journal of Internet Commerce*, *10*(1), 68–90. DOI: 10.1080/15332861.2011.558458

Kleiman, S. (2004). Phenomenology: To wonder and search for meanings. *Nurse Researcher*, *11*(4), 7–19. DOI: 10.7748/nr2004.07.11.4.7.c6211 PMID: 15227895

Ko, H., Cho, C. H., & Roberts, M. S. (2005). Internet uses and grafitications: A structural equation model of interactive advertising. *Journal of Advertising*, *34*(2), 57–70. DOI: 10.1080/00913367.2005.10639191

Koob, G. F. (2013). Negative reinforcement in drug addiction: The darkness within. *Current Opinion in Neurobiology*, *23*(4), 559–563. DOI: 10.1016/j.conb.2013.03.011

Kooli, C., Kooli, Y., & Kooli, E. (2025). Generative artificial intelligence addiction syndrome: A new behavioral disorder? *Asian Journal of Psychiatry*, *107*, 104476. DOI: 10.1016/j.ajp.2025.104476 PMID: 40174516

Kruglanski, A. W. (2004). *The Psychology of Closed Mindedness*. Psychology Press.

Küçükvardar, M., & Tıngöy, O. (2018). Teknoloji bağımlılığının semptomlar temelinde incelenmesi. *AJIT-e: Academic Journal of Information Technology, 9*(35), 111–123. DOI: 10.5824/1309-1581.2018.5.008.x

Kuijk, F., Van Broeck, S., Dareau, C., Ravenet, B., Ochs, M., Apostolakis, K., Daras, P., Monaghan, D., E O'Connor, N., Wall, J., Izquierdo, E., Kuijk, F., Van Broeck, S., Dareau, C., Ravenet, B., Ochs, M., Apostolakis, K., Daras, P., Monaghan, D., E O'Connor, N., Wall, J., & Izquierdo, E. (2013). A Framework for Human-like Behavior in an Immersive Virtual World.

Kukar-Kinney, M., Scheinbaum, A. C., & Schaefers, T. (2016). Compulsive buying in online social networking sites: An investigation of the role of social presence and social identification. *Journal of Business Research*, *69*(8), 2717–2723. DOI: 10.1016/j.jbusres.2015.11.005

Kuss, D. J., & Griffiths, M. D. (2011). Online social networking and addiction—A review of the psychological literature. *International Journal of Environmental Research and Public Health*, *8*(9), 3528–3552. DOI: 10.3390/ijerph8093528 PMID: 22016701

Kuss, D. J., & Griffiths, M. D. (2017). Social media addiction—An overview of prevalence, etiology and consequences. *Journal of Behavioral Addictions*, *6*(4), 529–543. DOI: 10.1556/2006.6.2017.069

Kuss, D. J., & Griffiths, M. D. (2017). Social networking sites and addiction: Ten lessons learned. *International Journal of Environmental Research and Public Health*, *14*(3), 311. DOI: 10.3390/ijerph14030311

Kuss, D. J., Griffiths, M. D., Karila, L., & Billieux, J. (2014). Internet addiction: A systematic review of epidemiological research for the last decade. *Current Pharmaceutical Design*, *20*(25), 4026–4052. DOI: 10.2174/13816128113199990617 PMID: 24001297

Kwon, M., Kim, D.-J., Cho, H., & Yang, S. (2013). The Smartphone Addiction Scale: Development and Validation of a Short Version for Adolescents. *PLoS One*, *8*(12), e83558. DOI: 10.1371/journal.pone.0083558

Laidler, J. (2019, March 4). Harvard professor says surveillance capitalism is undermining democracy. *Harvard Gazette*. https://news.harvard.edu/gazette/story/2019/03/harvard-professor-says-surveillance-capitalism-is-undermining-democracy/

Lang, A. (2000). The limited capacity model of mediated message processing. *Journal of Communication*, *50*(1), 46–70. DOI: 10.1111/j.1460-2466.2000.tb02833.x

Leclercq-Vandelannoitte, A. (2019). Is Employee Technological "Ill-Being" Missing from Corporate Responsibility? The Foucauldian Ethics of Ubiquitous IT Uses in Organizations. *Journal of Business Ethics*, *160*(2), 339–361. DOI: 10.1007/s10551-019-04202-y

Lefebvre, H. (1991). *Critique of everyday life* (Vol. 1; Moore, J., Trans.). Verso.

Lefebvre, H. (2004). *Rhythmanalysis: Space, time and everyday life* (S. Elden & G. Moore, Trans.). *Continuum.*

León-Mejía, A. C., Gutiérrez-Ortega, M., Serrano-Pintado, I., & González-Cabrera, J. (2021). A systematic review on nomophobia prevalence: Surfacing results and standard guidelines for future research. *PLoS One*, *16*(5), e0250509. DOI: 10.1371/journal.pone.0250509

Lepuschitz, R. (2010). BCIs – The New Ontological Dimension of Cyberspace.

Lestari, B., & Suratmini, D. (2024). The Relationship FoMO (Fear of Missing Out) and Nomophobia with Phubbing Behavior among Adolescent Instagram Users. [ICON Journal]. *Indonesian Contemporary Nursing Journal*, *8*(2), 82–89. DOI: 10.20956/icon.v8i2.30750

Licoppe, C. (2004). "Connected" presence: The emergence of a new repertoire for managing social relationships in a changing communication technoscape. *Environment and Planning. D, Society & Space*, *22*(1), 135–156. DOI: 10.1068/d323t

Liimatainen, L., Latvala, E., & Hopia, H. (2016). Reviewing the methodology of an integrative review. *Scandinavian Journal of Caring Sciences*, *30*(4), 662–669. DOI: 10.1111/scs.12327 PMID: 27074869

Limna, P., Jakwatanatham, S., Siripipattanakul, S., Kaewpuang, P., & Sriboonruang, P. (2022). *A review of artificial intelligence (AI) in education during the digital era.* Advance Knowledge for Executives, 1(1), 1–9. https://papers.ssrn.com/sol3/papers.cfm?abstract_id=4160798

Lin, L. Y., Sidani, J. E., Shensa, A., Radovic, A., Miller, E., Colditz, J. B., Hoffman, B. L., Giles, L. M., & Primack, B. A. (2016). Association between social media use and depression among U.S. young adults. *Depression and Anxiety*, *33*(4), 323–331. DOI: 10.1002/da.22466 PMID: 26783723

Lin, Y.-H., Chiang, C.-L., Lin, P.-H., Chang, L.-R., Ko, C.-H., Lee, Y.-H., & Lin, S.-H. (2016). Proposed Diagnostic Criteria for Smartphone Addiction. *PLoS One*, *11*(11), e0163010. DOI: 10.1371/journal.pone.0163010

Li, R., & Wang, C. (2022). Cultural and creative product design and image recognition based on deep learning. *Computational Intelligence and Neuroscience*, *2022*(1), 7256584. DOI: 10.1155/2022/7256584 PMID: 35865496

Liu, C., Bao, Z., & Zheng, C. (2020). Exploring the factors influencing consumers' social commerce intention: An integrated model. *Information & Management*, *57*(7), 103325. DOI: 10.1016/j.im.2020.103325

Liu, H., Chu, H., Huang, Q., & Chen, X. (2023). How social commerce features influence consumers' browsing behavior and purchase intention: An investigation from the perspective of social capital. *Information & Management*, *60*(3), 103762. DOI: 10.1016/j.im.2023.103762

Livingstone, S. (2008). Taking risky opportunities in youthful content creation: Teenagers' use of social networking sites for intimacy, privacy and self-expression. *New Media & Society*, *10*(3), 393–411. DOI: 10.1177/1461444808089415

Livingstone, S. (2009). *Children and the internet: Great expectations, challenging realities*. Polity Press.

Loewenstein, G. (1994). The psychology of curiosity: A review and reinterpretation. *Psychological Bulletin*, *116*(1), 75–98. DOI: 10.1037/0033-2909.116.1.75

Lorenz-Spreen, P., Mønsted, B. M., Hövel, P., & Lehmann, S. (2019). Accelerating dynamics of collective attention. *Nature Communications*, *10*(1), 1759. DOI: 10.1038/s41467-019-09311-w PMID: 30988286

Lupton, D. (2020). *Data selves: More-than-human perspectives*. Polity Press.

Lutz, C., & Tamó-Larrieux, A. (2020). The robot privacy paradox: Understanding how privacy concerns shape intentions to use social robots. *Human-Machine Communication*, *1*, 87–111. DOI: 10.30658/hmc.1.6

M Thomas, N., G Choudhari, S., M Gaidhane, A., & Quazi Syed, Z. (2022). 'Digital Wellbeing': The Need of the Hour in Today's Digitalized and Technology-Driven World!.

M. James, M. & Francis Leader, J. (2023). Do digital hugs work? Re-embodying our social lives online with digital tact.

Machidon, O. M. (2025). Beyond algorethics: Addressing the ethical and anthropological challenges of AI recommender systems. *Journal of Media Ethics*, 1–13. Advance online publication. DOI: 10.1080/23736992.2025.2584435

Maclachlan, R., Adams, R., Lauro, V., Murray, M., Magueijo, V., Flockhart, G., & Hasty, W. (2024). Chat-GPT: A clever search engine or a creative design assistant for students and industry? In *Proceedings of the 26th International Conference on Engineering and Product Design Education* (Article 70). DOI: 10.35199/EPDE.2024.70

Maignan, I., & Lukas, B. A. (1997). The nature & social uses of the Internet: A qualitative investigation. *The Journal of Consumer Affairs, 31*(2), 346–37. DOI: 10.1111/j.1745-6606.1997.tb00395.x

Manuel Sánchez-Sordo, J. (2019). Data mining techniques for the study of online learning from an extended approach.

Maral, S., Naycı, N., Bilmez, H., Erdemir, E. İ., & Satici, S. A. (2025). Problematic ChatGPT Use Scale: AI-Human collaboration or unraveling the dark side of ChatGPT. *International Journal of Mental Health and Addiction*. Advance online publication. DOI: 10.1007/s11469-025-01509-y

Markowitz, D. M., Hancock, J. T., Bailenson, J. N., & Reeves, B. (2019). Psychological and physiological effects of applying self-control to the mobile phone. *PLoS One, 14*(11), e0224464. DOI: 10.1371/journal.pone.0224464

Marsh, E., Perez Vallejos, E., & Spence, A. (2024). Overloaded by Information or Worried About Missing Out on It: A Quantitative Study of Stress, Burnout, and Mental Health Implications in the Digital Workplace. *SAGE Open, 14*(3), 21582440241268830. DOI: 10.1177/21582440241268830

Marwick, A. E., & boyd, . (2011). I tweet honestly, I tweet passionately: Twitter users, context collapse, and the imagined audience. *New Media & Society, 13*(1), 114–133. DOI: 10.1177/1461444810365313

Masuwd, M., & Putra, F. T. (2024). Improving the quality of education through teacher resource management: The strategic role of school principals. *Jurnal Manajemen Pendidikan Islam Almatani, 1*(1), 29–46. https://journal.yrpipku.com/index.php/jmpia/article/view/6148

Matar Boumosleh, J., & Jaalouk, D. (2017). Depression, anxiety, and smartphone addiction in university students- A cross sectional study. *PLoS One, 12*(8), e0182239. DOI: 10.1371/journal.pone.0182239

Matias, J., Quinton, J.-C., Colomb, M., Normand, A., Izaute, M., & Silvert, L. (2021). Fear of Missing Out Predicts Distraction by Social Reward Signals Displayed on a Smartphone in Difficult Driving Situations. *Frontiers in Psychology, 12*, 688157. DOI: 10.3389/fpsyg.2021.688157

Matsiola, M., Lappas, G., & Yannacopoulou, A. (2024). Generative AI in education: Assessing usability, ethical implications, and communication effectiveness. *Societies (Basel, Switzerland), 14*(12), 267. DOI: 10.3390/soc14120267

Mazhar, M., Farhan, M., & Raza, S. A. (2023). Fear of missing out, social media addiction and compulsive buying: The mediating role of digital window shopping. *Information Technology & People*, *36*(7), 2845–2867. DOI: 10.1108/ITP-10-2021-0815

McAlister, A. R., Alhabash, S., & Yang, J. (2024). Artificial intelligence and ChatGPT: Exploring current and potential future roles in marketing education. *Journal of Marketing Communications*, *30*(2), 166–187. DOI: 10.1080/13527266.2023.2289034

Medrano-Sánchez, E. J., Cuenca Silva, L. S., & Medrano-Sánchez, G. M. (2024). Towards Understanding Nomophobia: A Systematic Review of Its Prevalence, Causes, and Effects in Educational Settings. *Academic Journal of Interdisciplinary Studies*, *13*(6), 306. DOI: 10.36941/ajis-2024-0196

Meynadier, J., Malouff, J. M., Schutte, N. S., & Loi, N. M. (2025). Using social media to cope with psychological distress and fear of missing out: The role of social media reward expectancies in social media addiction. *International Journal of Human-Computer Interaction*, *41*(20), 12687–12696. DOI: 10.1080/10447318.2025.2464894

Milano, S., Taddeo, M., & Floridi, L. (2020). Recommender systems and their ethical challenges. *AI & Society*, *35*(4), 957–967. DOI: 10.1007/s00146-020-00950-y

Miller, W. R., & Rollnick, S. (2012). *Motivational interviewing: Helping people change*. Guilford Press.

Montag, C. & Diefenbach, S. (2018). Towards Homo Digitalis: Important Research Issues for Psychology and the Neurosciences at the Dawn of the Internet of Things and the Digital Society.

Montag, C., Błaszkiewicz, K., Sariyska, R., Lachmann, B., Andone, I., Trendafilov, B., & Markowetz, A. (2015). Smartphone usage patterns and personality: The context of cultural differences. *Frontiers in Psychology*, *6*, 33. DOI: 10.3389/fpsyg.2015.00033

Montag, C., Lachmann, B., Herrlich, M., & Zweig, K. (2019). Addictive features of social media/messenger platforms and freemium games: A design perspective. *Human Behavior and Emerging Technologies*, *1*(1), 23–31. DOI: 10.1002/hbe5.108

Montag, C., & Reuter, M. (2017). *Internet addiction: Neuroscientific approaches and therapeutic implications*. Springer., DOI: 10.1007/978-3-319-46276-9

Montague, P. R., & Berns, G. S. (2002). Neural economics and the biological substrates of valuation. *Neuron*, *36*(2), 265–284. DOI: 10.1016/S0896-6273(02)00974-1

Morales-García, W. C., Sairitupa-Sanchez, L. Z., Morales-García, S. B., & Morales-García, M. (2024). Development and validation of a scale for dependence on artificial intelligence in university students. *Frontiers in Education, 9*, 1323898. DOI: 10.3389/feduc.2024.1323898

Moretta, T., Buodo, G., Demetrovics, Z., & Potenza, M. N. (2021). Tracing the boundaries between problematic Internet use and its specific manifestations: A systematic review. *Comprehensive Psychiatry, 111*, 152274. DOI: 10.1016/j.comppsych.2021.152274

Moretta, T., & Wegmann, E. (2025). Toward the classification of social media use disorder: Clinical characterization and proposed diagnostic criteria. *Addictive Behaviors Reports, 21*, 100603. DOI: 10.1016/j.abrep.2025.100603 PMID: 40256627

Mostyn Sullivan, B., George, A. M., & Rickwood, D. (2025a). An exploration of motives that influence problematic smartphone use in young adults. *Behaviour & Information Technology, 44*(9), 1886–1900. DOI: 10.1080/0144929X.2024.2380102

Murimi, R. (2023). What makes AI addictive? The role of discounting, risk aversion and self-regulation. In Hsu, C. H., Xu, M., Cao, H., Baghban, H., & Shawkat Ali, A. B. M. (Eds.), *Big data intelligence and computing* (Vol. 13864, pp. 451–462). Springer., DOI: 10.1007/978-981-99-2233-8_32

Napoli, P. M. (2019). *Social media and the public interest: Media regulation in the disinformation age*. Columbia University Press. DOI: 10.7312/napo18454

Nash, J. (2019). Exploring how social media platforms influence fashion consumer decisions in the UK retail sector. *Journal of Fashion Marketing and Management, 23*(1), 82–103. DOI: 10.1108/JFMM-01-2018-0012

Navas-Echazarreta, N., Juárez-Vela, R., Subirón-Valera, A. B., Rodríguez-Roca, B., Antón-Solanas, I., Fernández-Rodrigo, M. T., De Viñaspre-Hernandez, R. R., Sabater, A. M., Echániz-Serrano, E., Saus-Ortega, C., Santolalla-Arnedo, I., & Satústegui-Dordá, P. J. (2023). Nomophobia in university students during COVID-19 outbreak: A cross-sectional study. *Frontiers in Public Health, 11*, 1242092. DOI: 10.3389/fpubh.2023.1242092

Naveed, A., & Al-Madfai, S. (2022). Influence of infinite scrolling on consumer browsing behavior: A study of e-commerce platforms. *International Journal of Marketing Studies, 14*(2), 45–62.

Naydanova, E., Beal, B. D., & Doty, D. H. (2018). Internet use for school-mandated and self-initiated learning: Good, bad, or both? *Cyberpsychology, Behavior, and Social Networking, 21*(7), 444–449. DOI: 10.1089/cyber.2017.0003

Newport Institute. (2024). *Brain rot*. https://www.newportinstitute.com/resources/co-occurring-disorders/brainrot/

Newport, C. (2019). *Digital Minimalism: Choosing a Focused Life in a Noisy World*. Portfolio.

Ngonso, B., Egielewa, P., Egenti, G., Uduehi, I., Sunny-Duke, F., Ukhurebor, K., Onwusinkwue, S., Odezuligbo, I., Abiodun, A., Talabi, A., Jokthan, G., Opateye, J., Nwankwo, U., Eneche, B., & Osemengbe, U. (2025). Influence of artificial intelligence on educational performance of Nigerian students in tertiary institutions in Nigeria. *Journal of Infrastructure. Policy and Development*, *9*(1), 9949. DOI: 10.24294/jipd9949

Ngo, T. T. A., Nguyen, N. T. A., La, U. N., Truong, D. N., & Nguyen, H. Q. B. (2024). Impacts of Social Media Experiences on Academically Related Peer Influence and Fear of Missing Out of Secondary and High School Students. [iJEP]. *International Journal of Engineering Pedagogy*, *14*(2), 112–129. DOI: 10.3991/ijep.v14i2.43567

Nurmalasari, E., Hartini, I., Putri, R. A., & Soesilo, P. K. M. (2024). Effect of FOMO and Hedonic Value on Impulsive Buying and Post Purchase Regret for Purchasing Skincare Products at the Online Shop. [Andalas Management Review]. *AMAR*, *8*(1), 1–21. DOI: 10.25077/amar.8.1.1-21.2024

Nutt, D., King, L. A., Saulsbury, W., & Blakemore, C. (2010). Development of a rational scale to assess the harm of drugs of potential misuse. *Lancet*, *369*(9566), 1047–1053. DOI: 10.1016/S0140-6736(07)60464-4 PMID: 17382831

Oberst, U., Wegmann, E., Stodt, B., Brand, M., & Chamarro, A. (2017). Negative consequences from social media use: Body dissatisfaction, self-esteem, and fear of missing out. *Journal of Adolescence*, *55*, 20–28. DOI: 10.1016/j.adolescence.2016.12.008 PMID: 28033503

Okazaki, S., Schuberth, F., Tagashira, T., & Andrade, V. (2021). Sneaking the dark side of brand engagement into Instagram: The dual theory of passion. *Journal of Business Research*, *130*, 493–505. DOI: 10.1016/j.jbusres.2019.11.028

Ökten, B. (2025). X,Y ve Z kuşağının dijital tüketim eğilimleri: Sosyal medya ve bilinçli harcama perspektifi. *Journal of Internet Applications and Management*, *16*(1), 31–53. DOI: 10.34231/iuyd.1615441

Oraison, H., & Wilson, B. (2024). The Relationship Between Nomophobia, Addiction, and Distraction. *Journal of Technology in Behavioral Science*, *9*(4), 745–751. DOI: 10.1007/s41347-024-00392-z

Orben, A. (2020). The Sisyphean cycle of technology panics. *Perspectives on Psychological Science*, *15*(5), 1143–1157. DOI: 10.1177/1745691620919372

Orben, A., & Przybylski, A. K. (2019). The association between adolescent well-being and digital technology use. *Nature Human Behaviour*, *3*(2), 173–182. DOI: 10.1038/s41562-018-0506-1

Organisation for Economic Co-operation and Development & Global Partnership on Artificial Intelligence. (2024). Algorithmic transparency in the public sector: A state-of-the-art report. https://wp.oecd.ai/app/uploads/2025/05/algorithmic-transparency-in-the-public-sector.pdf

Oulasvirta, A., Rattenbury, T., Ma, L., & Raita, E. (2012). Habits make smartphone use more pervasive. *Personal and Ubiquitous Computing*, *16*(1), 105–114. DOI: 10.1007/s00779-011-0412-2

Özer Canarslan, N. (2025). Online alışverişte kıtlık etkisi, FOMO ve sürü davranışının anlık satın alma üzerindeki rolü. *bmij 13*(1): 243-262 DOI: 10.15295/bmij.v13i1.2521

Özkent, Y., & Akdoğan, Y. (2025). Relationships between problematic binge-watching behavior with psychological and social states. *BMC Public Health*, *25*(1), 2309. DOI: 10.1186/s12889-025-23422-8 PMID: 40611062

Pandey, M., & Yadav, P. S. (2023). Understanding the role of individual concerns, attitude, and perceived value in green apparel purchase intention, the mediating effect of consumer involvement, and the moderating role of Generation Z and Y. *Cleaner and Responsible Consumption*, *9*, 100120. DOI: 10.1016/j.clrc.2023.100120

Panova, T., & Carbonell, X. (2018). Is smartphone addiction really an addiction? *Journal of Behavioral Addictions*, *7*(2), 252–259. DOI: 10.1556/2006.7.2018.49

Papacharissi, Z. (2015). *Affective publics: Sentiment, technology, and politics.* Oxford University Press.

Park, S., & Jung, Y. (2024). Digital engagement and the loss of temporal awareness: A longitudinal study of interface paradigms. *Computers in Human Behavior*, *151*, 108012. DOI: 10.1016/j.chb.2023.108012

Parks, L., & Starosielski, N. (Eds.). (2015). *Signal traffic: Critical studies of media infrastructures.* University of Illinois Press. DOI: 10.5406/illinois/9780252039362.001.0001

Patani, N. S. (n.d.). *Smartphone Use, Fear of Missing Out (FOMO) and Social Connectedness among College Students.*

Paulus, M. P., Zhao, Y., Potenza, M. N., Aupperle, R. L., Bagot, K. S., & Tapert, S. F. (2023). Screen media activity in youth: A critical review of mental health and neuroscience findings. *Journal of Mood and Anxiety Disorders*, *3*, 100018. DOI: 10.1016/j.xjmad.2023.100018 PMID: 37927536

Pearson, J., & Qadar, S. (2024). *Artificial intelligence has psychological impacts our brains might not be ready for*. ABC News. https://www.abc.net.au/news/health/2024-05-01/artificial-intelligence-ai-psychology-mental-health/103753940

Pérez-Castejón, M., Martínez-Alarcón, L., Molina-Rodríguez, A., & Jiménez-Ruiz, I. (2025). Job satisfaction among midwives in high-intervention birthing rooms: A qualitative phenomenological study. *Health Care*, *13*(11), 1318. DOI: 10.3390/healthcare13111318 PMID: 40508931

Pérez-Torres, V. (2024). Problematic use of social media in adolescents or excessive social gratification? The mediating role of nomophobia. *Cyberpsychology (Brno)*, *18*(4). Advance online publication. DOI: 10.5817/CP2024-4-2

Petcharat, N., & Leelasantitham, A. (2021). A retentive consumer behavior model of electronic commerce to influence sustainable purchase intention. *Sustainability*, *13*(16), 8695. DOI: 10.3390/su13168695

Pettman, D. (2018). *Sonsuz Dikkat Dağınıklığı: Gündelik Yaşamda Sosyal Medyaya Odaklanmak* (Y. Çetin, Trans.). Sel.

Phang, J., Lampe, M., Ahmad, L., Agarwal, S., Fang, C. M., Liu, A. R., . . . Maes, P. (2025). *Investigating affective use and emotional well-being on ChatGPT*. arXiv. https://doi.org//arXiv.2504.03888DOI: 10.48550

Pine, B. J., & Gilmore, J. H. (1998). Welcome to the experience economy. *Harvard Business Review*, *76*, 97–105. PMID: 10181589

Pittman, M., & Sheehan, K. (2015). Sprinting a media marathon: Uses and gratifications of binge-watching television through Netflix. *First Monday*, *20*(10). Advance online publication. DOI: 10.5210/fm.v20i10.6138

Plantin, J.-C., Lagoze, C., Edwards, P. N., & Sandvig, C. (2018). Infrastructure studies meet platform studies in the age of Google and Facebook. *New Media & Society*, *20*(1), 293–310. DOI: 10.1177/1461444816661553

Przybylski, A. K., Murayama, K., DeHaan, C. R., & Gladwell, V. (2013). Motivational, emotional, and behavioral correlates of fear of missing out. *Computers in Human Behavior*, *29*(4), 1841–1848. DOI: 10.1016/j.chb.2013.02.014

Putri, A. E., Dinata, W. W., & Basri, D. C. (2024). The influence of addiction to using artificial intelligence (AI) in generation z in guidance and counselling. *BICC Proceedings, 2*, 159–164.

PwC. (2025). Global entertainment & media outlook 2025-2029. https://www.pwc.com/gx/en/issues/business-model-reinvention/outlook.html

Rahman, K. S., & Thelen, K. (2019). The rise of the platform business model. *Politics & Society*, *47*(2), 177–204. DOI: 10.1177/0032329219838932

Raj, N., & Ida, S. (2022). A new era of viewing, binge watching: Review article. *International Journal of Health Sciences*, *6*(S6), 7831–7840. DOI: 10.53730/ijhs.v6nS6.11099

Ramos-Soler, I., López-Sánchez, C., & Quiles-Soler, C. (2021). Nomophobia in teenagers: Digital lifestyle, social networking and smartphone abuse. *Communicatio Socialis*, *34*(4), 17–32. DOI: 10.15581/003.34.4.17-32

Ricci, L., Gnisci, A., & Spagnoli, P. (2023). Digital consumer engagement: A systematic review of its antecedents and consequences. *Journal of Consumer Behaviour*, *22*(4), 841–858. DOI: 10.1002/cb.2141

Riemann, D., Krone, L. B., Wulff, K., & Nissen, C. (2019). Sleep, insomnia, and depression. *Neuropsychopharmacology : Official Publication of the American College of Neuropsychopharmacology*, *45*(1), 74–89. DOI: 10.1038/s41386-019-0411-y PMID: 31071719

Rifkin, J. R., Chan, C., & Kahn, B. E. (n.d.). *Anxiety About the Social Consequences of Missed Group Experiences Intensifies Fear of Missing Out*. FOMO. DOI: 10.1037/pspa0000418

Riva, G., Wiederhold, B., & Cipresso, P. (2015). 1. Psychology Of Social Media: From Technology To Identity. In *The Psychology of Social Networking Vol.1: Personal Experience in Online Communities* (pp. 4-14). Warsaw, Poland: De Gruyter Open Poland. https://doi.org/DOI: 10.1515/9783110473780-003

Roberts, J. A., & David, M. E. (2023). *The attention economy: A category blueprint*. Routledge.

Rodgers, W., & Nguyen, T. (2022). Advertising benefits from ethical artificial intelligence algorithmic purchase decision pathways. *Journal of Business Ethics*, *178*(4), 1043–1061. DOI: 10.1007/s10551-022-05048-7

Roll, I., & Wylie, R. (2016). Evolution and revolution in artificial intelligence in education. *International Journal of Artificial Intelligence in Education, 26*(2), 582–599. DOI: 10.1007/s40593-016-0110-3

Rosa, H. (2013). *Social acceleration: A new theory of modernity*. Columbia University Press. DOI: 10.7312/rosa14834

Rosen, L. D., Carrier, L. M., & Cheever, N. A. (2013). Facebook and texting made me do it: Media-induced task-switching while studying. *Computers in Human Behavior, 29*(3), 948–958. DOI: 10.1016/j.chb.2012.12.001

Roth, C. (2019). Algorithmic Distortion of Informational Landscapes.

Roy, G., & Sharma, S. (2021). The roles of utilitarian and hedonic values in enhancing mobile social commerce customer loyalty. *Journal of Retailing and Consumer Services, 58*, 102298. DOI: 10.1016/j.jretconser.2020.102298

Rozgonjuk, D., Sindermann, C., Elhai, J. D., & Montag, C. (2020). Fear of Missing Out (FoMO) and social media's impact on daily-life and productivity at work: Do WhatsApp, Facebook, Instagram, and Snapchat Use Disorders mediate that association? *Addictive Behaviors, 110*, 106487. DOI: 10.1016/j.addbeh.2020.106487

Rudolph, J., Tan, S., & Tan, S. (2023). ChatGPT: Bullshit spewer or the end of traditional assessments in higher education? *Journal of Applied Learning & Teaching, 6*(1). Advance online publication. DOI: 10.37074/jalt.2023.6.1.23

Ryan, R. M., & Deci, E. L. (2000). Self-determination theory and the facilitation of intrinsic motivation, social development, and well-being. *The American Psychologist, 55*(1), 68–78. DOI: 10.1037/0003-066X.55.1.68 PMID: 11392867

Ryan, R. M., & Deci, E. L. (2017). *Self-determination theory: Basic psychological needs in motivation, development, and wellness*. Guilford Press. DOI: 10.1521/978.14625/28806

Safaria, T., Saputra, N.E. & Arini, D.P. (2024). The Impact of Nomophobia: Exploring the Interplay Between Loneliness, Smartphone Usage, Self-control, Emotion Regulation, and Spiritual Meaningfulness in an Indonesian Context. *J. technol. behav. sci.* 10, 382–401 (2025). https://doi.org/DOI: 10.1007/s41347-024-00438-2

Sahibinden.com. (2025). *Sayılarla sahibinden*. https://www.sahibinden.com/kurumsal/sayilarla-sahibinden

Saidon, J., Musa, R., Hashim, H., Atory, N. A. A., Md Sohid, F., Mohd Yusof, N., & Syed Omar, S. A. (2023). Device Features and/or Personality Traits? Disentangling the Determinants of Smartphone Nomophobia and Pathology among Urban Millennials. *Information Management and Business Review, 15*(4(SI)I), 447–455. DOI: 10.22610/imbr.v15i4(SI)I.3619

Sain, Z. H., Vasudevan, A., erban, R. C., & Thelma, C. C. (2024). Integrating artificial intelligence in education: Understanding students' perceptions. *Journal of Educational Informatics*. Advance online publication. DOI: 10.62083/d62dea91

Salah, M., Abdelfattah, F., Alhalbusi, H., & Mukhaini, M. A. (2023). Me and my AI bot: Exploring the "Aiholic" phenomenon and university students' dependency on generative AI chatbots—Is this the new academic addiction? *Research Square*. DOI: 10.21203/rs.3.rs-3508563/v1

Sapmaz, F. (2023). The direct and indirect effects of workplace loneliness on FoMO: Nomophobia and general belongingness. *Journal of Educational Technology and Online Learning*, *6*(4), 947–965. DOI: 10.31681/jetol.1369184

Satani, A., Satani, K. K., Barodia, P., & Joshi, H. (2025). Modern day high: The neurocognitive impact of social media usage. *Cureus*, *17*(7), e87496. DOI: 10.7759/cureus.87496 PMID: 40777702

Sayan, N., & Uslu, A. (2025). Online Yeniden Satın Alma Niyetinde FOMO, Algılanan Kıtlık ve Online Anlık Satın Alma Davranışının Etkisi. *Journal of Research in Business*, *10*(1), 1–29. DOI: 10.54452/jrb.1510782

Schultz, W. (2007). Behavioral dopamine signals. *Trends in Neurosciences*, *30*(5), 203–210. DOI: 10.1016/j.tins.2007.03.007 PMID: 17400301

Schultz, W. (2016). Dopamine reward prediction error coding. *Dialogues in Clinical Neuroscience*, *18*(1), 23–32. DOI: 10.31887/DCNS.2016.18.1/wschultz

Secrest, J. (2000). Transformation of the relationship: The experience of primary support persons of stroke survivors. *Rehabilitation Nursing*, *25*(3), 93–99. DOI: 10.1002/j.2048-7940.2000.tb01877.x

Selwyn, N. (2022). *Education and technology: Key issues and debates*. Bloomsbury Academic. DOI: 10.5040/9781350145573

Sende, C. C., Ebner, K., & Soucek, R. (2024). *Development and Test of a Conceptual Model on the Emergence of Digital Stress: A Training Intervention Study. SSRN*. DOI: 10.2139/ssrn.4966638

Sequeira, S. L., Rodman, A. M., Nesi, J., & Silk, J. S. (2025). Social threat and adolescent mental health. *Nature Reviews Psychology*, *4*(10), 639–653. DOI: 10.1038/s44159-025-00484-4

Shaffer, H. J., LaPlante, D. A., LaBrie, R. A., Kidman, R. C., Donato, A. N., & Stanton, M. V. (2005). Toward a syndrome model of addiction: Multiple expressions, common etiology. *Harvard Review of Psychiatry*, *12*(6), 367–374. DOI: 10.1080/10673220490905705 PMID: 15764471

Shahzad, M. F., Xu, S., Liu, H., & Zahid, H. (2024). Generative Artificial Intelligence (ChatGPT-4) and social media impact on academic performance and psychological well-being in China's higher education. *European Journal of Education*. Advance online publication. DOI: 10.1111/ejed.12716

Shaker, K. S., & Bukhari, S. R. (2025). Binge Watching, Para Social Relationships and Psycho Social well-Being in Early Adults. *Journal of Development and Social Sciences*, *6*(2), 53–67. DOI: 10.47205/jdss.2025(6-II)06

Shanmugasundaram, M., & Tamilarasu, A. (2023). The impact of digital technology, social media, and artificial intelligence on cognitive functions: A review. *Frontiers in Cognition*, *2*, 1203077. DOI: 10.3389/fcogn.2023.1203077

Sharma, P., & Murano, P. (2020). Infinite scrolling vs. pagination: A comparison of user satisfaction and usability for mobile websites. *Journal of Universal Computer Science*, *26*(2), 237–254. DOI: 10.3897/jucs.2020.014

Shen, M. K., & Yoon, D. (2025). The dark addiction patterns of current AI chatbot interfaces. In *Conference on Human Factors in Computing Systems - Proceedings* (pp. 1–7). DOI: 10.1145/3706599.3720003

Siekpe, J. S., & Kamssu, A. A. (2005). The effect of culture & uses and gratifications in online shopping. *Southwest Decision Sciences Institute 2005: Proceedings of the 36th Southwest Decision Sciences Institute Annual Conference*, Southwest DSI, Dallas, USA, 370-378.

Sil, M., Mondal, A., & Kumar, M. (2025). Prevalence and psychological correlates of binge-watching: The digital era of entertainment. *Industrial Psychiatry Journal*, *34*(2), 215–220. DOI: 10.4103/ipj.ipj_36_25 PMID: 40861144

Simon, H. A. (1971). Designing Organizations for an Information-Rich World. In Greenberger, M. (Ed.), *Computers, Communications, and the Public Interest* (pp. 37–72). Johns Hopkins Press.

Singer, J. A., & Omary, A. (2026, April 16). *The case against social media "addiction."* Cato Institute. https://www.cato.org/blog/case-against-social-media-addiction

Singh, M., Michael, R. A., Saheb, S. S., Yadav, P. S., Kiran, P. B., & Malhi, A. (2025). A Study on Digital Intelligence and Influencer Marketing for Sustainable Diversification of India's Retail Economy: A Qualitative Study. In Pujari, P., Khan, S., Kumar, A., & Naim, A. (Eds.), *Fostering Economic Diversification and Sustainable Business Through Digital Intelligence* (pp. 1–22). IGI Global Scientific Publishing., DOI: 10.4018/979-8-3693-8492-3.ch001

Singh, M., Syed, S. M., Saheb, S. S., Yadav, P. S., & Kiran, P. B. (2025). Role of Influencer Marketing in the Indian Retail Business Sector: A Qualitative Study. In Hussain, Z., Albattat, A., Fakir, F., & Yi, Z. (Eds.), *Innovative Trends Shaping Food Marketing and Consumption* (pp. 105–130). IGI Global Scientific Publishing., DOI: 10.4018/979-8-3693-8542-5.ch005

Singh, P., & Thomas, R. (2025). Binge-watching behavior and the strategies adopted to overcome this among undergraduate students. *Journal of Health and Society*, *7*(2). https://jhas-nu.in/binge-watching-behavior-and-the-strategies-adopted-to-overcome-this-among-the-undergraduate-students/

Singh, S. (2025). Artificial intelligence and sustainable development: Opportunities and challenges. In Beniwal, A. (Ed.), *Artificial intelligence, ethics, and the digital society: Pathways to sustainable development*. Deep Science Publishing., DOI: 10.70593/978-937-1854-97-9

Siregar, Z. M. E., Syahputra, S., & Ginting, R. (2023). The impact of digital consumer engagement and affective value on social commerce. *International Journal of Data and Network Science*, *7*(2), 855–864. DOI: 10.5267/j.ijdns.2023.1.008

Skinner, B. F. (1953). *Science and human behavior*. Macmillan.

Slater, M., & Wilbur, S. (1997). A framework for immersive virtual environments (FIVE). *Presence (Cambridge, Mass.)*, *6*(6), 603–616. DOI: 10.1162/pres.1997.6.6.603

Smart, P., Heersmink, R., & Clowes, R. (2017). The Cognitive Ecology of the Internet. Holman, C. & de Villers-Sidani, E. (2014). Indestructible plastic: the neuroscience of the new aging brain.

Spada, M. M. (2014). An overview of problematic internet use. *Addictive Behaviors*, *39*(1), 3–6. DOI: 10.1016/j.addbeh.2013.09.007 PMID: 24126206

Spina, S. (2023). Homo-Loggatus. The anthropological condition of historians in the digital world. Ensslin, A., Bell, A., Smith, J., Van Der Bom, I., & Skains, L. (2019). Immersion, digital fiction, and the switchboard metaphor. Bell, A., Ensslin, A., Van Der Bom, I., & Smith, J. (2018). Immersion in digital fiction.

Stănculescu, E., & Griffiths, M. D. (2024). Problematic social media use and its relationship with psychopathology: A systematic review and meta-analysis. *Current Psychology (New Brunswick, N.J.)*, *43*, 1–18. DOI: 10.1007/s12144-023-05534-1

Starcevic, V., & Berle, D. (2013). Cyberchondria: Towards a better understanding of excessive health-related Internet use. *Expert Review of Neurotherapeutics*, *13*(2), 205–213. DOI: 10.1586/ern.12.162 PMID: 23368807

Starks, H., & Trinidad, S. B. (2007). Choose your method: A comparison of phenomenology, discourse analysis, and grounded theory. *Qualitative Health Research*, *17*(10), 1372–1380. DOI: 10.1177/1049732307307031 PMID: 18000076

Statista. (2025). *Number of social media users worldwide 2018–2025*. https://www.statista.com/forecasts/277694/number-of-internet-users-in-the-world

Statista. (2025). Video streaming – worldwide. https://www.statista.com/outlook/dmo/digital-media/video-on-demand/worldwide

Strong, C., & Bakhshi, S. (2023). S. B. (2023). Smartphones and the Future of Remembering: Frictions, Problems, and Pathways. *Conference Proceedings. Ethnographic Praxis in Industry Conference*, *2023*(1), 89–102. DOI: 10.1111/epic.12154

Subramanian, P.S. & Das, K. (2024). Binge Watching and Mental Health Among Late Adolescence and Early Adulthood. International Journal of Indian Psychology, 12(1), 1002-1030. DIP:18.01.095.20241201, DOI:DOI: 10.25215/1201.095

Sun, C., Sun, B., Lin, Y., & Zhou, H. (2022). Problematic Mobile Phone Use Increases with the Fear of Missing Out Among College Students: The Effects of Self-Control, Perceived Social Support and Future Orientation. *Psychology Research and Behavior Management*, *15*, 1–8. DOI: 10.2147/PRBM.S345650

Swedberg, R. (1997). New economic sociology. *Acta Sociologica*, *40*(2), 161–182. DOI: 10.1177/000169939704000203

Syahputra, Y., Miswanto, M., & Hafni, M. (2023). Exploration of the fear of missing out internet based on demography. [IJERE]. *International Journal of Evaluation and Research in Education*, *12*(4), 2186. DOI: 10.11591/ijere.v12i4.25353

Syed Hassan Raza, Muhammad Yousaf, Faryal Sohail, Rehana Munawar, Emenyeonu C Ogadimma & Jenny Marisa Lim Dao Siang (2021) Investigating Binge-Watching Adverse Mental Health Outcomes During Covid-19 Pandemic: Moderating Role of Screen Time For Web Series Using Online Streaming, Psychology Research and Behavior Management,, 1615-1629, DOI: To link to this article: https://doi.org/ DOI: 10.2147/PRBM.S328416

Szawłoga, T., Soroka, K., & Śliwińska, M. (2024). Relationship between fear of missing-out and adolescents mental health. *Medycyna Srodowiskowa*, *27*(1), 18–22. DOI: 10.26444/ms/187716

Tandon, A., Dhir, A., Talwar, S., Kaur, P., & Mäntymäki, M. (2021). Dark consequences of social media-induced fear of missing out (FoMO): Social media stalking, comparisons, and fatigue. *Technological Forecasting and Social Change*, *171*, 120931. DOI: 10.1016/j.techfore.2021.120931

Tang, T.-C., Chi, L.-C., & Tang, E. (2024). Office islands: Exploring the uncharted waters of workplace loneliness, social media addiction, and the fear of missing out. *Current Psychology (New Brunswick, N.J.)*, *43*(17), 15160–15175. DOI: 10.1007/s12144-023-05445-9

Tanhan, F., Özok, H. İ., & Tayiz, V. (2022). Gelişmeleri Kaçırma Korkusu (FoMO): Güncel Bir Derleme. *Psikiyatride Güncel Yaklasimlar*, *14*(1), 74–85. DOI: 10.18863/pgy.942431

Tashtoush, M. A., Wardat, Y., Aloufi, F., & Taani, O. (2022). The effectiveness of teaching method based on the components of concept-rich instruction approach in students achievement on linear algebra course and their attitudes towards mathematics. *Journal of Higher Education Theory and Practice*, *22*(7). Advance online publication. DOI: 10.33423/jhetp.v22i7.5269

Tateno, M., Kato, T. A., Shirasaka, T., Kanazawa, J., Ukai, W., & Hirota, T. (2022). A network analysis of problematic smartphone use in Japanese young adults. *PLoS One*, *17*(8), e0272803. DOI: 10.1371/journal.pone.0272803

Taylor, A., Hook, M., Carlson, J., Gudergan, S., & Falk, T. (2024). Appetite for distraction? A systematic literature review on customer smartphone distraction. *International Journal of Information Management*, *75*, 102722. DOI: 10.1016/j.ijinfomgt.2023.102722

Thaler, R. H., & Sunstein, C. R. (2008). *Nudge: Improving decisions about health, wealth, and happiness*. Yale University Press.

Thomas, S. (2020). Resolving tensions in phenomenological research interviewing. *Journal of Advanced Nursing*, *77*(1), 484–491. DOI: 10.1111/jan.14597 PMID: 33058245

Throuvala, M. A., Griffiths, M. D., Rennoldson, M., & Kuss, D. J. (2019). Motivational processes and dysfunctional mechanisms of social media use among adolescents: A qualitative focus group study. *Computers in Human Behavior*, *93*, 164–175. DOI: 10.1016/j.chb.2018.12.012

Tolba, A. A., & Zoghaib, S. Z. (2022). Understanding the Binge-watching Phenomenon on Netflix and Its Association with Depression and Loneliness in Egyptian Adults. *Media Watch, 13*(3), 264–279. DOI: 10.1177/09760911221117339

Townsend, D. M., & Hunt, R. A. (2019). Entrepreneurial action, creativity, & judgment in the age of artificial intelligence. *Journal of Business Venturing Insights, 11*, e00126. DOI: 10.1016/j.jbvi.2019.e00126

Trigueros, R., Aguilar-Parra, J. M., López-Liria, R., & Rocamora, P. (2019). The dark side of the Self-Determination Theory and its influence on the emotional and cognitive processes of students in physical education. *International Journal of Environmental Research and Public Health, 16*(22), 4444. DOI: 10.3390/ijerph16224444 PMID: 31726790

Tse, N., Pang, N. S., Wang, X., Li, Y., Lo, C. K., & Yang, X. (2025). Binge-watching and gender-specific effects on academic, social, and mental well-being in children and adolescents. *PLoS One, 20*(8), e0329655. DOI: 10.1371/journal.pone.0329655 PMID: 40845080

Tsitsika, A. K., Janikian, M., Schoenmakers, T. M., Tzavela, E., Olafsson, K., Iordache, A., & Richardson, C. (2014). Internet addictive behavior in adolescence: A cross-sectional study in seven European countries. *Cyberpsychology, Behavior, and Social Networking, 17*(8), 518–525. DOI: 10.1089/cyber.2013.0382 PMID: 24853789

Turkle, S. (2011). *Alone together: Why we expect more from technology and less from each other*. Basic Books.

Twenge, J. M., & Campbell, W. K. (2019). Media use is linked to lower psychological well-being: Evidence from three datasets. *The Psychiatric Quarterly, 90*(2), 311–331. DOI: 10.1007/s11126-019-09630-7 PMID: 30859387

Twenge, J. M., Martin, G. N., & Campbell, W. K. (2018). Decreases in psychological well-being among American adolescents after 2012 and links to screen time during the rise of smartphone technology. *Emotion (Washington, D.C.), 18*(6), 765–780. DOI: 10.1037/emo0000403 PMID: 29355336

Umesh, S., & Bose, S. (2019). Binge-Watching: A Matter of Concern? *Indian Journal of Psychological Medicine, 41*(2), 182–184. DOI: 10.4103/IJPSYM.IJPSYM_279_18 PMID: 30983669

Urfa, O., & Görgülü, R. (2025). From addiction to pervasiveness: Validation of the Smartphone Pervasiveness Scale in Turkish adolescents. *International Journal of Assessment Tools in Education, 12*(4), 926–941. DOI: 10.21449/ijate.1579992

Uslu, O. (2025). Understanding digital wellbeing: Impacts, strategies, and the path to healthier technology practices. *Discover Social Science and Health*, *5*(1), 145. Advance online publication. DOI: 10.1007/s44155-025-00259-5

Vagka, E., Gnardellis, C., Lagiou, A., & Notara, V. (2024). Smartphone Use and Social Media Involvement in Young Adults: Association with Nomophobia, Depression Anxiety Stress Scales (DASS) and Self-Esteem. *International Journal of Environmental Research and Public Health*, *21*(7), 920. DOI: 10.3390/ijerph21070920

van Dijck, J. (2014). Datafication, dataism and dataveillance. *Surveillance & Society*, *12*(2), 197–208. DOI: 10.24908/ss.v12i2.4776

van Dijck, J., Poell, T., & de Waal, M. (2018). *The platform society: Public values in a connective world*. Oxford University Press. DOI: 10.1093/oso/9780190889760.001.0001

Van Rooij, A. J., & Prause, N. (2014). A critical review of "Internet addiction" criteria. *Journal of Behavioral Addictions*, *3*(4), 203–213. DOI: 10.1556/JBA.3.2014.4.1

Vanden Abeele, M. M. P. (2021). Digital Wellbeing as a Dynamic Construct. *Communication Theory*, *31*(4), 932–955. DOI: 10.1093/ct/qtaa024

Vannucci, A., Flannery, K. M., & Ohannessian, C. M. (2017). Social media use and anxiety in emerging adults. *Journal of Affective Disorders*, *207*, 163–166. DOI: 10.1016/j.jad.2016.08.040 PMID: 27723539

Veissière, S. P. L., & Stendel, M. (2018). Hypernatural Monitoring: A Social Rehearsal Account of Smartphone Addiction. *Frontiers in Psychology*, *9*, 141. DOI: 10.3389/fpsyg.2018.00141

Vizcaíno-Verdú, A., & Abidin, C. (2022). Music challenge memes on TikTok: Media spreadability, iterativity, and user engagement. *New Media & Society*, *25*(12), 883–908.

Vogel, E. A., Rose, J. P., Roberts, L. R., & Eckles, K. (2014). Social comparison, social media, and self-esteem. *Psychology of Popular Media Culture*, *3*(4), 206–222. DOI: 10.1037/ppm0000047

Voinea, C., Vică, C., Mihailov, E., & Savulescu, J. (2020). The Internet as Cognitive Enhancement.

Volkow, N. D., & Baler, R. D. (2014). Addiction science: Uncovering neurobiological complexity. *Neuropharmacology*, *76*, 235–249. DOI: 10.1016/j.neuropharm.2013.05.007

Volkow, N. D., Wang, G. J., Begleiter, H., Porjesz, B., Fowler, J. S., Telang, F., & Logan, J. (2006). High levels of dopamine D2 receptors in unaffected members of alcoholic families: Possible protective factors. *Archives of General Psychiatry, 63*(9), 999–1008. DOI: 10.1001/archpsyc.63.9.999 PMID: 16953002

Wallinheimo, A.-S., & Evans, S. L. (2025). Mechanisms that link circadian preference to problematic smartphone and social media use in young adults. *PLoS One, 20*(9), e0331961. DOI: 10.1371/journal.pone.0331961

Walther, J. B. (1996). Computer-mediated communication: Impersonal, interpersonal, and hyperpersonal interaction. *Communication Research, 23*(1), 3–43. DOI: 10.1177/009365096023001001

Wang, Q., Khuu, A., & Jivotovski, M. (2023). The self online: When meaning-making is outsourced to the cyber audience.

Wang, Y., & Jia, J. (2023). Understanding the effects of hedonic and utilitarian values on consumer online impulse buying: A meta-analysis. *Frontiers in Psychology, 14*, 1118671. DOI: 10.3389/fpsyg.2023.1118671

Ward, A. F., Duke, K., Gneezy, A., & Bos, M. W. (2017). Brain Drain: The Mere Presence of One's Own Smartphone Reduces Available Cognitive Capacity. *Journal of the Association for Consumer Research, 2*(2), 140–154. DOI: 10.1086/691462

Wegner, D. M., & Ward, A. F. (2013). How Google Is Changing Your Brain. *Scientific American, 309*(6), 58–61. DOI: 10.1038/scientificamerican1213-58

Wen, F., Ding, Y., Yang, C., Ma, S., Zhu, J., Xiao, H., & Zuo, B. (2023). Influence of smartphone use motives on smartphone addiction during the COVID-19 epidemic in China: The moderating effect of age. *Current Psychology (New Brunswick, N.J.), 42*(22), 19316–19325. DOI: 10.1007/s12144-022-03355-w

Whitehead, M., & Hannah, M. G. (2025). New figurations of freedom: Ricoeurian perspectives on the digital society. *Dialogues in Human Geography*, 20438206251379592. Advance online publication. DOI: 10.1177/20438206251379592

Whittemore, R., & Knafl, K. (2005). The integrative review: Updated methodology. *Journal of Advanced Nursing, 52*(5), 546–553. DOI: 10.1111/j.1365-2648.2005.03621.x PMID: 16268861

Wiederhold, B. K. (2018). "Alexa, are you my mom?" The role of artificial intelligence in child development. *Cyberpsychology, Behavior, and Social Networking, 21*(8), 471–472. DOI: 10.1089/cyber.2018.29120.bkw PMID: 30110199

Williams, J. (2018). *Stand Out of Our Light: Freedom and Resistance in the Attention Economy*. Cambridge University Press., DOI: 10.1017/9781108453004

Williamson, B. (2017). Big data in education: The digital future of learning, policy and practice. *Sage (Atlanta, Ga.)*. Advance online publication. DOI: 10.4135/9781529714920

Wilson, A. (2015). A guide to phenomenological research. *Nursing Standard*, *29*(34), 38–43. DOI: 10.7748/ns.29.34.38.e8821 PMID: 25902251

Wu, T. (2016). *The attention merchants: The epic scramble to get inside our heads*. Knopf.

Wu, T. (2017). *The attention merchants: From the daily newspaper to social media, how our time and attention is harvested and sold*. Atlantic Books.

Xie, T., Pentina, I., & Hancock, T. (2023). Friend, mentor, lover: Does chatbot engagement lead to psychological dependence? *Journal of Service Management*, *34*(4), 806–828. DOI: 10.1108/JOSM-02-2022-0072

Yadav, P. S., Kiran, P. B. N., Sharma, A., Vemula, R., & Shrama, A. (2025). Customer Acceptance of Sustainable Fintech Innovation. In Financial Innovation for Global Sustainability (pp. 337–357). Wiley. https://doi.org/DOI: 10.1002/9781394311682.ch14

Yadav, P. S., Kiran, P. B., Vemula, R., Kumar, V., Kumari, P., & Michael, R. A. (2026). Leveraging AI and Digital Solutions to Enhance Sustainability in Green and Blue Economies. In Ordóñez de Pablos, P., Zhang, X., Anshari, M., & Almunawar, M. (Eds.), *AI and Digital Nomads Shaping Global Industrial Technology Transitions* (pp. 53–84). IGI Global Scientific Publishing., DOI: 10.4018/979-8-3373-0159-4.ch002

Yang, C., Mousavi, S., Dash, A., Gummadi, K. P., & Weber, I. (2025). *Studying behavioral addiction by combining surveys and digital traces: A case study of TikTok*. arXiv. https://arxiv.org/pdf/2501.15539

Yang, H., Tng, G. Y. Q., Khoo, S. S., & Yang, S. (2022). Multidimensional Profiles of Addictive Smartphone Use: A Latent Profile Analysis. *Current Psychology (New Brunswick, N.J.)*, *41*(12), 8410–8423. DOI: 10.1007/s12144-022-02881-x

Yao, M. Z. (2025). Regulating social media for minors: A comparative analysis of national approaches. *Journal of Information Policy*, *15*(1), 1–38. DOI: 10.5325/jinfopoli.15.1.0001

Yastıoğlu, S. (2023). Üretken yapay zekânın işletmelerde kullanımı: Fırsatlar ve tehditler. İ. Çeviktekin (Ed.), *Yönetim bilişim sistemleri: İşletmelerde dijital dönüşüm yönetimi* içinde (ss. 173-190). Özgür Yayınları.

Yeung, K. (2017). 'Hypernudge': Big data as a mode of regulation by design. *Information Communication and Society*, *20*(1), 118–136. DOI: 10.1080/1369118X.2016.1186713

Yıldırım, A., & Şimşek, H. (2016). *Sosyal bilimlerde nitel araştırma yöntemleri*. Seçkin Yayıncılık.

Yildirim, C., & Correia, A.-P. (2015). Exploring the dimensions of nomophobia: Development and validation of a self-reported questionnaire. *Computers in Human Behavior*, *49*, 130–137. DOI: 10.1016/j.chb.2015.02.059

Yılmaz, K., Filiz, N., & Yılmaz, A. (2012). Learning social studies via objects in museums: Investigation into Turkish elementary school students' lived experiences. *British Educational Research Journal*, *39*(6), 979–1001. DOI: 10.1002/berj.3018

Younes, F., Halawi, G., Jabbour, K., Osta, N. E., Karam, L. B., Hajj, A., & Khabbaz, L. R. (2016). Internet Addiction and Relationships with Insomnia, Anxiety, Depression, Stress and Self-Esteem in University Students: A Cross-Sectional Designed Study. *PLoS One*, *11*(9), e0161126. DOI: 10.1371/journal.pone.0161126 PMID: 27618306

Young, K. S. (1998). Internet addiction: The emergence of a new clinical disorder. *Cyberpsychology & Behavior*, *1*(3), 237–244. DOI: 10.1089/cpb.1998.1.237

Young, K. S. (2017). The evolution of Internet addiction. *Addictive Behaviors*, *64*, 229–230. DOI: 10.1016/j.addbeh.2015.05.016

Yue, H., Yue, X., Zhang, X., Liu, B., & Bao, H. (2022). Exploring the relationship between social exclusion and smartphone addiction: The mediating roles of loneliness and self-control. *Frontiers in Psychology*, *13*, 945631. DOI: 10.3389/fpsyg.2022.945631

Yu, H., & Alizadeh, F. (2024). Online Binge-Watching Among Chinese College Students: Implications for Loneliness, Anxiety, and Depression. *Psychology Research and Behavior Management*, *17*, 295–303. DOI: 10.2147/PRBM.S447311 PMID: 38292254

Yu, Y. (2021). The role and influence of artificial intelligence on advertising industry. In *Proceedings of the 2021 International Conference on Social Development and Media Communication (SDMC 2021)* (pp. 190–194). Atlantis Press. DOI: 10.2991/assehr.k.220105.037

Zandi, R. (2018). *The Parallel Mind. Cavagnetto, S. & Gahir, B. (2011). A Formalized Model of Multiple Selves in MUDs. Kuruc, K. (2010).* Identity VS E-dentity.

Zhang, K. Z., Benyoucef, M., & Zhao, S. J. (2019). Consumer behavior and social commerce: A systematic review of over a decade of research (2008–2018). *International Journal of Information Management*, *47*, 1–10. DOI: 10.1016/j.ijinfomgt.2019.01.001

Zhang, S., Zhao, X., Zhou, T., & Kim, J. H. (2024). Do you have AI dependency? The roles of academic self-efficacy, academic stress, and performance expectations on problematic AI usage behavior. *International Journal of Educational Technology in Higher Education*, *21*(1), 34. DOI: 10.1186/s41239-024-00467-0

Zhang, X., Wu, Y., & Liu, S. (2019). Exploring short-form video application addiction: Socio-technical framework. *Computers in Human Behavior*, *101*, 257–268. DOI: 10.1016/j.chb.2019.07.019

Zhang, Y., Fang, Y., Wei, K.-K., Ramsey, E., McCole, P., & Chen, H. (2011). Repurchase intention in B2C e-commerce—A relationship quality perspective. *Information & Management*, *48*(6), 192–200. DOI: 10.1016/j.im.2011.05.003

Zhao, N., & Zhou, G. (2021). Covid-19 stress and addictive social media use (SMU): Mediating role of active use and social media flow. *Frontiers in Psychiatry*, *12*, 12–85. DOI: 10.3389/fpsyt.2021.635546 PMID: 33633616

Zheng, X., Men, J., Yang, F., & Gong, X. (2019). Understanding users' satisfaction with social commerce sites from the perspective of social capital. *Computers in Human Behavior*, *91*, 217–228. DOI: 10.1016/j.chb.2018.10.011

Zhou, T., & Zhang, C. (2024). Examining generative AI user addiction from a CAC perspective. *Technology in Society*, *78*, 102653. DOI: 10.1016/j.techsoc.2024.102653

Zhou, X., Zhang, J., & Chan, C. (2024). Unveiling students' experiences and perceptions of Artificial Intelligence usage in higher education. *Journal of University Teaching & Learning Practice*, *21*(6). Advance online publication. DOI: 10.53761/xzjprb23

Zhu, C., Li, S., & Zhang, L. (2025). The impact of smartphone addiction on mental health and its relationship with life satisfaction in the post-COVID-19 era. *Frontiers in Psychiatry*, *16*, 1542040. DOI: 10.3389/fpsyt.2025.1542040

Zillmann, D. (1988). Mood management through communication choices. *The American Behavioral Scientist*, *31*(3), 327–340. DOI: 10.1177/000276488031003005

Zuboff, S. (2019). *The age of surveillance capitalism: The fight for a human future at the new frontier of power*. PublicAffairs.

Zuboff, S. (2019). *The Age of Surveillance Capitalism: The Fight for a Human Future at the New Frontier of Power*. PublicAffairs.

About the Contributors

Özgün Arda Kus, graduated from Maltepe University, Department of Public Relations and Advertising, with a full scholarship, and also pursued a double major in Psychology. He completed his first Master's degree in the Department of Sales and Marketing at Okan University, Business Administration Department. His second Master's degree is in Department of Addiction and Rehabilitation, Institute of Health Sciences. He completed his Ph.D. education in the Department of Public Relations and Advertising at Istanbul University with a thesis titled "Digital Games as an Interactive Communication Space; A study on the effects of playing motivations on digital game addiction." He is currently continuing his academic studies as an Assistant Professor at the Department of Public Relations and Advertising at Usküdar University Faculty of Communication. He has participated in various international and national certificate programs in the fields of marketing and psychology. He has authored the internationally published books "The Concept of Mobile Marketing, A Study for Istanbul and Generation Y," and "Relationships Among Game, Digital Game, Addiction, and Motivation Concepts," and has served as co-editor for the compilation books "Digital Forms of Games 1,2 and 3". He is also co-editor of "Critical Perspectives on Digital Culture and Gaming" and "Advancements in Digital Broadcasting and Content Platforms" published by IGI Global. He has also presented papers at international scientific conferences and contributed chapters and articles to various books. The areas of research and interest for Ozgün Arda Kus include: digital games, alienation, self, mobile marketing, consumer behaviors and generations, mood disorders, and behavioral addictions. He is a full member of the Turkish Psychological Association.

***

Gülsün Bozkurt is an academic specializing in media and communication studies. She received her undergraduate degree in Philosophy from the Faculty of

Literature at Istanbul University in 2009, and completed both her master's and doctoral studies in Journalism at the Institute of Social Sciences of the same university. Her academic background combines philosophical inquiry with communication and media research. Her research interests focus on digital media, communication ethics, social media practices, and the socio-cultural implications of platform-based communication. She has presented her work at national and international academic conferences and has contributed to scholarly publications and edited volumes. In addition to her research, she teaches undergraduate and graduate courses in communication and media studies, with a particular emphasis on digital culture and contemporary communication environments.

Neslihan Bulur Demirel, PhD, is a researcher at Üsküdar University. She holds a doctorate in Communication Sciences from Marmara University and an MA in Strategic Communication Management from Galatasaray University. Her research centers on communication sociology, techno-social systems, and the dynamics of platformization. Her doctoral dissertation examined the interplay between techno-politics and social identity within climate change discussions on digital platforms.

Özgül Dağli completed her undergraduate studies at Anadolu University, Faculty of Communication Sciences, Department of Communication Arts in 1999. She obtained her Master's and Ph.D. degrees from the Department of Public Relations and Advertising at the same university. Dağlı began her academic career as a Research Assistant at Anadolu University and was awarded the title of Associate Professor in 2018. Having attained the title of Professor in 2023, she currently serves as the Head of the Advertising Department at Üsküdar University, Faculty of Communication. Her research interests and areas of expertise include Advertising, Copywriting, Creative Processes in Advertising, and the Brand Building Process.

Gülden Demir holds a BA in English Language Teaching and an MA and PhD in Interpersonal Communication from Marmara University. She completed her doctoral degree in 2021. Her doctoral dissertation, Youth Perception: A Research of Young People on "The Lifeworld of Youth", was published as a book by the Municipality of Şişli in 2023 and included in the local government library. Her research interests focus on digital culture, digital communication, new media, and youth studies. She led the Şişli Youth Perception Research project and continues to explore critical approaches to youth discourses in digital media, as well as K-pop fan culture on social media. She teaches undergraduate and graduate-level courses on digital culture, cyberculture, media literacy, media analysis, and youth studies, adopting an interdisciplinary perspective.

Asena Irmak Kuş graduated from Üsküdar University, Faculty of Communication, Department of New Media and Communication in 2025. She is currently pursuing her master's degree at Marmara University, Institute of Social Sciences, in the field of Public Relations.

Utsav Krishan Murari is a gifted writer, dedicated life coach, motivational speaker, passionate educator, and, above all, an exceptional mentor. He holds a doctorate in communication and media studies from the Central University of South Bihar. Graced with a vivid imagination, he is a genuine catalyst for ideas and is always open to trying new things. His one such initiative is Saarthi, which began as Saarthi Entertainment. Saarthi is a Delhi-based creative media production start-up that wants to leave a legacy of artistry in the production industry.

Sumit Kumar Pandey is an Assistant Professor at the Department of Media, Communication and Fine Arts, Manipal University Jaipur. He holds a Ph.D. from Kashi Vidyapith University, Varanasi, and is a UGC NET qualifier. He earned an M.Phil. and Master's in Journalism & Mass Communication (both Gold Medals) and a PG Diploma in Electronic Media Management & Film Production. With nine years of experience in academia and research, his focus areas include AI & Media, Media Literacy, Political Communication, New Media, Print Media, and Radio. He has published 36 papers/chapters in Scopus-indexed, UGC Care-listed, and peer-reviewed journals/books. He has authored three books: 1. Atal Bihari Vajpayee's Contributions to Journalism and Nation-Building (Greenleaf Publication, India) 2. Democracy by Design (Special Publication, USA) 3. AI and the Future of Print Media: Disruption, Adaptation, and Strategic Transformation (LPU Publication, India) Dr. Pandey holds three patents/designs: an AI-based multimedia kiosk for wildlife tourism (2024), a cloud-based digital display branding device (2025), and an IoT-Based Solar Rotating LCD Interactive Tourist Guide Standee (2025). A former Radio Presenter at All India Radio and IGNOU Gyan Vani FM, he has organised over 40 and participated in over 80 national/international academic events, showcasing expertise in teaching, communication, and research.

Hemlata Parmar is an Assistant Professor in the Department of Artificial Intelligence and Machine Learning at Manipal University Jaipur, India. Her academic specialization is in Network Security and Cryptography, with research interests encompassing artificial intelligence–enabled cybersecurity, IoT security architectures, encryption techniques, and secure computing systems. She has contributed to national and international conferences and scholarly publications addressing topics such as sensor-based IoT security frameworks, image-based encryption methods, and intelligent security models integrating machine learning and neural network approaches. In addition to her research contributions, Dr. Parmar is actively involved in teaching, curriculum delivery, academic mentoring, and departmental coordination activities. She participates in professional academic bodies and engages in institutional service initiatives that support student development and technical learning. Her work focuses on advancing applied artificial intelligence and secure digital infrastructures, emphasizing practical technological solutions to contemporary cybersecurity challenges in networked environments. Through her teaching and research, she contributes to the development of robust and trustworthy computing ecosystems aligned with evolving technological demands.

Deeksha Ranga is a final-year Master's student in Psychology at Lovely Professional University (LPU), Punjab, India. Her academic interests span multiple areas of psychology, with a particular focus on understanding psychological processes in everyday life. She is interested in integrating theoretical perspectives with practical applications across diverse fields of psychology. Her work reflects a strong interest in connecting psychological theory with real-world practice.

Pinnika Syam Yadav is a distinguished researcher and academician specializing in business and marketing analytics. He holds a Ph.D. and gained over three years of teaching experience at the Mittal School of Business, Lovely Professional University and School of Business and Management, Christ University, where he made significant contributions to academia. Currently, Dr. Yadav serves as an Assistant Professor at Christ University, continuing to excel in research and education. He has notably guided and awarded two Ph.D. scholars, further demonstrating his profound commitment to his field. His innovative approach and extensive knowledge have established him as a leading figure, inspiring young researchers to follow in his footsteps.

Muhammed Enes Yılmaz is a Research Assistant at the Department of Communication and Design, Nişantaşı University, Istanbul, Türkiye and a PhD student in Public Relations and Publicity at Istanbul University, Turkiye. His research interests include digital media, artificial intelligence in communication practices, and human–computer interaction.

Index

T

V

www.ingramcontent.com/pod-product-compliance
Lightning Source LLC
LaVergne TN
LVHW080904300926
849162LV00003B/544